Judy Garland

World's Greatest Entertainer

By John Fricke

MJF BOOKS NEW YORK

For Christopher

++++++++++++++++++++++++++

Also by John Fricke
The Wizard of Oz: The Official 50th Anniversary Pictorial History

Published by MJF Books
Fine Communications
Two Lincoln Square
60 West 66th Street
New York, NY 10023

Library of Congress Catalog Card Number 97-72763
ISBN 1-56731-204-7
A Book from Puck Productions

This edition published by arrangement with Henry Holt and Company, Inc.

Art direction and interior design by Michaelis/Carpelis Design Associates, Inc.

Front Matter illustrations: page 1: Garland in costume for "Gotta Have Me Go with You," *A Star is Born*, Warner Bros./1954. Title page: Between takes of "It Never Was You" for *I Could Go On Singing*, United Artists/1963. Page 5: Singing "Get happy" in *Summer Stock*, MGM/1950.

Manufactured in the United States of America on acid-free paper

MJF Books and the MJF colophon are trademarks of Fine Creative Media, Inc.

10 9 8 7 6 5 4 3 2 1

Contents

Introduction

FACING PAGE: *Portrait, 1941.*

BELOW: *During a personal appearance at the Chicago Theatre, Chicago, 1938.*

Just given the bare facts, Judy Garland's career was a beautiful success story.

So wrote a critic for *Saturday Review* in 1975. The quality of Garland's work was often rapturously acknowledged and heralded during her lifetime. After her death, in 1969, her unique gifts earned her even greater recognition.

Posthumous acclaim, however, arrived without the aid of Garland's biographers. Rather than chronicle her career, the majority elected instead to analyze her personal travail. This is to some extent understandable, given the extremes of Judy Garland's life and the excesses of the media. But what has been lost in journalistic attempts to explain a life gone awry is the scope and detail of her professional achievements.

This book offers a complete and chronological record, in words and pictures, of that career. (Those who desire treatises—of varying accuracy—on husbands and hospitalizations, prescriptions and problems, are directed to the bibliography on page 254.)

Judy Garland was capable of volatile, unpredictable, erratic, irrational, even monstrous behavior. Yet, as she suggested in 1962, "For an 'undependable,' I certainly made a lot of pictures. The only time I was undependable was when I was ill and couldn't work. Everyone is undependable when they're ill." If hardly an in-depth perspective, it's the same stand always taken by the majority of Judy's co-workers, associates, and three children. They explain that when Garland was healthy—eating, working on a reasonable schedule, being treated with respect and humor—she was fine. Things would go wrong only when, time and again, she would have to seek escape from the overwhelming professional, financial, physical, and emotional pressures her talent made almost inevitable in mid-century America. Ethan Mordden makes passing reference to her sometimes tempestuous reputation in his fine 1990 *New Yorker* profile and then is careful to note that the brutal, mean-spirited Garland was "not herself. [But] something about a terrible Judy Garland [is] supposed to fascinate us, and surely that is a testament to how nice she must have been." Even more succinctly, Garland's longtime California houseman told a journalist in 1982, "The bad things she did, that was her head, not her heart. . . . At heart, she was a wonderful woman."

There are those who see her as victim or victimizer, and they condemn Metro-Goldwyn-Mayer Studios, her mother, her father, her husbands and lovers, her doctors, her management, or Judy herself. Others cast her as a Hollywood icon, symbolically aligning the dissolution of her MGM contract with the collapse of the studio system. Others see in her life a condemnation of a commercialized society (Garland as exploited pawn, forced to work as a child); others credit *or* dismiss her death as a motivating factor in New York's Stonewall riots in 1969. Every theory and approach has its adherents.

Part of Garland's burden grew out of her profligate talent and a career that spanned almost five decades. Her abilities came so easily, so naturally, that she eventually doubted them. Coupled with that doubt was the continual pressure to top herself, or to be as good as she had been five, ten, twenty, and thirty years earlier. Her genuine terror of being unable to live up to expectations, of failing to please audiences, directors, and co-workers, led to those occasions she would refuse to leave her dressing room or have to be forced onto a concert stage or film set.

Judy Garland worked for nearly forty-five of her forty-seven years. She made thirty-two feature films, did voice-over work for two more, and appeared in at least a half dozen short subjects. She received a special Academy Award and was nominated for two others. She starred in thirty of her own television shows (the programs and Garland herself garnering a total of ten Emmy Award nominations) and appeared as a guest on nearly thirty more. Between 1951 and 1969, she fulfilled over eleven hundred theatre, nightclub, and concert performances, winning a special Antoinette Perry (Tony) Award for the first of three record-breaking Broadway engagements at the Palace. She recorded nearly one hundred singles and over a dozen record albums; *Judy at Carnegie Hall* received an unprecedented five Grammys in 1962 (including Album of the Year) and has never been out of print. Her radio work encompassed several hundred broadcasts, and she sang at countless benefits and personal appearances for the military. Earlier, between the ages of two and thirteen—and prior to signing her MGM contract in 1935—she fulfilled hundreds of live vaudeville and radio dates with her two older sisters.

Behind the scenes, those exposed to Garland remember most her humor and warmth, her compassion and care, her sincerity and sensitivity, her laser-direct awareness, and her intelligence. She had profound influence on those whose lives she touched, on the industry in which she worked, and on the audiences who watched and heard her perform.

One of Garland's hallmarks was, of course, an ability to convey in song the heartrending pathos of human existence. But she could also convey joy with unparalleled success, and epitomize the determination to rise above and carry on with unequaled force. Those who thrilled to her as an entertainer came away from the exposure—on film, on record, or (supremely) onstage—in an exultant,

FROM LEFT: *The "You Stepped Out of a Dream" production number,* Ziegfeld Girl, *MGM/1941. At her dressing room door during filming of* Presenting Lily Mars, *MGM/1943. At the Talk of the Town in London, January 1969.*

Singing "Hello, Bluebird" at the London Palladium for I Could Go On Singing, *United Artists/1963.*

transported, celebratory state. Almost unconsciously, she invariably appealed to the best qualities of the human condition.

Today those affected by the Garland touch fall into two categories: those who experienced her career with her, and those who have discovered her in the last two decades. Both factions respond to her in the same way. The millions of all ages who crowd revival houses, purchase videotapes and compact discs, and revel in television retrospectives gather to pay tribute to her matchless talent, her communicative ability, and—in the word used repeatedly by her professional associates—her genius.

This book is intended for those who feel that the most significant aspect of Judy Garland's life is her professional legacy—and for any who would explore the facts behind the career of the "world's greatest entertainer." It is hoped that, whether new fan or veteran admirer, the reader will feel the book can be best summarized as "*This* is what she was all about. This is what she *did*."

Chapter One

Sing, Baby, Sing

Friday, December 26, 1924:

The two-and-a-half-year-old stood quietly onstage, carefully hidden behind her two sisters. The feature film and short subject were over, the theatre houselights had come up, and she could hear her father on the other side of the curtain, welcoming the audience to the Christmas show at the New Grand.

Tonight was the little girl's first "formal" performance. She was wearing a new white-net outfit, finished just days earlier for this special occasion by her mother. And when her father concluded his introduction, it was her mother who struck up the opening music on the piano in the tiny orchestra pit to begin the stage act.

The curtains slowly parted, and the child heard welcoming applause from friends and neighbors for her sisters. As planned, however, she remained tucked away out of sight as the two older girls began their song, "When My Sugar Walks Down the Street."

The audience settled in to enjoy the show. But those who had seen the Gumm sisters on earlier occasions were quick to notice that nine-year-old Mary Jane and seven-year-old Dorothy Virginia were not moving about the stage with their usual verve. Tonight, they simply stood side by side and sang.

Then, midway through the chorus, a third voice chimed in. The two older girls let the sound register for a moment and then suddenly stepped aside. There, walking unabashedly forward to meet her first theatre audience, was Baby Gumm.

The crowd "oohed" and "ahhed" but grew more impressed as the tiny girl joined her sisters in their entire routine. After some simple song and dance, Baby offered a brief tap number and ran offstage; Mary Jane and Virginia encored with a dance duet and then they, too, bowed out. But the audience, in a friendly uproar, called for more, and Baby returned alone, carrying a tiny dinner bell and walking to center stage near the footlights. Ethel Gumm hit an introductory piano chord to quiet the crowd, and Baby began her solo: *"Dashing through the snow / in a one-horse open sleigh. . ."*

The crowd in Grand Rapids, Minnesota, was enraptured. The tot sang out loud, clear, and on key, prompting affectionate laughter as she reached the chorus and rang her bell on every title phrase: *"Jingle bells, jingle bells, jingle all the way. . ."*

There was genuine applause as she finished, and Baby—rather than settle for such approval and get off as rehearsed—spontaneously began the number again. Her mother, choking back a burst of laughter, quickly jumped into the accompaniment; her proud father, manager of the little theatre and watching from the rear of the house, roared with the rest of the crowd.

At the end of the second chorus, Baby once more segued to the top. Then she did it yet again, beginning the complete number for the fourth time. The audience response grew with each reprise, and the louder their hysteria, the louder Baby sang, ringing her little bell and finally running around in a circle in excitement.

FACING PAGE: *"Baby" Frances Ethel Gumm in her debut costume, 1925.* BELOW: *The Grand Rapids* Herald-Review *for December 24, 1924, printed the first advertisement for a Judy Garland performance.*

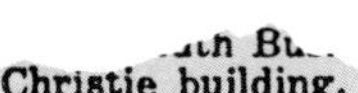
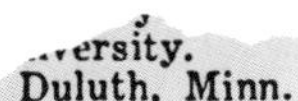

Christie building. Duluth, Minn.

AT THE NEW GRAND

Tonight.

STRONGHEART, the wonder dog, in "The Love Master" a thrilling romance of the land of the eternal snow. An excellent human cast supports "Strongheart" in this production. The News weekly completes the program.

Thursday and Friday.

MARY PICKFORD, "America's sweetheart," in one of the prettiest pictures she has ever appeared in, entitled, "Thru, the Back Door." A two-reel comedy, "Motor Mad" completes the program. Special for Friday night; the three Gumm children in songs and dances; featuring "Baby Frances" two years of age.

Saturday Night and S...

Ethel and Frank Gumm, from a series of family publicity photos taken by Eric Enstrom in nearby Bovey, Minnesota, in 1925. More than forty years later, a pianist who filled in for a week at the New Grand during Frank's tenure as manager would recall the showman's warm personality and vocal appeal. Even when audiences were small due to snow and cold weather, Ruth Gunderson remembered that "the building rocked. . . when he sang."

Midway through her fifth chorus, Baby's amused father strode down the theatre aisle and signaled to the wings. The girl's grandmother, waiting there during the act to assist backstage (and as entertained as anyone by Baby's hammy performance), marched out, picked up the child, and unceremoniously carried her off; the crowd's laughter and applause smothered the girl's tearful protest from behind the curtain: "I wanna sing some *more*!"

Proud father Frank Gumm, by now in the wings himself, comforted Baby and then escorted all three of his daughters onstage for a final bow. Bolstered by the cheers, Baby broke into a smile and, secure in her father's arms, alternately waved to the crowd and rang her little bell until the curtains closed.

++++++++

So began the career of Judy Garland.

It was neither as mythical nor as magical a start as the journalistically creative Metro-Goldwyn-Mayer press corps would later claim. But her gifts, her talent for spontaneity, her appeal to an audience —and its eager response—were already in evidence. And, although there was certainly no sense in December 1924 that Baby Gumm would one day be acclaimed as the world's greatest entertainer, her affinity for the stage was a natural one. A number of her relatives were active in what was then called "the show business" and, as she later sang in Roger Edens's special material for *Babes in Arms*, *"My daddy was a minstrel man / when minstrels were the thing. . ."*

Frank Avent Gumm, born March 20, 1886, in Murfreesboro, Tennessee, did indeed pursue a minstrel career while a young man, dropping out of college at eighteen to seek work as a performer. He found only sporadic success, however, and frequently settled into nontheatrical jobs instead. By 1912, his travels had led to the Parlor Theatre in Superior, Wisconsin, where he conducted audience sing-alongs. His pianist was nineteen-year-old Ethel Marion Milne, who had moved with her family from upper Michigan to Superior several years earlier. Born November 17, 1893, Ethel demonstrated early musical aptitude, prompting her mother to arrange for her to take piano lessons. The girl eventually became a fixture at local theatres, accompanying silent films as well as any live act.

The professional association between Frank and Ethel warmed into a courtship. Married in Superior in January 1914, they settled in Grand Rapids, Minnesota, two months later; Frank took over the New Grand, the local movie house, and Ethel played piano in the pit. The Gumms were well received and active in the little town and, in time, created a duo act for themselves: Jack and Virginia Lee, Sweet Southern Singers. Although Ethel's voice ranked second to her skills as accompanist/arranger, Frank's lyric baritone was well suited to such sentimental tunes of the day as "Let Me Call You Sweetheart" and "Danny Boy."

The Gumms' family life began when daughter Mary Jane was born on September 24, 1915; she later changed her first name to Suzanne (or Susie). Dorothy Virginia, eventually nicknamed Jimmie, came along on July 4, 1917, and, by the early 1920s, both girls were performing locally (if infrequently and informally) with their parents.

In autumn 1921, Ethel found herself pregnant for the third time. The news wasn't welcome. A strain had developed between husband and wife, triggered by Ethel's discovery of Frank's homosexual activities. The demand for self-denial and the need for secrecy (or at least discretion) must have put enormous pressure on Frank; the situation made Ethel certain she did not want another child. She tried to induce a miscarriage, and Judy, fully aware of this in later years, laughingly commented, "She did *everything* to get rid of me. She must have rolled down nineteen thousand flights of stairs, jumped off of tables. . ." Frank even discussed the advisability of abortion with family friend Marc Rabwin, but the second-year medical student knew the dangers of such an operation in 1921 and convinced him to talk Ethel out of the idea.

Resigned to a full-term pregnancy, the Gumms hoped for a boy, whom they planned to name Frank, Jr. Instead, a baby girl arrived at 5:30 A.M. on Saturday, June 10, 1922. She was christened Frances Ethel (after both parents) and baptized at the Episcopal church. From the beginning, however, everyone called her Baby—Baby Gumm.

All three Gumm girls led happy, normal lives in Grand Rapids. Judy recalled in 1940 that "certainly my first sort of large, blurry memory is of music, music all the time, music all over the house." In a much-loved bedtime ritual, she would nightly crawl into Frank's lap for a lullaby before he went off to the theatre. He also figured in her first music lesson; as Judy remembered, "I had a little girlfriend who was just about my age; we couldn't have been any more than two. And this particular day, my father decided to teach us both to sing 'America' while he played it on the upright piano in the parlor. After we had run through it a couple of times, he called my mother and my sisters in to listen. And I was terribly proud, because it had only taken a few times for me to learn the song. After I finished, they all kept saying, 'Baby's *good.* She can sing!' "

As a result, Susie and Jimmie added Baby to their amateur theatrical performances in the garage; she had already been "*full* of infant rage at being left out!" Jimmie recalled. "That was really where Judy got her start, in those little backyard shows for our friends and Mama's bridge guests. [After a while] there was no way we could have left her out, even if we'd wanted to. And she was *good,* too. She picked everything up so quickly—and what a ham!"

Jimmie remembered as well that, around the time of Baby's second birthday, their father booked an out-of-town act, The Blue Sisters, into the New Grand. "We joked about them coming out all dressed in blue—and they did! They were a trio of harmony singers, just about our ages; the oldest couldn't have been more than eleven and the youngest about five. They weren't anything special, by any means, but they absolutely freaked us out. Here, right before our eyes, was just what we wanted to be. Judy, especially, was all but uncontrollable. She sat there, bouncing up and down, humming along. Then, just before they finished their turn, the little girl sang a solo. We all could see how this was really going to send Judy into a fit, and it did. She sat transfixed. When it was over, she turned to Daddy and—I'll never forget it—said, 'Can I do that, Daddy?' We all laughed at her remark (which made her mad as hell, I'm afraid!). But there wasn't any doubt that she already knew exactly what she wanted."

The neighborhood shows, the music around the house, and the appearance of The Blue Sisters all led to Baby's debut on December 26, 1924, but the eager child almost jumped the gun. Ethel's mother, Eva Milne, had come from upper Michigan to spend the holidays and see the act. She encouraged Baby to spontaneously join in a children's matinee show on the twenty-fourth, sending her down the theatre aisle with an assertive "Go on, get up on the stage!" (There are two legends about the effect of that directive: in one, Baby scampered right

BELOW: Baby Gumm, 1925. BOTTOM: Baby's first notice, from the Herald-Review, *December 31, 1924. A year earlier, she had sung "Tie Me to Your Apron Strings Again" in a backyard show. But she would always recognize her formal debut as the night "I took one look at all those people, laughing and applauding, and I fell hopelessly in love with audiences. . . the lights and the music and the whole thing."*

Gumm Children Please.

The three young daughters of Mr. and Mrs. Frank Gumm delighted a large audience at the New Grand theater last Friday night with 20 minutes of singing and dancing. Mary Jane and Virginia, the two oldest girls are becoming accomplished entertainers, while the work of Frances, the two year old baby, was a genuine surprise. The little girl spoke and sang so as to be heard by everyone in the house and she joined in the dancing both alone and with her older sisters. The audience expressed their appreciation of the work of all three girls by vigorous applause.

LEFT: Susie, Jimmie, and Baby—the Gumm Sisters, 1925. After Baby's debut, local newspapers were quick to announce her subsequent appearances with such laudatory (and foreshadowing) phrases as "[She] will sing and dance. . . in the way that she alone can perform." RIGHT: The Gumms in a family snapshot, circa 1925. Judy later characterized Grand Rapids as "beautiful. . . wonderful—a gracious little town, full of trees and porches and people who knew how to live in simple goodness."

out and interrupted the show with "Jingle Bells"; in the other, she stopped en route at the piano and asked her mother's permission. Ethel recommended that she wait until her new dress was finished for the formal presentation.)

A month after her Christmas show debut, Baby did make an unscheduled reappearance at the New Grand, running onstage unannounced during an amateur-night competition. She launched directly into "Jingle Bells" once again, and this time Frank himself had to walk out and retrieve his errant child. (The local audience, already firmly in Baby's corner, awarded her first prize at the end of the show. Her diplomatic father refused to let her accept it.)

Later, Judy's memories of events at the New Grand in December 1924/January 1925 would merge and mingle; MGM publicity simply declared her first appearance had been a momentous surprise to all. But, as Jimmie later confirmed, Baby's debut "was just another Christmas show at Dad's theatre. We didn't attach any particular significance to it. And neither was it spontaneous; it was carefully planned and rehearsed for about two weeks before."

Baby quickly became part of every family performance. Over the next eighteen months, she gave approximately twenty shows—usually with her sisters—both in Grand Rapids and in nearby towns. Entertaining became an integral, though hardly regimented aspect of her life, and something in which she reveled. The only traumatic event she experienced during that time was a case of acute acidosis so severe that she was rushed eighty miles to a Duluth hospital where the initial prognosis was poor. After several days, she began to recover, but the memories of the illness and the separation from home reportedly haunted her for some time.

In June 1926, the five Gumms took a summer vacation, traveling by train across the northwestern United States to the West Coast and stopping en route for seven performances. Frank and Ethel resurrected Jack and Virginia Lee for the occasion, this time sharing billing with The Three Little Lees. In Los Angeles, they enjoyed a reunion with Marc Rabwin, visited several movie studios, and saw the famed Duncan Sisters in a performance of "Topsy and Eva." That matinee provided another early indication of Baby's prodigious appeal: the Duncans spontaneously picked her out of the crowd of juveniles visiting them onstage after the act and suggested the Gumms keep in touch. The Duncans felt sure they would be able to place Baby in "the show business" during the next season.

The sunshine of southern California made the prospect of another Minnesota winter highly undesirable. Shortly after the Gumms returned to Grand Rapids in July, they announced a permanent move West. Ethel later claimed their decision was predicated solely on climate, but evidence exists that Frank's local indiscretions had reached a point that such a move was necessary. The Gumm Sisters concluded their New Grand appearances with gala farewell shows in October. There were also a dozen going-away parties for the family; a number of the local citizens obviously held them in high regard and were sorry to see them leave.

After a few months of searching in southern California, Frank found another theatre to rent. But instead of the hoped-for Los Angeles location, the family ended up eighty miles to the north, in Lancaster—considerably removed from the professional opportunities they could seek in the city. Despite the initial disappointment, they quickly fell into a familiar routine. Frank managed what he renamed the Valley Theatre, Ethel played the piano, and the girls performed, all to local enthusiasm.

Over the next eight years, the foundation of Judy Garland's career would be established: Baby sang in stage shows, on radio programs, at social events, and in grammar-school productions. The infrequent performances in Grand Rapids gave way in California to an increasingly rigorous schedule, and Ethel also arranged for additional training; she and the girls often made the three-hour car trek into Los Angeles for various theatrical lessons.

Ethel's efforts on behalf of her daughters came to be regarded with a measure of disdain and suspicion by some residents of Lancaster, who saw her as an obsessive stage mother. The general public received the same impression in later years when, during periods of illness, overmedication, and financial pres-

The Gumms clown for a Los Angeles camera in 1927, a few months after their move to California. LEFT TO RIGHT: *Frank; Baby and Susie; Baby and Jimmie. In the Gumms' brief cross-country tour during June 1926, Baby had already been billed as the "three-year-old Charleston stepper."*

sure, Judy Garland would claim she had been forced into her career by a driven, talentless mother. (Her accusations were supplemented by other negative memories of Ethel, voiced by many who knew her during Judy's years at MGM.) If the opinions are to some degree accurate, it is equally true to say that Ethel's motives—at least during her days in Lancaster—have been misunderstood. There's little doubt she was growing more ambitious. But by 1928, Ethel's discontent was at least partly due to her perplexing and complex marital problems. Frank's liaisons had been sporadic, but they must have seemed to her a source of potential, dreadful humiliation. Her need to spend time away from Lancaster probably grew out of a desire to protect herself and her daughters as much as possible. She found such an opportunity in an active pursuit of their performing careers.

Further, the professionals with whom Ethel associated in Los Angeles during this time regarded her not only as a solid musician but as the very antithesis of the average stage mother. Jimmie would later concur: "My mother was wonderful. She didn't push us at all, and we owe everything we are to her." Judy, during the healthy and happy portions of her adult life, was also quick to acknowledge this: "My mother is a strong-minded woman, but she was never a 'stage mama.' She was part of an era that was hard on women. She wanted so desperately to be a person in her own right, and I can understand that. If I weren't in a business that has always accepted women as people, that would have been one of my bothers, too. Mother had to succeed at whatever she undertook . . ."

During her young childhood, however, Baby Gumm was occasionally unhappy with her mother's actions and periodically came to resent the demands of rehearsals, auditions, travel, classes, and the literally hundreds of performances she gave during those early years. She adored her father and, even into the 1930s, was too young to grasp the reasons for her parents' separations. She eventually came to equate Lancaster with increasing familial problems and career activity.

LEFT: Lobby card for the first film made by the Gumm Sisters; they are shown in their specialty number, "The Good Old Sunny South." The eighteen-minute Big Revue *premiered at Hollywood's Fox Belmont Theatre on August 14, 1929. In subsequent two-reelers, the girls sang "Storyland Holiday" and "When the Butterflies Kiss the Buttercups Goodnight" in* A Holiday in Storyland, *the title song in* The Wedding of Jack and Jill, *and "The Land of Let's Pretend" in* Bubbles. *RIGHT: Baby in 1929.*

(During her first year there, she was also struck by a recurrence of the viral infection she had suffered in Minnesota. Rabwin got her admitted to Los Angeles County Hospital, and her case was serious enough to require weeks of care.)

Whatever Baby's feelings, or Ethel's, or Frank's, Lancaster loved the Gumms in 1928. Frank made an instant success of the Valley Theatre and, once the town's doubts about show people were dispelled, the girls were quickly accepted. At least initially, there was time to enjoy the sort of life they'd left behind.

By September 1928, however, the Gumm Sisters were also working in Los Angeles with The Meglin Kiddies, a group of children culled from the Ethel Meglin Dance School. During a prestigious appearance at Loew's State Theatre, Baby was given a coveted solo spot and dressed as Cupid to sing "I Can't Give You Anything but Love." Later, in mid-1929, the Meglin association also led to the girls' first film work. Shot over three days at Tec-Art Studios in Hollywood, *The Big Revue* showcased 140 Meglin star pupils accompanied by an all-children orchestra. The Gumm Sisters had their own brief number, introduced by a young mistress of ceremonies: "Now you will see a dancing and singing number by The Gumm Sisters. . . not The Wrigley Sisters!" As the orchestra scraped out an introduction, Jimmie sang the verse to "The Good Old Sunny South"; at the chorus, the camera cut away to show Baby's entrance. The seven-year-old matched both her sisters step for step, at one point jumping a singing entrance in her enthusiasm and shooting a sheepish "Did anyone notice that?" glance at Jimmie. Though historic only as the film debut of Judy Garland, the number is notable for the power of Baby's voice as she shouts "Yassuh!" to punctuate several lyrical points, all but drowning out her sisters and the band. Her attitude is nothing so much as vintage minstrel; there is a lingering (if apocryphal) sense that it was a moment inspired, if not taught, by Frank. She also carries out her choreography in a totally second-nature manner, giving the stodgy steps a flow and ease that the two older girls can't quite manage.

During the next few years, Ethel and the girls went from school to school, leaving Meglin's for Flynn O'Malley's Hollywood Starlets and then moving on to I. C. Overdorff's Hollywood School of the Dance, the Maurice Kusell Theatrical Dance Studio, and the Fanchon & Marco School of the Theatre. Ethel frequently joined the various teaching staffs as a combination pianist, arranger, coach, and conductor, and each school association led to more work and recognition for the Gumm Sisters. O'Malley sent them to Warner Bros. where, in late 1929 and early 1930, they appeared for Roy Mack in three two-strip Technicolor Vitaphone Kiddie shorts. The girls, billed as The Three Kute Kiddies, sang in *A Holiday in Storyland, The Wedding of Jack and Jill,* and *Bubbles;* seven-year-old Baby also had a solo in each short: "Blue Butterfly," "Hang On to a Rainbow," and "Lady Luck." The films were released by First National–Vitaphone Pictures.

The Gumms also began to be heard regularly on Los Angeles-area radio, winning praise for their appearances on "Big Brother Ken's Kiddie Hour" over KFI and "Junior Hi-Jinx" over KFWB. One reviewer commended their vigor and found "nothing on the air at the moment. . . so original" as the Gumm Sisters. There were further film auditions as well. Famed impresario Gus Edwards interviewed the girls as candidates for a series of MGM musical shorts in 1929 and, although he couldn't use them, advised Ethel to develop three-part harmony-numbers as the core of the girls' act. (They began rehearsing on the way back to Lancaster.) In 1931, Jack Hayes at Universal liked Baby's audition but had nothing for her

Baby in 1930. By this time, the Gumm Sisters' repertoire featured close harmony trio songs, eventually including "In a Little Spanish Town," "Bye, Bye Blackbird," "When the Red, Red Robin Comes Bob-Bob-Bobbin' Along," and "Shuffle Off to Buffalo." But the act quickly became a showcase for Baby, and Ethel chose her solos. Over the years, these included "My Mammy," "I Can't Give You Anything But Love," "Rain, Rain, Go Away," and "Brother, Can You Spare a Dime." (The latter, as Judy wryly noted in 1968, was "perfect for a little girl" of ten or eleven. She also laughingly remembered the occasion she had to sing reprise after reprise of "Trees" to appease an insistent drunk. The man sat in an otherwise empty theatre, weeping and calling, "Tha's beautiful, honey, tha's beautiful.*")*

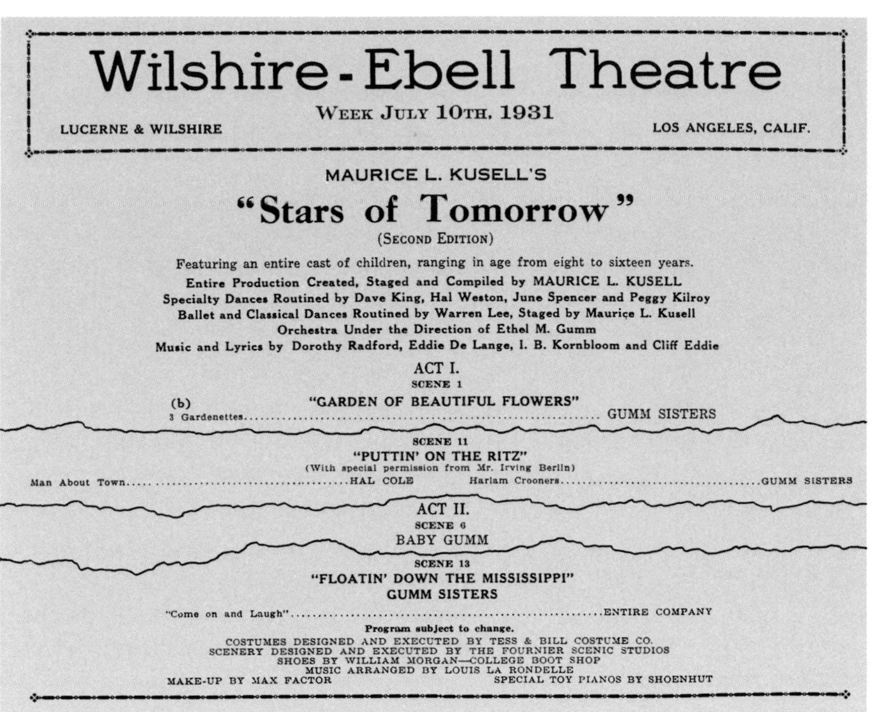

Wilshire-Ebell Theatre

LUCERNE & WILSHIRE — WEEK JULY 10TH, 1931 — LOS ANGELES, CALIF.

MAURICE L. KUSELL'S

"Stars of Tomorrow"

(SECOND EDITION)

Featuring an entire cast of children, ranging in age from eight to sixteen years.
Entire Production Created, Staged and Compiled by MAURICE L. KUSELL
Specialty Dances Routined by Dave King, Hal Weston, June Spencer and Peggy Kilroy
Ballet and Classical Dances Routined by Warren Lee, Staged by Mauriçe L. Kusell
Orchestra Under the Direction of Ethel M. Gumm
Music and Lyrics by Dorothy Radford, Eddie De Lange, I. B. Kornbloom and Cliff Eddie

ACT I.
SCENE 1
(b) "GARDEN OF BEAUTIFUL FLOWERS"
3 Gardenettes........ GUMM SISTERS

SCENE 11
"PUTTIN' ON THE RITZ"
(With special permission from Mr. Irving Berlin)
Man About Town........HAL COLE Harlam Crooners........GUMM SISTERS

ACT II.
SCENE 6
BABY GUMM

SCENE 13
"FLOATIN' DOWN THE MISSISSIPPI"
GUMM SISTERS

"Come on and Laugh"........ENTIRE COMPANY

Program subject to change.
COSTUMES DESIGNED AND EXECUTED BY TESS & BILL COSTUME CO.
SCENERY DESIGNED AND EXECUTED BY THE FOURNIER SCENIC STUDIOS
SHOES BY WILLIAM MORGAN—COLLEGE BOOT SHOP
MUSIC ARRANGED BY LOUIS LA RONDELLE
MAKE-UP BY MAX FACTOR SPECIAL TOY PIANOS BY SHOENHUT

ABOVE: Ethel Gumm and her daughters, circa 1931. RIGHT: Excerpts from the playbill that marked the Gumms' first association with Maurice Kusell. The teacher-impresario later remarked that, even then, "it was plainly obvious to everyone that Judy would one day be the biggest thing that ever came along."

to do; the same year, she made it to the final cut for the lead in *The Unexpected Father,* a ZaSu Pitts/Slim Summerville feature, but the role went to Cora Sue Collins. In 1933, there was brief but truncated interest from MGM.

So vaudeville remained the most important aspect of the Gumm Sisters' career, with ever-increasing response to Baby's unique abilities. As early as 1930, the San Diego *News* termed the girls "the highlight of [a Hollywood Starlets] presentation. Their smallest member is a feisty little miss who also sang solo in a surprisingly powerful voice and all but stopped the show." (In 1968, Judy would self-deprecatingly recall her early volume: "Well, I could always be *heard.* We had to practically *scream* the place down because half the time there were no mikes!")

The Gumm Sisters began their most advantageous association when they met Maurice Kusell in summer 1931. Recognizing the girls' ability, he unhesitatingly added them to the already enormous cast of his current children's revue. In December, Baby was chosen over thirty-five other acts to headline his presentation at the Hollywood Theatre, where her singing and dancing literally stopped the show.

The year 1932 began auspiciously. Baby's impromptu appearance at a Cocoanut Grove tea dance led to work during the bistro's regular Saturday "Star Night." That summer, Kusell got the girls booked on a California tour arranged by Fanchon & Marco. The Gumm Sisters were the hit of the bill, receiving their first notice in *Variety* while at the Los Angeles Paramount: "Selling end of the trio is the ten-year-old with a pip of a lowdown voice. Kid stopped the show. . ."

Kusell next put Baby in his "Juvenile Christmas Revue" at the Los Angeles Million Dollar Theatre, where the Los Angeles *Record* rated her "astounding. Her singing all but knocks one for a loop, her dancing is snappy and clever. She handles herself onstage like a veteran pro." Having noticed what would later be termed "the wail" in Baby's voice, Kusell also arranged for her to be coached by cantor Oscar Blanco, feeling he could help expand such a soulful sound.

There must have been some experiments with a new approach or inappropriate material during the trio's summer engagements in 1933, for several critics came down hard on the girls for the first time. Their voices and style were described as "mediocre," and one reviewer bemoaned "the little girl who had been trained to sing 'Stormy Weather' in a leather-lunged blues voice." Fortunately, there were redeeming comments as well: *Junior Professionals* noted that Baby was billed as "a wonder in disguise," but observed that "this remarkable tot is anything but incognito. . .with twice the charm and genuine ability of all the [movie child stars] put together."

Up to this point, the girls had always spent most of the school year in Lancaster, performing at the Valley Theatre. By 1933, however, the situation at home had deteriorated to such an extent that Ethel took a house for them in suburban Los Angeles, at Silver Lake. (There had been earlier separations from Frank during some of their tours and longer Los Angeles sojourns.) Ostensibly, Frank made the move with them, but he actually spent most of his time managing the theatre and living in a small shack in Lancaster. In Los Angeles, Baby and Jimmie enrolled in Lawlor's Hollywood Professional School, where Mickey Rooney was also a student. He and Baby first shared the bill at a Lawlor recital on October 21.

In early 1934, the Gumm Sisters toured the Northwest, a trip that later gave Judy a raft of anecdotes to tell television and concert audiences. In truth, she never appeared with most of the acts she described; the stories were usually adapted from tales told by other vaudevillians. But the Garland humor and penchant for embellishment and emphasis made the jokes her own; thus she would mischievously discuss the cowboy "who had a singing *coyote* with him. . .until the humane society took the coyote *away*, and the man went into the business of becoming a *fire*-eater." She also loved remembering Hadji Ali, "the man who *threw up* for a living." Assisted by his wife and in full view of the audience, Ali would drink "an *enormous* fishbowl full of fluid which was half kerosene and half water, and then 'bring up' the kerosene," projecting it clear across the stage to "a sort of Oriental outdoor *barbecue*." The fire in the barbecue would flare up in fine fashion until "he'd bring up the *water*. . .and put the fire *out*." Ali, Judy ruefully noted, finally "died of ptomaine poisoning—in a *cafeteria!*" But her most famous saga was probably appropriated from Bert Lahr. It concerned Harry Rose—by Garland's description, "the most *depressed* comedian I've ever known." For his entrance, Rose always burst through the stage curtains at top speed, greeting the audience with "HelloeverybodythisisHappyHarry!" On one memorable occasion, he misjudged the space between the velour drapes and footlights, barreled out onto the stage, and kept right on going into the orchestra pit. In Judy's recounting, "he broke his leg in three places, very badly. Now the manager of the tour would make us *wait* all through his act every night to make sure we were ready. So we were in the wings, and the manager said, *'GO ON!'* So we had to sing 'Dinah.' And we walked on, '*Di*-nah. . . is there anyone *fi*-nah. . .?' And this poor thing in the pit is yelling, *'AHHHHHHHHHH!'* "

Evidently, the girls heeded the criticisms of their 1933 tour, for they returned to consistent raves by 1934. Baby's new featured number created a sensation, and Judy later described the setting: "[I was] wrapped in a black shawl, sitting on [mother's] piano on a dark stage, only my face spotlighted." Then, in what

A candid snapshot of Baby, circa 1932. By this point—in her eighth year of performing—Baby's singing and dancing were almost invariably reviewed as show-stealing or show-stopping, no matter where the Gumm Sisters appeared.

A portrait taken during the girls' successful Chicago engagements, summer 1934. During their weeks in town, Baby was chosen special guest of honor at the July 19 Children's Day at the World's Fair; by August, the trio was sharing a first-class bill at the Oriental Theatre with singer-monologist George Jessel. Twenty years later, he would refer to Baby as "a combination of Helen Hayes and Al Jolson and Jenny Lind and Sarah Bernhardt."

George Jessel would soon hear as "the voice of a woman . . . a woman who had been hurt," eleven-year-old Baby sang Helen Morgan's "Bill" from *Show Boat*. "At the song's conclusion, I threw off my shawl and the lights came up." The audience, realizing for the first time that they'd been listening to a child, invariably went wild.

Following a spring tour in southern California, the girls decided to go East. There were brief bookings in Colorado, but it was their work in Chicago that led—in the words of the local Lancaster paper—to "one of the proverbial 'breaks' in the show business."

The initial stretch of their stay was rocky. Contest auditions in July won them several engagements at the Chicago World's Fair, but the Gumms were only paid for the first of their three weeks at the Old Mexico Nite Club, and Ethel turned down a Lido booking because of its scantily clad chorines. Frank—worried about four women driving alone across the country—had given Ethel several hundred dollars in travelers checks for any emergency, but she was determined not to use his money. By mid-August, however, when reduced to washing their clothes by hand and with only a couple of eggs and moldy bread for breakfast, she finally broke down, cashed a check, and took the girls out to eat.

Twenty years later, in *A Star is Born*, Judy would sing *"Then something happened: Dame Fortune showed her face."* On August 17, as the Gumms prepared to leave Chicago in defeat, the phone rang. Mary Jane had been dating trumpeter Jack Cathcart, and a friend had just called to tell him that The Three 'C's trio had been fired after their first appearance at the Oriental Theatre. The Gumms could audition to replace them and, if hired, go on for the second house. They rushed to get ready and were quickly added to the program; though slotted second on the bill (a far from desirable spot), they stopped the show cold.

George Jessel, headliner at the Oriental that week, never forgot the impression Baby made on him and the audience. He quickly had the girls' position in the show changed to next to closing and volunteered to correct the one flaw he found in their act: the audience had laughed when he'd introduced "The Gumm Sisters," and he promised the girls a new name for their next appearance. (Jessel later joked that, when he approached Ethel with the idea of renaming Baby, Mrs. Gumm replied, "Well, Mr. Jessel, she's just starting; call her anything you like.") That afternoon, Jessel announced "The Garland Sisters," a name appropriated from that of New York *World-Telegram* drama critic Robert Garland. The girls were delighted, and it was a welcome change; over the years, they'd been incorrectly billed as the Gum Sisters, Gunn Sisters, Drumm Sisters, and Glumm Sisters.

(In 1935, when Judy signed with MGM, the studio developed its own story of her name change. They claimed that Jessel met Baby as she wept over the sight of "The Glumm Sisters" in electric lights on the Oriental marquee; he decided on the spot she was "pretty as a garland of roses." Jessel later maintained that his inspiration at the Oriental grew out of a flowery wire he'd sent to congratulate actress Judith Anderson on her reviews for a new play: "These critical paeans become you like garlands of roses." He then combined Anderson's first name with a word from the telegram to come up with "Judith Garland." While Judy herself always warmly acknowledged Jessel's contribution, she actually selected her own new first name—in the summer of 1935.)

Jessel lined up other Chicago dates for the trio, and they worked three midnight shows at the Chez Paree Club with Morton Downey, until the management realized Baby was a minor. The girls were also taken up by the local William Morris agency, which arranged for several suburban bookings and a brief Midwestern tour. Jessel next suggested that the girls go on to New York with him to play the Paramount, but Baby's age made it impossible for them to work in Manhattan without hiring a tutor for her. So "Mrs. Garland" and the girls returned to California and an emotional reunion with Frank.

But the momentum of their latest successes continued all autumn. *Variety* published a rapturous review of Baby's work during a November engagement at Grauman's Chinese Theatre, and the girls were also invited to participate in Irving Strouse's "Sunday Nite Vaudeville Frolics" at the Wilshire-Ebell Theatre. On December 10, the Los Angeles *Evening Express* ran the headline, "Twelve-Year-Old Girl Is Sensation at Frolics." Critic W. E. Oliver wrote, "Little Frances. . . sang in a way that produced in the audience sensations that haven't been equalled in years. Not your smart, adult-aping prodigy is this girl, but a youngster who had the divine instinct to be herself on the stage, along with a talent for singing, a trick of rocking the spectators with rhythms, and a capacity for putting emotion into her performance that suggests what Bernhardt must have been at her age. It isn't the cloying, heavy sentiment her elders so often strive for, but simple, sincere feeling that reaches the heart. The three girls together are an act anyone would want to see. Frances alone is a sensation, and last Saturday's audience realized it by the way they encored. Much of her individual style of singing was culled by the little girl from her parents' old act, although she must have the divine spark to be able to sing as she did. . . She would make any show."

Strouse briefly took a version of the "Frolics" to San Francisco, where the *Call-Bulletin* reported that "Frances [has become] the talk of the town in no time at all. . . as much the sweetheart of the stage as Shirley Temple is of the screen, with less renown and, naturally, with more maturity in her appeal, but no less charm."

The girls' work for Strouse also led to a successful screen test at Universal

Both the renovation of the family name and the kind of mistake that inspired it are apparent in ads for several of the girls' 1934 Chicago engagements. In earlier years, Baby's name had also been briefly, experimentally changed, and she had been alternately billed as Baby Marie Gumm, Alice Gumm, Gracie Gumm, and Frances Gayne.

BELOW: *Baby, and* BOTTOM: *Ethel and the Garland Sisters, Chicago, 1934. On November 6,* Variety *reviewed Baby at Grauman's Chinese Theatre: "[She] gets every note and word over with a personality that hits audiences. . . . She has never failed to stop the show."*

in January 1935, and they were signed for *The Great Ziegfeld*, scheduled to film that spring. In March, with Ethel at the piano, they tackled a new medium and cut three test records for Decca. The trio sang "Moonglow"; Baby did "Bill" and a medley of "On the Good Ship Lollipop," "The Object of My Affection," and "Dinah," but the tests were rejected. Shortly thereafter, the nearly bankrupt Universal sold off the *Great Ziegfeld* property to MGM, who, in turn, dropped the girls from the picture.

Consolation came when The Garland Sisters were featured at the Los Angeles Paramount Theatre in May and then held over two extra weeks—an astounding achievement at that time. Baby was reviewed as "about as talented an entertainer as one could imagine," and the trio won another film contract, this time for a Louis Lewyn Technicolor short subject to be filmed in August.

Meanwhile, Frank's life in Lancaster had become increasingly difficult. Due to the expenses incurred by the girls' career and the maintenance of separate residences for the family, he had been unable to keep up his payments on the Valley Theatre. In March, he lost the lease and left town. His departure was also attributed to the same kind of disquieting rumors heard nine years earlier in Grand Rapids, although many in Lancaster maintained warm memories of his community spirit and personality. By May, he'd found a new theatre within commuting distance of Silver Lake, and the family was once again living together. The girls inaugurated Garland's Lomita Theatre on June 8 and then left for a summer booking at Lake Tahoe's Cal-Neva Lodge.

The engagement was notable on two counts. Determined once and for all to get away from the "Baby" sobriquet, thirteen-year-old Frances refused to answer to anything but "Judy," a self-termed "peppy" tag she had taken from a new Hoagy Carmichael song. More important, she was seen during her final performance at Cal-Neva by songwriter Harry Akst and agent Al Rosen. After the show, the two men requested an introduction, and Rosen asked Judy if she knew "Dinah" (Akst had written it). The composer himself accompanied her and later said: "I was. . . three feet away. The volume nearly knocked me flat. Her pitch was perfect, her breathing and timing naturally flawless. And she had those saucer-shaped brown eyes swimming with anxiety and love." The captivated Rosen would ever after refer to Judy as "the greatest discovery" of his career.

The two men had actually gone to Tahoe as moral support for songwriter Lew Brown, whose wife was there establishing residence for a divorce. Unable to effect a reconciliation, the depressed Brown had gone to bed and missed the girls' show. The next day, when the Garlands unexpectedly returned to Cal-Neva to retrieve their forgotten orchestrations (and a hat box), club manager "Bones" Remer dragged Judy into the lounge so that Brown could hear her as well. Akst reprised a hasty chorus of "Dinah" for the girl, and she then ran back to the family car.

In August, the Garland Sisters filmed three choruses of "La Cucaracha" for Louis Lewyn's *La Fiesta de Santa Barbara*. It marked the girls' last professional association. While in Tahoe, Susie had met musician Lee Cahn, and she married him there on August 15. Jimmie was also going steady by this time, and the act broke up.

Al Rosen, however, had already begun to work on Judy's behalf. At Columbia, his cohorts from Cal-Neva were doing a musical for singer Harry Richman, and Akst and Brown arranged for the headliner to hear her. Though much impressed,

Richman thought her a tomboy type: "What can we do with a little Huckleberry Finn?" Harry Cohn, the head of Columbia, felt she was too young for pictures, and Judy would later say that most of the studio heads she met at that time "didn't know what to do with twelve-year-old girls. There was no such thing. You either had to be a *Munchkin* [à la young juvenile stars like Shirley Temple] or you had to be [at which point she pantomimed a large bosom] . . . *eighteen.* There was no in-between!"

The situation was much the same at RKO, Warners, and Paramount; everyone (including Cecil B. De Mille) loved her, but there were no roles she could fill. At Fox, the tables turned: they felt Judy was too mature in voice and appearance for a cameo role in Jane Withers's *Paddy O'Day.* (Rosen was irate about the audition anyway: "She's good enough for the lead; why give her a stooge part?")

The agent next approached MGM, where legitimate interest in Judy had already been manifested. Writer/producer/director Joseph L. Mankiewicz had taken Ida Koverman and George Sidney to hear her sing at the Wilshire-Ebell nine months earlier, and they had wanted to sign her then—Koverman as adjunct to studio head Louis B. Mayer and Sidney as ace screen-test director for the lot. Sidney clearly remembers filming Judy (with Ethel at the piano) as she performed a musical baseball routine built around "Casey at the Bat." It's difficult now, however—nearly sixty years later—to determine if that test was made in 1934 (*Variety* noted in December that "Metro tested Frances Garland for a featured part in *Broadway Melody*"), or as a result of Judy's subsequent Metro interview, arranged by Rosen in September 1935.

On that day, Ethel was at the Pasadena Playhouse, rehearsing a new Maurice Kusell revue. Judy, home working in the garden, got the call from Rosen to get out to MGM quickly and, more or less "as is," was taken to Culver City by her proud father. He accompanied her as she sang "Zing! Went the Strings of My Heart" for Koverman and Jack Robbins, head of Metro's music department.

The timing couldn't have been more propitious. Robbins was in the process of creating a stock company of musical performers, training them for feature film work in a series of short subjects. He called his assistant, Roger Edens, to replace the self-admittedly amateur Frank at the piano, and Judy sang again. In 1961, Edens said, "I knew instantly, in eight bars of music. The talent was that inbred. I fell flat on my face. She was just so high and chubby, wearing a navy blue middy blouse and baby-doll sandals, with lots of hair and no lipstick. It was like discovering gold at Sutter Creek."

Koverman next phoned Louis B. Mayer and insisted he hear Judy. (When he agreed, Judy recalled an awed reaction. "They said, 'He's *coming!*' Like it was the Resurrection!") Mayer supposedly listened impassively, but he knew talent. A succinct order reached the legal department almost immediately: "Please prepare contract for the services of Judy Garland as an actress."

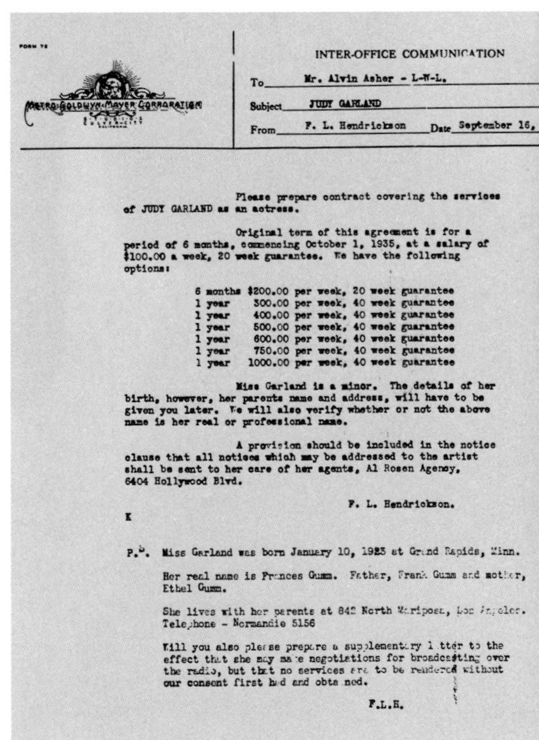

FORM 72

METRO-GOLDWYN-MAYER CORPORATION

INTER-OFFICE COMMUNICATION

To Mr. Alvin Asher - L-N-L.

Subject JUDY GARLAND

From F. L. Hendrickson Date September 16, 193

Please prepare contract covering the services of JUDY GARLAND as an actress.

Original term of this agreement is for a period of 6 months, commencing October 1, 1935, at a salary of $100.00 a week, 20 week guarantee. We have the following options:

6 months $200.00 per week, 20 week guarantee
1 year 300.00 per week, 40 week guarantee
1 year 400.00 per week, 40 week guarantee
1 year 500.00 per week, 40 week guarantee
1 year 600.00 per week, 40 week guarantee
1 year 750.00 per week, 40 week guarantee
1 year 1000.00 per week, 40 week guarantee

Miss Garland is a minor. The details of her birth, however, her parents name and address, will have to be given you later. We will also verify whether or not the above name is her real or professional name.

A provision should be included in the notice clause that all notices which may be addressed to the artist shall be sent to her care of her agents, Al Rosen Agency, 6404 Hollywood Blvd.

F. L. Hendrickson.

K

P.S. Miss Garland was born January 10, 1923 at Grand Rapids, Minn.

Her real name is Frances Gumm. Father, Frank Gumm and mother, Ethel Gumm.

She lives with her parents at 842 North Mariposa, Los Angeles. Telephone - Normandie 5156

Will you also please prepare a supplementary letter to the effect that she may make negotiations for broadcasting over the radio, but that no services are to be rendered without our consent first had and obtained.

F.L.H.

TOP: December 1934: Although still working as a trio, the Garland Sisters were by this point yielding solo billing to Baby. BOTTOM: The intracorporate memo that would make Judy Garland an MGM contract player.

Chapter Two

When a Star Is Born

Baby Gumm reached a new level of success when she signed her MGM contract in 1935. It was the biggest and best of all the movie studios and, although her ability could have easily led to eventual fame onstage or radio, working at MGM meant potential worldwide film celebrity. The studio boasted "more stars than there are in heaven," and possessed every necessary professional coach and adviser to best create a "Judy Garland" palatable to the public. It also provided supervision from the alternately paternalistic/despotic Louis B. Mayer, vice president in charge of production. (While Mayer held forth in Culver City, MGM was, in effect, run from New York by its parent company, Loew's, Inc., and president Nicholas M. Schenck.)

Whether acting at Al Rosen's suggestion or endeavoring to make Baby's talent seem even more prodigious, Frank and Ethel gave her birthdate as January 10, 1923, when providing initial background information for the studio. As a result, actor Wallace Beery introduced her as "only twelve years old" when she made her network radio debut on "The Shell Chateau Hour" on October 26. He also added a scripted "I think she's going to be the sensation of pictures." Judy responded with some giggly patter ("I wanna be a singer, Mr. Beery—and I'd like to act, too"), but the naive tones vanished when she sang "Broadway Rhythm." Attending the broadcast was MGM child star Jackie Cooper (who would shortly thereafter begin to date Garland); he remembered that she performed "with the energy of seven hundred Mack trucks" and approached the song as if "it was the last time anyone would ever sing it again."

Judy made a return visit to "Shell Chateau" on November 16, and Beery intimated that her Metro contract had been signed as a result of the first appearance. Her rendition of "Zing! Went the Strings of My Heart" was all the more impassioned that night; her father had been taken to the hospital earlier in the day, and Marc Rabwin had called to say that Frank would be listening.

He died the next afternoon of spinal meningitis. The experience was shattering for the whole family, especially Judy. A relative stability had been established in their lives in the preceding months, and she herself was finally reaching an age when she could have better comprehended some of her parents' problems. Frank's death made such a mature resolution impossible.

Meanwhile, she continued her daily coaching at Metro. Roger Edens and Ida Koverman were Judy's particular champions, the latter keeping her "alive" in Mayer's mind whenever possible. The industry outside MGM maintained its interest as well: Decca made test records with Judy on November 27, but the songs "No Other One" and "All's Well" were rejected. In December, MGM agreed to loan Garland to Hal Roach for an *Our Gang Follies* film but pulled her out at the last minute.

Legend has it that Metro virtually ignored Garland during her first months at the studio, bypassing her for films at every opportunity. It's true they weren't initially certain what to make of her; George Sidney remembers a corporate feeling that "audiences wouldn't believe that it was really her singing." By mid-1936,

FACING PAGE: A full-fledged seventeen-year-old MGM star in late 1939. BELOW: A fourteen-year-old Metro contract player in early 1937.

even the *Hollywood Reporter* was taking Mayer to task: "The greatest individual talent in Hollywood—Judy Garland—is going to waste due to MGM's negligence during the past year in not spotting her in a picture or accepting one of the many major studio offers for her services." Metro had actually announced Garland for several pictures, including *This Time It's Love* and *Born to Dance*. But the roles never materialized, and she grew increasingly frustrated at such inactivity. Ethel finally asked for Judy's release, later explaining, "I was sure she'd be happier on the stage. She liked it better because of the audiences." But Mayer asked for a little more time; he later summed up his own estimation of Garland as "a girl [with] all the talent in the world."

In spring 1936, the studio produced a one-reel test, teaming Judy with another teenage vocalist, Edna Mae Durbin. The picture's simple premise contrasted Garland's "jazz" with Durbin's opera, and the difference between the two extended to the physical as well. Judy later offered a tongue-in-cheek description of their characters: "*I* had an apple in my hand and a dirty face, and *she* was the Princess of Transylvania!" The film was seen solely by those attending an MGM exhibitors' convention.

In June, MGM sent Judy (with Ethel) on a brief promotional trip to New York, where, two days after her fourteenth birthday, she and Bob Crosby's orchestra cut her first accepted and released sides for Decca: "Stompin' at the Savoy" and "Swing, Mr. Charlie." She was scheduled for East Coast radio appearances, when the studio abruptly called her back to team again with Durbin in a one-reel musical short designed to test their audience appeal. The songs for *Every Sunday* were prerecorded at the end of June; filming was completed over a few days in July but, by that time, Durbin's contract with Metro had lapsed. It's unclear whether the studio dropped or inadvertently neglected to pick up her option, but she was quickly signed by Universal, which changed her first name to Deanna

LEFT: Garland, Mickey Rooney, and Edna Mae Durbin at Metro in March 1936. Judy would later wonderingly refer to Deanna's pre-glamorized eyebrows as "just like a caterpillar." RIGHT: As Judy Dale, singing "Waltz with a Swing"/"Americana" in Every Sunday, *1936. FACING PAGE, TOP LEFT: With Durbin and a Metro script clerk during production of* Every Sunday.

and cast her in the feature *Three Smart Girls.* Ironically, producer Joe Pasternak had seen the earlier exhibitors' reel of both girls and decided Judy was "warm, lovable, natural, and charming." He wanted her for his film, only to be told that MGM was keeping Garland and only Durbin was available.

Three Smart Girls was an enormous success when released later in 1936, and there was some backlash comment at Metro. Stanley Kramer, then an assistant film editor, remembers an executive saying, "Mayer let Tiffany go and held on to Woolworth." But such corporate mutterings seem to have been in the minority; by October 1936, Judy had a successful feature in release as well. The studio had agreed in July to loan her to 20th Century-Fox for a supporting role in the collegiate football comedy *Pigskin Parade.* The powers at Fox must have been aware of and thoroughly impressed by Garland; the part was created for her, and the script describes her sequences in such phrases as "This is where Judy will do her stuff . . . giv[ing] out a thrilling rendition like it's never been done before." Their estimation of her ability was so strong that in one plan—later abandoned—the film finale medley built to Judy singing the last eight bars to close the picture.

Garland spent five weeks at Fox, completing a half-dozen scenes and four songs by September 15. One ensemble number ("Hold That Bulldog") was cut before release, but her vocal remained to top the "Balboa" dance routine, and she was given expert showcasing in two no-holds-barred solos: the powerhouse ballad "It's Love I'm After" and the "thrilling rendition" of "The Texas Tornado." Judy was reportedly horrified by her own freckled, pigtailed, chunky appearance on screen ("I didn't wear any make-up, and I sure looked it" was her unhappy comment), but critics enjoyed the film, and a number of them singled out Garland for special praise. The New York *Sun* found her "piquant face and surprising voice. . .one of the film's biggest assets"; *Script* declared that "[Judy] grasps her [chance] with both hands and great effect," and the *Hollywood Reporter* decided that "one of the loftiest [high spots] is little Judy, who captured the preview audience with a brace of nifty songs."

TOP RIGHT: As Sairy Dodd, singing "The Texas Tornado" to (among others) Tony Martin, Arline Judge, Dixie Dunbar, Betty Grable, Patsy Kelly, and Jack Haley. ABOVE: Judy's encore solo, "It's Love I'm After"; both scenes from Pigskin Parade, *1936.*

TOP: In appearances with Jack Oakie, Garland sang such songs as "Some of These Days," "Slap That Bass," "They Can't Take That Away from Me," "Play, Orchestra, Play," "Always," "There's a Lull in My Life," and "Alabamy Bound." ABOVE: On the set of Parnell, *after singing "Dear Mr. Gable: You Made Me Love You" for the first time. (Garland's voice on her Decca recording provided the inspiration for Harry James's later hit single.)*

The treatment afforded Judy by Fox, the resultant reviews, and the overnight sensation caused by Durbin all contributed to the pressure on Metro to do more with Garland. Late in 1936, she was written into *Broadway Melody of 1937,* scheduled for production early the next year; meanwhile, she continued to appear at Hollywood benefits and parties. In January 1937, she guested on "Jack Oakie's College" radio show and was such a hit she was added to the regular cast for the remainder of the season. George Sidney remembers that Metro saw such exposure as an important way to accustom the public to Judy's ability: "You couldn't see if she was twelve years old or twenty. No one would know what age she was."

On the strength of her initial success with Oakie, she was also signed for a February 2 radio appearance with orchestra leader Ben Bernie and All the Lads. Garland hoped to sing "Drums in My Heart," a sophisticated arrangement Roger Edens had first done for Ethel Merman. Her request brought about the only conflict she and Edens had encountered. As he later recalled, "Judy came to MGM with the firm conviction that she was a 'hot' singer, and no amount of explaining that she was a little young for that could convince her otherwise." Edens wanted instead to help her develop a vocal identity both suitable to her age and appearance and faithful to her mature talent. It was his idea to use the Bernie program as a step toward creating such an image and, when she pleaded for the Merman routine, he countered, "Look—I'll write you a special song all your own. Go to lunch; if I haven't written something you like better by the time you get back, you can sing 'Drums.' " When she returned, he had already sketched out most of an arrangement of "You Made Me Love You," which paid tribute to the orchestra leader in a special verse titled, "Dear Mr. Bernie." (Edens had taken the premise from a musical radio monologue he had written for Carmel Myers a couple of years earlier; the Edens/Myers routine, "Gee, Mr. Gable," had been built around the song "Let's Fall in Love," and dealt with a Los Angeles chambermaid's infatuation with MGM star Clark Gable.) Bernie was delighted; his office approved the song the last week in January, and it was slotted for the program.

A near scandal and a birthday party changed everything. On January 26, Clark Gable was accused of fathering an illegitimate child. The supposed mother, Mrs. Violet Norton, was arrested shortly thereafter and charged with suspicion of attempted extortion and mail fraud; she had been writing the actor since 1934 in an effort to secure film work for her and their alleged daughter. Gable denied the woman's charges as "preposterous," and the case came to nothing. But his thirty-sixth birthday fell on February 1, and he was due back at the studio that day after a week away with influenza. To take the edge off the newspaper headlines about Norton's accusations, a surprise party was scheduled on the set of *Parnell,* Gable's current film. Mayer asked Ida Koverman to prepare some entertainment; she immediately thought of Judy, called Roger, and he "hit upon the idea of substituting Gable's name for Ben Bernie." He switched the title to "Dear Mr. Gable," as a humorous play on Norton's letters; further irony came in the fact that the actor's alleged daughter was roughly the same age as Garland. Edens's treatment of "Dear Mr. Bernie" was at best tongue-in-cheek and poked fun at the old maestro. His birthday rewrite for Gable was in the same vein, and, not unnaturally, Judy protested: "I can't sing that—he might not understand." But Roger convinced her that the song would work as long as she maintained an aura of guileless innocence. (They also decided to abandon the original number for the February 2 Bernie program to avoid learning two versions of the song back-to-back.)

On his birthday, Gable and fiancee Carole Lombard walked back onto the *Parnell* set after lunch to find the cast, crew, and MGM's upper echelons assembled in the actor's honor. A piano flourish drew attention to a corner of the soundstage; from the keyboard, Roger introduced Judy, sitting atop the upright and by her own admission "trembling like a leaf . . . stage-frightened for the first time. [But] I gave it all I had, because I admire him so." By the time she got to Roger's last refrain, *"You can have the Tones, the Colmans, and the Taylors. / Compared to Gable, they are only good for trailers. . . ,"* the crowd was cheering, and Gable, his eyes wet with tears, went directly to her. Judy remembered, "He put his arms around me and said, 'You are the sweetest little girl I ever saw in my life.' Looking at him up close, my knees almost caved in. And then *I* cried, and it was simply heavenly!" Years later, Gable recalled, "I was in a hell of a state in my life [at that time] and hated making *Parnell.* When little Judy was brought on the set to sing, I just about dropped, I was so surprised and really *touched.* She was so nervous and eager to please that you couldn't help but fall in love with her."

That night, Judy sang the number publicly for the first time at a benefit at the Trocadero. The bill included George Jessel, Eddie Cantor, Sophie Tucker, Bill Robinson, and George Burns and Gracie Allen, but Sidney Skolsky reported Garland as "the sensation of the evening, [singing] as terrific a piece of special material as I ever heard." Edens then rewrote the lyric in a more straightforward and less-industry-oriented fashion, and Judy sang it with great success on the Oakie show, at an MGM dinner-dance on February 22, and at an exhibitors' conclave in early May. By then, *Broadway Melody* producer Jack Cummings had long since worked the number into the film.

The reception for "Dear Mr. Gable" was the turning point in both Judy's relationship with MGM and in the creation of her public persona. Roger Edens's contribution cannot be overstated; as George Sidney remembers, "Roger was the

BELOW: A detail from Garland's Bancroft Junior High School class photograph, spring 1937. BOTTOM RIGHT: Costume test for "Dear Mr. Gable," Broadway Melody *of 1938, May 1937. BOTTOM LEFT: Judy sings "You Made Me Love You" to pictures of Gable in her scrapbook.*

most important man in Judy's life. He helped to discover and refine her musical style. He really developed it [and] let her try different things." Edens's own talent and influence were further exemplified by the material he repeatedly turned out for Judy's Oakie appearances. At least one routine each week incorporated his special material: verse, patter section, or medley melange of additional songs. The numbers were thus personally identified with Judy's personality and interpretation and were instrumental in creating a public image for her.

Prerecordings for *Broadway Melody of 1937* finally began in March 1937, although the lengthy preproduction schedule meant that Cummings had to retitle the feature *Broadway Melody of 1938.* The extra preparation, however, did not extend to the script; it remained an innocuous story of a prospective Broadway hoofer (Eleanor Powell), her producer (Robert Taylor), and her pet racehorse. Judy was cast in a vaguely autobiographical role as the daughter of a veteran entertainer (Sophie Tucker) who is working to place her child in show business. Though Garland appeared in only four sequences in the nearly two-hour film, three involved musical numbers. (Two of her other songs were cut from the release print.)

If Judy's role was peripheral to the main plot, her presence was essential to the entertainment value of the finished product, and Garland's co-workers were again in awe of her on- and off-camera gifts. Tucker found Judy "so eager and so determined to get ahead in pictures, it made me proud to work with her. [She was] the only one in the cast in whom I saw great possibilities." Whether in earnest or for the sake of publicity, the grande dame of vaudeville labeled Judy her successor—"America's next 'Red Hot Mama.' Not only has she one of the best voices I've heard, but she understands the value of lyric lines as if she were a grown-up." Actor George Murphy first met Judy at the time of her MGM audition, and *Broadway Melody* was the earliest of their three pictures together. He later described her as "the greatest all-around talent I have ever encountered. She could do anything. All of us who watched her on the set knew immediately that [she] had that extra something that would make her one of the screen immortals. Her voice could make you laugh or cry almost at the same time. There was never anyone like her."

BELOW: With Sophie Tucker. BOTTOM LEFT: Between takes in Broadway Melody. *BOTTOM RIGHT: Her (eventually deleted) finale number, "Your Broadway and Mine."*

The film was finished in late July; Judy was billed seventh in the credits and ads, but when the reviews and reports of audience reaction began to come in, MGM hastily designed new ad copy that featured her second only to Taylor and Powell. General critical comment was pleasant, although the film was not considered the caliber of previous Metro spectaculars. Virtually everyone, however, took notice of Garland. The *Hollywood Reporter* called her "a certain new picture star" and singled out "her sensational work" before that of anyone else in the cast. Harrison Carroll in the Los Angeles *Herald-Express* reported that Judy "really walks away with the picture. Here is not only a complete artist, but a personality that takes you by storm." "Dear Mr. Gable" was a highlight for many; the *New York Times* called Garland "amazing" and the song "a tour de force." But at least one reviewer missed the point of the number: the conservative Hollywood *Spectator* self-righteously warned, "A child sing[ing] seriously of her love for Gable [is] an exhibition of extremely bad taste which will shock the sensibilities of all parents."

Given her burgeoning radio audience, Judy was offered a long-term Decca recording contract, which went into effect on August 30, 1937. That day, she recorded "Everybody Sing," from *Broadway Melody,* and "All God's Children Got Rhythm," from MGM's *A Day at the Races.* On September 24, she did two additional sides, including "Dear Mr. Gable." Judy stayed with Decca until MGM began issuing its own records in 1947; starting in 1937 and continuing for a decade, she recorded more than seventy additional songs for the label and frequently hit the charts with both singles and souvenir albums.

By August, Judy was also simultaneously at work on two new pictures. The less elaborate *Thoroughbreds Don't Cry* was in release by November. It marked her first screen appearance with Mickey Rooney, who played a brash jockey living in a boardinghouse run by Sophie Tucker (this time cast in a nonsinging role as Garland's aunt). When Rooney's father feigns illness, the boy is conned into throwing a race; he then joins forces with Garland and Australian child actor Ronald Sinclair to right the situation at a subsequent event. (Sinclair's role as the British grandson of a racing enthusiast was originally intended for Freddie Bartholomew, but as Judy wryly explained later, "Freddie's *voice* was changing. . .")

TOP LEFT: With Tucker and Barnett Parker. TOP RIGHT: Singing "Yours and Mine" in Broadway Melody of 1938. *The latter sequence was also cut from the release print. ABOVE: En route to school at Metro with Rooney. When Rooney chided her for being at the bottom of the class, she shrugged, "They teach the same thing at both ends."*

ABOVE LEFT: *With Ronald Sinclair, Tucker, and Rooney in publicity for* Thoroughbreds Don't Cry, *1937.* ABOVE RIGHT: *"Sun Showers," the song cut from the film.* BELOW: *In costume for The Russian Dolly Sisters number, abandoned for* Everybody Sing, *1937.*

Though the script called for Garland to play some brief puppy-love scenes with Sinclair, there were more sparks in her snappier and defiant passages with Rooney. Off camera, he nicknamed her "Joots," and, ever after, she would credit him with helping her to feel as comfortable acting on the screen as she felt singing. Garland was also given two songs in *Thoroughbreds,* both rejects from *Broadway Melody.* ("Got a Pair of New Shoes" had been a deleted Eleanor Powell solo and "Sun Showers" a showcase for Igor Gorin; Garland's version of "Showers" would be cut from *Thoroughbreds* as well.) The film—little more than an eighty-minute programmer for the top half of double bills—hardly called for major attention, but most reviewers responded to its pace and expert performances. Garland was noticed as "volatile and versatile" in the role of Cricket West.

The concurrent production, *Everybody Sing,* had been in the works as a specific Garland showcase since late 1936; it cast her as swing-singing Judy Bellaire, youngest daughter of a madly theatrical family. Their precarious financial standing is further jeopardized when actress/mother Billie Burke insists on casting foppish Reginald Gardiner in her playwright husband's new production. Judy saves the day by going out on her own as a performer, aided by family cook Allan Jones and Russian maid Fanny Brice. It was a senseless but dazedly effective screwball comedy. (The plot lines were even more intertwined in early, abandoned scripts, in which Freddie Bartholomew appeared as the Bellaire offspring and Judy was a street kid paired with Mickey Rooney to sing Cole Porter's "Swinging the Jinx Away." Classical singers Mary Garden and Mme. Ernestine Schumann-Heink originally vied—at least on paper—with May Robson for the easily adaptable role of the maid; Spanky McFarland was considered as another Rooney sidekick, and Igor Gorin almost got the Jones role.)

The working title of the film, *The Ugly Duckling,* gave way to *Swing Fever* before becoming *Everybody Sing* after Judy's *Broadway Melody* song and Decca recording. (The script, however, retained several odd references to Judy as an "ugly duckling," which must have done wonders for her self-esteem.) Prerecordings and filming ran from late August 1937 into early January 1938, and the finale centered on a revue in which Jones, Garland, and Brice attain stardom.

PRECEDING PAGE AND LEFT: *Fourteen-year-old MGM contract player Judy Garland, circa 1936–37.* *BOTTOM LEFT:* *The Garland Sisters sing "La Cucaracha" to Paul Porcasi in* La Fiesta de Santa Barbara, *August 1935.* *BELOW LEFT AND RIGHT:* *Posters for* Everybody Sing, *MGM/1938.*

FACING PAGE: *MGM touted Garland's approaching star status in a four-page trade-paper supplement in February 1938.*

The Girl Who Makes

EVERYBODY SING

THE STORY OF JUDY GARLAND

It is May, 1937! A 12-year-old girl, with her mother, faces M-G-M casting directors to beg for a "singing audition." The studio is overrun with girls who want an audition. But Judy has something.

Anything can happen in magic Hollywood. One man has a hunch. One man writes a page in screen history when he says "Let's hear this kid!"

Such is the romance of the discovery of Judy Garland! In just three pictures, topped by "Broadway Melody" her fame was national. Now, after smashing new triumphs on the air, she comes into her glorious own—in M-G-M's lavish, spectacular musical—"Everybody Sing!"

Another story of JUDGE HARDY'S FAMILY
"How d'you like her, Pop... $8 more and she's mine!"
Love FINDS ANDY HARDY
A Metro-Goldwyn-Mayer PICTURE
COUNTRY OF ORIGIN U. S. A.

SUNDAY NEWS
NEW YORK'S PICTURE NEWSPAPER

Alhambra
Canonsburg
Sun. Mon. Dec. 18 · 19
SEE IT WITH A SONG IN YOUR HEART!
LISTEN DARLING
WITH Freddie BARTHOLOMEW
Judy GARLAND
MARY ASTOR
ALAN HALE
WALTER PIDGEON
A Metro-Goldwyn-Mayer PICTURE

FACING PAGE, TOP: Lobby card for Love Finds Andy Hardy, *MGM/1938; the quote in the bottom left-hand corner refers to Andy's car and not to any of the three girls in the front seat. BOTTOM LEFT: Rotogravure cover taken while Judy was in New York to play Loew's State, February 1938. BOTTOM RIGHT: Poster for* Listen, Darling.

Posters for Listen, Darling, *MGM/1938.*

Sparkling with ear-tingling music and laughter to make you happier than you have been in years, the story beloved by millions now comes to the screen in a surpassingly beautiful Metro-Goldwyn-Mayer Technicolor film.

THE WIZARD OF OZ required a cast of 9200, the brains and brawn of 165 different arts and crafts, a symphony orchestra of 120 pieces and a chorus of 300 voices...to bring you 100 minutes of unparalleled entertainment.

Whirl from the everyday on the black wings of a tornado—to the mystic land of Oz! See an old lady knitting on a cloud; a cow milked sky-high!

In Munchkinland you meet Toto, the wonder dog, and the White Witch (*Billie Burke*), who may give you magic slippers like Dorothy's to take you safely to Oz.

Meet the harum-scarum Scarecrow, hanging on a post. Hear him sing his sorrowful song. He is searching for a brain.

Dance down the Yellow Brick Road with Dorothy and the Scarecrow, thru orchards of apple trees which pick their fruit and throw it, too!

Greet the rusty Tin Man. Oil him up a bit so he can creak out his sad tale—he seeks a heart and doesn't know where to find it.

Laugh at the plaintive Cowardly Lion —in need of courage—the things that befall this merry-mad company fairly set his tail on end . . .

Beware the dangers of the Haunted Forest as you go. Don't let the Black Witch (*Margaret Hamilton*) and her guards, the Winged Monkeys and the Giant Winkies head you off! Just beyond is the glistening Emerald City—and the wonderful Wizard of Oz who makes every wish come true.

• • •

Screenplay by Noel Langley, Florence Ryerson and Edgar Allan Woolf. From the Book by L. Frank Baum. A VICTOR FLEMING Production. Produced by MERVYN LE ROY. Directed by VICTOR FLEMING. *Sing and whistle these gay, tuneful Arlen and Harburg song hits: "Over the Rainbow", "We're Off to See the Wizard", "The Merry Old Land of Oz", "Ding Dong".*

JUDY GARLAND (as Dorothy)

FRANK MORGAN (as the Wizard of Oz)

JACK HALEY (as the Tin Woodman)

BERT LAHR (as the Cowardly Lion)

RAY BOLGER (as the Scarecrow)

FACING PAGE: The Wizard of Oz *ad art, September 1939.*

LEFT AND BELOW: Kodachromes of "Dorothy Gale" and the principal cast of The Wizard of Oz, *MGM/1939. BOTTOM LEFT: Poster for* Babes in Arms, *MGM/1939. BOTTOM RIGHT: Rotogravure cover taken while Judy and Mickey Rooney were appearing at New York's Capitol Theatre, August 1939.*

FOLLOWING PAGE: Publicity art of Garland and Rooney drawn by Jacques Kapralik for Strike Up the Band, *MGM/1940. Kapralik did collage-like renderings to promote many MGM films.*

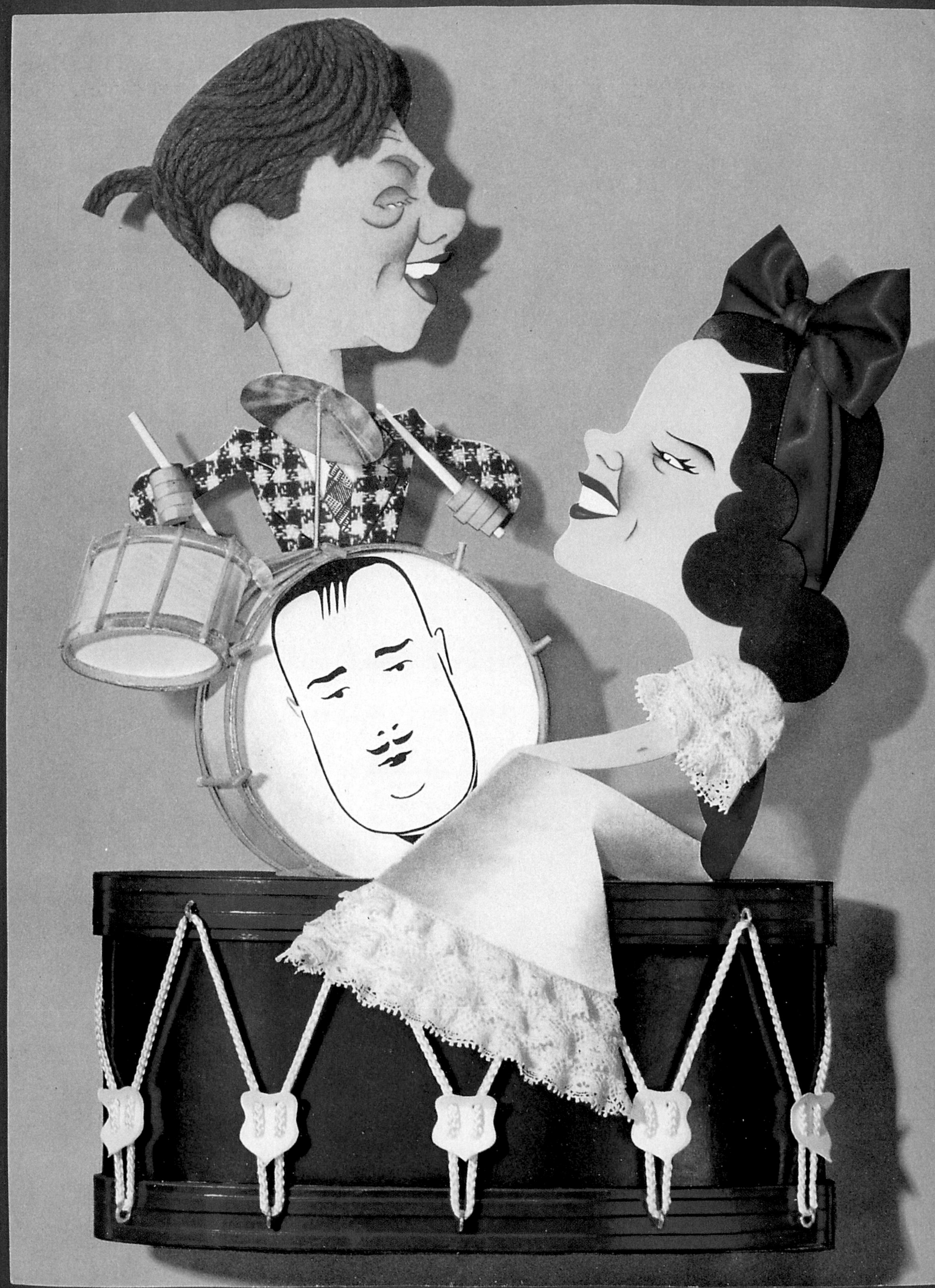

Its premise was reworked several times, and with the film over budget and behind schedule, the studio abandoned at the last minute a plot complication that saw no one turn up for the Jones & Company opening. Lost from the picture as a result was Judy's parade with the cast through the streets of New York to draw a crowd, plus a Garland/Brice duet in which Roger Edens had them do a takeoff on a famous vaudeville team. Billed as The Russian Dolly Sisters, they were to sing, *"We're the Tootsie-Wootsy Twins From the Ballet Russe: / I'm Yatchka the Swan, / I'm Katchka the Goose. . . We used to dance before the court / for the dukes and prince-skies. / Now we do three shows a day / on the gangplank down at Minsky's."*

The preview trailer for *Everybody Sing* capitalized on Judy's popularity in its promotional claim: "Judy will become an overnight sensation . . . Welcome Judy Garland to the Royal Family of Movie Stardom!" When the picture was previewed in Westwood in January, the audience apparently concurred; she carried off top honors, and one reviewer described her as "astonishingly good." At the conclusion of the screening, Judy went straight through the crowd to Louis B. Mayer and planted a kiss on his cheek. The film was released the next month and even publicized as the "mad-as-a-hatter" musical. Its noise and energy annoyed some critics, but Garland was heralded by the British *Kinematograph Weekly:* "She has a sense of character, a sense of humor and, above all, an amazing flair for hot rhythm." *Variety* found the entire picture "first class entertainment" and labeled the coupling of Garland and Brice as "an audience-rocker."

To help promote *Everybody Sing,* Metro sent Judy, Edens, and Ethel on a seven-week, seven-stop personal-appearance tour of movie theatres, opening on Broadway at Loew's State on February 10. *Variety* raved, "Youngster is a resounding wallop [with] the personality and skill to develop into a box office wow in any line of show business. She encored twice, finally begging off . . . she could have stayed on indefinitely." Edens remembered that, despite Garland's experience and professionalism, she had the sensitivity to be "petrified" of her first New York opening—so much so that she couldn't control her voice, and the audience was initially unimpressed. Then, during her second song, he heard "a baby begin to cry somewhere in the balcony—shuddering and whining, exactly like Judy was singing. Somebody in the audience tittered. Judy took a breath but couldn't

LEFT: Shooting the title sequence for Everybody Sing, *1937. RIGHT: In November 1937, Judy sang "Silent Night" with the Saint Luke's Episcopal Church Choristers of Long Beach for MGM's* 1937 Christmas Trailer*—the studio's holiday greeting to the world. Conductor William Ripley Dorr later wrote, "She told me she had sung in a church choir since she was very small and loved church music."*

Stills and production photographs from Everybody Sing. *TOP LEFT: Asking the musical question, "Shall I Sing Swing?" in the finale. TOP RIGHT: With Fanny Brice and Allan Jones in the latter's dressing room.*

BOTTOM LEFT: As Little Lord Fauntleroy to Brice's legendary Baby Snooks in "Why? Because!" CENTER: A deleted section of Garland's opening number, "Swing, Mr. Mendelssohn." BOTTOM RIGHT: Portrait taken during Garland's 1938 tour to promote the film.

get the next note out. I didn't know whether she was going to panic. She didn't. She broke into her infectious, little-girl grin and started to giggle. The audience laughed. Judy laughed with them. The house roared. That did it. I never heard such an ovation for an unknown kid as she got."

Garland drew superlative crowds in every venue, usually on a four-a-day schedule. (Between shows, she made miscellaneous side appearances and did homework; a tutor traveled with the entourage.) Her stage demeanor continued to delight audiences, especially when she poked fun at a scripted plug for *Everybody Sing* by suddenly switching to a monotone voice and deadpan face to announce, "And-I-hope-you'll-see-my-latest-picture-which-will-open-at-this-theatre-Monday," before adding an apologetic "if you don't mind the commercial." In Columbus, Ohio, she was made a Sweetheart of Sigma Chi, and the tour concluded with a brief, nostalgic visit to Grand Rapids.

Back in Culver City, she went immediately into preproduction work for *Love Finds Andy Hardy,* the fourth film in an increasingly popular series about small-town family life. Mickey Rooney played the title role, irrepressible teenage son of Judge James K. and Emily Hardy (Lewis Stone and Fay Holden). The low-budget Hardy pictures began a year earlier with *A Family Affair;* the succeeding titles, *You're Only Young Once* and *Judge Hardy's Children,* brought in grosses far in excess of many of Metro's more lavish offerings. Adding Garland to the series was another studio step in establishing her with the public. As Betsy Booth, thirteen-year-old daughter of a musical-comedy star, Garland again played someone younger than her own age, a sort of visiting girl-next-door. Although hopelessly in love with Andy, she finds he has eyes only for local girls—in this case played by Lana Turner and series regular Ann Rutherford.

Although the script was built around Garland, she was almost dropped from the film. Shooting had only been under way for a couple of weeks when she suffered three broken ribs, a sprained back, and a punctured lung in a May 24 automobile accident; the studio was at first unsure if the picture could wait for her. But she returned June 11 and, within two weeks, had finished her scenes and prerecorded four songs. One of these was dropped from the picture; Betsy was to have pointedly sung "Bei Mir Bist Du Schön" through an open parlor window in an attempt to attract Andy's attention. Metro borrowed Mack Gordon

Love Finds Andy Hardy, *1938.* *BELOW LEFT:* *"Maybe I'll shave!" exults Rooney as Andy prepares to squire Betsy Booth to a Christmas Eve dance.* *TOP:* *At the dance.* *ABOVE:* *Her songs, with Don Castle in support, are a Carvel sensation.*

and Harry Revel from Fox to write her three other numbers, two of which she sang in a party sequence ("Meet the Beat of My Heart" and "It Never Rains but What It Pours"). The third, "What Do You Know About Love?," was never recorded, and its spot in the film usurped by "In Between," an Edens routine loosely based on an earlier Morey Amsterdam song, "I'm Fourteen."

As Betsy, Garland helped Rooney out of several family and romantic snafus and, in the eyes of many critics, came "close to taking the [film's] honors out of [his] hands" *(Motion Picture Daily).* The *Los Angeles Times* found her "a fine foil . . . [in] a very fine performance," and the *Examiner* called the picture "one of the funniest movies we've seen this year." *Love Finds Andy Hardy* came to be regarded as the best and most representational of the series.

From *Andy Hardy,* Judy rushed into another film, planned for her since August 1937. *Listen, Darling* was a B picture at best but boasted the kind of cast that made even MGM's minor efforts among the most memorable in Hollywood. In cahoots with Freddie Bartholomew, Judy sought an eligible husband for her widowed mother, played by Mary Astor. (The task was made easier when an impromptu family trailer trip parked them next to Walter Pidgeon.)

Listen, Darling took over two months to complete—four weeks longer than intended, as Astor was laid up for nearly a month after a fall from a horse. The screen veteran remembered Garland as "sheer joy: young, vital, warm, affectionate, and exuberant. A real kid" whose sense of humor was so genuine and strong that production would be suspended when "she got the giggles. 'There goes Judy!' would be the cry! And we just had to wait until she got over it."

Only seventy minutes long, *Listen, Darling* was pleasant, mild entertainment, enhanced by Garland's three numbers. "Zing! Went the Strings of My Heart"—recorded at several lengths and tempos, including a hot swing version—was cut to a gentle chorus and a half for the final print. The film was released in October, and although *Cue* labeled it "preposterous, quite silly, and dull," most critics found it unpretentious and engaging. The *Christian Science Monitor* summed it up as "a little laughter, a little tears, a little singing by the fair Judy," and the *Hollywood Spectator* warmed considerably from its *Broadway Melody* appraisal: "Metro at last seems to have awakened to a realization of what it has in [her]." Of course, MGM's knowledge of Garland's potential dated from her signing, but now, nearly three years later, all of the studio's power was behind her.

LEFT: "Remember: we're neighbors," offers Lewis Stone as he doffs his Judge Hardy hat in Garland's direction. RIGHT: Having makeup adjusted on the set of Love Finds Andy Hardy. *FACING PAGE, LEFT COLUMN: Costume tests for* Listen, Darling, *1938; the center photo shows Judy with Mary Astor. FACING PAGE, TOP RIGHT: Astor, Alan Hale, Sr., Barnett Parker, Scotty Beckett, Judy, and Freddie Bartholomew in a scene cut from the film.*

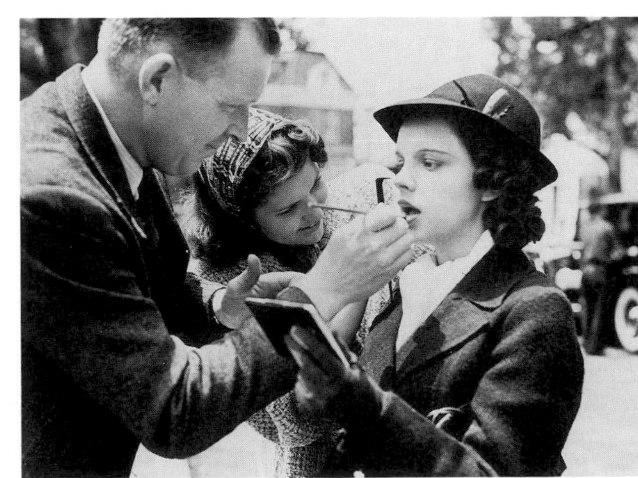

LEFT: The Listen, Darling *cast also included Walter Pidgeon. BELOW RIGHT: As Pinkie Wingate, Judy consoles "little brother" Beckett during a thunderstorm by singing "Ten Pins in the Sky."*

Judy's next film was designed from conception to be her supreme stellar showcase.

Negotiations for *The Wizard of Oz* as a Garland vehicle began with the autumn 1937 success of *Broadway Melody.* Metro songwriter Arthur Freed wanted to produce musical films and to work specifically with Judy. At the same time, producer Mervyn LeRoy was being wooed to MGM from Warner Bros. Both men told Mayer they wanted to film L. Frank Baum's classic fantasy, with Garland in the role of Dorothy Gale. In early 1938 (and buoyed by the recent success of Walt Disney's *Snow White and the Seven Dwarfs),* Mayer authorized purchase of *Oz* for $75,000. LeRoy was made producer of the film, and Mayer assigned the fledgling Freed as his unbilled assistant. By the time LeRoy officially started at MGM on February 1, Freed had already planned casting suggestions, and the budget for the film had passed $2 million.

At that point, MGM president Schenck and the Loew's offices entered the action, horrified at the prospective costs. They suggested abandoning the idea—or at least giving it some box-office insurance by starring the nation's top attraction, nine-year-old Shirley Temple. Temple's connection to *Oz* has since been embellished into a complex legend, but it was in truth a very brief, intracorporate, nonpublicized affair. On February 15, Freed grudgingly dispatched Edens to Fox to hear Temple sing. A day later, with Edens declaring the child's "vocal limitations. . . insurmountable" (and Fox point-blank refusing to loan her for an MGM film), Garland got the role. Her casting and the production were announced on February 24, and Freed later confirmed, "I bought [*Oz*] for the studio with only one person in mind for Dorothy. It was finally decided, *by all,* that *Oz* should be used to establish a good box office reputation for Judy."

MGM's *The Wizard of Oz* has since become the most-viewed and arguably best-loved motion picture of all time. Its story has been told in countless articles, two television documentaries, and three full-length books. *The Wizard of Oz* (New York: Warner Books, 1989) offers a concise day-by-day history of the nearly two years required to create the film.

Challenges and changes in concept, script, costuming, scenery, and casting consumed the spring and summer of 1938. Principal photography began in October and continued into March 1939. At least five directors were assigned to the film: Norman Taurog did tests before being replaced by Richard Thorpe. The latter filmed for two weeks and was replaced by George Cukor, who oversaw more tests and proved a special boon for Garland. He felt she had been directed in "a fancy-schmancy" manner during Thorpe's tenure; Cukor changed her blond baby-doll look and frilly wardrobe, suggesting she had only to be herself to be believable as Dorothy. The picture was then taken over by Victor Fleming, a known savior of troubled MGM pictures. He completed the majority of the film before being reassigned to *Gone With the Wind* in February 1939, and *Oz* was finally finished by King Vidor. Garland enjoyed a special rapport with Fleming ("I had a terrible crush on him—a lovely man"), and felt she had learned more from him than from any of her other early directors.

Rehearsals for *Oz* had begun in September 1938 while Judy was still working on *Listen, Darling.* On October 7, she recorded Harold Arlen and E. Y. Harburg's "Over the Rainbow," a ballad that the *Oz* songwriters felt was needed to balance the lighter, more whimsical numbers in the score. The "Rainbow" scene wasn't filmed until March 1939, and the song was briefly cut from the picture when *Oz* was sneak-previewed the following June. (Judy later quoted studio executives

BELOW: The Scarecrow (Ray Bolger), Cowardly Lion (Bert Lahr), and Tin Man (Jack Haley) join Garland and script clerk Wallace Worsley, Jr., on the set of The Wizard of Oz, *1939. Worsley would work on several Garland films; in 1988 he recalled, "She was naturally brilliant. In fact, she never had to try hard to do anything. Where other people had to really work hard to do something, she picked it up like that." FACING PAGE, BOTTOM LEFT: Between takes of* Oz, *Judy poses with skater Gloria Nordkog in publicity for a March 1939 Mt. Sinai Hospital benefit. FACING PAGE, BOTTOM RIGHT: The Munchkinland set swarms with midgets and technicians; Garland listens to director Victor Fleming while choreographer Bobby Connolly looks on, December 1938.*

TOP AND ABOVE LEFT: "Lolita Gale of Kansas"—the early (and quickly abandoned) concept of Dorothy as an overly rouged blonde. Both stills were taken during Richard Thorpe's two weeks of Oz direction, and Garland is shown left with Bolger and top with Buddy Ebsen (originally cast as the Tin Man), Bolger, and Lahr. The three men are disguised as the Wicked Witch's Winkie guards.

who thought the number took "up too much time with this little *fat* girl singing.") Freed and LeRoy argued it back into the film, and "Rainbow" ultimately topped the "Hit Parade," won the Academy Award for best film song of the year, and became a best-selling Decca single and theme song for Garland.

Oz was a difficult picture to make. Early Technicolor required blindingly hot lights. On-set accidents incapacitated Wicked Witch Margaret Hamilton, her stand-in, and several of the Winged Monkeys. Buddy Ebsen, who played the Tin Woodman under Thorpe's direction, was hospitalized after suffering a severe allergic reaction to the aluminum dust in his silver makeup; he was replaced by Jack Haley. Throughout the adversities, Garland was the joy of the set. Her co-workers always remembered her admiringly as a professional and fondly as a person. Good Witch Billie Burke offered, "From the moment she walked on the soundstage, there was no question she was a star. I think she knew it, too, yet [when the work was a strain, there was] never a complaint, never a murmur." Haley concurred: "She was so sweet—a darling. Everyone was enchanted by her."

BELOW: Judy celebrates her seventeenth birthday on the set of Babes in Arms *with Rooney and director Busby Berkeley, June 1939. BOTTOM LEFT: June ("just getting the kinks out") Preisser was Garland's foil for Rooney's affection in the film. BOTTOM RIGHT: Garland, Douglas MacPhail, Rooney, and Betty Jaynes in the title song production number.*

But the six-day-a-week schedule of filmmaking, plus school and personal appearances, took their tolls. By the time *Oz* was completed, there were implications in the press that Judy was exhausted and in need of a vacation. After a few days off, however, she left Hollywood for a five-week tour. Police had to be called to control the crowds during her return to New York's Loew's State in April 1939, and the *Variety* critic found her even more polished than a year earlier: "The impression of voice, singing style, and personality is all in her favor. Response heightens in intensity and volume as [she] proceeds. She's potent box office . . . a refreshing performer."

Judy returned to Los Angeles on April 30 and went right into rehearsals for *Babes in Arms.* It was Arthur Freed's first film as a producer, and his adaptation of the Broadway musical had been in the works for Garland and Rooney since the preceding summer. The ninety-six-minute film took just eleven weeks to complete and showcased the two teens as children of vaudevillians. With their families in financial straits, the characters played by Garland and Rooney join forces with other teenagers to stage a fund-raising show in a Long Island barn—and end up on Broadway. Other "Babes" in the cast included Betty Jaynes and Douglas

LEFT: Garland and Betty Jaynes sing an Edens-arranged medley, "Opera Versus Jazz" in Babes in Arms. *(The two were originally scripted to do a similar routine in an early draft of* Oz, *with Jaynes as a classical singing princess. They were also announced to costar in the never-produced* Topsy and Eva.*) RIGHT: Judy as Patsy Barton with Ann Shoemaker as her mother in a scene cut from the film. Garland's big ballad in* Babes *was "I Cried for You."*

MacPhail as a doughy duo of legit singers and June Preisser as Baby Rosalie—a wicked takeoff of a Temple-esque child star past her prime. (Freed originally considered Lana Turner for the part.)

Babes in Arms was the first Metro film directed by Busby Berkeley—a highly respected film talent, an often vague and regimented taskmaster, and an off-set alcoholic. Berkeley fondly remembered that the Garland of 1939 "would not do a scene unless I stood by the camera, and afterward she would ask me how she looked and if she had done all right." But Rooney—while acknowledging the director's genius—recalls him as "impossibly demanding. . . He was always screaming at Judy: 'Eyes! Eyes! Open them wide. I want to see your eyes!' When the cameras started grinding away, he wanted us to do the numbers from beginning to end, nonstop. [And] we had to go through some very elaborate, very exhausting rehearsals before anyone even bothered to put film in the cameras."

While Garland worked on *Babes in Arms,* MGM was fine-tuning *Oz* for an August premiere. Final cost for the film, including prints and advertising, would top $3.5 million; to ensure a boffola Broadway opening, Metro decided to send Garland and Rooney to New York to appear between showings of the film at the Capitol Theatre. They traveled with their mothers, Roger Edens, and Metro's Georgie Stoll as conductor, breaking in the act during one-day stops in Washington, D.C., and three cities in Connecticut. The duo was reviewed on the road as "a lesson in showmanship." They took stage together, and after some brief patter, Mickey would urge Judy to sing, "while I go get a cold root beer or something." After her vocals, his drum solo, and his imitations of Clark Gable and Lionel Barrymore ("so terrible," per *Variety*'s dry comment, "that house applauds every line"), they dueted tunes to promote *Babes in Arms.* Thousands greeted their arrival in each locale; extra police were invariably summoned to handle the crush. The press summed up contemporary reaction to Garland: " 'She's the most wonderfullest girl I've ever seen,' panted one high school sophomore. 'Hey, she smiled at me!' screamed another."

Heralded as "the Garbo and Gable of Hollywood High," Garland and Rooney opened in New York on August 17. Their two-week engagement broke every attendance record, as lines of waiting fans encircled the block like a moat. The two teens did five thirty-minute shows a day, interspersed with promotional ap-

TOP LEFT: *The two stars head East for their August 1939 promotional appearances.* TOP RIGHT: *Garland and Rooney as Eleanor and President Franklin D. Roosevelt in the "God's Country" finale of* Babes in Arms. *Five minutes of this routine (including "My Day," the stars' spoof of a fireside chat) was later deleted from the film negative after Roosevelt's death and is now missing.*

BOTTOM LEFT: *With Jack Haley, emcee of the Waldorf Astoria luncheon where specially selected teenagers welcomed Garland and Rooney to Manhattan.*

pearances all over town. The critics were much impressed by their stage dynamics, and *Oz*—which had already debuted cross-country to primarily rapturous response—won mostly raves in New York as well, particularly for Judy and for Bert Lahr's outrageous Cowardly Lion. (When Rooney returned to Hollywood, Garland remained at the Capitol for a third week, teamed with Lahr and Scarecrow Ray Bolger.) The basic tenor of Garland's *Oz* reviews was prophetically summarized in the Daily *Oklahoman:* "[Her] career, I think, will be dated by this picture. Her fine performance is going to win further big parts for her. [She is] sweet and thoroughly convincing, [and] good use of her grand voice is made in a half-dozen clever light songs."

Babes in Arms opened across the country in September. Rooney's versatility won special praise and, in early 1940, an Academy Award nomination as Best Actor. Reviews for the film itself were equally enthusiastic. *Cue* found it "the best musical to come to the screen in many years," and the New York *Herald Tribune* decided *Babes* was "a complete delight from beginning to end." Most critics echoed *Variety*'s estimation that Judy was "most effective," and the *Hollywood Reporter* declared "Judy Garland does Judy Garland which is enough for any ticket buyer." The film broke box-office records everywhere; the daylong lines waiting to see *Babes* included more adults than children so, while *Oz* smashed attendance records, the low-budget *Babes* actually brought in more money. (The film's success also established Arthur Freed as the studio's foremost movie musical producer, and he and his associates—the Freed Unit—would ultimately be responsible for nearly twenty years of quality MGM product.)

The Hollywood premiere of *Babes in Arms* was held at Grauman's on October 10, and Judy was invited to join past screen luminaries by leaving her hand- and footprints in cement in the theatre forecourt. She inscribed her message, "For Mr. Grauman / All Happiness," but her participation was not without incident. "I had the habit of biting my fingernails," she later admitted, "and I was just sick that I couldn't have long glittering fingertips. So the studio manicurist gave me false nails. After I placed my hands in the cement, we went inside to see the picture. I thought creeping paralysis had set in—my fingertips were numb and heavy. Then I realized that some of the cement had crept under the false nails and hardened on my own. The next day I had to have my 'glamour' chipped off!"

The Grauman's ceremony was confirmation that Garland had arrived, but her new rank had already been recognized at Metro. The studio had taken her off their list of featured players and elevated her to star status in November 1938, presenting her with her own trailer dressing room. In January 1939, her fan mail at MGM reportedly topped that for any other star—a public response that was underscored when the box-office records for 1939 were posted. *Oz* and *Babes in Arms* were both on the list of the top ten pictures, and Bette Davis and Judy Garland were the only two women on the exhibitors' list of the top ten stars.

It had taken MGM just four years to turn "Frances Gumm—known professionally as Judy Garland"—into a major movie star.

FACING PAGE, BOTTOM RIGHT: *Singing "I'm Just Wild About Harry" in the* Babes Minstrel Medley. *The sequence played badly in previews until the Metro hierarchy realized that the audience was unsure of who they were watching. A hasty insert was filmed showing Garland and Rooney applying their blackface.*

ABOVE: *With Mickey at the Grauman's premiere of* Babes in Arms; *Garland was the seventy-fourth star immortalized in cement. After the film, Hedda Hopper remembered, "The house lights came on, and Judy was crying through the applause. 'I know what you're thinking,' Mickey said to her. 'We're two kids from vaudeville, and we didn't mean a damn thing for so long, and now it's happened to both of us.' "*

CHAPTER THREE
TOP TEN

Judy Garland's ascent to stardom provided a potent payoff for her decade-plus of work. But those first years at MGM also saw the beginnings of problems that would plague her for the rest of her life. One immediate difficulty was Garland's self-image. Whatever normal teenage insecurity she might have developed about her looks and figure was immeasurably heightened by Metro's constant corporate carping about her weight. (She later acknowledged, "I had baby fat"—and wryly added, "That's not exactly a criminal offense.") But by 1935, Judy had grown to her full height of four feet eleven inches; as a result, any weight gain was instantly visible. Though she seldom appears much more than thick-waisted in her early films, the legend endures that Garland was referred to as "the fat one" during her preliminary days at MGM. The studio had a special, painful corset-like contraption made to both slim her and (in her first pictures) minimize her bosom. She was also put on a stringent diet, and between the front-office complaints and her self-comparisons to Hollywood femmes fatales, Judy became convinced that she lacked real allure and beauty. The situation was further compounded by her roles in *Love Finds Andy Hardy* and *Babes in Arms,* where she was cast as either Mickey Rooney's pal or the girl he (however briefly) passes over for someone prettier or more successful.

After her years of stage triumphs, Judy was also rankled by her comparative inactivity during her first months at Metro. At the time, she publicly and gratefully acknowledged that Deanna Durbin's overnight success created interest in (and parts for) teenage girls. But she was immediately—if privately—envious as well. Durbin's *One Hundred Men and a Girl* premiered at Grauman's in autumn 1937, and the young soprano was invited to put her handprints in cement that evening. The next day, Judy sobbed to Ida Koverman, "I've been in show business ten years, and Deanna's starred in a picture, and I'm nothing." (With more humor, Garland later admitted, "I was *very* jealous of her. . . but not for long!")

FACING PAGE: The glamorous box office sensation, 1942. BELOW: On February 29, 1940, Rooney presented Garland with a miniature Oscar (or, as she later described it, "the Munchkin Award") for her "outstanding performance" as a juvenile actress in Oz.

Koverman and Ethel Gumm continued to fight for work for Judy during those early months, incurring Mayer's wrath on several occasions. He even had Ethel temporarily barred from the lot, although she persisted in defending Garland against any seeming slights (or, in the years to come, any heavy demands). A veteran Metro clerk remembers filing innumerable letters written by Ethel to the MGM hierarchy on behalf of her daughter. Conversely, others recall Mrs. Gumm as playing the studio's game, switching Judy's professional representation to an agency run by a friend of Mayer's and striving to implement every front-office directive as she heavy-handedly pushed Judy along.

There are similar diverse opinions about Mayer and his rotating disinterest in/manipulation of Garland. In her later, difficult times, he would offer her his personal financial support. But the complex chieftain also maintained definite opinions about the appropriate behavior and appearance of his stars; the studio literally controlled the lives of its leading players. When they had grievances,

TOP: With James Stewart and Louis B. Mayer, circa 1940. Stewart remembers that when Judy first arrived at Metro and would daily practice songs with Roger Edens, "a lot of us used to go down to [his] office. We weren't allowed in, so we'd just listen from outside around the windows. And it got to be about fifty of us there every day when Judy would be singing." ABOVE: Judy and her mother, Ethel Gilmore (right), at the July 1938 premiere of Marie Antoinette, *accompanied by Freddie Bartholomew and his Aunt Millicent.*

Mayer was capable of weeping with them, either in genuine sympathy or in an effort to circumvent their requests. (Judy would comically refer to Mayer's "*steel* tears.") He could also rail against their complaints or react with little or no regard for their feelings. Studio songwriters Bob Wright and Chet Forrest remember that the teenage Judy once demonstrated a new score of theirs for Mayer. As she sang, he made negative comments about her, reducing her to tears. Appalled, Wright and Forrest walked out, urging Garland to join them; she said she couldn't—her mother wouldn't like it. When Mayer later apologized to the men, it had nothing to do with his treatment of Judy; he had just discovered that they were the lyricists of MGM's hit song "The Donkey Serenade."

By 1938, the inactivity of Judy's initial months at Metro had given way to frequent overwork. As a minor, her Monday-through-Saturday daily schedule was by law divided into four hours of film work, three hours of studio schooling, and an hour of recreation. (The agenda did not take into account the additional time required for makeup, wardrobe fittings, photo sessions, radio and recording work, and personal appearances.) The situation would worsen when Judy turned eighteen in June 1940, and there were no legal restraints on the hours she could be kept on-set or on call. Rooney remembers the two of them returning "for hours of night work, sometimes until eleven P.M. A couple of times we worked until three in the morning." Robert Stack, then a Metro contract player and a friend of Garland's, recalls her as "the prize possession" of MGM but feels the studio both "pushed" and "misused" her. "They made her work practically twenty-four hours a day; they worked that kid until she just fell down." Those who would defend MGM point out with alacrity and accuracy that other stars made as many movies and kept the same schedule as Judy Garland without falling prey to her problems. Few of those other stars, however, began to work at age two, had their formative years regulated and molded by the studio, or made predominantly musical films with their requisite weeks of taxing dance and vocal rehearsals. The talent, sensitivity, and genius that made Garland unique perhaps ultimately made her less than adept at coping with the mounting demands of her stardom. She was, at this time, still a teenager, and was later to remark, "I met wise and learned people in every field, and you automatically pick up things from them. So when I was seventeen, I guess I *seemed* older. But underneath, I was pretty young and not much different from other girls my age."

Judy was also dealing with changes in her personal life. After a number of teenage romances, she was by 1939 much in love with bandleader Artie Shaw, but his affection for her was at best that of a brother. This only deepened Garland's uncertainties about her desirability and worth. Then the loss of Frank Gumm was accented once again when, four years to the day after his death, Ethel remarried. Her new husband, Will Gilmore, had been a neighbor in Lancaster whose invalid wife had died in the late 1930s. Fervently loyal to Frank's memory, Judy did not particularly like Gilmore and, even as a girl, had been aware of rumors that linked him with Ethel while both their respective spouses were still alive.

Finally, all of Judy's problems—her appearance, personal considerations, studio politics, and overwork—were critically underscored when, sometime in the late 1930s, she was encouraged by MGM to take prescription medication to help control her weight. Benzedrine was then regarded as a new miracle appetite suppressant; no one seemed to be aware that such medication was not only addictive but nerve-destroying. An intense stimulant, it also made sleep impossible. So Garland began taking sleeping pills to counteract both the diet pills and her natural insomnia. (Her early years in theatre had accustomed Baby Gumm to working late and sleeping in—a routine much at odds with the sunrise schedule required for filmmaking.) She eventually developed a dependence on the pills and found herself requiring larger doses in order to maintain her professional obligations.

The adult Garland would—when ill or destitute—frequently blame her mother for her problems. MGM came in for its share of invective as well, and there was real justification for some of her charges. Yet, despite the complaints, she could also laugh about the studio. When remembering such fellow child stars as Rooney, Bartholomew, Turner, and Elizabeth Taylor, she once rhetorically gibed, "Have you seen us since we've come out? We were a very peculiar group!" (When later asked if one of her fellow female stars was a nymphomaniac, Garland shot back, "Only if you can calm her down.") She loved telling the story of a private studio luncheon and MGM's "anxious producer," Harry Rapf: In an effort to flatter his host, the nervous Rapf wholeheartedly declaimed, "Oh, Mr. Mayer—this is the best piece of apple pie I've ever had in my whole mouth." And she reveled in the memory of a dazed Keenan Wynn, shaking his head over an encounter with sometimes-dour executive Benny Thau: "Benny opened his mouth to laugh, and *dust* came out."

On both her good and bad days, Garland could also credit MGM for her success. In 1968, she quite earnestly and sincerely told Johnny Carson that the studio had been the greatest influence on her career and, six months later, further summarized her feelings for a British reporter: "We were overworked and underfed . . . Still, I mustn't complain. We all did well out of Metro, and Metro did well out of us. There were lots of good times, too."

Judy enjoyed a brief lull in her film work in autumn 1939; *Good News* had been announced as her next vehicle with Rooney, but while the script was being devised, MGM approved her for a regular spot on Bob Hope's popular radio show. She completed a full season as the comedian's foil and resident vocalist, appearing on more than twenty-five broadcasts between late September and mid-May 1940. Garland was reviewed as "radio's newest important personality"; many years

BELOW: After a 1937–38 stint on Metro's "Good News" radio program, Judy spent a season as Bob Hope's vocalist. He quipped, "I learned to love Judy so much her mother met her after each program." BOTTOM LEFT: Director George B. Seitz oversees Garland and Rooney in Andy Hardy Meets Debutante, *1940. BOTTOM RIGHT: With Georgie Stoll, prerecording "All I Do Is Dream of You" for that film.*

BELOW: *As Mary Holden, singing "Nobody" in* Strike Up the Band. BOTTOM LEFT: *Hairstyle test for the film, April 1940.* BOTTOM RIGHT: *The "La Conga," much of which was shot by Berkeley with multiple cameras in an extended take. Edens recalled, "He rehearsed it with a complete crew for five days. It soon became like the opening number of a Broadway show. When the morning came to shoot, the whole studio was down there. The scene went without a hitch. Even now, it has an unforgettable something extra about it."*

later, Hope paid tribute to Judy's "natural talent," rating her "at the forefront of all the performers I've been associated with over the course of fifty years." Her radio success also boosted sales of her records, and Garland's Decca version of "Over the Rainbow" spent twelve weeks on the charts that fall.

The script for *Good News* was finished in late October; in short order, a dissatisfied Arthur Freed abandoned the project and, at Mayer's suggestion, began developing a different Garland/Rooney property called *Strike Up the Band.* By early December, he had established an April start date for the film. While waiting, Judy returned to Judge Hardy's family for *Andy Hardy Meets Debutante,* which began shooting in February 1940. On this go-round, Betsy Booth meets Andy on her own turf when the Hardys travel to New York for one of the judge's court cases. Andy has bragged about his involvement with Manhattan debutante Daphne Fowler to hometown friends. When they demand proof of the relationship, Andy is forced to attempt to meet the girl. He is continually thwarted until he takes Betsy into his confidence. The deb turns out to be her close friend, and Andy once again wakes to Betsy's charm and vocal ability.

Roger Edens wrote "How Much Longer?" for Judy to sing in the film, but it was bypassed in favor of "All I Do Is Dream of You" (which was cut before release), "Buds Won't Bud" (which was cut after the sneak preview and replaced by "Alone"), and "I'm Nobody's Baby," which became Judy's next chart hit for Decca. When *Debutante* was released in July, *Daily Variety* opined, "Neither Rooney nor Miss Garland has ever turned in a more carefully-etched portrayal," and *Time* commended Judy ("prettier by the picture") for managing to steal scenes even from the celebrated Mickey.

Retakes for *Debutante* bled into prelim work for *Strike Up the Band* in April. In the new film, Mickey played a drummer who converts his high-school band into a modern dance orchestra with Judy as lead vocalist. Their efforts propel the group to the top spot in a nationwide band contest conducted by Paul Whiteman.

Judy Garland

PRECEDING PAGE: Judy in costume for "It's a Great Day for the Irish," Little Nellie Kelly, *MGM/1940.*

RIGHT: Lobby card for Andy Hardy Meets Debutante, *MGM/1940. BELOW LEFT: Poster for* Strike Up the Band, *MGM/1940. BELOW RIGHT: Kapralik art for* Little Nellie Kelly.

FACING PAGE: A Garland/Rooney publicity portrait for Strike Up the Band.

Help Wanted—Male
Commercial—Miscellaneous
Help Wanted—Male
Commercial—Miscellaneous
Help Wanted—Male
Commercial—Miscellaneous
Help Wanted—Male
Technical—Industrial
Help Wanted—Male
Technical—Industrial
CHIEF INSPECTOR
Cost Analyst & Estimator
INDUSTRIAL ENGINE
STAGE MAN
COIL WINDER
COUNSELORS
SET-UP MAN
FEDERAL SHIPBUILD
AND DRY DOCK C
KEARNY, NEW JERSEY
ANDY HARDY

FACING PAGE: Kapralik art of Garland and Rooney for Life Begins for Andy Hardy, *MGM/1941.*

LEFT: Belgian and U.S. posters for Little Nellie Kelly, *MGM/1940. BELOW: Poster for* For Me and My Gal, *MGM/1942.*

STAGE
LOEW'S THE
PRESENT
NOW SH

FACING PAGE: Kapralik art of Garland and Rooney for Babes on Broadway, *MGM/1941. ABOVE: Belgian poster for* For Me and My Gal, *MGM/1942. FOLLOWING PAGE: Kapralik art for* For Me and My Gal.

En route they must deal with lack of funds, the necessity of an emergency operation for a friend, and Mickey's preoccupation with new-girl-in-town June Preisser. Most admired of the film's songs was "Our Love Affair," which built from a Garland/Rooney living-room duet to a fantasy rendition played by an imaginary fruit orchestra. The segment was the inspiration of Broadway director/designer Vincente Minnelli, who had just arrived at MGM to work as a musical film adviser under Freed's aegis.

Directed by Busby Berkeley, *Band* was completed in August and previewed in September. Audience reaction cards included such exclamations as "You might show this to Hitler—it might cheer him up," and "If only high school was like this!" Professional reviewers found the film a trifle long, but concurred it was "one of the top money pictures of the year." *Daily Variety* enthused, "While all the young principals do themselves proud, Garland particularly achieves rank as one of the screen's great personalities. Here she is for the first time in the full bloom and charm which is beyond childhood, as versatile in acting as she is excellent in song—a striking figure and a most oomphy one in the wild abandon of the 'La Conga.' " Jack Moffitt, Kansas City correspondent for the *Hollywood Reporter,* summarized the local press reaction by noting, "Metro was praised for at last developing a leading woman who didn't remind you of your mother." But perhaps the most telling praise came from a U.S. Navy lieutenant commander on board the USS *Melville,* who wrote MGM to say, "I have never seen any audience of Navy Men give any picture the ovation [it] received. They started applauding and wound up standing and cheering. I have been in the Navy twenty-four years; this is the first time I have ever witnessed such a demonstration."

The production schedule for *Band* and Garland's next picture overlapped by three weeks; *Little Nellie Kelly* was a 1922 George M. Cohan stage musical that Arthur Freed had purchased expressly for her. Unfortunately, *Nellie Kelly* was saddled with a drawn-out, two-generation plot in which Garland, as the daughter of Charles Winninger, defies her father to marry George Murphy. The old man summarily refuses to speak to his son-in-law, although he emigrates to America with the newlyweds. When Nellie dies in childbirth, her daughter is named for her; Garland played the daughter as well, finally effecting a reunion between her father and grandfather. Winninger was frequently grating in his irascible role (Garland and Murphy had originally requested and tested with Barry Fitzgerald for the part); equally drab was Douglas MacPhail as Little Nellie's contemporary suitor.

MGM's adaptation kept only one Cohan song ("Nellie Kelly, I Love You") and interpolated three others, including Freed's "Singin' in the Rain." Judy's first number was originally scripted as "The Stars Look Down," but it was quickly dropped in favor of her poignant "Danny Boy." This was in turn supplanted in the final film by a chorus of "A Pretty Girl Milking Her Cow," a reprise of which also displaced her scheduled rendition of "By Killarney's Lakes." (She would later describe "Pretty Girl" as one of Roger Edens's discoveries, "an *obscure* Irish folk song that fit the picture quite well. And we did it, and they released the picture, and the song became. . . an *obscure* Irish folk song!") Garland's version of "Rings on My Fingers"—which she was to sing to fellow immigrants on the boat to America—was also eliminated from the shooting script. But Edens created a big number, "It's a Great Day for the Irish," which she and MacPhail sang with maximum gusto during a St. Patrick's Day parade; the song became a standard.

Two numbers cut from the "Nell of New Rochelle" parody in Strike Up the Band. *TOP: Judy sings "The Curse of an Aching Heart." ABOVE: Garland and Rooney in "Strolling Through the Park." The film's song hit, "Our Love Affair," was one of seven songs introduced by Garland nominated for an Academy Award. (The others: "How About You?" "The Trolley Song," "The Man That Got Away," "The Faraway Part of Town," "Over the Rainbow," and "On the Atchison, Topeka, and the Santa Fe." The last two won the Oscar.)*

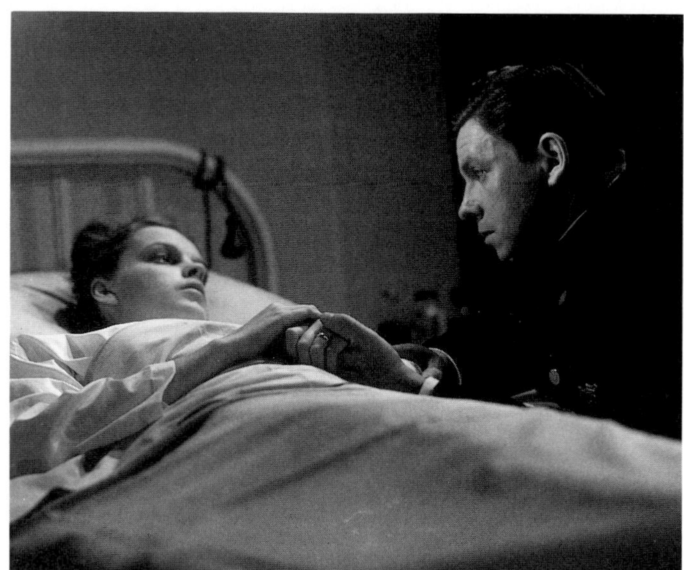

Little Nellie Kelly. *TOP LEFT: Garland and George Murphy in the only on-screen death scene she ever played, August 1940. TOP RIGHT: With producer Arthur Freed, Douglas MacPhail, and Murphy. ABOVE: Wardrobe test.*

Garland's death scene was deeply moving and, as Murphy later wrote, "so emotional and effective that it wrung the hearts of all those watching. When it was finished, the complete set was empty, with the exception of the director, Judy, and myself. All these so-called hard-bitten workers were so affected that they had to get away so that their sobs would not disturb the soundtrack."

The film was finished by the end of September and previewed shortly thereafter. A small earthquake hit Inglewood during the "sneak," but audience reaction cards included comments such as, "It would take more than an earthquake to shake me out of seeing it through," and "The quake could not drive us out." Some patrons were worried that Garland was growing up too fast on the screen (Mayer himself had purportedly ranted, "We can't let that baby have a child!"), but they found her performance "magnificent." When the film was released in November, critics found it long but easy-going family entertainment. The *Los Angeles Times* congratulated Judy on "a very fine performance," and the *Examiner* found her "a beauty, unsurpassable in her many talents and fresh young appeal."

Two months earlier, Metro had torn up Judy's original contract. She was making $600 a week; they raised her to $2,000 a week, with options for seven years that would eventually bring her up to $3,000. Her preceding films had brought the studio several million dollars in profit (Garland would once again place in the top-ten box-office poll for 1941), and MGM's willingness to pay her a total of $680,000 over seven years (for forty-week years) was indication of this. The new contract forbade regular radio work, so Garland bowed off the Hope show but continued occasional guest appearances and began to be heard as well in broadcast adaptations of such films as *Merton of the Movies, Morning Glory,* and *A Star is Born.*

From *Nellie Kelly,* Judy went directly into rehearsals for *Ziegfeld Girl,* which had originally been announced as a 1938 vehicle for Eleanor Powell, Joan Crawford, Margaret Sullavan, and Virginia Bruce. Now the leading women's roles were assigned instead to Garland, Lana Turner, Hedy Lamarr, and Eve Arden; James Stewart played opposite Turner. The story followed the careers of three young women, personally selected by (the never-seen) Ziegfeld to appear in his annual

Broadway revue. Turner falls prey to alcohol and stage-door Johnnies before a dramatic end; Lamarr deserts the stage to return to her musician husband; and Garland perseveres to become a front-ranking star vocalist. Her principal ballad was a heartfelt "I'm Always Chasing Rainbows," but the extravaganza was highlighted by three lavish production numbers. Tony Martin sang "You Stepped Out of a Dream" to accompany the girls' debut; a lengthy montage of West Indian music and motifs led to Garland's first specialty, "Minnie from Trinidad"; and a colossal seven-minute finale, "We Must Have Music," featured Garland and Martin and included brief reprises of "Dream" and "Rainbows." ("We Must Have Music" was dropped from the finished film and hastily replaced in March 1941 by an entirely different finale; footage and songs from the 1936 *Great Ziegfeld* were intercut with a new Garland/Edens number, "Ziegfeld Girl.")

Busby Berkeley did the film's musical staging, and at a running time of two and a quarter hours, *Ziegfeld Girl* was labeled lengthy and overdone but enormously effective entertainment. The picture was released in April 1941 and recognized largely as a showcase for Lana Turner. But *Variety* found Garland "a youthful but veteran trouper [who] carries the sympathetic end most capably and delivers her vocal assignments in great style." Thirty years later, film historian David Shipman coolly summarized the *Ziegfeld Girl* plot, noting that of the three "aspirants to stardom . . .only [Judy] made it, which gave the film a conviction it lacked elsewhere."

Garland made her final appearance as Betsy Booth in *Life Begins for Andy Hardy,* shot over six weeks in spring 1941. Andy, fresh out of high school, decides to work in New York for the summer, and Betsy once again provides solid companionship during his seemingly unavoidable difficulties. (Now a sixteen-year-old "sub-deb," the girl is full of snappy slang and sleek sophistication.) Not unexpectedly, Andy rejects the big-city advances of a previously married "wolfess" (Betsy's term) and returns to Carvel, wiser and ready to start college in the fall. Except for a brief a cappella rendition of "Happy Birthday to You," Garland was songless in the film, although she recorded and filmed four num-

Ziegfeld Girl, *1941.* LEFT: *Garland as Susan Gallagher in a portion of the deleted original finale, "We Must Have Music." (Clips from the number were later used in an identically titled short subject, released in 1942 to explain the workings of the studio music department.)* RIGHT: *Judy and Tony Martin at the finale of the extended "Trinidad" segment.*

Life Begins for Andy Hardy. BELOW: *Relaxing on set, May 1941.* BOTTOM LEFT: *With Fay Holden, Mayor Fletcher Bowron of Los Angeles, Rooney, Lewis Stone, Ann Rutherford, and Sara Haden at the film's Grauman's premiere, August 1941. The mayor and a bronze plaque proclaimed "the family of Judge James K. Hardy, the first family of Hollywood." (The Hardy series also received a special Oscar for its "achievement in representing the American way of life.")* BOTTOM RIGHT: *Garland sings "America," a number deleted from the film.*

bers: "America" (which was to open the movie); "Easy to Love" (sung to Rooney to the accompaniment of his car radio as they make their initial approach to New York); and "Abide with Me" and "The Rosary" (offered during the funeral service Rooney arranges for his ill-fated New York roommate). The songs were deleted at the last minute; some of the studio ad copy for the film still carried the pronouncement "Mickey Woos! Judy Sings!" as part of its come-on.

Released in August, *Life Begins* won praise for its comparatively somber approach to Andy's maturing years. Though Garland had outgrown such a supporting role, her work was reviewed as "helpful" and "solid" (if by no means a challenge). But there is a sharp contrast between this Betsy and that offered by Garland in the other Hardy pictures. Though still younger than Andy, the girl has been considerably, becomingly seasoned by her New York existence. *Life Begins* was also noteworthy for the trouble it incurred with the National Legion of Decency. Judge Hardy's on-screen discussion of marital fidelity and Andy's near dalliance with the "wolfess" gave the film an "unobjectionable for adults" rating, thus serving notice that some of its content might be unsuitable for children.

By June, Garland was in preproduction for *Babes on Broadway,* the third in her Rooney/Berkeley trilogy of "backyard" musicals. In this case, Mickey and song-and-dance partners Ray McDonald and Richard Quine enlist Garland as their costar in a showcase for the troupe of actors who hang out at New York's Pitt-Astor Drug Store. The performance is designed by an exploitative Rooney as a means of sending inner-city settlement-house kids on a country vacation. (Virginia Weidler—in a role intended for Shirley Temple—appeared as the kids' ringleader.) Complications involving a group of British war-refugee children and an aborted performance in a condemned theatre melt away when the Babes arrive on Broadway.

Berkeley began shooting in July and finished by early October. Minnelli again lent a hand, scripting the "Ghost Theatre" segment wherein Garland and Rooney offered impressions of legendary stage favorites. Veteran vaudevillian Elsie Janis was employed to coach the duo; she was especially appreciative of Garland and wrote, "She can be anything she wants to be, and it will be very interesting to watch her heart and head battle it out. The former is enormous—the latter is

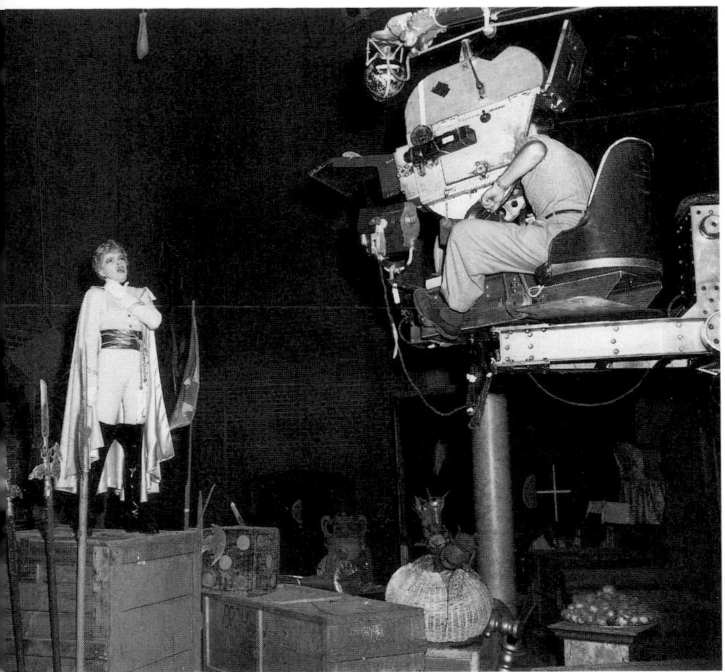

surprisingly small, considering the crowns and laurels it has to hold up. Judy has gone farther, faster than anyone I know—and she has not yet started."

When *Babes* was released in December, critics were again overwhelmed by the sheer energy, length, and occasional corn of it all; some took special exception to the footage of the refugee children superimposed over sights of London, although the sequence (and Garland's rendition of "Chin Up, Cheerio, Carry On") were undeniable crowd-pleasers. The *Hollywood Reporter* was entirely laudatory: "As great a job as has ever been put into one picture. The audience wore themselves out applauding." Editor Billy Wilkerson especially liked Garland's brief tribute to Sarah Bernhardt and editorialized, "Blurbs could never measure up to the performance of that ever-surprising Judy. The shivers go up and down your spine in admiration." *Babes* was held over in many of its initial engagements, accruing over 200 percent better-than-average business for the theatres in which it played.

Judy was late or ill on ten occasions during filming; the corporate notation that the *Babes* company enjoyed a layoff on Monday, July 28, "due to Judy Garland" is especially significant. Garland (with her mother and stepfather) had flown to Las Vegas late Sunday night, where she was married to conductor/arranger/composer David Rose. The two had been dating since February 1940, when Rose was newly separated from wife Martha Raye, and Garland was in emotional shock over the elopement of Lana Turner and Artie Shaw. (For well over a year, Garland had employed the aid of sister Jimmie and old flame Jackie Cooper in helping her to keep her secret meetings with Shaw. His unexpected marriage shattered her.) Metro, worried about the effect the Garland/Rose union would have on her box-office appeal, was furious about the alliance and refused her a honeymoon. She was summoned back from Las Vegas to resume work the next day.

Rose, twelve years Judy's senior, had been conducting her recording sessions

Babes on Broadway. *TOP LEFT: As Penny Morris, Judy offered an impression of Sarah Bernhardt's "La Marseilles," October 1941. TOP RIGHT: Rooney played four different roles in the deleted sketch, "The Convict's Revenge," filmed in September 1941. BELOW: In costume for the "Yankee Doodle Dandy" duet with Mickey.*

Babes on Broadway. *TOP: "And I'll sweep up the stage," Garland once declaimed while having her professional abilities listed. She is shown in costume between takes of a rip-roaring "Franklin D. Roosevelt Jones," September 1941. The hit song from the film was the Garland-Rooney duet, "How About You?" ABOVE: Garland and veteran vaudevillian Elsie Janis.*

and benefit performances since late 1940. He was also with her for a live "Chase and Sanborn Hour" broadcast from Fort Ord on December 7 when news came of the Japanese attack on Pearl Harbor. The two of them finally took time to have a brief honeymoon early in 1942, but spent most of it touring army camps throughout the Midwest with a USO troupe. Garland was the first Hollywood star to make such a commitment, and she averaged four shows a day. With Rose at the piano, she sang a dozen songs per performance, including "Blow, Gabriel, Blow," "This Love of Mine," "Blues in the Night," "Chattanooga Choo-Choo," and "Abe Lincoln Had But One Country"; she got the most requests for "Over the Rainbow" and "Dear Mr. Gable." After several weeks, she collapsed with strep throat and was taken back to Los Angeles.

In February 1942, Judy began work on *For Me and My Gal,* the first film in which her name would be billed alone above the title (another indication of her star power). In development for over a year as *The Big Time* and then *Applause,* the story originally featured two leading ladies, a singer and a dancer; Eleanor Powell tested for the latter role. When it was decided Garland could handle any requirements, the roles were combined. Dan Dailey had tested to play opposite Powell, but the role went to George Murphy, who later wrote that *Gal* was the film "that disappointed me most." At the last minute, he was abruptly shifted "to the part of the schnook who never gets the girl" and replaced by newcomer Gene Kelly, the Broadway star of *Pal Joey,* who was making his screen debut.

Whatever the casting uncertainties, Busby Berkeley later claimed *For Me and My Gal* as his own favorite of the more than fifty films in which he was involved as director and/or choreographer. He was blunt, however, in his preference for Murphy as the male lead, and Kelly's consequent discomfort was much alleviated by Garland's consideration. Kelly says now that Judy "pulled me through. She was very kind and helpful, more than she even realized, because I watched her to find out what I had to do. I was amazed at her skill; she knew every mark and every move. All I could do for her was help with the dancing. She wasn't a dancer, but she could pick up a step instantly. She was a very relaxed, marvelous person . . . the most talented performer we've ever had."

For Me and My Gal told the tale of vaudevillians Garland and Kelly, who team up after Murphy dissolves the act in which she appeared with him, Ben Blue, and others. The new duo finds it rough going; she almost loses Kelly, romantically and professionally, to classical singer Marta Eggerth. Just as Garland and Kelly finally fall in love, click as an act, and are booked into New York's Palace Theatre, he receives a draft notice and, to avoid induction, crushes his hand in the lid of his wardrobe trunk. When Garland realizes that the action was intentional, she leaves him to entertain the World War I troops in France. Kelly, unable to enlist because of his injured hand, goes abroad as an entertainer as well. In a burst of heroism, he is wounded while en route to warn an ambulance brigade about an ambush and barrage. After the war, Garland and Kelly are reunited and join forces with Murphy and Blue for an act that finally plays the Palace.

During filming, Garland missed sixteen days due to illness and was late on several occasions. (Although there would be future trouble over her tardiness, such behavior was not unique. Production logs show that such Metro stars as Norma Shearer and Greta Garbo were frequently late as well.) Despite the delays, shooting was done by the end of May; then there was new trouble after the first sneak preview. Murphy remembers that "about eighty-five percent of

For Me and My Gal, *1942.* CLOCKWISE FROM TOP RIGHT: *With George Murphy and Gene Kelly in the original (eventually deleted) finale; Garland as Jo Hayden sings "After You've Gone," April 1942; and "Smile, Smile, Smile"; the northwest corner of 45th Street and Broadway in New York, October 1942; relaxing between takes.*

RIGHT: Busby Berkeley works with Garland before she tears into "How Ya Gonna Keep 'Em Down on the Farm?" in For Me and My Gal. *BELOW: On the* Babes on Broadway *set, Mickey seems to be mocking columnist Louella Parsons. BOTTOM: Judy and husband David Rose return from their Las Vegas elopement, July 1941. FACING PAGE, TOP: Singing "How Ya Gonna Keep 'Em Down on the Farm?" FACING PAGE, BOTTOM: Garland and Kelly in* For Me and My Gal*'s title song.*

the preview cards submitted by the audience contended that [I] should have gotten the girl and not Gene Kelly." The film unit reassembled to shoot a sequence that would make Kelly more of a hero: at the end of July, he completed a scene wherein he hand-grenades a machine-gun nest of Germans who are firing on the ambulances. An entirely new finale (which mingled "When Johnny Comes Marching Home" and the title tune) was created for Garland, who spots Kelly in the Palace audience and brings him onstage for their romantic reunion and the realization of his lifelong dream. (Garland recorded "For Me and My Gal" with Kelly; their Decca record was on the charts for twenty-one weeks.)

Gal opened in New York on October 20; on the first night, Metro arranged a midnight Times Square community sing of World War I favorites, followed by a late showing of the film for vaudevillians and Broadway celebrities. As a result, the Astor Theatre hit a house record; receipts exceeded those for every type of engagement in its history. Reviewers carped about the film's "maudlin, dusty, oft-repeated, two-bit story," but most found Kelly a promising newcomer and were unanimous in acclaiming Garland's "personal triumph." The Los Angeles *Daily News* found that "she has the faculty (wonderful for her but tough on an audience) of melting your heart. And in a sympathetic part, she's murder." *Daily Variety* wrote, "She continues to gain impressiveness as a persuasive and skillful actress." *Gal* broke box-office records everywhere as Garland's biggest hit to date. In a front-page editorial, Billy Wilkerson of the *Hollywood Reporter* credited her with the success of the film: "It would not attract such sales without Judy. Nor would audiences go out so satisfied if Judy was not in there punching as only she can punch out a hit performance."

While final retakes were being made for *Gal,* Garland was already at work on *Presenting Lily Mars.* Based on a Booth Tarkington novel, the film was originally intended as a straight dramatic vehicle for Lana Turner; producer Joe Pasternak, working with Judy for the first time, had the story softened and musicalized.

She played ambitious, stagestruck nineteen-year-old Lily Mars, who manages to hitchhike to New York and infiltrate the Broadway chorus of producer Van Heflin's newest show. He falls in love with her, much to the egomaniacal displeasure of the show's star, Marta Eggerth. When Eggerth walks out, Heflin tries Judy as the lead. In a nice twist of reality, the quintessential American girl is unable to fill the operatic European-princess role, and Eggerth returns. Though disappointed and disheartened, Lily stays on to do her one-line bit; the film concludes with a number from a later show, which Heflin has produced as a showcase for her.

Pasternak had just come to MGM from Universal after making a huge success of Deanna Durbin's early films. He would rave about his association with Judy, calling her "an authentic cinema genius, born with what might be called perfect theatrical pitch." He is one of many who became quickly aware of Garland's photographic memory: "Once she read a script, she knew every speech and cue in it." Norman Taurog, who directed Garland as Nellie Kelly, was assigned to *Lily Mars;* he succinctly labeled his star "the finest girl-actress of my whole experience." Additionally, Garland was at her physical peak during much of *Lily Mars.* Several reviewers had noted her frail appearance in *For Me and My Gal;* she gained weight for the Pasternak picture and perhaps looks better than in any other film.

Lily Mars, however, was not on a par with the more lavish Arthur Freed product of Garland's past. A patriotic number, "Paging Mr. Greenback," was recorded and shot as the finale in front of one of the old *Babes in Arms* backdrops. Pasternak remembers that members of the Freed Unit "ran to Judy with wails of pain and distress" over the way she had been misemployed. As a result, he worried that Garland might feel "that this new producer from a lot that specialized in inexpensive pictures had let her down." Mayer diplomatically suggested to Pasternak that a new finale be shot, and Roger Edens devised an eight-minute medley of standards. He capped it with Freed's song "Broadway Rhythm," in which

Garland offered a sophisticated dance routine with Charles (Chuck) Walters, a choreographer new to the studio. At first unsure of herself, Judy was coaxed into the number when Walters suggested she think of it as an imitation of ace ballroom dancer Tony DeMarco. This gave her the image she required to make herself comfortable. The finale was recorded and filmed in March 1943 while Judy was simultaneously working on *Girl Crazy* (and cut to five minutes before *Lily Mars* was released in late April).

Not all reviewers responded to *Lily*'s low-key charm, but the *Motion Picture Herald* felt that "Judy grows better and better, and this picture registers a new high in performance and charm. She exhibits a dancing talent that is delightful in its grace and poise." Though the *New York Times* found the film "glorified monotony," it admitted, "This is tasty gingerbread at the box office, and it is not going to diminish Miss Garland's popularity one bit."

BELOW: With Bob Crosby, musical mentor Roger Edens, and producer Joe Pasternak at the prerecordings for Presenting Lily Mars, *autumn 1942.* *BOTTOM: With José Iturbi in* Thousands Cheer, *December 1942.*

After filming most of *Lily* and prior to beginning *Girl Crazy* in January 1943, Judy also did one number for *Thousands Cheer,* a Gene Kelly/Kathryn Grayson starrer concluded by an army camp show featuring much of Metro's star roster. Garland was paired with classical pianist José Iturbi for the boogie-woogie jump tune, "The Joint Is Really Jumpin' Down at Carnegie Hall." When the film was released, the *Hollywood Reporter* declared the camp show was "climaxed by the great delivery of a song by Judy"; nevertheless, several reviewers noticed that Garland was again too thin.

Meanwhile, the Freed Unit had reworked *Girl Crazy* into a new vehicle for Garland and Rooney. The plot was much changed from that of the original 1930 Broadway show but retained seven songs by George and Ira Gershwin. Rooney appeared as a Yale student and fledgling playboy whose father sends him West to Cody College to keep away from women. At first, he rankles everyone (while falling in love with Garland as the dean's granddaughter), but when lack of enrollment threatens closure of the school, he produces a Wild West rodeo and carnival to attract new students. The school goes coed, and the influx of female students saves Cody.

Freed imported Tommy Dorsey and His Orchestra for *Girl Crazy*'s specialty numbers (one of which also featured Metro newcomer June Allyson). There was much script revision as well; the producer eliminated a stereotypical black sidekick for Rooney along with one of Garland's songs: she was to have sung "Boy! What Love Has Done to Me" after once again losing Rooney to another girl (in this instance, Frances Rafferty). "I've Got a Crush on You," a quartet for Garland, Rooney, Nancy Walker, and Rags Ragland, was also dropped from the script, as were Walker's solo and duet with Gil Stratton.

Busby Berkeley was assigned as director and began by filming the "I Got Rhythm" number. According to Edens, however, Berkeley was ill and combative, overembellishing the routine with extraneous chorus, whip, and blasting-gun and cannon effects. The projected four days of shooting stretched to nine; the film was immediately $60,000 over budget. More important, Garland became ill after a week of Berkeley's demands. She told columnist Hedda Hopper, "I used to feel he had a big black bullwhip, and he was lashing me with it." Hopper later confirmed, "I saw him work her over. He watched from the floor with a wild gleam in his eye, while in take after take he drove her toward the perfection he demanded. She was close to hysteria; I was ready to scream myself. But the order was repeated time and time again: 'Cut. Let's try it again, Judy. Come on, move! Get

Presenting Lily Mars, *1943.* CLOCKWISE FROM TOP LEFT: *"Ev'ry Little Movement" with Connie Gilchrist; playing Lady Macbeth ("Who would've thought that the old man had so much blood in 'im?") to Annabelle Logan's pianistics and an unimpressed Van Heflin; in the "Where There's Music" finale, February 1943, which replaced "Paging Mr. Greenback"; Garland making up and on set for the latter number.*

On Palm Springs location for Girl Crazy, *1943.* FACING PAGE, CLOCKWISE FROM TOP LEFT: *Studio memo detailing Judy's frailty and health problems; as Ginger Gray, filming "I Got Rhythm" before Berkeley's dismissal, January 1943; singing "But Not for Me" to "Rags" Ragland; the "Embraceable You" sequence with Ragland, Gil Stratton, and Robert E. Strickland (April 1943); a portion of the original (junked) finale with Rooney and Frances Rafferty; and a scene with Nancy Walker, Rooney, and Guy Kibbee.*

the lead out.' " By January 26, Berkeley had been replaced by Norman Taurog, and Chuck Walters came in to stage the musical numbers.

Garland was now so thin and weak that Dr. Marc Rabwin ordered her not to dance for six to eight weeks. She took some time off—*Girl Crazy* shot around her until the second week of February—but then returned to continue the film (and rehearse and shoot the new finale for *Lily Mars*). Her health remained precarious; she missed a dozen days during the spring (although Rooney was out ill for a time, too, as was Ragland). A location shoot in Palm Springs offered new difficulties: sandstorms, dust, wind, and haze. But Garland's humor remained a saving grace. When Rooney first saw her in a white cowgirl costume, he kidded, "You look like a vanilla ice cream cone." She took in his diminutive frame, scarlet jacket, and chaps and rebutted, "You look like a rationed bottle of catsup."

Girl Crazy was judiciously edited prior to release. "I Got Rhythm" ended up as the finale of the picture even though it was intended for an earlier spot in the plot (prior to the coronation of "Queen of the Rodeo"). The originally scripted finish was scrapped; it featured the coronation of Garland as "Cody's first and most beautiful coed," and a Judy/Mickey reprise of "Embraceable You."

When released in November 1943, *Girl Crazy*'s grosses topped those for *Babes in Arms* and *Strike Up the Band.* The film was reviewed as "a blockbuster for pep" and "escapist in the happiest and most joyous sense of the word." Garland was commended for "her new-found maturity" and a performance "far above standard"; the Los Angeles *Daily News* found that, "away from Rooney, she loses her ingenue tricks and becomes a smart, poised, sophisticated leading lady."

While in the throes of *Girl Crazy* and *Lily Mars* in February 1943, Garland announced her separation from David Rose; there had been several months of rumors about their troubled marriage. (According to some reports, Garland had terminated a pregnancy when Rose seemed indifferent to the idea of a child, and MGM and Ethel suggested it might interfere with her work schedule.) She found solace in love affairs with two married men, actor Tyrone Power and Metro producer/director/writer Joseph Mankiewicz. The latter would later write, "In many ways, I've never met anyone like Judy at that time. She was just the most remarkably bright, gay, happy, helpless, and engaging girl I've ever met." Mankiewicz was also quick to pick up on Garland's off-camera insecurities ("She reacted to the slightest bit of kindness as if it were a drug"), and he suggested that she see a psychiatrist, who agreed that Judy required professional counseling. Both Ethel and Mayer took exception to this, the latter screaming uncontrollably at Mankiewicz during a couple of confrontational meetings. As a result, Mankiewicz left MGM, and his affair with Garland slowly died out. For the time being, Judy abandoned her therapy as well.

Professionally, Garland embarked on a new challenge by accepting her first concert date at the outdoor Philadelphia Robin Hood Dell on July 1, 1943. The event provided both a flashback to the response garnered by Baby Gumm a decade earlier and a thorough preview of her stage performances of the 1950s and 1960s. The audience began to line up five hours prior to the show. Judy more than doubled the previous Dell attendance record when fifteen thousand people filled the sixty-five-hundred-seat amphitheatre, and an additional fifteen thousand sat on adjoining grass knolls and in parking lots. (Somewhere between five and ten thousand other patrons left when they could find no spot within listening distance of the stage.) Acoustics weren't perfect; some had trouble hearing

INTER-OFFICE COMMUNICATION

To T BUTCHER-cc B Ryan-E Woehler-J Pasternak
A Freed-E Mannix-B Thau

Subject JUDY GARLAND

From FRED DATIG Date 1-29-43

I have just talked with Mrs. Gilmore, Judy's mother, who advises me that Judy's physician, Dr. Marcus Rabwin, has expressed the desire that she do no dancing for at least six or eight weeks. Mrs. Gilmore, however, feels that if Judy, who is now down to 94 pounds, is given the proper food, rest and exercise, that she should be able to dance by three weeks from Monday, which would be approximately February 21st. This is in reference to the scenes for LILY MARS.

Mrs. Gilmore advises that Judy is still confined to her bed and will be unable to again render services in GIRL CRAZY before next Wednesday, February 3rd.

Datig

"Judy in Concert," July 1943. TOP LEFT: *Judy looks on while her accompanist Earl Brent confers with conductor Andre Kostelanetz.* TOP RIGHT: *"Excited. . . and* awfully *scared; I've never seen such a big place!" Judy sings at the Robin Hood Dell. She wears the finale dress that was not seen in* Presenting Lily Mars. ABOVE: *Meeting the press in her suite at Philadelphia's Hotel Warwick.*

Judy over the orchestra. But everything but her presence was apparently immaterial. A journalist wrote, "She was cheered by her admirers. . .when her car drove in the private entrance; she was cheered at every appearance onstage; hearty applause always drowned out the final notes of each selection." André Kostelanetz conducted several selections to begin the show, but reporters described with awe "the tense atmosphere of expectancy that permeated the audience, [indicating] where the public's interests lay."

Judy began her Edens-arranged program with a Gershwin medley: "Someone to Watch Over Me"/"Do, Do, Do"/"Embraceable You"/"The Man I Love," and then swung into "Strike Up the Band." Reviewers found her poised and assured but "scared stiff" for the first couple of numbers; by "Band," she had warmed to the crowd, offering what one paper gleefully described as "an experience in rhythmic vitality." Her second spot included a medley of her own film songs, opening with the complete "Over the Rainbow" and segueing into one chorus each of "For Me and My Gal," "You Made Me Love You," and "It's a Great Day for the Irish." She concluded with "Our Love Affair," "I'm Nobody's Baby," and "The Joint Is Really Jumpin'," but response was so strong that she said, "I think it would be sorta fun if we did the last number over again." (At one point in the reprised lyric, she spontaneously substituted Robin Hood Dell for Carnegie Hall.) When the audience demanded yet another encore, she offered "But Not for Me."

The music critic for the Philadelphia *Bulletin* warmly acknowledged that "a good little artist she is, indeed. . . and her sense of rhythm and projection is simply amazing." Another journalist described the "hundreds of persons [who] fought their way down the aisles to get a nearer look; after the last number had been repeated, and the entire audience seemed to move forward as in a gigantic ocean wave, the lights were finally lowered to an accompaniment of quasi-hysterical cries and shrieks."

Garland spent July and early August on her second army-camp tour. After a performance at Fort Hancock, New Jersey, one of the commanding officers wrote to tell her that "two days after the event, the hubbub has increased rather than subsided, and all over camp one sees the eager faces of those who were unfortunate enough not to have heard you listening intently to those who did. . . It must make you very proud, Miss Garland, to realize how much good you are doing for our soldiers. . ."

Almost immediately after her return to Los Angeles, Judy was asked to join a dozen other stars on the Hollywood Bond Cavalcade/Third War Loan campaign. The company kicked off a sixteen-city tour in Washington, D.C., on September 8, ultimately playing to more than seven million people and selling over a billion dollars in bonds. In each town, the stars participated in a two-hour afternoon parade, mid-afternoon hotel press conference, and evening show. Despite the talent on the bill, Judy and Mickey were selected as the next-to-closing act; she sang solo and with José Iturbi at the piano, Mickey did impressions, and the two of them worked together prior to the "Star Spangled Banner" finale with the entire cast. To kill time on the train, Judy, Greer Garson, and Lucille Ball wrote a song parody deprecating their reputations as Mickey Rooney's girlfriend, Walter Pidgeon's wife, and Red Skelton's sidekick. Garland's solo couplet offered, *"I sing to Mr. Gable, / But he's never really there. / I'm longing to enchant him / With sophisticated flair. / But ev'ry time I turn around, / Andy Hardy's in my hair!"*

On her return to MGM, Judy began work on *Meet Me in St. Louis.* Arthur Freed had purchased the rights to Sally Benson's autobiographical "Kensington Stories" in March 1942 and planned to use the material for an intimate family musical. The finished film would become Judy's most important vehicle since *Oz,* but she initially rejected the part. Legend has it that she objected to playing another seventeen-year-old, but at least some of her discontent can be traced to early drafts of the *St. Louis* script, which were far from the careful, simple tale that ended up on screen. Although true to Benson's vignettes, there was much silliness in the roles originally designed for Garland and her film sisters; this was slowly excised, as was a romantic subplot wherein Garland (as Esther Smith) attempts to align her older sister with a local colonel. After being discovered while hiding in the married colonel's hotel closet, Esther is arrested for her trouble.

LEFT: Leaving Los Angeles with the Hollywood Bond Cavalcade. The troop includes James Cagney, Kathryn Grayson, Betty Hutton, Lucille Ball, Greer Garson, José Iturbi, Fred Astaire, Harpo Marx, Mickey Rooney, Paul Henreid, Kay Kyser, His Orchestra (including Ish Kabibble, Harry Babbit, and Sully Mason), and a flock of starlets. RIGHT: Judy joins Mickey for "How About You?"—after kicking off her heels so as not to be taller than her partner. She would do the same thing twenty years later during their reunion on her TV series.

BELOW: *Costume test for Esther Smith and* Meet Me in St. Louis, *November 1943.* BOTTOM LEFT: *Between takes, February 1944. The music in her lap, "It's Getting Hot in Tahiti," was a song under consideration for her next film,* Ziegfeld Follies. BOTTOM RIGHT: *Garland is joined by Tom Drake at the conclusion of "The Trolley Song." The actor was third choice for the role—after Robert Walker and Van Johnson.*

The final script told the unadorned story of a year in the life of the Smiths, whose serene existence is threatened when the father of the family decides to move them from St. Louis to New York. Preliminary work on the film began in November 1943; Vincente Minnelli was assigned as director (after George Cukor went into the service) and shooting began in December. He demanded eleven takes of Garland's first scene with Lucille Bremer, and Judy was crushed, terrified she had lost her talent. In truth, Minnelli was trying to help her abandon her more contemporary satiric line readings and settle into the character of a turn-of-the-century teenager. She gradually came to understand his approach, and as the picture progressed, their mutual professional respect led to romance.

But Garland continued her late arrivals at the studio on many occasions and was out sick for a total of three weeks during the filming. Singer Margaret Whiting, a friend of Judy's during the early 1940s, explains why, at that point, "the studio put up with" her tardiness. On the day she was to prerecord "The Trolley Song," Garland missed her morning call completely, apologetically arriving after lunch with her two little poodles in tow. Vocal coach Kay Thompson was new to the Freed Unit but had immediately become one of Garland's closest friends and (ultimately) strongest performing influences. Whiting recalls, "Kay asked her, 'Do you want a rehearsal?' 'We'll run it down once,' Judy agreed. They did. She was letter perfect." Garland, conductor Georgie Stoll, the chorus, and the forty-piece orchestra went for a take. "The music started," says Whiting. "Judy listened attentively and then raised her head. Her eyes were shining and she sang [with] all the delicate urgency of a young girl in love and the joy of performing that was [her] hallmark. It was a perfect take. . . She did another, as good as the first. She collected her two poodles and went home. She had been there all of fifty minutes. And they had been waiting for five hours. But when she worked, she *worked.* And *it* worked. The results were effortless magic."

PRESENTING
LILY MARS

PRECEDING PAGE: *Kapralik art of Garland and Van Heflin for* Presenting Lily Mars, *MGM/1943.*

Kodachromes of Judy taken during the early 1940s. She is shown with Jackie Cooper and with her niece Judalein Sherwood, sister Jimmie's daughter.

ABOVE RIGHT: *Poster for* Ziegfeld Girl, *MGM/1941.* *ABOVE LEFT:* *Poster for* Presenting Lily Mars, *MGM/1943.* *LEFT:* *Poster for* Girl Crazy, *MGM/1943.*

ABOVE: Kapralik art of Garland and Rooney for Girl Crazy, *MGM/1943. RIGHT: Poster for* Presenting Lily Mars, *MGM/1943.*

FACING PAGE: Publicity art by famed caricaturist Al Hirschfeld for Meet Me in St. Louis, *MGM/1944. From left: Garland, Tom ("boy next door") Drake, and Margaret ("I killed 'im!") O'Brien.*

Love makes the
world go 'round
For you
pine and
Balsam

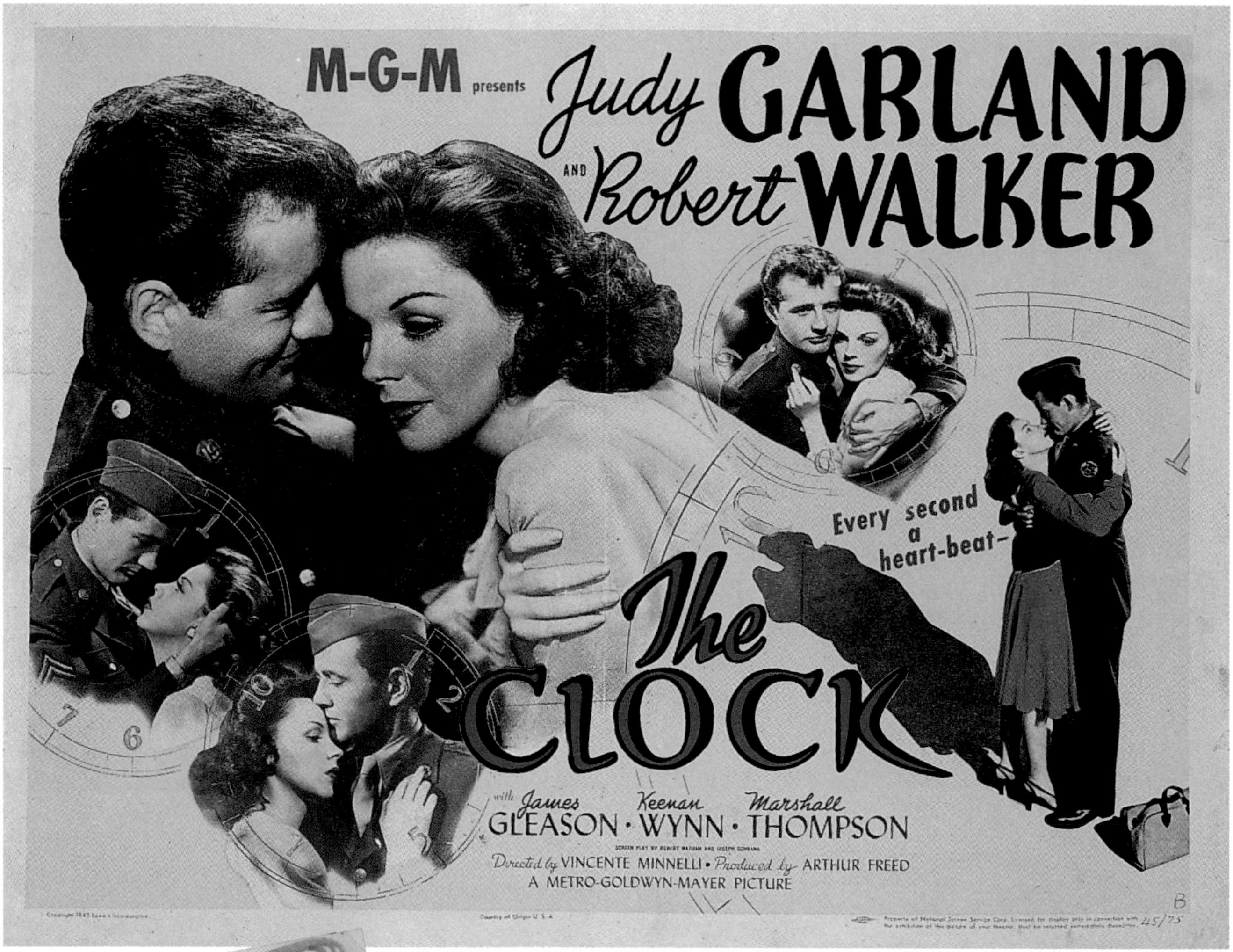
M-G-M presents
Judy GARLAND
AND Robert WALKER
Every second a heart-beat—
The CLOCK
with James GLEASON · Keenan WYNN · Marshall THOMPSON
Directed by VINCENTE MINNELLI · Produced by ARTHUR FREED
A METRO-GOLDWYN-MAYER PICTURE

M·G·M's MEET ME IN ST. LOUIS
GLORIOUS LOVE STORY WITH MUSIC
Starring JUDY Garland
MARGARET O'BRIEN
MARY ASTOR LUCILLE BREMER
TOM DRAKE MARJORIE MAIN
DIRECTED BY VINCENTE MINNELLI
PRODUCED BY ARTHUR FREED
A METRO-GOLDWYN-MAYER PICTURE
Photographed in TECHNICOLOR

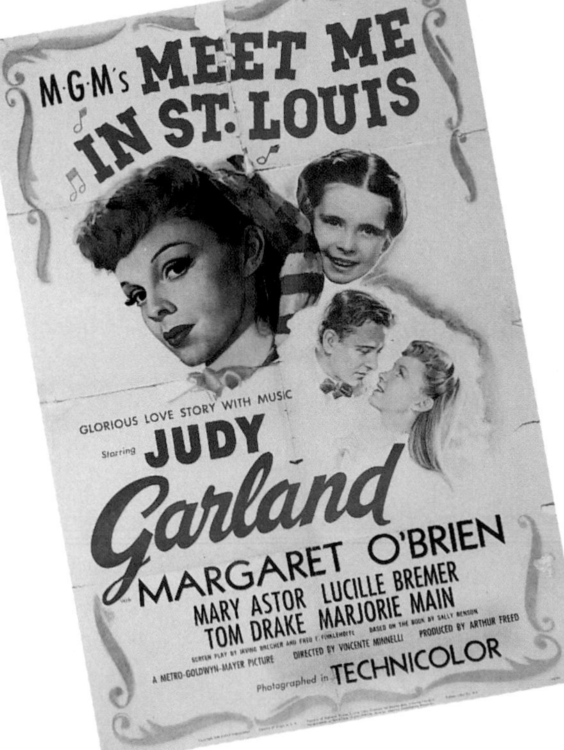

ABOVE: Poster for The Clock, *MGM/1945. LEFT: Poster for* Meet Me in St. Louis, *MGM/1944. RIGHT: Portrait, circa 1943.*

FACING PAGE: Foldout ad art for The Clock, *showing TOP LEFT: the front cover, BOTTOM LEFT: the back cover, and RIGHT: the interior. Kapralik created the portraits of Judy and Robert Walker.*

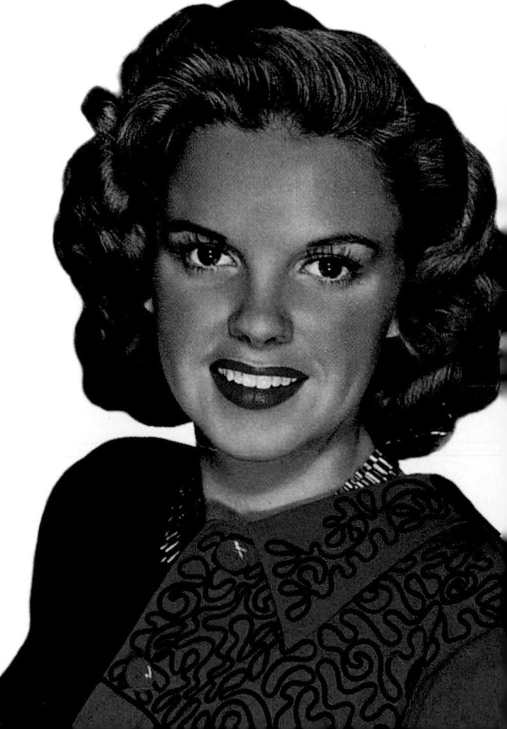

THE CLOCK

"... Unusual ... an attraction which exhibitors will exploit to advantage ... delightful ..."
MOTION PICTURE HERALD
"...one of the most entertaining to be shown in a long time"... should do well for every theatre privileged to show it ..."
SHOWMEN'S TRADE REVIEW
"... special treat for women ... absorbing ... action and suspense ..."
FILM DAILY
"... highly entertaining ... delightful, romantic drama ..."
THE EXHIBITOR
"... charm, sweetness, heart tug and wholesomeness ..."
MOTION PICTURE DAILY
"... one of those pictures about which the romantic will rave..."
BOXOFFICE
M·G·M
MERRILY PRESENTS
JUDY GARLAND
ROBERT WALKER
in "THE CLOCK"
with JAMES GLEASON · KEENAN WYNN · MARSHALL THOMPSON
Screen Play by ROBERT NATHAN & JOSEPH SCHRANK · A METRO-GOLDWYN-MAYER Picture
Directed by VINCENTE MINNELLI · Produced by ARTHUR FREED
"TIME TO SET IT FOR A LONG RUN!"
RINGING THE BELL AT ITS CAPITOL, N. Y. WORLD PREMIERE!
MGM
MOTION PICTURE DAILY, MAY 16, 1945
With all your might!
MIGHTY 7th WAR LOAN

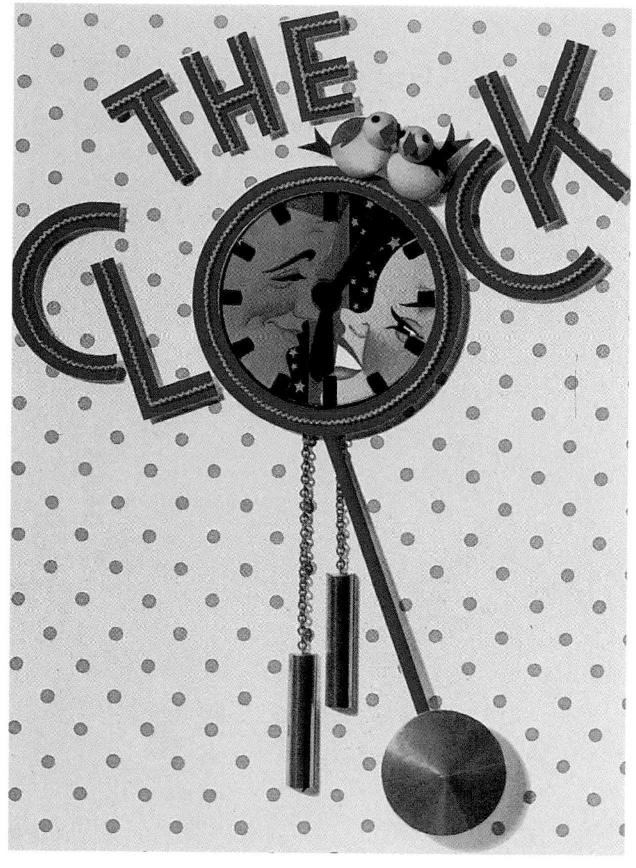

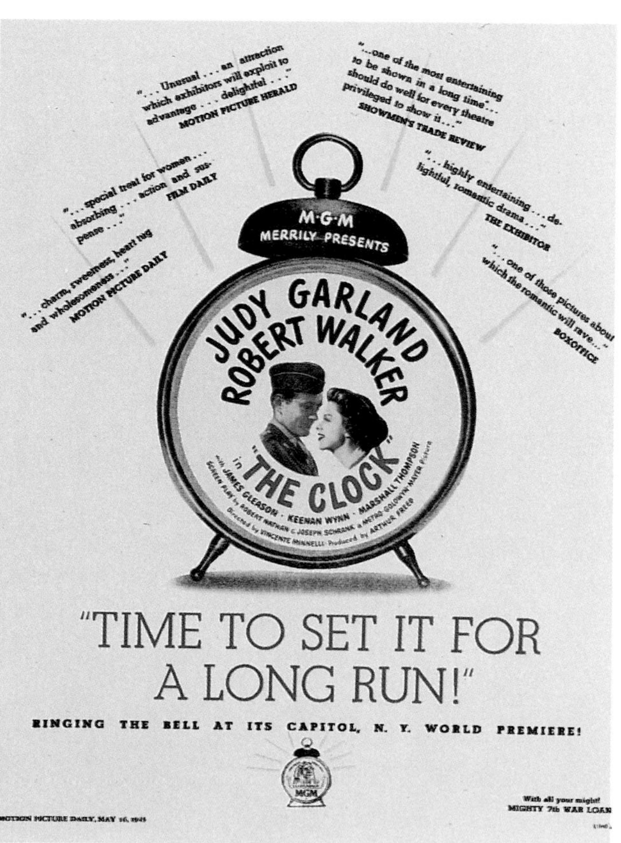

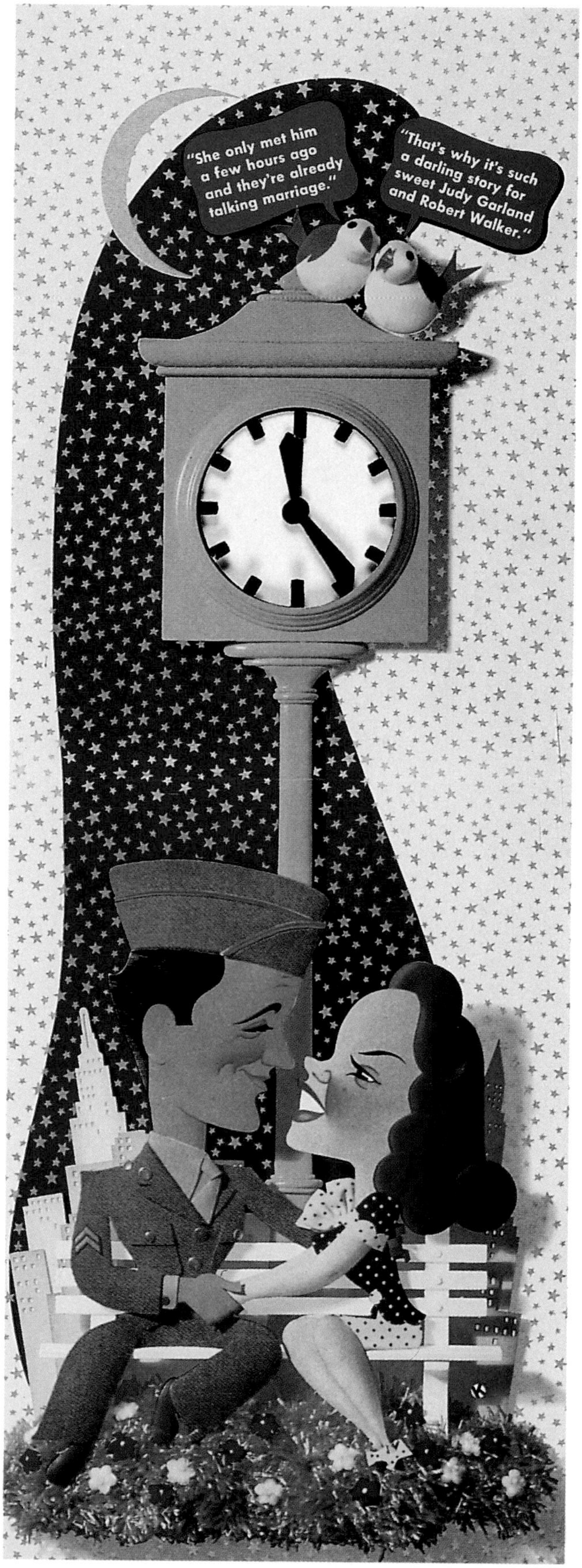
"She only met him a few hours ago and they're already talking marriage."
"That's why it's such a darling story for sweet Judy Garland and Robert Walker."

TOP: Hirschfeld ad art for The Harvey Girls, *MGM/1946. ABOVE LEFT: Poster for the same film. RIGHT: Hirschfeld also provided the poster caricatures for the all-star* Till the Clouds Roll By, *MGM/1947.*

Other illnesses plagued the set as well. Mary Astor, again cast as Garland's mother, missed almost a month with recurring pneumonia. Little sister Joan Carroll was out most of a month after an appendectomy, and grandfather Harry Davenport was out for a week. Garland's immediate costar, seven-year-old Margaret O'Brien, was briefly taken out of the picture by her mother, who feared the child was being overworked at MGM. (At one point, Garland had watched the child from the sidelines and quietly commented to several of the chorus, "I hope they don't do to her what they did to me.")

Minnelli finished the film in early April, and it premiered in St. Louis on November 22, 1944. Garland was ultimately very proud of her work, noting that "actors with musical talent should be given better material to work with," and citing *St. Louis* as an example of such quality. The movie was reviewed as Minnelli intended: an ensemble piece with Garland's contributions essential and in the forefront but always within the context of the script and in proportion to the other characters. If the past was never as perfect as Minnelli here painted it, general critical consensus held that his beautiful vision was indeed how it *should* have been. The *Hollywood Reporter* called *St. Louis* "a warmly human entertainment which has captured a nostalgic charm rarely if ever equaled on the screen," while *Variety* said in praise, "Miss Garland achieves true stature with her deeply understanding performance." Their appreciation was echoed in the New York *Daily Mirror:* "Bremer is a standout, [but] she's no challenge to the star. No one alive could be."

St. Louis broke box-office records all over the country as not only Garland's greatest hit to date but Metro's top moneymaker after *Gone With the Wind.* Her recordings of "The Trolley Song" and "Have Yourself a Merry Little Christmas" both made the charts.

Scheduled to begin *Ziegfeld Follies* immediately after *St. Louis,* Garland took time between the two pictures to file for divorce from David Rose on June 7, 1944. The charges were "incompatibility and clash of careers," but the couple had simply grown apart.

Ziegfeld Follies had been in discussion at MGM since early 1939; when Freed finally got the ball rolling in 1943, he solicited or was inundated with scores of numbers, sketches, and ideas. Garland was suggested for many of the routines: a takeoff on *Lady in the Dark* with Rooney and Fred Astaire; a minstrel number with Rooney, Astaire, and Lou Holtz (Garland and Nancy Walker would sing "Mrs. Gallagher and Mrs. Shean" in blackface); an "Album of Familiar Songs" medley with Marilyn Maxwell, Eddie (Rochester) Anderson, Lena Horne, and Kathryn Grayson; "The Babbitt and the Bromide" with Astaire (ultimately, Fred would partner Gene Kelly for the song); a "Firehouse Chat" sketch with Lucille Ball and Ann Sothern; a "Reading of the Play" sketch with Frank Morgan; a musical number, "It's Getting Hot in Tahiti"; "Lady in the Clouds," with Garland, Ball, and Greer Garson visiting a psychiatrist's office to sing the number they'd concocted on the War Bond train, "I've Got Those Rooney/Pidgeon/Skelton Blues"; appearances with Rooney in a backstage opening sequence and the finale, "There's Beauty Everywhere" (in which they'd ride through the set in a gondola); "Pass That Peace Pipe" with Garland (or Ball or June Allyson) and Astaire, Robert Walker, Gene Kelly, Rooney, or Chuck Walters; "Sand," a Harlem song and sketch in blackface with Astaire; and "Children's Park," riding on swings with Tom Drake and miscellaneous other Metro stars (including Katharine Hep-

The northwest corner of 45th Street and Broadway in New York, December 1944. As of 1992, St. Louis *is one of fourteen Garland films cited in* Variety*'s list of all-time film rental champs. (Others include* Love Finds Andy Hardy, The Wizard of Oz, The Clock, Girl Crazy, In the Good Old Summertime, Words and Music, Thousands Cheer, Ziegfeld Follies, The Harvey Girls, Easter Parade, Till the Clouds Roll By, Pepe, *and* A Star is Born.*) The film included such subsequent standards as "Have Yourself a Merry Little Christmas" and "The Boy Next Door."*

Deleted scenes from Meet Me in St. Louis. *TOP LEFT: The song "Boys and Girls Like You and Me." TOP RIGHT: Tootie (Margaret O'Brien) tells her sisters Esther and Rose (Lucille Bremer) about her encounter with one of their idols, Colonel Darly. ABOVE: Vincente Minnelli directs Garland and Drake in "Boys and Girls Like You and Me." LEFT: Esther helps her mother (Mary Astor) prepare to go out.*

burn, Walter Pidgeon, Basil Rathbone, and Esther Williams). Tenor James Melton also suggested that he do a number with her or Grayson.

Only one Garland item was specifically developed—a sketch and song (to be directed by Norman Taurog) in which she would play herself. The opening moments were to show her onstage, completing a performance. Once offstage, she turns down after-theatre dates with Metro players John Craig, Van Johnson, and John Hodiak to keep an appointment with "an old friend . . . a boy I used to know 'way back when." It turns out to be Mickey Rooney, whom she greets and entertains in a lofty manner à la Gertrude Lawrence, while he attempts to rekindle their past with clips from the *Babes* pictures and *Strike Up the Band.* He mentions his recent discomfort at seeing her "make love to another fellow. . . in Technicolor," and notes that "I haven't kissed you . . . since black and white." Judy comes out of her grande dame pose to duet the Hugh Martin/Ralph Blane number, "I Love You More in Technicolor Than I Do in Black and White."

Meanwhile, Greer Garson was penciled in for a *Follies* routine as a "glamorous, amorous" great lady of the cinema, giving an interview to a singing and dancing press corps and bemoaning her constant appearance in films that pay "monumental, biographical tribute to a monumental biographical woman." (The ensuing song heralded her supposed next picture as *Madame Crematante,* inventor of the safety pin.) The entire routine was written by Roger Edens and Kay Thompson, but Garson rejected the number in early April 1944; a week earlier, Rooney went into the service before he could even prerecord the "Technicolor" song. With Garland's sketch summarily dropped from the *Follies,* and Garson out of "The Interview," Edens and Thompson taught the latter number to Judy. Chuck Walters staged the routine, and Minnelli filmed it over three days in July.

The uncut *Ziegfeld Follies* ran nearly three hours during its first preview in November 1944; it would ultimately be cut to 110 minutes. The film finally premiered in Boston and Pittsburgh in August 1945 as a two-a-day road show; it was nationally released in April 1946. Although many critics noted the uneven quality of the film, they admired the lavish production; the New York *Herald Tribune* particularly disliked "The Interview" and thought Judy had "some mighty unpleasant stuff to do." That specific opinion, however, was much in the minority. The Los Angeles *Herald-Express* welcomed its "snap of pace after the slow-moving spectacle" elsewhere in the film, and Bosley Crowther of the *New York Times* offered that "Miss Garland's trenchant spoofing gives promise of a talent fast approaching that of Beatrice Lillie or Gertrude Lawrence." The *Hollywood Review* directed, "Just watch her slay 'em with subtlety. The number is Judy Garland all the way and at her tip-top best. And that's 'best' enough to make it the prime standout of the whole production."

As a further stretch, Garland next tackled her first straight dramatic role in *The Clock,* the story of a wartime romance between a secretary and a soldier (Robert Walker) who meet during his forty-eight-hour leave in New York City. She told an interviewer at the time, "You take your life in your hands, but it's fun to see what you can do. I like taking a crack at something different." Director Jack Conway fell ill in June while shooting backgrounds on location in New York; principal photography finally began at Metro in early August 1944 under the direction of Fred Zinnemann. Minor roles were filled by Audrey Totter as Garland's New York roommate, and by Hume Cronyn and Connie Gilchrist as the milkman and his wife who briefly befriend the young couple.

Garland in costume for her sketch in Ziegfeld Follies *(filmed in 1944 but not released until two years later). Her over-the-top portrayal of a sophisticated star poked fun at Tallulah Bankhead and Greer Garson and was heavily influenced by the theatrical coaching of her new compatriot Kay Thompson.*

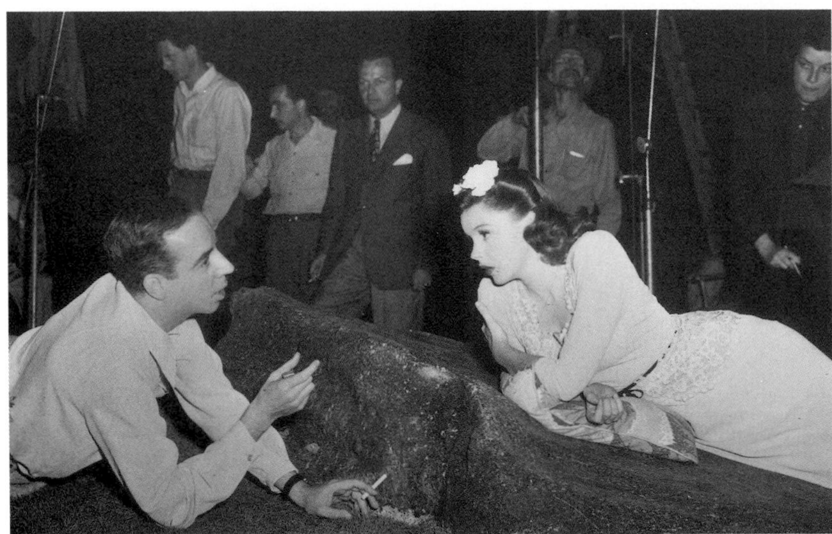

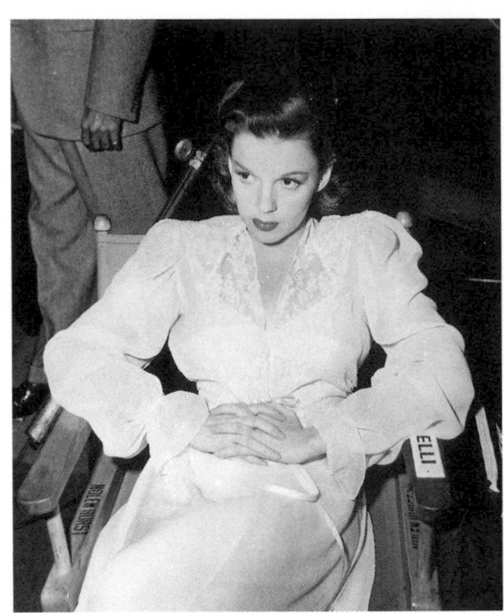

The Clock. *LEFT: Minnelli directs Garland as Alice Mayberry in the Riverside Park sequence. RIGHT: On set, October 1944.*

During the third week of August, with nearly a third of the picture shot, Zinnemann was taken off *The Clock.* (Garland told producer Freed that she and the director had "no compatibility.") At Judy's request, Minnelli replaced Zinnemann on September 1. She had begun to fall in love with Vincente during *St. Louis;* now the affair would blossom. But on a purely professional level, she felt the original *Clock* script "hadn't played very well: it was all talk and no action," especially in her scenes with Walker. In an interview just subsequent to their work on the film, she lavishly praised Minnelli as "a wonderful director. He killed himself thinking up ways to give [*The Clock*] movement." She also affectionately and humorously described him as "a little peculiar and hard to get used to. He talks fast, and then he gets excited and stutters and doesn't finish his sentences—just says, with a wave of his arm, 'Well, you know what I mean.' Fred Astaire said, 'Vincente's so good—if I just knew what he was saying!' "

Minnelli reworked many of *The Clock*'s script points in an effort to make New York City "the third character" in the story. He also humanized and added humor to the supporting characters, recasting the older couple and Garland's roommate with, respectively, James Gleason, his wife Lucile, and Ruth Brady. And he continued to marvel at Garland: "I would tell her a hundred things while she was being made up, and I felt I wasn't getting through to her. Yet, when she got before the cameras, everything was there, all the subtleties and the pathos—she was magnificent."

The director began the film from the top. Judy was frequently late to the set during filming, and out sick for ten days; Minnelli missed several days as well, but the real problem on the film was Robert Walker. Despondent over his pending divorce from Jennifer Jones, the young actor began to drink. Minnelli remembers how Garland would "reach out to people," in this case tracking Walker to a bar by night and working to sober him up in time for his call in the morning.

Nonetheless, *The Clock* was completed in late November 1944 and released in May 1945. One critic yawned, "The incurably romantic will rave, 'how sweet,' the dilettantes will declare, 'how artistic,' but the rank and file of theatregoers will undoubtedly turn thumbs down." The positive reviews, however, far outweighed the negative. *Time* found *The Clock* "so good at its best that it inspires ingratitude for not being great. Few films in recent years have managed so movingly to combine first-rate truth with second-grade fiction." The *Los Angeles Times* liked the film more than the much-vaunted *Since You Went Away* and called it "nearly everything that a picture should be about young romance during wartime." Many asked "why one of the greatest singers of songs on the screen was shut out of singing," but Garland's acting brought her much appreciation: "To say she is superb is an understatement in two syllables. She need never sing or dance again" (the New York *Daily Mirror*).

From *The Clock*, Judy segued directly into rehearsals for another film. Originally conceived as a straight drama for Lana Turner, *The Harvey Girls* became a Garland picture when Arthur Freed—influenced by the success of *Oklahoma!*—decided to attempt a vintage Americana musical. Principal photography began in January 1945, and Garland played a prospective mail-order bride who becomes instead a waitress at one of the Fred Harvey restaurants established along the Atchison, Topeka, and the Santa Fe railroad during the 1890s. She wins the affections of the local saloon keeper, played by John Hodiak (in a role originally intended for Clark Gable); by film's end, the bar and its horde of dance-hall harlots have relinquished the town to the Harvey Girls. Angela Lansbury played the leader of the saloon contingent, with Preston Foster as wicked Judge Purvis. (The parts were first suggested for Ann Sothern and Edward Arnold.)

Director George Sidney had done Judy's screen test ten years earlier. He relished the progress made by the Freed Unit in developing the film musical, noting that such movies once required "thousands of girls kicking together. . . until somewhere along the line we found out that you could just have a close-up of Judy—and let it run for three minutes because she had talent." After Garland and company prerecorded the mammoth "Atchison, Topeka, and the Santa Fe" production number, Sidney "spent days lining up" the shooting. "We had hundreds of dancers, cowboys, Indians, horses, God knows what. Judy saw a 'dance-in'—a dancing stand-in—do a run-through once. Then she said, 'I'm ready,' and she

BELOW: Robert Walker and Garland in a scene cut from The Clock. *BOTTOM LEFT: Garland and Walker look on as Keenan Wynn and James Gleason begin to tangle; on the far left is Moyna MacGill, mother of Angela Lansbury. BOTTOM RIGHT: Minnelli (second from right) oversees a rehearsal of the couple's application for a marriage license.*

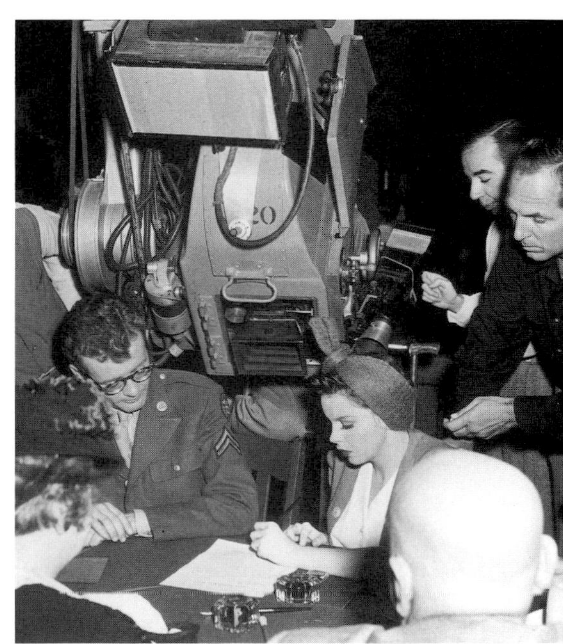

The Harvey Girls, *1946.* BELOW AND BOTTOM LEFT: *Two different endings for the "March of the Doagies" production number, reworked as changes were made in the script. The number was ultimately cut.* BOTTOM RIGHT: *Also cut was Garland's rescue of her wedding dress from the burning Harvey House. John Hodiak is the confrontational leading man.*

went right through it, every movement matched to the subtle changes in her voice, every movement of the dance-in memorized at a glance. I never saw such concentration; it was incredible."

Seven screenwriters made considerable script revision as shooting progressed, and Garland later joked that "they couldn't come up with one plot; we had seven plots, one plot per person." Last-minute rewrites eliminated "Hayride," a six-minute production number that had already been prerecorded and rehearsed; late changes also necessitated shooting two versions of another four-minute routine, "March of the Doagies," which was ultimately deleted entirely. (This left the last portion of the film virtually without songs, and a well-turned musical became in its last reels just an average Western.)

Problems abounded. Virginia O'Brien was pregnant, and her scenes had to be rushed through. Ray Bolger was burned by steam from the train. Foster and Hodiak were hurt during their fight scene. According to a production memo, Judy was frightened by a "very fractious" horse and retired briefly from the set. She missed eleven days during the five-month shooting schedule and was late on nearly forty occasions. But the film remained a happy experience for most of the company. Lansbury today rhapsodizes, "What an education it was to work with Judy; I loved her. I was like a sponge in those days and picked up a lot of wonderful stuff from her. She was a total pro, and her talent was the one thing that always saw her through."

The film was another monetary bonanza and, when it debuted at New York's Capitol Theatre in January 1946, scored the biggest nonholiday opening in history. Judy's recording of "Atchison, Topeka" hit the charts, and the song itself sold three-quarters of a million copies of sheet music in six months. Virtually every critic validated Freed's approach; *Liberty* began, "Move over, Broadway, and make room for a great, wide, wonderful musical comedy. It's a certainty that if Judy gets any more talented, she'll probably explode." *Box Office Digest* called the film "showmanship to the bursting point," and Garland was praised by *Motion Picture Daily* for her "sharpened demonstration of comic ability." *Hollywood Review* raved, "Her winsome beauty and little girlishness make the best

vehicle she has had in moons out of all this. And you'll see some acting from her that will gain your respect for real talent." Only the *Hollywood Reporter* dissented: "Judy has never looked worse. . . all the things, photogenically, a leading lady should not be."

The Harvey Girls finished principal photography on June 4, 1945. Eleven days later, twenty-three-year-old Judy and forty-two-year-old Minnelli were married at her mother's home. Corporate MGM looked with favor on the union; Mayer himself gave away the bride, and the newlyweds departed the same day for a New York honeymoon.

It was a new beginning for Judy, and there was hope in Hollywood that her marriage would provide both stability and peace. The preceding five and a half years had made immeasurable demands on her. There had been over seventy-five radio appearances (many of them on a volunteer basis for Armed Forces Radio) and hundreds of benefit, service-camp, and war-bond shows. She cut over thirty-five sides for Decca. And she starred or costarred in twelve films, guest-starring in two others. Professionally, she was at a new high; the success of *St. Louis* and *The Clock* would once again place her among the top-ten box-office stars for the year.

But her increasing absences and late arrivals, her weight losses, her emotional highs and lows had become cause for concern; there were increasing signs that Joe Mankiewicz had been correct in his appraisal of her emotional fragility. Many thought that the gifted, gentle Minnelli could help assuage some of Garland's personal insecurities and keep her professionally fulfilled as well.

TOP, LEFT TO RIGHT: Harvey Girls *director George Sidney looks on as Garland's Susan Bradley challenges Hodiak; Garland chats with the film's villainess, Angela Lansbury (who later offered that "People used to hiss me in public for being mean to Judy"); Garland and Hodiak duet another deleted song, "My Intuition," April 1945. BOTTOM RIGHT: Garland in the dress designed for her marriage to Vincente Minnelli.*

Chapter Four

Quintessential Triple Threat

Minnelli and a pregnant Garland arrived back in Los Angeles in September 1945 to participate in *Till the Clouds Roll By,* Arthur Freed's all-star biography of composer Jerome Kern. The picture—at various times called *I Hear Music* and *Silver Lining*—had been in development since 1940; Garland was cast as legendary Broadway dancer Marilyn Miller, and Minnelli had agreed to direct her sequences. She began rehearsals in early October and, within five weeks, completed four musical numbers and three brief scenes.

Minnelli first showcased Judy in a dressing-room episode. as Miller receives admirers during intermission of the Kern hit, *Sally.* She then changes from glamorous dressing gown to scullery costume, and the camera tracks with her as she moves through the backstage area to an onstage set of sink and dirty dishes for the number "Look for the Silver Lining." Later Garland returned as a circus equestrienne for "D'Ye Love Me?" and the title song from *Sunny,* finally appearing in feathered evening gown for a lavish "Who?" The pregnant star was partnered in the latter by a dancing male chorus and delighted in twirling up to different men to ask the musical question *"Who. . . stole my heart away?";* off camera, she laughed to costume designer Helen Rose, "What a song to sing in my present condition!"

FACING PAGE: Metro's "biggest asset," circa 1945. BELOW: Garland sings "Look for the Silver Lining" in Till the Clouds Roll By *(filmed in 1945; released in 1947).*

When the film premiered in January 1947, critical estimation ranged from "elephantine" (the New York *Herald Tribune*) to "pretty as a king-size lollipop" (the New York *Journal-American*), but all agreed that *Clouds* was distinguished chiefly by its score and the execution of some of the songs. Garland was singled out by everyone. *Film Daily* found her numbers "superb. . . paragons of [Minnelli's] ability and style"; *Hollywood Review* named her the "high point in an entertainment unbelievably full of high points. [It's] the greatest work she has ever done. She is radiantly beautiful, winsomely appealing, [and] for twenty minutes, the picture is all hers." *Clouds* established new box-office records everywhere, including New York's Radio City Music Hall.

There was brief radio and recording work in autumn 1945; then Judy retired to await the Cesarean birth of her six-pound ten-ounce daughter Liza May, on March 12, 1946. Garland suffered postpartum depression but, by late spring, had settled into a happy period of vibrant domesticity. Gradually, however, she was drawn into plans for her return to work in December. MGM had again torn up her contract and created a new, impressive pact, effective at the start date of her first film after maternity leave. The agreement guaranteed her $300,000 annually and called for starring roles in ten pictures over five years.

As December drew nearer, the thought of such a commitment became increasingly unpleasant. Prior to her marriage, Judy had told friends she had no intention of signing another term contract when her 1940 pact expired in 1947: she planned to work independently, limiting herself to one picture a year and possibly a radio series. She recognized the treadmill she had been on and was determined to avoid future overwork and any dependency on medication. (During their

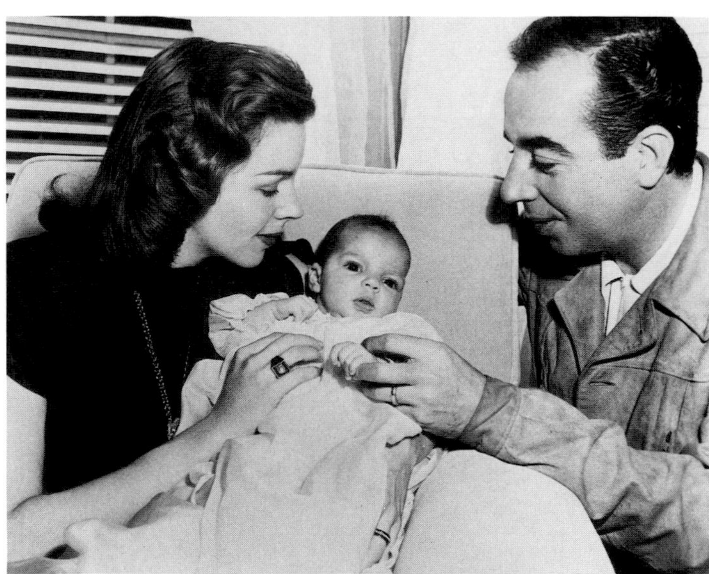

ABOVE LEFT: With John and Renee Arnaut in "D'Ye Love Me," deleted before release from Till the Clouds Roll By. *ABOVE RIGHT: Mr. and Mrs. Vincente Minnelli and daughter, Liza May, June 1946.*

honeymoon, Garland went walking with Minnelli one evening and threw a vial of pills into the East River, pledging to abandon them forever.) When MGM executives heard of her plans for professional freedom, they were stunned. The Loew's hierarchy immediately went into action, romancing Judy during the Minnellis' New York sojourn, laying a foundation for a new contract. In addition to the obvious financial rewards, they offered an implied artistic control; Garland could continue to work with her husband, and Metro would mount specialized vehicles created specifically for her. The first of these—at the Minnellis' request—would be an adaptation of S. N. Behrman's sophisticated Broadway comedy, *The Pirate.* Given such concessions, Garland was persuaded to accept the studio's bid. However, even before production began on the picture, she regretted her decision and commitment to five more years in Culver City.

The project itself was (at least initially) an exciting one. Garland would be partnered with Gene Kelly, and Freed contracted Cole Porter for the score. Anita Loos and Joseph Than worked on the script for more than six months, producing an unusable reversal of Behrman's original premise: their central character was a dancing pirate who pretends to be an entertainer rather than a touring actor who impersonates a legendary seaman. They also fashioned a role for Lena Horne as a Caribbean dressmaker, and a subplot concerning Horne's boyfriend, the village mayor, and local political intrigue. Minnelli, Freed, Porter, and the stars were speechless at a reading of the Loos/Than script, and Albert Hackett and Frances Goodrich were hastily summoned to rework the scenario from scratch. Their version cast Garland as a romantic island girl, betrothed to a fat and pompous mayor but in love with her fantasies of the ruthless buccaneer Mack the Black Macoco. Kelly, as a strolling player, meets and falls in love with the girl; when he discovers her obsession, he poses as the pirate and then discovers that the mayor himself is really the retired Macoco.

Judy's problems began to slowly escalate as soon as she returned to the studio. She was out ill for nine days during wardrobe and prerecordings in December and January. In February and March, she missed eight more days and was late on many occasions. It was increasingly obvious that the frail Garland was back on medication, whether in frightened realization of the work commitment ahead of her, uneasiness about the potential success of her marriage, or in a growing awareness that *The Pirate* was shaping up poorly—for all its high-powered cast and staff. Her deteriorating condition led her to drop out of the Academy Awards ceremony the night before the annual event on March 12; she was slated to sing the Oscar-nominated "On the Atchison, Topeka, and the Santa Fe." (The song, like "Rainbow," won the award.)

Kelly later explained, "Judy only worked when she thought she was going to be good. If she felt she wasn't up to giving her best, she didn't appear on the set." But if Garland was insecure about her own performance, she also grew paranoid about Minnelli and Kelly's close working relationship. She even briefly quarreled with Porter over the score, although the composer told Roger Edens he found her rendition of "Love of My Life" very beautiful. (Porter was merely tactful about arranger Kay Thompson's manic approach to "Mack the Black"; he just commented that her treatment "has me in a dither.")

Garland suffered a public, pill-induced collapse during the filming of "Voodoo," a song-and-dance-under-hypnosis routine with Kelly. She burst onto the set, reared in panic at the flames that had been lit for the number, and begged for Benzedrine from the assembled extras before being led away. "Voodoo" created another problem as well. The song began in a tent where Kelly's troupe was presenting its show; Garland's rendition built to their duo dance, which was to grow so wild and abandoned that it spilled out onto the town plaza. Hedda Hopper later described the number as "a hair curler. Gene and Judy flung themselves too eagerly into the spirit of things. It looked like a torrid romance." When Ida Koverman saw the rushes, she dragged Louis B. Mayer out of an executive conference to see them, too. "Burn the negative!" he cried. "If that exhibition gets on any screen, we'll be raided by the police!" He later gave Kelly a lecture on how to behave while dancing, and "Voodoo" was restaged.

The Pirate, *1948.* FACING PAGE, BOTTOM AND BELOW RIGHT: *Costume tests for Garland's Manuela Alva; she did not wear the latter outfit in the finished film.* BELOW LEFT: *Garland and Kelly in the throes of "Voodoo" and* BELOW CENTER: *Minnelli discusses staging of the number with them between takes.*

BELOW: *Fred Astaire, in rehearsal for* Easter Parade, *visits Judy and Gene Kelly during retakes on* The Pirate, *December 1947.* BOTTOM: *Garland and Kelly in the knockabout "Be a Clown."*

During the last two weeks of March and the first week of April, Minnelli shot around Garland whenever possible. When she did work, it was sometimes only for an hour or two or under duress. At one point, Hopper visited Judy's dressing room and found her hysterical, accusatory of her co-workers, suspicious of her mother, and "shaking like an aspen leaf. She was carried out, put in a limousine, still wearing make-up and costume, and put to bed." She missed seven days in May; on the thirty-first, Freed held a long meeting with her, and she rallied until June 30. Then she was out for eight days in a two-week period, finally making one last push to finish the picture. On July 15, she appeared for the finale, "Be a Clown," completing thirty-three takes of five different camera setups between mid-afternoon and midnight. Two days later, she returned to finish "Clown" and to do retakes and pickups on five other scenes, changing wardrobe, hairstyle, and makeup at least three times for more than twenty-five takes.

Her work completed, Garland made a quiet, unpublicized attempt at suicide and was sent off to Las Campanas, a California sanitarium. Her stay there was followed by a trip to the Austen Riggs Center in Stockbridge, Massachusetts; the press was told she was exhausted and had suffered a breakdown. Her sometimes high-strung manner during interviews and her occasionally too-thin appearance in preceding years had prepared them for such news, although Hollywood columnists, at least, were aware that overmedication and insecurity had played a large part in the story. This time, MGM encouraged Judy to seek psychiatric help (Mayer had earlier arranged for a therapist to visit Garland on the set of *The Pirate*), but she abruptly left Riggs after a few weeks.

She would later compare therapy to "taking strong medicine for a disease I didn't have. It just tore me apart." The truth is found more in the latter statement, and there is much evidence that Garland alternated between sincerely working at her analysis and inventing horror stories to unnerve (or entertain) her doctors. Whatever her actions, and whatever her reasons, there were undeniable and mounting pressures at this point in her life. She had been performing for over twenty years, and more than a decade of that time had been spent at MGM. Everyone in the business wanted to work with her, but the need to live up to their enormous expectations brought increasing terror. (When director George Cukor later asked Judy why someone with her extraordinary capabilities should be so frightened, she told him, "I'm always afraid this is the time they're going to catch me.") The demands on her energy and time since she was Baby Gumm had also caught up with her. Mankiewicz refers to "the complete obliteration of her childhood," when Garland lost years of gentle maturation while in vaudeville. Then, in her early days at Metro, the publicity department reinvented so much of her past that what little anchor Judy had in reality had all but disintegrated. She later admitted, "You get to doubting your actual personality. You can't go around denying the stories your studio releases when it is doing all it can to make you a star."

Her relationship with her mother became increasingly stormy as well. Minnelli remembered Ethel Gilmore as "a strong-willed woman who attempted to dominate Judy. . . [a woman who] hadn't adjusted to her daughter's coming of age." He felt Ethel "tended to agree with everything Mayer wanted Judy to do. . . and had been making a career of her own by 'keeping Judy in line.' Judy felt betrayed."

Of course, medication remained a major problem. It had become an escape and a false buffer, a counterfeit means of making herself feel energetic and confident. But Garland required larger and larger doses as her tolerance grew, and the strength and/or combination of the pills could lead to hallucinatory anxiety and dreadful behavior. "I don't want to act like this," she once cried. "I don't even know why I do." Her deep guilt about her dependency was not alleviated by the fact that some co-workers were also taking pills, and medication was comparatively easy to obtain. (Several Metro stars remember a doctor on the lot whose pharmaceuticals were all too accessible.) Due to the pills and the pressures of work, Judy's insomnia continued to flourish; unable to sleep, she began a pattern of nocturnal phone calls to friends, seeking someone to talk her through the night. Still unsure of her physical attractiveness, she would often rant to them about being wanted and important only because of her voice.

While at Riggs, Garland had also discussed her father and the rumors of his homosexual activities. She would never resolve her conflicted feelings about Frank, and the problem was compounded by the creative, brilliant, and sensitive people of varied sexual natures whom she encountered on a daily basis in her professional environment. She was intensely attracted to some of the men and occasionally found fulfilling romances and relationships with them. But such associations were ultimately dissatisfying, and this contributed enormously to her instability over the years. (It has additionally been suggested—both by Mickey Rooney as well as by her intelligent biographer, Christopher Finch—that Judy was vulnerable to some bisexual experimentation of her own. This created further angst for her.)

Typically, Garland could also make light of her experience in sanitariums and took pleasure in telling about her late-night admission to Las Campanas. Though attendants supported her on either side as she walked across the front lawn, she felt something continually tugging at and tripping her feet. The sensation terrified her and, once inside, she collapsed, sure she had finally gone around the bend. By daylight, she looked across the expanse of grass she had traversed; it was pockmarked with croquet wickets.

The Pirate was sneak-previewed in October and November 1947 to mostly positive but widely diverse public reaction. As a result, Freed and Minnelli did several weeks of additional editing and retakes in November and December. Kay Thompson's arrangement of "Mack the Black" was dropped completely; it had originally opened the film as underscoring for a filmed montage of Macoco in action. (The sequence then dissolved to the daydreaming Garland, singing about the fabled pirate.) A new version was prepared for Garland, and it replaced the deleted "Voodoo." The initial complete version of Garland's "Love of My Life" was dropped, leaving only a reprise; her slightly double-entendre rendition of "You Can Do No Wrong" was also cut and then refilmed as a sincere ballad for a new slot in the script. Even Kelly's "Pirate Ballet" was deleted for one preview and then reinstated.

Finally released in June 1948, *The Pirate* was received with much enthusiasm by most critics. The Philadelphia *Bulletin* called it "a dazzling phantasmagoria," and *P.M.* thought it "the best big-time musical show presented on screen or onstage in years." "Be a Clown" was the acknowledged highlight of the film, and where some reviewers found it Kelly's picture, others praised Garland. If critically acclaimed, *The Pirate* didn't always please audiences; perhaps they concurred with Garland, who felt the film too rarefied for the average taste.

TOP: With Louis B. Mayer, Irving Berlin, and Arthur Freed. Until the day she died, Judy was Freed's choice to star in his long-planned Berlin film cavalcade, Say It with Music. *"I always thought that Judy would come back. I thought she was made out of iron. She came back so many times. She was going to play Irving Berlin's wife. Vincente was going to direct it. We'd be working together." ABOVE: Hair and makeup test for Garland's Hannah Brown,* Easter Parade, *November 1947.*

BELOW: *Garland's makeup expert and confidante Dottie Ponedel joins hairdresser Helen Young in preparing the star for her stellar* Easter Parade *solo, "Mr. Monotony."* BOTTOM LEFT: *Astaire, Garland, and director Chuck Walters.* BOTTOM RIGHT: *"When the Midnight Choo-Choo Leaves for Alabam'."* Easter Parade, *December 1947.*

FACING PAGE, TOP: *Peter Lawford toys with Garland's troublesome feather.* BOTTOM: *Costume test for* Easter Parade, *November 1947.*

Though the picture grossed well, its high budget made it her first, and only, MGM film to lose money. (The final cost of $3.7 million did not reflect Garland's problems alone. The project's account was charged with several earlier abandoned treatments. The first of these, prepared in 1943 by Joe Mankiewicz, was intended as a straight comedy for William Powell and either Hedy Lamarr or Myrna Loy. The salaries of Loos and Than for the unused script were also charged to the cost, as were the weeks of retakes.) *The Pirate* has since gained status as the perfect exemplification of Minnelli's genius and as a grand Kelly showcase. But Robert Kotlowitz of *Show* offered another analysis in 1961: "The movie threatened to collapse under its own swollen weight . . . every five minutes. What saved it [was] a gay, corny, tongue-in-cheek performance by Garland that . . . gave a kind of hilarious panacea to the whole nonsensical book." Nearly thirty years later, historian Ethan Mordden stated bluntly that, without Garland, *The Pirate* would be "a cult movie without a cult."

On her return from Riggs in September 1947, Garland began rehearsals with Kelly for *Easter Parade.* Arthur Freed had bought the title song from Irving Berlin and signed him to write the score for $500,000 plus a percentage of the film's profits. The producer later acknowledged that "the reason I got Irving to agree to *Easter Parade* was on account of Judy." Roger Edens selected eight Berlin standards for the film, which Berlin augmented with eight additional songs-some new and some early, unused material. When Garland posed for publicity pictures with Berlin, she remembered that "the photographer asked us to stand in a dancing position. I quipped, 'Maybe this will inspire one of the new songs.' Irving laughed and said, 'Maybe.' Then as I was leaving, he slipped a small piece of paper into my hand, saying, 'Don't show this to anyone yet.' When I looked at it, I read the words, 'It Only Happens When I Dance With You.' I've always considered this my very own beloved melody."

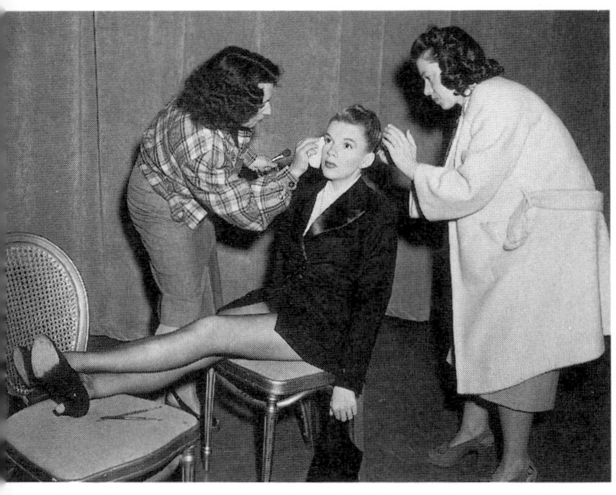

The cast for *Easter Parade* underwent considerable revision. Roles for Frank Sinatra, Kathryn Grayson, and Red Skelton gave way to parts for Peter Lawford and Cyd Charisse; the latter broke a bone in her foot and was supplanted by Ann Miller. After several weeks of rehearsal, Gene Kelly broke his ankle on October 12 in a home football game. Overnight, Freed contacted the nominally retired Fred Astaire, who delightedly accepted the chance to work opposite Garland. He later exulted, "Judy's not primarily a dancer. But she's the best of her type;

an amazing girl. She could do things—*any*thing—with*out* rehearsing and come off perfectly. She could learn faster, do *everything* better than most people. It was one of the greatest thrills to work with her."

By then, there had been another important replacement in the *Easter Parade* company. Judy's psychiatrist advised Freed that both working and living with Minnelli would be detrimental for her, and on September 18, the producer removed Vincente as the film's director. His replacement, Chuck Walters, had just made his directorial debut with *Good News* and was thrilled at the assignment. Better still, Judy adored him (although kidding him about the grand treatment she expected to receive at his hands); he found her "very cooperative; just toss Judy the ball, and she carried it for a home run." Walters was also instrumental in bringing Sidney Sheldon to the project, asking for a complete rewrite of the original Albert Hackett/Frances Goodrich screenplay: "The first script I saw was terrible! The hero was a real heavy." Sheldon, Walters, Freed, and Edens worked to make a straightforward musical comedy out of the story of a vaudeville headliner (Astaire) whose female partner deserts him for a Broadway contract. He vows to make a new costar out of an unknown, picks Garland out of a chorus line, and misguidedly tries to mold her into an exotic danseuse. The act finally takes off when he realizes her musical-comedy potential, but their success is complicated by her love for him, his for former partner Miller, Miller's for mutual friend Lawford, and Lawford's for Garland.

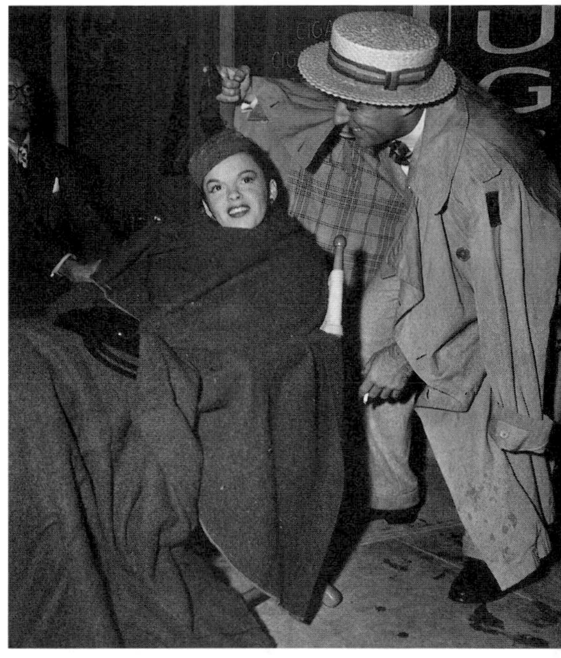

The first Garland/Lawford encounter was scripted to occur during a rainstorm, thus cueing in one of Berlin's new tunes, "A Fella with an Umbrella." Judy later remembered it as "not *too* great a song, but we had it choreographed, and [the studio] had tarped in four blocks of buildings and put in pipes under that to make it rain. I was wearing a red skirt, a black jacket, and a little black Scottish hat with a red plume. At the very end of the number, all I had to do was turn and do a sort of lovely look at Peter. Suddenly, everyone yelled *'Cut!'*; I thought, 'What have I done?' Well, it turned out the dye off the red feather had run all over [my face and] the back of the jacket; it looked like there was just *blood* everywhere. So then they had to reset, and get more rain. And they couldn't figure out what to do with this bloody feather—so they put *Vaseline* on it! Which I thought was kind of unattractive!"

Prerecording and shooting for *Easter Parade* began in November. On the twenty-first and twenty-second, Judy filmed sixty-three takes to complete her first major solo, "Mr. Monotony." (It was later cut from the picture, but she would wear the costume again more than two years later for "Get Happy" in *Summer Stock.*) Throughout November and December, Garland was also involved in the *Pirate* retakes, but *Easter Parade* was completed by mid-February 1948. Despite the competing schedules and Garland's absence on more than fourteen days, the film was under budget by nearly $200,000.

Easter Parade was released in June 1948, and critics everywhere rated it the top screen musical of the year. Astaire was much celebrated, and the *Hollywood Reporter* declared, "*Easter Parade*. . . firmly establishes Judy as the screen's first lady of tempo and tunes. It's her picture, and it's to Astaire's everlasting credit that he let it be that way." The New York *Sun* wrote, "Judy is at her youthful best again," and the *Journal-American* found Garland "the happiest choice yet as an Astaire dancing partner." The film outgrossed all her preceding films.

Despite her satisfaction in making the picture, Garland was rail-thin and depleted, occasionally seeking refuge in the home of agent Carleton Alsop and his wife, actress Sylvia Sidney. She faced two more immediate screen assignments, with a third set for autumn. The first was a guest shot in another Freed musical biography, *Words and Music,* which fictionalized the careers of Richard Rodgers and Lorenz Hart. MGM had withheld some $50,000 of Garland's salary for the preceding year in connection with the difficulties incurred during *The Pirate;* they agreed to pay her that amount if she would appear as herself in two sequences of *Words and Music.* The first segment, a Hollywood party, reteamed Garland with Mickey Rooney. He'd been cast as Lorenz Hart and was set to join her for either "You Took Advantage of Me" or a medley of "This Can't Be Love," "Mimi," and "I Wish I Were in Love Again." (By the time prerecording took place, their spot had been whittled down to just the last song.)

BELOW: The highlight of Easter Parade: *"A Couple of Swells," which Irving Berlin hurriedly wrote as a replacement for "Let's Take an Old-Fashioned Walk." Garland's tramp jacket was part of an old Wallace Beery costume retrieved from MGM wardrobe.*

Garland's initial scenes were scheduled to be taken the first week in June; she arrived late and unable to work and then was out ill the next two days. (Alsop remembers that Garland was so frail at this time that she was confined to bed at his house, receiving glucose intravenously.) Finally, on June 8, she shot a brief dialogue scene in the morning; Janet Leigh, playing wife to Tom Drake's Richard Rodgers, remembers Judy as "warm and open and dear—and nervous and thin and drawn. It never occurred to me that someone as proficient in her profession as Judy could be insecure or unsure. [But] she was pure magic; I was hypnotized. She always gave one hundred fifty percent of herself." After lunch, Garland and Rooney filmed the entire "I Wish I Were in Love Again" segment.

The *Words and Music* script followed the party sequence with a trip to MGM by Rodgers and/or Hart so that they could discuss making a film with "Judy Garland." Their conversation was to segue to Judy and a male chorus of twenty in a blackface minstrel rendition of "Johnny One Note." But she was much too drained to shoot any scenes; furthermore, she faced a June 12 start date for rehearsals with Astaire for her next major film. *The Barkleys of Broadway* boasted an original screenplay by Betty Comden and Adolph Green, and cast Judy and Fred as a contemporary Broadway musical comedy couple who go their separate ways when the wife renounces singing and dancing for drama. Disguising his voice, the husband secretly coaches her by phone for a triumphant debut, and they are reunited; the working title of the film had been *You Made Me Love You.*

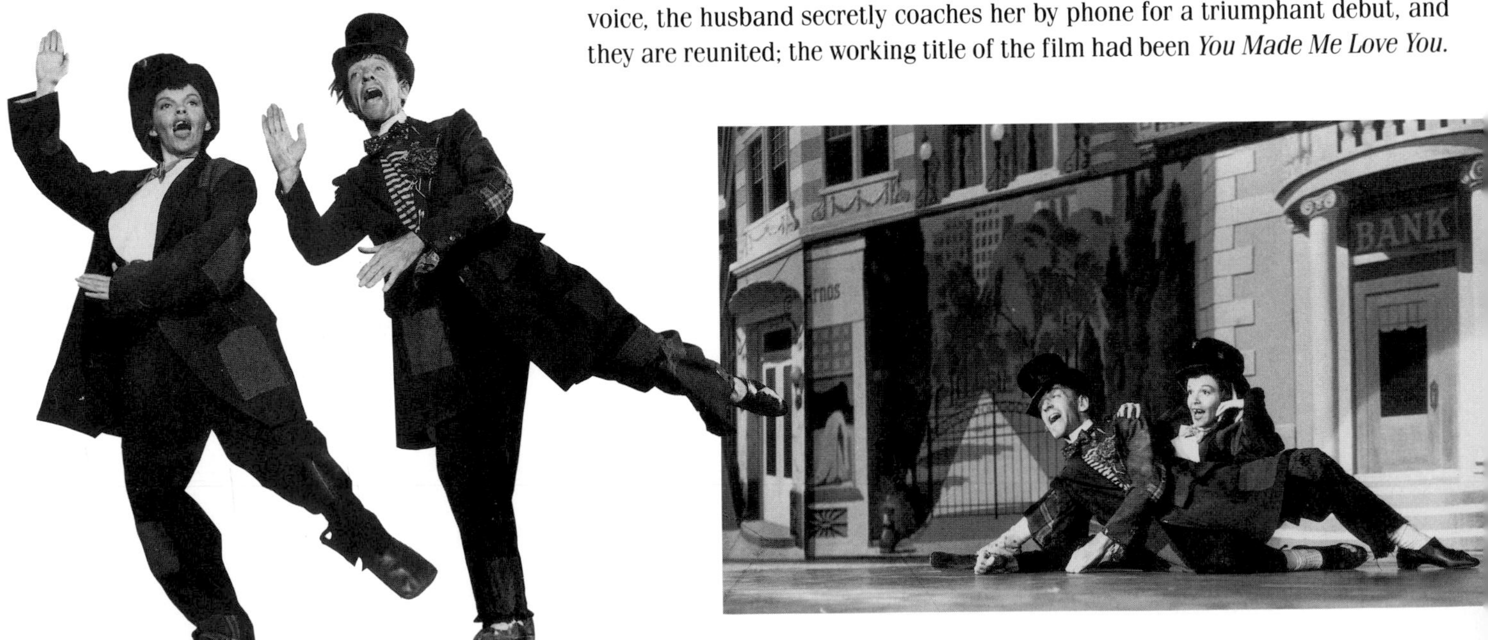

Promotion for The Pirate, *MGM/1948.* LEFT: *Poster.* BELOW: *Rotogravure cover.* BOTTOM: *French film magazine.*

JUDY GARLAND
GENE KELLY
THE GREAT MGM MUSICAL ROMANCE
The PIRATE
TREASURE CHEST OF TECHNICOLOR ... SONGS BY COLE PORTER
WALTER SLEZAK
GLADYS COOPER · REGINALD OWEN
Directed by VINCENTE MINNELLI · Produced by ARTHUR FREED

EASTER PARADE
FRED ASTAIRE
JUDY GARLAND
PETER LAWFORD · ANN MILLER
LA PARADE DU PRINTEMPS
Technicolor
MISE EN SCÈNE
CHARLES WALTERS
MUSIQUE
IRVING BERLIN
"LENTEPARADE"

SONGS!
TECHNICOLOR!
JUDY GARLAND
VAN JOHNSON
Fall in Love
IN THE GOOD OLD SUMMERTIME
M·G·M
S.Z. SAKALL · SPRING BYINGTON
A ROBERT Z. LEONARD PRODUCTION

FACING PAGE, TOP LEFT: Poster for The Pirate, *MGM/1948. TOP RIGHT: Belgian poster for* Easter Parade. *BOTTOM LEFT: 1947 portrait of Judy and Arthur Freed on* The Pirate *set. BOTTOM RIGHT: Poster for* In the Good Old Summertime, *MGM/1949.*

Posters for Easter Parade, *MGM/1948.*

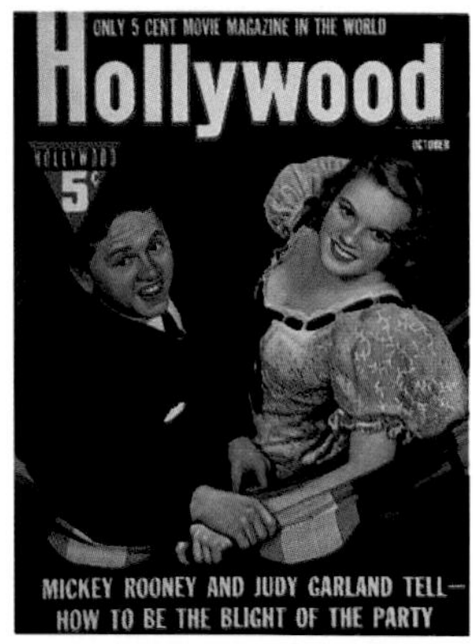

HOLLYWOOD WHO'S WHO

"The Girl on the Magazine Cover": Twenty-five years of Garland promotional art.

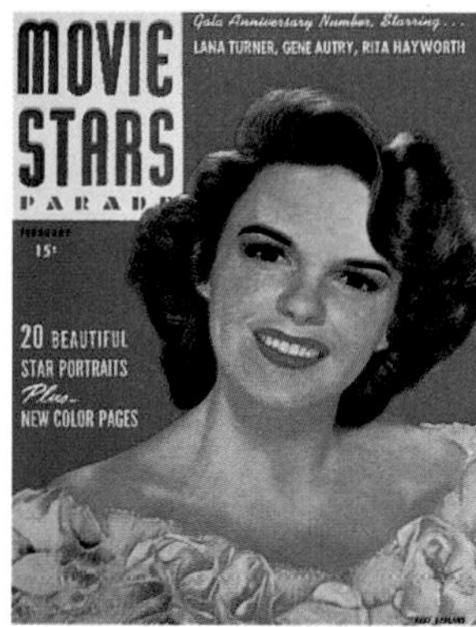

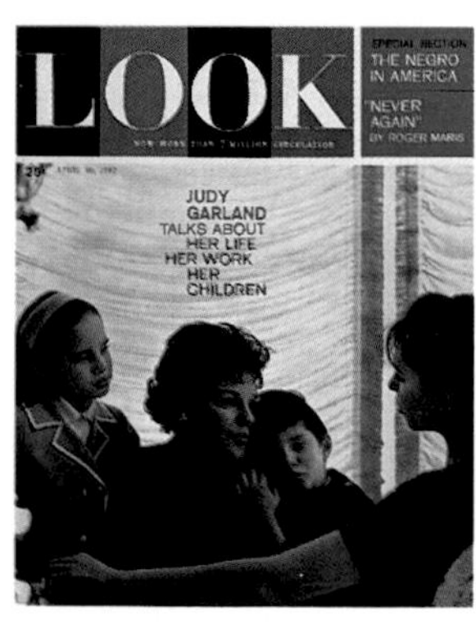

She is shown with Mickey Rooney, Ann Rutherford, Lana Turner, David Rose, her three children, and Danny Kaye.

FACING PAGE, TOP LEFT: Judy at home with daughter Liza Minnelli in 1946. TOP RIGHT: Portrait, circa 1945. BOTTOM LEFT: Judy and Mickey Rooney sing "I Wish I Were in Love Again" in Words and Music, *MGM/1948. BOTTOM RIGHT: Liza visits the set of* Easter Parade, *MGM/1948.*

RIGHT: A surprisingly racy (and totally unrepresentative) poster for In the Good Old Summertime, *MGM/1949. BELOW: Poster for* Summer Stock, *MGM/1950.*

TOP LEFT: Poster for Garland's debut at the London Palladium, April 1951. *TOP RIGHT:* Facade and marquee of New York's Palace Theatre for Garland's first engagement, 1951–52. *CENTER LEFT:* Judy and Sid Luft, June 1952. *ABOVE:* Judy with George Jessel. *LEFT:* With George Burns at the Friars Club "Miss Show Business" testimonial, June 29, 1952.

Judy began rehearsing the Harry Warren/Ira Gershwin score as scheduled and worked happily with Astaire. Within three weeks, however, the strain had become too much for her, and she was ill and away from July 7 through 17. On the twelfth, her doctor told Arthur Freed that it would be a "risky procedure" for her to start on an important picture, that she "could possibly work four or five days, always under medication, and possibly blow up for a period and then work again for a few days." On the nineteenth, Astaire's former partner Ginger Rogers was hastily signed to replace her. ("There I was," Rogers cooed to thc prcss, "up on my ranch in Oregon with the cowsies and the chickensies, all perfectly content.")

Suspended by MGM, Garland collapsed, too weak to leave her bed. In August, the scurrilous newspaper *Hollywood Nite Life* printed three front-page articles, referring to her only as "Miss G.," but announcing her "dope addiction," her surveillance by the Federal Bureau of Investigation, and a Bureau order that MGM provide proof within ninety days that Judy was being helped to overcome her addiction. The paper's editor, Jimmie Tarantino, also quoted a studio spokesman who told the FBI that $14 million was tied up in current and pending productions involving "Miss G." (*Nite Life* was rag journalism at best, but a few weeks after Garland died in 1969, former commissioner of narcotics Harry Anslinger confirmed that he had indeed discussed Judy with Mayer during the late 1940s. Anslinger insisted that Garland needed a year's vacation if the studio expected her to be a productive star. The studio head told him, "A vacation simply isn't possible" and—corroborating the Tarantino report of more than twenty years earlier—he added, "We have fourteen million dollars tied up in this girl. She's the biggest asset the studio has at the moment.")

Garland, under doctors' care, was yet again weaned away from medication by September. Cosseted by Minnelli and Alsop (and fed by Sylvia Sidney), she gained twenty pounds and made a remarkable recovery. MGM had meanwhile sneak-previewed *Words and Music;* the Garland/Rooney duet had won far and

ABOVE: On set, December 1947. TOP LEFT: A candid snap of Garland and Astaire walking through MGM to the Easter Parade *soundstage. TOP RIGHT: The east side of New York's Seventh Avenue between 45th and 46th streets, June 1948.*

Words and Music, *1948.* BELOW: *With Liza and Arthur Freed at the "I Wish I Were in Love Again" prerecording session, May 1948.* BOTTOM LEFT: *With Mickey and director Norman Taurog; the latter defined Garland as "most brilliant. . . and the better talent you put with her, the better she was."* BOTTOM RIGHT: *Judy and Mickey in their final film number together, June 1948.*

wide the greatest response from audiences, and the studio wanted to add another Judy song to the picture. A studio memo suggested she appear either in the film's concert finale or sing another number on the party set; in addition to the aforementioned "Johnny One Note," "You Took Advantage of Me," and "This Can't Be Love," the songs under consideration included "My Romance," "Ten Cents a Dance," "There's a Small Hotel," and "It Never Entered My Mind." It was decided to reassemble the party set and extras; the wardrobe department recut Garland's party dress and eliminated its belt to accommodate her increased weight. After five days of rehearsal and wardrobe tests the last week in September, Judy recorded "Johnny One Note" in thirty minutes on the thirtieth and shot the number the next day.

Words and Music premiered in December 1948, and its stars and hit songs resulted in strong box office. Critics dismissed (or panned) the plot and some of the acting, but the *Hollywood Reporter* sagely realized that this was "about the biggest musical of the year. Judy could sing 'I Wish I Were in Love Again' four or five times and still not wear out her welcome." And though *Daily Variety* found Garland's routines "badly staged," they were "well worth seeing because of her great artistry."

Although she had lost *Barkleys,* another plum production still belonged to Judy in autumn 1948. MGM had purchased Irving Berlin's Broadway smash *Annie Get Your Gun* specifically for her for $650,000, the most they had ever paid for a musical property. *Annie* was originally scheduled to begin in October, but script and casting problems delayed the film until late winter. Garland immediately began work instead on Joe Pasternak's production *In the Good Old Summertime.* Originally titled *The Girl from Chicago,* the picture was a musicalized version of MGM's 1940 comedy *The Shop Around the Corner,* and had been intended for June Allyson and Frank Sinatra. The latter was replaced by Van Johnson. Spring Byington was first cast as Garland's aunt but instead displaced Mary Astor in the featured role of a music-store cashier. Garland and Johnson played combative clerks in the same store, not knowing that each was the other's "Dear Friend" in a fervid lonely-hearts correspondence.

Summertime rehearsals began in October, with prerecording in November.

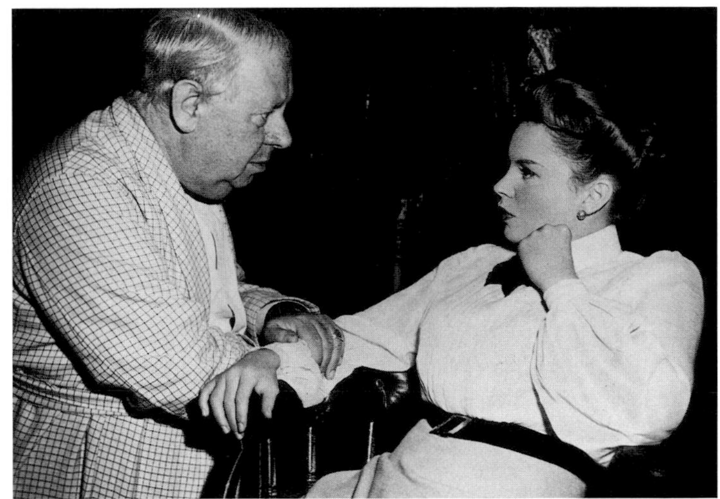

In the Good Old Summertime, 1949. *LEFT: With S. Z. "Cuddles" Sakall. RIGHT: With Van Johnson. BELOW: Singing "I Don't Care."*

Garland completed four of her six songs for the film in one session, never requiring more than three takes. She also managed to breeze through the filming, completing the picture by the end of January despite sixteen days away for illness. Mayer summoned Johnson to his office to ask how such a miracle had been wrought; the actor replied, simply, "We made her feel wanted and needed. We joked with her and kept her happy." Pasternak's appreciation for Garland was a contributing factor as well. "A great artist is entitled to a lot more latitude," he said. "The quality that makes her great makes her feel more deeply. All of us felt—and you don't often feel this way in Hollywood—that we would accommodate ourselves gladly to work with Judy. There was never a word uttered in recrimination when she was late, didn't show up, or couldn't go on. We knew her magical genius and respected it."

Summertime was released in August 1949. Critics raved, and audiences everywhere applauded Garland's on-screen numbers as if the film were a live show. All the reviews approved her added weight; *Motion Picture Daily* decided, "She has not been seen to such overall advantage in quite a spell. She is tops here and outdoes all others." *Film Digest* referred to Judy as "the little bundle of genius," and to the film as "one of the most solid hits of her career"; the *Hollywood Reporter* cheered, "Great troupers come seldom in a theatrical generation, but when one does arrive on the scene, there is no mistaking the special magnetism that is their art. [The film] is a Garland triumph . . . her show from start to finish."

By the conclusion of *Summertime, Annie Get Your Gun* was waiting. Judy remembered: "[I] had seen the show on Broadway and had my heart set on doing it. Rehearsals started, and I knew I wasn't good. I was so very, very sick. I'd begged them to postpone the starting date, but they wouldn't. [And] I knew I wasn't going to make it. I hadn't slept one night in fourteen." (Garland even underwent a series of electroshock therapy sessions prior to her work on the picture.) Further complicating the situation was the assignment of Busby Berkeley as *Annie*'s director. Though he'd just completed Arthur Freed's *Take Me Out to the Ball Game,* Berkeley's limitations and his tactless past handling of Garland make his appointment to the film a mystery.

After John Raitt had been tested (and Bing Crosby, Dan Dailey, Perry Como,

In the Good Old Summertime, *1949. TOP LEFT: Garland sings "Last Night When We Were Young," deleted from the release print. TOP RIGHT: Garland's Veronica Fisher surges through "Play That Barbershop Chord." ABOVE: James Mason, at Metro for Vincente Minnelli's production of* Madame Bovary, *visits with Judy four years before they would begin* A Star is Born.

and Roy Rogers rumored) for the part of Frank Butler, newcomer Howard Keel was signed for his film debut opposite Garland. Both Buster Keaton and Boris Karloff auditioned for the role of Chief Sitting Bull before it went to J. Carrol Naish. At one point, even three-year-old Liza was announced for the role of Judy's kid sister; it was decided that she was too young.

In the midst of rehearsals and prerecordings, Judy's difficulties were compounded by a personal crisis. She'd been estranged on and off from her mother, and on March 30, she and Minnelli announced their separation. Given Garland's problems, such a decision was not unexpected. Despite the genuine love that existed between the two, there were shortcomings on both sides. The high-strung, gentle Minnelli had never been the most likely candidate for matrimony, and his professional strengths (like Garland's) weren't always matched by the personal traits required for a happy husband/wife relationship. If studio executives had smiled on the wedding in 1945, there were many other Metro co-workers who admired the couple's talents but couldn't understand the union. ("We all knew how lonely Judy was" is the only explanation proffered by a dancer who worked on many Garland and Minnelli films during the 1940s.) Garland had certainly responded initially to Minnelli's gifts, flair, and sophistication; their first real work together in 1943–44 coincided with her own emotional independence and attempts at sophistication. Garland's close friends grew to include the elite (or pseudo-elite) of Hollywood; Minnelli's included those of the theatre. It's possible that the couple envisioned and cast themselves in a sort of Noel Cowardesque design-for-living scenario among their personal and professional associates, including such friends as Kay Thompson and her producer/husband, Bill Spier. After more than four years with Minnelli, Garland may well have come to realize that the scenario just didn't work for either of them. And Minnelli—though recognizing her failures, "her indulgences and compulsions"—would agree that "I'd obviously failed Judy. Those periods in her life when she'd been least able to cope with the world coincided with the years of our marriage. It was an indictment I couldn't ignore." Though they reconciled later in 1949, their marriage would continue to wane.

Meanwhile, studio production records detail the effort Judy was making to play Annie Oakley. Between early March and mid-April, there were few sick days, few late days, and a number of days she arrived early. She made the prerecordings in good humor and goodwill, but her enthusiasm couldn't compensate for her physical exhaustion. The situation was exacerbated the second day of principal photography, when Keel's horse stumbled and fell on him, injuring the actor's right leg. Keel recalls, "After the accident, the only other person they could shoot was Judy, and they just wore her out." Over the next month, Judy filmed the song "Doin' What Comes Natur'lly" and the scene around it; scenes of the Buffalo Bill troupe leaving for Europe and meeting Queen Victoria; scenes in a Pullman car, as Annie is taught to read by her little brother; and miscellaneous scenes of the troupe's travel montage. During the fourth week, she began the lavish "I'm an Indian Too" production number, working with choreographer Robert Alton, whom she adored.

Everyone involved with the film soon became dissatisfied with Berkeley. Freed decided the director "had no conception of what the picture was all about," and he called in Chuck Walters as a replacement. Walters found that "none of Berkeley's footage was usable. The rushes were awful, and Judy had never been worse." (Surviving footage shows a game Garland, similar in physical frame to the real Annie Oakley, working to portray the character as a human being and not a musical-comedy cartoon. After takes, she often jokes and mugs, although there are moments after Berkeley or Alton yell "Cut" that she seems fatigued or snappish. There must have been difficult days and unusable material as well; Freed later said there were times "you could run up to her screaming the earth was caving in, but she wouldn't have known it. [But] none of us really wanted to take her out of the picture.")

The day after Walters was assigned, however, Garland admitted to him, "It's too late; I haven't got the energy or the *nerve* anymore." She called Berkeley "a monster," and complained that he had treated her "the same as when I was fifteen." Walters convinced her to make another try, but on May 10, when she

Annie Get Your Gun, *1949.* BELOW: *Costume test.* BOTTOM LEFT: *Visiting the set with Liza (Arthur Freed is at left).* BOTTOM RIGHT: *Trade ad.*

BELOW: Garland as Annie Oakley and J. Carrol Naish as Chief Sitting Bull. BOTTOM: Memo from Annie's assistant director, detailing Garland's final day on the project.

arrived more than two hours late, Metro's front office went into action. Formal notice was delivered to her dressing room that she would be removed from the film unless she could arrive when scheduled. She cried and raged, furious at such treatment, and refused to return to the set. (There is some question as to the subsequent chain of events that afternoon. In the most likely version, the studio, crew, and Garland were suddenly miscommunicating. The front office apologized for sending the letter, although the distraught Garland refused to perform. The company was then dismissed. In the interim, Garland had calmed down and decided to return to the set. When she arrived, it was virtually deserted.)

Whatever the specific progression, Judy was put on suspension that afternoon. Ten days later, MGM announced they would borrow Betty Hutton from Paramount to play Annie Oakley. A wan and dispirited Garland—via Hedda Hopper—wished Hutton happiness and success and said she didn't blame the studio for their decision: "They can't take chances with careless people like me."

Ten days later, Judy entered Peter Bent Brigham Hospital in Boston. Mayer had been a patient there a few months earlier; he arranged for Garland's stay, assuring her that the studio would pick up the bill for her care and recovery and loan her an additional $9,000 to cover her immediate bills. (Garland was broke, with taxes, doctor bills, and maintenance apart from Minnelli contributing to her debts.) In addition to the loan, MGM ultimately paid over $42,000 for Garland's three months of treatment. She gave a Boston press conference to announce her tenancy at the hospital and freely confessed the dependency she'd developed on pills. Judy told the press she was "learning to sleep all over again" without medication.

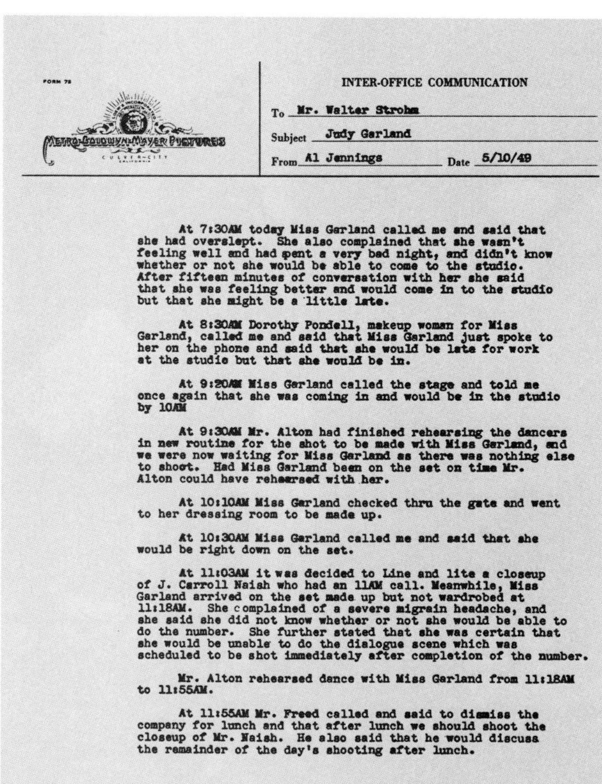

INTER-OFFICE COMMUNICATION

Metro-Goldwyn-Mayer Pictures, Culver City

To Mr. Walter Strohm
Subject Judy Garland
From Al Jennings Date 5/10/49

At 7:30AM today Miss Garland called me and said that she had overslept. She also complained that she wasn't feeling well and had spent a very bad night, and didn't know whether or not she would be able to come to the studio. After fifteen minutes of conversation with her she said that she was feeling better and would come in to the studio but that she might be a little late.

At 8:30AM Dorothy Pondell, makeup woman for Miss Garland, called me and said that Miss Garland just spoke to her on the phone and said that she would be late for work at the studio but that she would be in.

At 9:20AM Miss Garland called the stage and told me once again that she was coming in and would be in the studio by 10AM

At 9:30AM Mr. Alton had finished rehearsing the dancers in new routine for the shot to be made with Miss Garland, and we were now waiting for Miss Garland as there was nothing else to shoot. Had Miss Garland been on the set on time Mr. Alton could have rehearsed with her.

At 10:10AM Miss Garland checked thru the gate and went to her dressing room to be made up.

At 10:30AM Miss Garland called me and said that she would be right down on the set.

At 11:03AM it was decided to Line and lite a closeup of J. Carroll Naish who had an 11AM call. Meanwhile, Miss Garland arrived on the set made up but not wardrobed at 11:18AM. She complained of a severe migrain headache, and she said she did not know whether or not she would be able to do the number. She further stated that she was certain that she would be unable to do the dialogue scene which was scheduled to be shot immediately after completion of the number.

Mr. Alton rehearsed dance with Miss Garland from 11:18AM to 11:55AM.

At 11:55AM Mr. Freed called and said to dismiss the company for lunch and that after lunch we should shoot the closeup of Mr. Naish. He also said that he would discuss the remainder of the day's shooting after lunch.

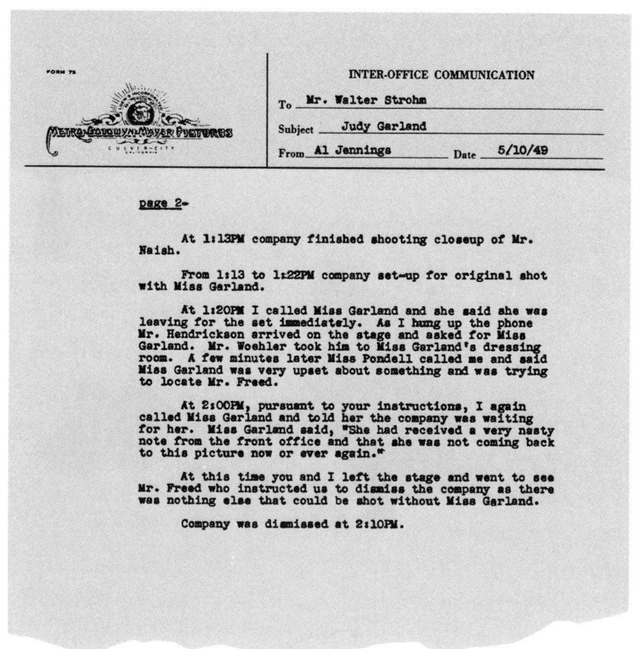

INTER-OFFICE COMMUNICATION

Metro-Goldwyn-Mayer Pictures, Culver City

To Mr. Walter Strohm
Subject Judy Garland
From Al Jennings Date 5/10/49

page 2-

At 1:13PM company finished shooting closeup of Mr. Naish.

From 1:13 to 1:22PM company set-up for original shot with Miss Garland.

At 1:20PM I called Miss Garland and she said she was leaving for the set immediately. As I hung up the phone Mr. Hendrickson arrived on the stage and asked for Miss Garland. Mr. Woehler took him to Miss Garland's dressing room. A few minutes later Miss Pondell called me and said Miss Garland was very upset about something and was trying to locate Mr. Freed.

At 2:00PM, pursuant to your instructions, I again called Miss Garland and told her the company was waiting for her. Miss Garland said, "She had received a very nasty note from the front office and that she was not coming back to this picture now or ever again."

At this time you and I left the stage and went to see Mr. Freed who instructed us to dismiss the company as there was nothing else that could be shot without Miss Garland.

Company was dismissed at 2:10PM.

On June 14, Louella Parsons announced that Garland would star in Joe Pasternak's production of *Summer Stock* at MGM; Judy interrupted her stay at Brigham for two weeks in Los Angeles in early August to discuss the picture. By early September, she was home again for good and reunited with Minnelli.

Summer Stock rehearsals began the first week in October; by the end of the month, she had almost lost the picture. There were daily reports filed on her arrival and departure times and her activities on the lot. Executives were worried that she had missed six days in the first twenty of preproduction; they were particularly concerned that her Boston treatment had added a healthy twenty pounds to her frame, and she was ordered to reduce. All this culminated in another warning letter on October 31. As a result, Judy went to Mayer later that day and requested a release from both *Summer Stock* and her MGM contract. There were no histrionics, but Garland was aware she was losing whatever ground she'd gained in Boston. She told Mayer that she really was not fully recuperated from her illness, that she didn't want to work for a couple of years, and that she would let Vincente support her and Liza. Mayer did not want to let her go and spent ninety minutes convincing her to stay, to continue to work, to lose weight, and to report on time. It was a conversation he would later rue. She finally agreed to try again, but the filming struggled on for an additional four months.

The plot of *Summer Stock* was a throwback to the early Garland/Rooney pictures; in fact, Pasternak had considered Mickey for the lead, but Gene Kelly was stronger box office at the time. Judy played a struggling Connecticut farmer whose barn is overwhelmed by a New York acting troupe. Led by her younger sister (played by Gloria De Haven), they plan to use the barn as a summer theatre. Ultimately, Garland replaces Gloria in the show, saves the production, and finds love with leading-man Kelly. Chuck Walters was set as director, and he and Gene took turns in helping Garland through the filming. She gratefully recalled that they "encouraged me to forget what people might be saying, laughed with me, helped keep down the friction. I was late, and there were fights over that. I was wobbly and unsure and desperately trying to prove to myself that I was making good as a person."

Despite Judy's determination, there were so many lost days that Walters remembered, "It was all over the lot that the picture would never be finished." Pasternak knew Judy "was not a happy girl; I had to handle her differently than anybody else. Delay with Judy is something that is within her—something you know she can't help. Everybody at the studio said to me, 'How can you stand these delays?' I replied, 'When I look at the rushes, I pray she'll come back *any* day.' " As shooting stretched into a third month, even Pasternak wanted to abandon the project, but Mayer himself encouraged the producer to "stay with it. Finish it, no matter what it costs." He had one of Judy's Boston doctors brought to the set in the hopes of providing her some aid, and Garland settled in and completed the film. It includes perhaps the best dance duet of her career, "The Portland Fancy." Kelly staged the challenge act himself and recalls, "It wasn't easy; I gave her some very difficult turns to do. But she danced magnificently, much better than in *For Me and My Gal*. She was in a good mood that day, and it was hard to believe she had anything on her mind but her work."

A month after finishing the picture, Judy returned to *Summer Stock*. Pasternak wanted a "payoff" routine for her in the finale; she had suggested the standard "Get Happy," and Saul Chaplin worked out an exacting, exciting vocal

Statement made by Les.ie Peterson May 10, 1949.

Between 1:15 and 1:30 p.m. May 10, 1949 I accompanied Mr. Hendrickson to Judy Garland's dressing room and personally saw him deliver to her a letter dated May 10, 1949, which letter Mr. Hendrickson had permitted me to read prior to going to Miss Garland's dressing room, and he had explained to me that he wanted me to be present at the time he personally delivered the letter to Miss Garland. A copy of the letter of May 10, 1949 which I read and which was delivered to Miss Garland is attached hereto as "Exhibit A".

Mr. Hendrickson handed the letter to Miss Garland and before opening it she asked Mr. Hendrickson to wait while she read it. I also waited, and Miss Garland's make up girl and hairdresser were also present. While reading the letter Miss Garland asked Mr. Hendrickson the meaning of "condone". She also asked who signed the letter. Mr. Hendrickson told her L.K. Sidney signed the letter.

When she finished reading the letter she said, "I do not accept the responsibility for the delays and confusion because I have told them for weeks that the director was wrong and that is proved by the fact that the director was removed." She said, "They can take me out of the picture" and added, "It'll break my heart" and began to cry. She then got out of her make up chair and became hysterical and shouted about the letter and how the company could send her such a letter after she had worked here for 14 years, the money she had made for them, and that it was Irving Berlin that had wanted her to play the part and that it was because of her that the company had acquired ANNIE GET YOUR GUN. She went on to say that after receiving a letter like this she would not go back on the set and did't want to work any more and that she was leaving the studio and not coming back.

She wanted to give the letter back to Mr. Hendrickson but he told her she should give it to Mr. Alsop and she said he was out of town. Mr. Hendrickson tried to calm her and told her that she should keep the letter and contact Mr. Alsop.

As we were leaving she said she was sorry that Mr. Hendrickson had had to deliver the letter, and that Les could tell him how hard she had worked these 14 years as he had been there.

Les Peterson

mb 5-11-49

TOP: Les Peterson's formal report of Garland's reaction to her dismissal. (Scenarist Sidney Sheldon later summed up the situation: "Judy was very warm, wonderful, very shy. She wasn't difficult; she had emotional problems.") ABOVE: Garland clowns between takes of "I'm an Indian Too."

Summer Stock, *1950.* TOP: *Garland in a makeup and hairstyle test as Jane Falbury, November 1950.* ABOVE: *Chuck Walters, Judy (in partial costume for "If You Feel Like Singing, Sing"), Minnelli, and Joe Pasternak toast the first day of filming.*

arrangement. He knew, however, it would be no problem for Garland. "She learned music like a vacuum cleaner," he has noted. "You played something to her, and she sang it right back the way you did it—like a Xerox machine." He regarded his "Get Happy" as "very complicated. Judy heard it three times but never sang it. Then she got sick. Two weeks later, she came in, rehearsed it *once,* and recorded it in about four takes."

When *Summer Stock* was previewed in August 1950, United Press put out a wire-service report that "the Hollywood press gave Judy the kind of ovation that any big star dreams of." On the East Coast, reaction was the same; the preview audience "raised the roof with tremendous bursts of applause at every one of her numbers, certain proof that this young lady still holds the warmest spot in the hearts of millions." If the film was slight, reviewers nonetheless found it immensely entertaining and described Garland as "pleasingly plump and as pretty as ever." Some even preferred her chunkier appearance to that in the slimmed-down "Get Happy" routine, although that number was the favorite of all. The Rochester *Democrat and Chronicle* opined that "hers is the genuinely satisfying performance of a seasoned, generously endowed trouper who instinctively knows what it's all about and who has a personality and an individuality of style which can't be replaced." "The mere flash of [her] name on the screen created excitement," exulted the *Los Angeles Herald-Examiner,* "but when the little star went into action—zounds!" The *Los Angeles Times* stated more quietly, "There can be no rivalry for the individuality she brings to a musical film." In its initial one hundred engagements alone, *Summer Stock* grossed more than a million dollars.

Throughout her career, such critical and audience response to Garland had been commonplace. But there was additional reason for the impassioned depth of reaction to *Summer Stock.* In June 1950, two months prior to the preview, Garland had made another attempt at suicide. The resultant front-page headlines created a unique public empathy and an awareness of her private turmoil; when audiences coupled that knowledge with her demonstrated on-screen professionalism and singular ability, they had no recourse but to cheer and rally in support.

Garland's doctors had recommended she take eight months off after completing *Summer Stock.* She had been in Carmel for just three weeks when the call came to replace a pregnant June Allyson, who was starring opposite Fred Astaire in *Royal Wedding.* Judy later admitted, "That was when I made one of the really *classic* mistakes of my life. I reasoned that I had been so humiliated by the studio and the press that if I returned, maybe everything would be all right." She began rehearsing the third week in May; when she arrived, Chuck Walters asked to be removed as the *Royal Wedding* director. He felt no animosity toward Garland and would always maintain that "she could not help herself when she was behaving badly. And you will *never* know anyone wittier and sharper and better company than Judy: terrific, fun, bright as a button." But he knew he couldn't handle another experience like *Summer Stock,* and Arthur Freed replaced him with Stanley Donen.

By June, Judy's strength was already beginning to falter. She was minutes, sometimes hours late for rehearsal, and more front-office warnings were drafted. Her efforts to continue despite it all must have at times been superhuman. John Green was then general music director at Metro and had already "worked a great,

great deal with Judy and never had one minute's trouble with her. During her worst periods of falling apart, she was never late, even to a piano rehearsal in my office.''

On Friday, June 16, she appeared for wardrobe tests. Helen Rose oversaw her first ensemble from hat to hairdo: ''Her head-to-toe look was one of sophistication and extreme chic. She opened the door to her dressing room, posed for a second in the doorway, and everyone burst into applause! Some of the crew whistled. Judy was never really confident about her looks, and she was simply delighted; it was just the boost she needed. At that moment, Arthur Freed came on the set, very angry about something and preoccupied. He glanced at her and said, in a rather sarcastic tone, 'What are you made up for?' Though I'm sure he did not mean it the way it sounded, she took it as a direct insult, burst into tears, and ran back to her dressing room.'' The next day, Garland canceled a rehearsal call; that afternoon, the studio dropped her from *Royal Wedding* and suspended her once again.

On Monday evening, June 19, while at home with Minnelli and secretary Myrtle Tully, Garland locked herself in the bathroom, smashed a drinking glass, and made a slight cut across her throat. Minnelli broke down the bathroom door, and Garland collapsed in his arms. A doctor and Carleton Alsop were summoned, although the latter had to deal with the hysterical Minnelli before tending to Garland. The injury was minor enough to be covered with a Band-Aid, and the situation would have ended there had not columnist Florabel Muir of the Los Angeles *Mirror* heard a rumor about the incident at three o'clock on Tuesday morning. She traced and cornered Alsop, and he was forced to confirm her facts. The *Mirror* hit the streets at seven-thirty that morning with an extra edition, headlining Judy's despair.

''Get Happy'' was the last routine Garland filmed at MGM. (To put her at ease, Walters gave her the image of Lena Horne to use as her attitude for the routine.) The director felt that Judy's unhappiness while making Summer Stock *stemmed from her knowledge that the film was not a worthy vehicle and that her involvement in anything was directly predicated by her estimation of its value.*

TOP: The reprise of "You, Wonderful You" with Kelly. He sang the song in Judy's memory at the world premiere of That's Entertainment *in 1974 and, to this day, calls Garland "our greatest talent. . . my favorite partner." ABOVE: On the* Summer Stock *set with Gene Kelly and Phil Silvers.*

The Los Angeles press corps and MGM publicity representatives immediately gathered at the Minnelli home. The official statement issued by Garland's physician, Dr. Francis Ballard, offered that the "several minor scratches on Judy's neck. . . required no treatment." He noted as well that her act was more a cry for help than any wish for self-inflicted injury; as Judy put it later, "I felt humiliated and unwanted—and faced with the bitter knowledge that I'd come to that unhappy position by my own actions."

Many journalists unequivocally blamed MGM for the whole situation, although a few of the trade papers pointed out that Metro had "for several years done everything conceivably possible" to help Judy. Not unnaturally, the studio defended itself, enumerated Garland's previous hospitalizations, and noted their efforts to come to her aid. Their case was somewhat hindered when Alsop pointed out to a reporter that the official MGM statement conveyed no personal sympathy or concern whatsoever for Garland. Metro's stand was further undermined by a quote from an anonymous executive who rather casually told Louella Parsons that Judy had "at least ten times before. . . pretended to end her life when she was in trouble with the studio." Unidentified Garland co-workers from the lot then jumped in with their viewpoint on the studio as well: "They won't leave her alone until she drops dead. If the [executives] must pick on one of their stars, a lot of us could give out with some good names. We see the bad ones as they really are—and Judy isn't one of them."

Garland was sedated for several days and horrified when eventually told about the international headlines. Friends rallied around, including Ida Koverman and the Rabwins; her mother, Ethel, flew in from her new home in Dallas; and Mayer not only visited but asked Katharine Hepburn to call on Garland as well. Hepburn knew Judy from the lot and considered her "an enormously complicated creature. By the time all this began to catch up with her, she was twenty-odd years old. She had worked hard. She had lived a lifetime. She was spent." The actress rushed through the photographers outside the Minnelli home, calling out, "If you take a picture of me, I'll kill you." (One reporter later commented that no one had planned to.) Hepburn delivered a straight pep talk to Judy: "You're one of the three greatest talents in the world. And your ass has hit the gutter. There's no place to go but up. Now, goddammit. Do it!" Garland was also cheered by a telegram from scenarist Fred Finklehoffe: "Dear Judy: So glad you cut your throat. All the other girl singers needed this kind of break."

For weeks, the story generated sympathy and compassion from both the press and the public. As Hedda Hopper wrote, Garland had long since become "a national institution. Hers is the greatest talent ever developed in this town, and I've known them all. So much talent, so much pressure, so much bad advice." Even Hopper's competition agreed; Louella Parsons wrote, "Judy is an appealingly wonderful person when she is not harassed by worry and fear." And NBC vice president John Royal offered Garland television and radio work, and wrote, "We all love you [and] would make things enjoyable for you."

Garland was soon out in public with Vincente and Liza. At the end of July, mother and daughter vacationed in Sun Valley, and Judy then set off by herself for a New York visit in early September. Prior to her arrival, she was addressed in an open letter that filled the entire September 1 newspaper column written by Broadway impresario Billy Rose. He'd just seen *Summer Stock* and offered, "It's probably silly of me to address you as if you were a two-bit Joan of Arc, but to my bedazzled eyes, that's about the way you show up in the entertainment world. In an oblique and daffy sort of way, you are as much a national asset as our coal reserves—both of you help warm up our insides."

The most important element of the Manhattan visit came when Baby Gumm's age-old public charisma once again made itself apparent. On September 5, Judy crept into a midnight showing of *Summer Stock* at the Capitol. The audience had no idea she was present, but the film and Garland's performance were playing to spontaneous ovations anyway. Syndicated columnist Hy Gardner noted that, when the picture was over, "the balcony and loge loungers started to stream out. Suddenly all movement stopped and a rumbling noise—one part cheers, two parts applause—worked its way up to a crescendo that rocked the rafters." Garland had been recognized, and the crowd followed her down the marble steps, through the lobby, and out onto Broadway, calling, "We love you," "We're all for you," "Keep your chin up," and "Keep making pictures." She shouted back, "I love you, I love you," and retreated to her car, which slowly nosed its way through the still-growing throng. Judy found the incident "so astonishing and so wonderful, so encouraging. It wasn't like a mob," she reflected the next day. "It was like a lot of friends." The press termed the event an "astonishing and probably unprecedented public demonstration," and Judy asked the media to "just say 'thank you' to [the public] because they've made me feel so happy—and well."

She arrived back in Los Angeles September 18 to an MGM still undecided about her future. (She had quipped in New York, "I'm suspended so often, my feet are practically never on the ground.") There had been meetings at the studio since August 1 about retaining Garland; they considered revising her contract for a single picture with options for two more. But president Nick Schenck was afraid the stockholders would claim the studio was running its business on sympathy and not intelligence. Jane Powell, Judy's replacement in *Royal Wedding,* was nearly finished with that film; this meant Garland would go back on salary after the twenty-eighth if still under contract. In late September, Arthur Freed and George Sidney put in a request to call Judy to work on their planned production of *Show Boat;* however, the corporate powers felt Garland was "unrecognizable" at her increased weight. Ignoring the critics' *Summer Stock* comments, the executives thought that she could not be photographed "in her physical condition . . . it would materially detract from her appearance on the screen." Judy Garland was no longer cost-effective.

On September 29, she was released by mutual consent from her MGM contract. Mayer had wanted to keep her. But he was fast losing power to new production chief Dore Schary, and the studio system itself was collapsing under the weight of television and from the government-ordered divestiture of its theatre chains. Mayer admitted, "It became too much to ask my producers and directors to work with her. She had to go; it broke my heart." More formally, he announced, "It is with great reluctance that Judy's request has been granted, and we wish her all the success and happiness in the continuance of her career." If she privately felt cut adrift after fifteen years at Metro, Judy was at least publicly glad to leave Culver City: "I was a very tired girl, and now maybe Metro realizes that. They were terribly nice about letting me out of my contract—it was fine of them and good for me. I feel like I've shed a suit of armor."

Judy did her final portrait sittings at MGM in spring 1950, costumed in the "All for You" wardrobe from Summer Stock.

Chapter Five

That Little Something Extra

In October 1950, Judy returned to New York. There were rumors of possible films and recordings, and actual meetings with Rodgers and Hammerstein, who wanted her to replace Mary Martin in *South Pacific.* But Abe Lastfogel, her new representative at the William Morris Agency, booked Judy as a guest on radio, avoiding for her any long-term pressure or the need to reduce to "camera-slim" weight. She made more than a dozen broadcasts between November and March; notable among them was an adaptation of *The Wizard of Oz.* Charlotte Stevenson, in the studio audience for the program, later wrote that Garland seemed "the consummate professional," while enjoying "an easy-going camaraderie with her supporting cast."

The most important of the radio shows were the half-dozen programs Judy did with Bing Crosby. He provided her with an ideal, secure showcase, both musically and comedically, and she gained enormously in professional self-confidence under his patronage. The regard was mutual; when asked in 1977 to name the most talented person with whom he had ever worked, Crosby immediately cited Judy.

The Crosby shows opened the door to a reunion between Garland and the people that would, in the next eighteen years, make show business history. Her performances gave ample indication that time, overwork, and illness had done nothing to impair the abilities exhibited by Baby Gumm twenty years earlier; her communicative power had, in fact, been much in evidence throughout Judy's MGM era. But there was now a new, enthusiastic response to Garland from studio broadcast audiences—a small-scale continuation of the hysteria created by her September appearance at the Capitol. It was suggested at the time (and has since been argued) that, beginning in 1949, Garland's appeal and fame were largely founded on sympathy, a response to her much-reported personal problems, or even on a public hope to see her fail or fall apart. While rumors about her private life and her much-headlined press would ultimately work both for and against her, her multitude of post-MGM successes grew primarily from a maturing and singular talent, an astounding reserve of energy, and an unexplainable magnetism and electricity. There would be future rifts and write-offs in Garland's relationship with the public and media—always at times when her health and resources were exhausted. But it became apparent that Garland could meet a live audience and overcome virtually any obstacle—their prejudices, negative journalism, and her own fluctuating weight and offstage reputation; this is repeatedly underscored by contemporary reviews and audience comments. Her ability to reach out to a crowd through a camera or microphone would also become stronger and more refined, but it was "in person" that her gifts were uniquely experienced. For all her worldwide MGM fame, Judy's tenure in Culver City had in some ways been an interruption of Baby Gumm's career and her happy, unique relationship with anyone who heard and saw her.

Throughout her radio engagements, Garland had a new escort. She first met

FACING PAGE: Garland as Vicki Lester acknowledges her ovation after singing the finale of "Born in a Trunk" in A Star is Born, *1954. BELOW: In Los Angeles with Liza and Sid Luft's son, Johnny, circa 1951.*

Sid Luft on the set of *Broadway Melody of 1938,* when he was serving as secretary to Eleanor Powell. In the intervening years, Luft had been a test pilot, produced a couple of films, and manifested an interest in and knowledge of Thoroughbred racehorse breeding and training. Judy and Sid met again in New York in autumn 1950. He was a significantly different type for her: strong, confident, and an aggressively charming, masculine businessman. They dated secretly until official announcement was made in December that Garland and Minnelli had separated (they divorced the following February).

In early 1951, Lastfogel urged Judy to accept a long-standing invitation to play the London Palladium. Encouraged as well by Luft and Fanny Brice, Garland agreed; then, just prior to departure, she had second thoughts. It was Brice who stormed into her house and told her off: "You're going over there, with the voice and the talent God gave you, and make everybody proud of you. Keep your head up and your eyes on tomorrow—and to hell with yesterday." The engagement had already made front-page trade-paper news: Garland was to be paid more than $70,000 for four weeks. Her act was assembled by Roger Edens and Oscar Levant; the still-admiring Minnelli offered his encouragement and counsel as well.

When the *Ile de France* docked in Plymouth, England, on April 5, fellow passengers crowded the railings to cheer Garland as she disembarked, and sirens from nearby ships Morse coded J-U-D-Y in salutation. Judy marveled to the waiting press, "They told me that people had a warm feeling for me in England, but I never thought it would be anything like this." Newspaper accounts of her arrival were interlaced with comments on Garland's increased weight ("tubby," "plump and jovial"). Judy laughingly commented to her accompanist, Buddy Pepper, "I feel like the fat lady from Barnum & Bailey's. . ." But she told one writer, "I've been trying to [be] slim for years. When I'm slim, the studios have been happy, but I've felt ill and unhappy. When I am plump, I've been happy."

On April 9, hundreds of fans waited in the rain at the stage door for Judy to arrive for the opening. Luft flew in to surprise her. Kay Thompson, in London to appear in cabaret, joined her in the wings and may have provided the push that got a self-admittedly "numb" Garland onstage. While waiting for her cue, Judy later remembered that "my knees *locked*—like Frankenstein's wife—and they *wouldn't* bend. So I walked on with two stiff legs. . .and just stood there in terror." She received what theatre manager Val Parnell described as "the biggest ovation I have ever seen or heard," but remained frozen at the microphone through her first set of numbers. Nothing mattered to the audience; they cheered mid-song as she offered Roger's special opening: *"I never thought I'd see / what we call Buckingham— / But that's past— / so hold fast— / At long last / here I am!"* Presaged by Edens's biographical verse *("For almost twenty years, I've been a minstrel girl, / Singing for my supper in the throngs. . ."),* she segued to a medley of "You Made Me Love You," "For Me and My Gal," "The Boy Next Door," and "The Trolley Song." (A variation of the medley, known as "Judy's Olio," would remain in her repertoire for the rest of her life.) Finally, still lock-kneed center stage, Judy launched into "Get Happy" and "Love Is Sweeping the Country." At that point, "I was supposed to bow slightly and go off—and then come back and sing three *other* outrageous arrangements. Well, I began one little curtsy, and one nerve 'undid,' and I just kept going! I wound up sitting on the floor—for *no* reason. If there'd been a wire going across the stage or a rope or something, I could have made something of it. But I was standing there, and simply *sat* down

on the stage! I was blushing like a baby and feeling like a fool. I wanted to cry, but I laughed instead—and the audience laughed with me." Their affectionate laughter turned to cheers when Pepper hoisted her to her feet, and she quipped, "That's one of the most ungraceful exits ever made." She began a second set of numbers, leading off with a tribute to Al Jolson in "Rock-a-Bye Your Baby with a Dixie Melody." (Garland had originally sung the song on a Crosby program the preceding December; Jolson had died on October 23.) She concluded with "Limehouse Blues," "Just One of Those Things," "Embraceable You," "But Not for Me," "Easter Parade," and, finally, "Over the Rainbow." The numbers were interspersed with Garland's byplay with the audience—that Grand Rapids-old, down-to-earth attitude that became a hallmark of her performances. Such spontaneity was the capper; the crowd yelled, "Good old Judy," "We love you," and "God bless you" at every pause.

The reviews the next day made passing reference to her Brunnhilde figure and wardrobe but primarily underscored the audience response. "She gave a more vital performance than anyone I have heard since Sophie Tucker, making me aware that what I have always imagined to be a fortissimo was merely a forte. It was not only with her voice but with her whole personality that she filled the theatre," wrote The *Daily Telegraph.* The *Evening Standard* decided, "Miss Garland is now better than her material. This quality of vibrant sincerity opens up possibilities which probably she, herself, has failed to realize. We saw a brave woman but, more than that, we saw a woman who has emerged from the shadows and finds that the public likes her as she is, even more than what she was."

Judy did two thirty-five minute sets a night, six nights a week for the next four weeks. The final performance on Saturday, May 5, was interrupted by shouts, "Stay with us, Judy—don't go," and Lorna Smith, one of Garland's most compassionate and intelligent friends, noted that the entertainer had "gained poise and confidence without losing the friendly warmth and diffidence" evident at her premiere.

At Judy's entreaty, Luft became her personal manager. Her new success brought immediate film offers, but he encouraged her instead to undertake a two-month tour of the provinces. The response to Judy live continued to burgeon. Hundreds of people who couldn't get into the sold-out Dublin theatre congregated under

FACING PAGE, TOP: At the Dorchester Hotel, London, April 1951. BOTTOM: Backstage at the Palladium with Maurice Chevalier, April 1951.

"She can command pathos without being maudlin. . . . In fact, she is an artist," wrote the Daily Telegraph *of Garland's London engagement. ABOVE, LEFT TO RIGHT: Receiving congratulations from Danny Kaye after a Palladium performance; greeting longtime friend and associate Kay Thompson after the latter's show at London's Café de Paris; backstage with Douglas Fairbanks, Jr., after the Sid Field benefit.*

TOP: Signing autographs for young British fans. ABOVE: An informal study taken during her stay in Great Britain.

her dressing room, and she sat on the window ledge to sing for them. In Edinburgh, scores of children recognized her as "Dorothy" but couldn't afford tickets to the show, so she bought out a section of the house and had them as her guests for a matinee. In gratitude, they brought little bouquets down the aisle, and by the end of the performance, the stage floor was covered with flowers. Finally, on the last night in Birmingham, the audience stood up, joined hands, and sang "Auld Lang Syne," while Judy cried happily.

On June 25, she returned to the Palladium in a "midnight matinee" benefit for the family of late comic Sid Field. Although fifty stars took part (Vivien Leigh, Laurence Olivier, Danny Kaye, Orson Welles, and Richard Attenborough among them), the evening's highlight came with Judy's "Rock-a-Bye." Attenborough wrote, "It wasn't just the song, or the way she sang it; it had nothing to do with pathos or memories: it was just magic." Witnesses compared audience response to a wall of noise so great that it physically forced Judy back from the apron until she bumped into the dais of stars behind her; Leigh rose and sank in a deep curtsy. (Luft was already aware of Garland's "uncanny" standing as The Star among even her most celebrated peers. "No matter who was on—it could have been the President of the United States—they didn't belong there when Judy was performing. The stage belonged to Judy.")

She sailed home on August 7, with quiet gratitude for her acceptance: "I came full of fear, I left full of joy." But her success abroad counted for little in New York. Abe Lastfogel hoped to launch Garland on a major concert tour or see her showcased at Broadway's Winter Garden Theatre. But there were no immediate plans until Sid Luft took a casual stroll down Seventh Avenue. He passed the Winter Garden and discovered that the theatre would be occupied for months with the musical *Paint Your Wagon.* A block or so later, however, he looked up to see in the distance the marquee of an even more fabled showplace—and the unexpected solution to Judy's professional dilemma.

The Palace Theatre had become the goal of every vaudevillian shortly after its opening in 1913. By the early 1930s, with vaudeville passe, the theatre had switched to a film policy; in 1951, it was halfheartedly presenting several live acts between movies. Audiences were small, response smaller. But Luft was well aware of its glorious history and of Judy's MGM roles as the girl who, with Rooney, Heflin, Kelly, or Astaire, made it on Broadway. He went to a phone booth and called RKO vice president Sol Schwartz, who immediately came down to the theatre from his office above the Palace. Schwartz knew instinctively what Luft had in mind, and on August 28, Lastfogel announced that Judy Garland would bring vaudeville back to the RKO Palace, headlining an all-star "two-a-day" reserved-seat bill for four weeks in October. There was nostalgic excitement in the trade, but everyone realized the success of the concept depended on Judy. *Variety* enthused, "If anyone can do it, this little bundle of talent can," but there was skepticism as well. One columnist stated bluntly, "Judy Garland's idea for a flash return to Broadway has wiser heads wagging negative"; he continued by invoking the biggest names in television and show-business spectacle: "Even Milton Berle wouldn't dare to try to fill those seventeen-hundred Palace reserved seats . . . two-a-day without Dagmar, Minsky, and Ringling." But Judy—thrilled to her Baby Gumm foundation—swept ahead. "Of course, I have qualms," she said. "But *vaudeville.* You have that feeling of bringing back something that's been missing from show business."

A Star is Born, *Warner Bros./1954.* FACING PAGE: *"Now we have a stunning shot with a clock. . ." —Garland sings "Someone at Last."*

LEFT AND BELOW RIGHT: Judy with costar James Mason. CENTER LEFT: Publicity portrait, 1954. BOTTOM RIGHT: Between takes with director George Cukor.

PAGE 129: Judy in costume for "Born in a Trunk."

A Star is Born, *Warner Bros./1954.* TOP: *Judy and chorus sing "Swanee."* ABOVE: *The legendary Garland sense of humor is captured between takes of "My Melancholy Baby."*

FACING PAGE: *The actual performance of the same song.*

WARNER BROS. PRESENT
JUDY GARLAND
JAMES MASON
in
"A Star is Born"
in
CINEMASCOPE
COLOR BY
TECHNICOLOR
ALSO STARRING
JACK CARSON ★ CHARLES BICKFORD
WITH TOM NOONAN SCREEN PLAY BY MOSS HART DIRECTED BY GEORGE CUKOR PRODUCED BY SIDNEY LUFT
NEW SONGS BY HAROLD ARLEN AND IRA GERSHWIN
MUSICAL DIRECTION BY RAY HEINDORF
A TRANSCONA ENTERPRISES PRODUCTION DISTRIBUTED BY WARNER BROS.

A Star is Born, *Warner Bros./1954.* *FACING PAGE: Early poster art, later abandoned in favor of a new design, shown BOTTOM. LEFT: Trade paper ad for the Los Angeles premiere. BELOW RIGHT: Jack Warner, Judy, and Sid Luft arrive at the Pantages Theatre, September 29, 1954. BOTTOM RIGHT: Kapralik publicity art for* Star.

FOLLOWING PAGE: Garland between takes of "Born in a Trunk."

Roger Edens and Chuck Walters were her equals in creative excitement; it took the three of them just two weeks to assemble her act. Hugh Martin, then writing for the theatre, read about the show and "called Judy to get house seats for opening night. She said, 'Why don't you sit on the stage with me instead?' " and Martin became her Palace pianist. He describes the job as "the greatest experience of my life, watching that woman. She was such a genius."

Schwartz refurbished the Palace from top to bottom for Judy's October 16 premiere, and Chuck taxied with her to the theatre on opening night. They were abruptly stopped by police barricades, holding back an estimated five thousand people in Times Square. "There were sawhorses across Broadway," Walters remembered, "and we asked the cab driver, 'What's this? Why can't we get through?' The cabbie said, 'Well, Judy Garland's openin' tonight, and them's the fans out there waitin'. ' Well, it hit us both. We both just froze. We realized then what opening night was going to be. And we had to get out of the cab and walk to the stage door."

A star-studded audience enthusiastically received the five variety acts in the first half of the show, but it was the second act for which they were waiting. The curtain went up on Judy's Eight Boy Friends, a tuxedoed re-creation of a typical Metro chorus line. For their opening, Edens rewrote the basic premise of "Madame Crematante" from *Ziegfeld Follies,* and the Boys (as members of the press) once again provided an introduction to "a great lady": *". . . Born in Minnesota, moved out to sunny California. / Got her Ph.D. at dear old MGM. / But we've stalled long enough, / So without further ado, / We introduce / that lallapaloos- / a, /* JUDY */ to you!"* Walters routined the number with great imagination. The Boys moved back and forth across the stage, and during their final surge toward the wings, Judy slipped out behind them, creeping along out of sight until they returned center. Then, in the same unexpected entrance that marked the debut of Baby Gumm in 1924, she suddenly appeared. The ovation lasted so long that

Judy at the Palace, 1951. ABOVE: *The preliminary newspaper ad.* FAR LEFT: *Garland swings into her opening numbers.* LEFT: *The "Rainbow" finale. The opening night crowd included Jimmy Durante, Gloria Swanson, Sophie Tucker, Martha Raye, Dorothy Lamour, Eva Gabor, Broderick Crawford, and the Duke and Duchess of Windsor.*

TOP: Judy acknowledges her flowers and ovations on opening night. Within hours of the premiere, Billy Wilkerson once more editorialized Garland on the front page of the Hollywood Reporter *and attempted to explain the crowd's response: "[They] reacted as no other audience had ever reacted to a performer. They applauded, they cried out of sheer delight. [Finally,] they stood on their feet at the conclusion of her show and yelled at the top of their voices." ABOVE: Onstage at the Palace with Sid Luft after the show.*

she was forced to cup her hands and holler "Hello!" before sailing into Edens's "Call the Papers" *("Call the* Mirror. / *Call the* News: / *You can say I've still got* ninety *pounds to lose. . .")* and the title song from MGM's *On the Town.* In the same biographical mode, she sang Roger's "Judy at the Palace": *"I played the State, the Capitol, / But people said, 'Don't stop! / Until you've played the Palace, / You haven't played the top. . .' "* The verse led to the signature songs of vaudevillians Nora Bayes ("Shine On, Harvest Moon"), Sophie Tucker ("Some of These Days"), Fanny Brice ("My Man"), and Eva Tanguay ("I Don't Care"). "Rock-a-Bye" was a subsequent showstopper (and by now well on its way to becoming a Garland standard); Judy finished her first set with the Olio and "Love Is Sweeping the Country." The Boy Friends returned for a tongue-in-cheek solo routine, "This Is Our Spot" *("We were sent out here to stall / While Madame's changing her dress. . .")* until an offstage whistle informed them, *"She must be set now. / We better get now."* The curtain opened on the "Get Happy" backdrop from *Summer Stock,* and the number was reprised as in the film. When later asked how she liked the sight of Garland in her black silk tights, the legendarily leggy Marlene Dietrich sighed, "Those legs are mine."

The Boys remained onstage for another Edens "filler" until Judy—with Chuck—returned for "A Couple of Swells." (Jack McClendon, one of the Boy Friends, partnered her after the first night.) Then she approached the edge of the stage alone. It was Luft's suggestion that she sit there for the final song; admittedly tired one evening in Dublin, Judy had simply plopped herself down along the footlights for a couple of numbers, and the audience loved her unassuming proximity. When she did it at the Palace, however, it became a moment of unforgettable theatre. Microphone forsaken, she sang "Rainbow" in her tramp costume, her dirty face and disheveled wig picked out of the darkness by a pin spot.

Clifton Fadiman later attempted to describe the significance of Garland's first Palace act and, specifically, its finale: "[She] worked the miracle of the playhouse, enforc[ing] the attention of the audience, an attention condensed, absolute, and . . . so uniform that it created a force peculiar to itself . . . transforming that audience into something beyond and above the separate selves of which it was made. . . We forgot who she was and indeed who we were ourselves. As with all true clowns, she seemed to be neither male nor female, young nor old, pretty nor plain. She had no 'glamour,' only magic. . . She wasn't being judged or enjoyed, not even watched or heard. She was only being felt, as one feels the quiet run of one's own blood, the shiver of the spine. . . When she breathed the last phrases of 'Over the Rainbow' and cried out its universal, unanswerable query, 'Why can't I?,' it was as though the bewildered hearts of all the people in the world had moved quietly together and become one, shaking in Judy's throat, and there breaking."

Judy herself "was thinking how lucky I was" as she sang the song on opening night. She later grew more introspective. "When I sing ['Rainbow'], the audience and I become (and share the optimism of) children. We have a flash of understanding that sets us [all] to weeping. I know many people think it's strange I can turn the tears on at performance after performance—but the really strange thing is that I couldn't sing [it] dry-eyed if I *wanted* to."

Inundated by flowers at the close of the show, Garland could only quaver out "Bless you all" before leaving the stage. And when the final curtain fell, Walters recalled that, "Judy did a beautiful thing. She changed into an evening gown and went out the front of the theatre and across to the [Duffy Square] island on Broadway and greeted all the fans who had been waiting there all night." The crowd responded with awed quiet as if for royalty, which surprised Judy until Chuck explained to her the honor of such a "silent tribute." A policeman told a newswoman in the crowd, "I've been on this beat twenty years, and I've never seen anything like this."

The reviews happily confirmed what *Life* magazine quietly termed "a miracle." *Variety* editor Abel Green called the act "a tour de force"; the New York *Post* found it "the greatest to have ever played the Palace." The *Hollywood Reporter* enthused, "No sir, not since the day World War I ended, the morning Lindbergh came down in Paris, the night *As Thousands Cheer* exploded in Times Square, or the afternoon Bobby Thomson sailed into a chin-high pitch and made history has there been a thrill like this." Robert Garland, whose last name George Jessel had appropriated seventeen years earlier for the Gumm Sisters, wrote in the New York *Journal-American:* "[The day after the opening], all Broadway seemed to be happy. It is as if vaudeville had been waiting somewhere for [Judy] to come along. And she, in turn, for vaudeville."

LEFT: A soulful portrait reflects what Variety*'s Abel Green reviewed on opening night as "simon-pure stellar quality. Miss Garland is a singer's singer. The late Lorenz Hart must have had her in mind in his lyric about 'love to hear the melody'—and with her, you also hear every phrase and word." RIGHT: With General Douglas MacArthur, his wife, and son after the October 20 Palace performance.*

TOP: Sid Luft, who had been in Los Angeles on business when Judy fell ill, returned to escort her to the theatre for the November 16 reopening; Palace management added "Welcome back, Judy" to the Times Square marquee. ABOVE: In her dressing room on her return to the Palace.

Garland's success was termed unprecedented; she was, in Luft's words, "the toast of New York with her peers and everybody." Each night, she made her exit out the Palace lobby onto Broadway, where hundreds of people waited to see her. The box office, originally worried that the ticket top of $4.80 might keep theatregoers away, found that Garland's success enabled scalpers to get three and four times that price. The engagement was quickly extended indefinitely.

Although Judy basked in such a reception, the strain of doing two shows a day, thirteen shows a week (there was no Monday matinee) became too much. She had begun seeing a new doctor in an attempt to diet. Sid was warned by another physician that the new doctor would involve Judy in medication that wouldn't be good for her. (There had been no such problems during the months Luft had known her.) After her Sunday matinee on November 11, Judy collapsed backstage with suspected heart palpitations. She later remembered that her doctor advised that she skip the evening performance and gave her a shot of sodium Pentothal to put her out. But when she heard slow hand-clapping from the audience, urging the beginning of act two after a long intermission, she rose from her dressing-room couch and said, "That does it. I've got to go on." Some years later, she wryly recalled, "The doctor gave me another shot—adrenalin—to bring me around. Can you *imagine?* Talk about being jolted!" She managed to get through the opening number feeling "halfway between the sky and the floor"; finally, her voice began to trail off completely, she stumbled to the wings and collapsed. Vivian Blaine, on a night off from *Guys and Dolls,* came up from the audience and did twenty minutes to help complete the show, as did comic Jan Murray. When the auditorium was empty, Judy was taken by stretcher to a waiting ambulance and the hospital.

Her doctor urged that she be given a real rest, and the Palace closed for four days. Most of the press was sympathetic, although Mike Connolly publicly advocated "a *complete* cure for this great performer," and pleaded in the *Hollywood Reporter* for Judy to "take at least a year away from it all." Although her doctor would label the brief illness "nervous exhaustion, similar to combat fatigue," Luft convinced Judy to stop seeing him, and there were no further problems with medication during the engagement. The Palace willingly cut back to a ten-show-per-week schedule, and Garland returned on November 16. It was, according to the press, "even more of an emotional experience than opening night," again replete with barricades and bouquets. Columnist George Minot found a simple explanation for Judy's success: "[This] is an age where much of your entertainment is shoddy and half-hearted, where too many radio and television programs are plain mediocre; where many big name players on the stage play down to their audiences as if they were casting gems into a pig pen; where movie stars on tour give you a bow and an artificial smile and flee the platform. It is duck soup for an honest entertainer like Judy to carry away her audiences in her hip pockets. She gives all she has inexhaustibly."

On Tuesday, November 27, in an unprecedented alliance, all seven theatrical unions of the American Federation of Labor joined in honoring Judy at a testimonial luncheon. She was presented with a silver lifetime membership card for the unions and acknowledged the tribute by admitting, "I can sing a pretty fair song, but I'm terrible at making speeches. Thank you; God bless you."

By early winter, Judy was battling laryngitis and, when there was no other recourse, canceled several matinees. (On at least one occasion, however, she apologized to the audience for the condition of her throat at the top of the act, told them she would do the best that she could, but that anyone who wanted to leave would gladly be given a refund. No one left.) She ultimately took five days off prior to Christmas, but returned for all the holiday-week shows. On January 1, she began her twelfth week at the theatre, breaking the long-run record set by Kate Smith in 1931. In late January, Garland finally dropped back to an eight-show-per-week schedule, and feeling the need for a real vacation (and then anxious to "sing in every town that has a theatre"), she decided to conclude her Palace run in mid-February. RKO executives were suddenly faced with the fact that most big-name entertainers considered the theatre "too hot" and refused to follow Judy. Betty Hutton told Harrison Carroll, "The audience is in tears before she opens her mouth, and when she sits down without a microphone and starts 'Over the Rainbow,' you can hear people all over the audience saying, 'God bless you, Judy.' Who can follow that? If you did four flips in the air, cut your head off and sewed it on again, it wouldn't mean a thing." (Ultimately, the theatre booked a combination of variety acts to immediately succeed the Garland show.)

The Palace tallied a gross of nearly $800,000 for Garland's nineteen weeks (184 performances); RKO felt she could have easily remained another nineteen weeks had she desired. To meet the demand for tickets, Judy did eleven shows during her final week, bringing in around $54,000 and breaking her own box-office record. She played her last show on February 24; some two hundred standees stood four deep at the back of the theatre, and *Variety* estimated that half of the house had seen the show before. (So attuned was the audience that they cued Judy into even the supposedly ad-lib moments of the act, calling out for her to take off her shoes at the point in the act where she always asked permission to do so.) She mocked the length of her Palace run after the opening song ("I think I got too old to do that number during this engagement") and, at the end, offered to answer some of the shouted requests for encores "if you'll let me talk for a minute afterwards: I have lots of *speeches* prepared!" Sorting the calls from out front, she asked if the crowd wanted to hear "Love" or "Liza"; a little boy, around eight years old, piped up forcefully, "Do *both* of 'em!" After "Love," she introduced Sid in the front row ("Let's make *him* take a bow for a change") before singing "his favorite," "A Pretty Girl Milking Her Cow." Finally, she dedicated "Liza" to a "particularly good friend of mine—my little girl."

Throughout the encores, Garland jubilantly joked with the crowd. She removed the tramp wig ("They *nail* it on back there") and propped her huge tramp shoes on the piano in the shape of a pyramid ("It dresses up the act"). Just before "Pretty Girl," she went to the wings, exchanged the tattered oversize jacket for a crumpled robe, and asked, "Do you think we're too informal?" As a finale, Lauritz Melchior joined her onstage; the former Metropolitan Opera tenor was following her into the Palace. But even after his bow, the audience frantically asked Judy for just "one more," and several requests were made for "Auld Lang Syne." One voice suggested the patrons sing it to her, so she stood back, folded her arms, and kiddingly challenged, "Okay. . . let's see you do it!" Jack Cathcart, who had taken over conducting chores for Judy in December, led the orchestra into the song, and the whole auditorium chimed in. Midway, Melchior stood up at his front-row seat; the rest of the Palace followed suit, continued singing, and began to applaud. *Variety* called it "one of the more memorable experiences in

A publicity portrait for the post-Palace 1952 tour.

the history of the two-a-day. . . one of the warmest tributes ever given a headliner in New York." Judy left the stage in tears.

The Palace management commemorated Garland's engagement by presenting her with a plaque for her dressing room. After a brief Florida vacation and prior to appearances on the West Coast, Judy also accepted a special Antoinette Perry (Tony) Award for her "important contribution to the revival of vaudeville."

She opened the show again on April 21 at the Los Angeles Philharmonic, where the entire four-week run was sold out in advance (a gross of $220,000). Scalpers got $100 a pair for opening-night tickets, and it was an occasion described in the *Herald-Express* as "a night of nights for star and audience alike—the great, big audience that cried." "Some [in the audience] may have intended to be kind. Some may have meant not to be," wrote Patterson Greene in the *Examiner.* "As it turned out, they had no choice in the matter. Within ten minutes of Judy's arrival on the stage, the audience found itself taken on a trolley ride. Not since Jolson was in the prime of his reign have I heard a singer of popular songs split a house wide open as Judy did repeatedly last night." There must have been a pocket or two of resistance somewhere in the Philharmonic, for *Daily Variety* thought the evening "never caught fire emotionally," and Bob Williams—who reviewed the show as "one of those rare and electrifying nights"—reversed his opinion a few days later and decided the performance was "something less than superlative."

BELOW: Judy at the Palace. BOTTOM: Ben Blue looks on appreciatively while Lauritz Melchior embraces Garland after her closing night Palace performance. Blue and Melchior topped the bill that followed Judy into the theatre, continuing the revival of "two-a-day" vaudeville.

But mass reaction was entirely positive. All Hollywood was on hand, from Louis B. Mayer on down, and Judy saluted them at the close of the show: "I think you know how much it means to me to be singing for you. I've missed you." Among her opening-night telegrams was one from the Duncan Sisters, who so many years before had been impressed by the sparkle of Baby Gumm.

On May 26, the show moved to the San Francisco Curran Theatre and similar sell-out receptions. During the run, a doctor confirmed that Judy was pregnant, and she and Luft were secretly married on June 8. News about the wedding broke four days later and brought a new spate of headlines about Garland's personal life. She and Luft had already been in and out of court over his child-support payments to ex-wife Lynn Bari for their son, John. Judy's mother created news of her own when, during Garland's Los Angeles engagement, the press revealed that Ethel was working as a clerk at Douglas Aircraft in Santa Monica for "a little over a dollar an hour," while Judy was "making twenty-five thousand dollars a week" at the Philharmonic. When told Judy had married Luft, Mrs. Gilmore informed newsmen, "He's a bad guy. I've been hoping it wouldn't happen." Her opinion was probably influenced by the headlines of the preceding summer, when Luft was arrested following a three-car collision and fisticuffs fracas in which Garland had also become embroiled. The resultant media reports and comments from Ethel contributed to a growing wonder about Judy's new manager/husband. There was, however, ready acknowledgment of his contribution to her career, and Garland herself gave Sid all credit for her success.

However volatile her offstage life, Garland was once more professionally on top. She was given a signal honor on June 29 when the Friars Club selected her as the second woman in their fifty-year history to be honored at a formal testimonial dinner. (The first had been Sophie Tucker.) Garland's event raised nearly $30,000 for Friars' charities and also marked the first time women were allowed to sit on the club dais. Speakers included Rosalind Russell, Olivia de Havilland,

Ed Wynn, Ronald Reagan, Eddie Cantor, and Jack Benny (the latter in a prerecorded tribute from London). George Burns garnered laughs when he reminded Judy, "Louis B. Mayer discovered you when you were ten [sic]. He could have discovered me, too, except that when I was ten, Louis B. Mayer was ten." The comic also congratulated Sid on his recent marriage: "I married a girl with talent, too. It's wonderful." Frank Sinatra and Marie Wilson offered parodies of "You Made Me Love You"; *South Pacific* star Ezio Pinza sang a new version of his song hit from the show: *"Some enchanted evening, / You may see a mogul / Pleading with Lastfogel / Across a crowded room. / A tear fills his eye as Abe shakes his head: / 'We're sold out for Garland for six months ahead . . .' "* The crowd cheered the bass into a reprise, but it was left to Judy to wrap up the evening with the Palace medley and "Rainbow." Presented with a pearl necklace and the pearl emblem of the Friars, she was dubbed "Miss Show Business"; a week later, she took a full-page ad in the trade papers to ask her "brother Friars," "Can you possibly know, each and every one of you, the good you have done my heart? I am very honored, I am very grateful, and I am very proud."

Garland's pregnancy was announced to the press in July, and Luft canceled touring plans for the Palace act. He pursued instead Judy's return to films, and they discussed her decade-old ambition to appear as Esther Blodgett in a remake of *A Star is Born.* Most of the rights to the original David O. Selznick film had been acquired in 1940 by Edward Alperson, and in early 1952, Alperson, Garland, Luft, and Luft's business partner, Ted Law, formed Transcona Enterprises as a film production company. They arranged a nine-picture option deal at Warner Bros.; three of the contemplated films would star Judy, and the first of these was to be *Star.*

In her ninth month of pregnancy, Judy received an unexpected chance to repay Bing Crosby's earlier kindnesses. His wife, Dixie Lee, was near death in her bout with cancer, and Garland agreed to replace him on his radio program for October 30. Three weeks later, at 4:17 P.M. on November 21, 1952, Dr. Daniel Morton performed a Cesarean section delivery of Judy's second daughter at St. John's Hospital. The six-pound four-ounce baby was named Lorna Luft.

But the general upswing of Garland's life was decimated on January 5 when news came that Ethel Gilmore had been found dead of a heart attack in the parking lot of Douglas Aircraft. The financial gulf between mother and daughter was again much headlined; it was seldom if ever mentioned that Ethel had received a portion of Judy's MGM salary for nearly fifteen years; that Garland had at one point bought her both a house and a car; and that Ethel had reportedly refused financial help from Judy during 1952. (Family friends confirmed that Garland was trying to circumvent the situation by purchasing income property for her mother.) Ethel's death was the final complication in a volatile mother/daughter relationship. They shared many traits. Both were strong-willed, determined women; both had fallen in love with and married creative men incapable of providing the emotional stability they required. Both had been divorced, Ethel from Will Gilmore in 1949 after a long separation. Ethel had also attempted suicide during the 1940s. For the rest of Judy's life—and depending on her own state of mind, her health, and her finances—she would alternately speak against her mother or blame herself for their separations and problems. The circumstances were too complex for any clear-cut resolution, however, and neither tack provided Judy any comfort or reassurance.

TOP: Judy at the Los Angeles Philharmonic, 1952. ABOVE: With newborn daughter, Lorna Luft, in early 1953. Eleven years later, Garland planned a musical salute to her three children for an episode of the CBS-TV "Judy Garland Show." When no appropriate song could be found for her second child, Judy asked Johnny Mercer to write a lyric for the series' theme melody—and Mort Lindsey's composition "A Song for Judy" became "Lorna."

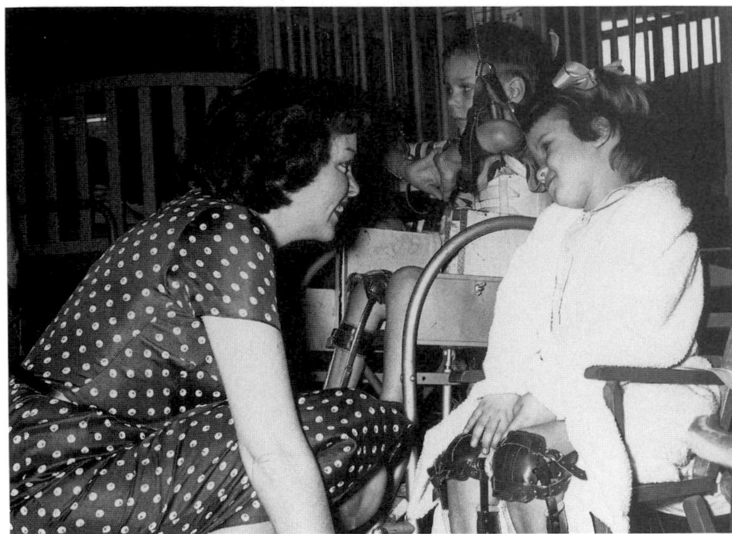

ABOVE LEFT: *Visiting the Shriners' Hospital, Lexington, Kentucky, April 1953.* ABOVE RIGHT: *Singing with Vaughn Monroe and His Orchestra at "The Blue Grass Festival."* BELOW: *Sharing ice cream with costar James Mason between takes of the elopement sequence in* A Star is Born*—Piru, California, December 1953.*

Garland remained under doctors' care for weeks after Ethel's death. In February, she went back to radio work in *Lady in the Dark;* in April, she cut four sides for Columbia. (The songs created no jukebox sensation, although one was co-written by Fred Ebb, Liza Minnelli's eventual musical mainstay.) On April 29, Garland headlined "The Blue Grass Festival," a new Derby Week event in Lexington, Kentucky. She closed her set with "My Old Kentucky Home," accompanied by a single violin. According to *Variety,* the "entire house rose as if on cue, and many could be seen wiping their eyes."

Preparations for *A Star is Born* were by this time well under way. Although Arthur Freed had privately predicted, "Those two alley cats can't make a picture," Luft and Garland had carefully and intelligently assembled a remarkable pool of talent. George Cukor, so instrumental in focusing Judy's image and performance for *The Wizard of Oz,* was their first choice as director and, when approached, didn't even give Sid a chance to describe the project. He simply said, "If it's for her, I'll do it, no matter what it is." (In 1932, the director had guided *What Price Hollywood?,* a forerunner to the original *Star.*) Playwright/scenarist Moss Hart expertly expanded and reinforced the original screenplay by Dorothy Parker, Alan Campbell, and Robert Carson. Harold Arlen and Ira Gershwin wrote eleven songs from which Garland's seven musical interludes could be selected, and Richard Barstow signed on as choreographer after Robert Alton, Jack Cole, and Michael Kidd had been considered. A host of leading men were either rumored in the running or approached to play opposite Garland in the role of Norman Maine, including Humphrey Bogart, Frank Sinatra, Laurence Olivier, Richard Burton, Tyrone Power, James Stewart, Glenn Ford, Stewart Granger, Robert Taylor, Gregory Peck, Henry Fonda, Ray Milland, Marlon Brando, Burt Lancaster, and Robert Young. After weeks of discussion, Cary Grant turned down the part; James Mason was finally signed in August 1954.

There were only three other major roles. Charles Bickford was cast as Oliver Niles, the studio head sympathetic to both the personal and professional plights of Blodgett and Maine. Jack Carson provided the appropriate cynicism for studio public-relations representative Matt Libby. Ray Walston, Dort Clark, and Ronny Graham were considered for the part of Danny McGuire, Esther's accompanist,

but the job went to Tommy Noonan, recently featured opposite Marilyn Monroe in *Gentlemen Prefer Blondes.*

Although Garland began preproduction work in August, principal photography was postponed into October. CinemaScope—the new process by which a film could be exhibited at twice the width of a standard movie screen—had burst upon Hollywood earlier in the year. Jack Warner had refused to rent the required lenses for his studio, experimenting instead with his own gimmicks (including Warnerscope). Weeks were spent deciding which would be best for *Star.* The film finally began shooting on October 12 in the older, comparatively intimate widescreen process. Then, with the completion of a dozen sequences, Warner decided to acquire the CinemaScope lens after all; two weeks of *Star* footage was scrapped, a new photographer was hired, and the film began again.

Star was planned from the start as Garland's valedictory, and Hart's script made her a hopeful singer rather than a fledgling actress. With minor modifications, his scenario told the same basic story as the 1937 feature: alcoholic screen-legend Norman Maine meets unknown Esther Blodgett when she saves him from public disgrace at a Hollywood benefit performance. He later hears her sing and exults, "You've got 'that little something extra' that Ellen Terry talked about; she said that's what star-quality is. . ." Maine helps Esther establish a film career; they marry, and her professional life soars while his declines. She plans to abandon her work to save him; overhearing this, he commits suicide, and though heartbroken, she rallies and introduces herself at another benefit as "Mrs. Norman Maine."

It took ten months to complete *A Star is Born,* and widespread rumors implicated Garland's instability and temperament as the cause for virtually every delay. Throughout the initial months of production, however, this was hardly the case. She was at the "floor" of her medication, working determinedly and well. When she missed a few days during November, December, and January, Cukor was able to use most of them to reshoot the footage scrapped in late October. Judy's absences invariably came after she had been called upon to perform such

LEFT: With Mason, Jack Carson, and Charles Bickford during early rehearsals for Star. *RIGHT: Exchanging beams with Doris Day on the New Orleans set for* Star*'s "Lose That Long Face." Day has written, "Some Hollywood faces seem to have been made for cameras. Judy had such a face—right, left, up, down, it didn't matter. . . . She was one of the funniest, wittiest ladies I have ever known, a marvelous conversationalist who would set me laughing until I actually doubled over." Day also found Judy "the most tightly wound person I ever knew. . . . She kept so much of herself locked up, but what she did let out was beautiful."*

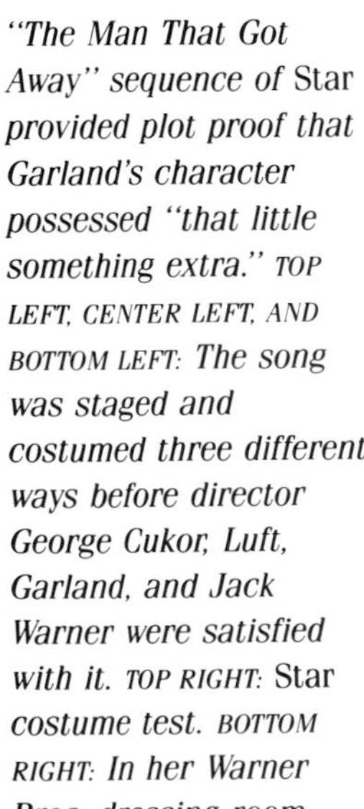

"The Man That Got Away" sequence of Star *provided plot proof that Garland's character possessed "that little something extra."* TOP LEFT, CENTER LEFT, AND BOTTOM LEFT: *The song was staged and costumed three different ways before director George Cukor, Luft, Garland, and Jack Warner were satisfied with it.* TOP RIGHT: Star *costume test.* BOTTOM RIGHT: *In her Warner Bros. dressing room.*

an emotionally exhausting scene as the one that took place in Esther's dressing room, confessing to Niles her growing ambivalence toward Maine. Cukor demanded multiple takes of almost every sequence, and he frequently shot many minutes of film without a break—an excellent approach but wearing for all concerned. (Garland appreciatively termed the director a perfectionist, a label she also applied to Luft and herself.)

Cukor always maintained a "very warm and affectionate feeling" for Judy and found her "a very complicated, modest little creature, with an absolute lack of chi-chi . . . , who works with the greatest intensity." Both he and Jack Carson understood Garland's sometime hesitation about coming to the set; the actor explained, "When Judy didn't think she was ready for a scene, she wouldn't do it. That's good sense, not temperament." Cukor agreed, referring to Garland's self-awareness: "She can only work when [her interior] 'light' goes on." Conversely, the director also remembers Garland's ability to rise above extenuating circumstances. While filming the Academy Award sequence wherein Esther is inadvertently slapped by a drunken Maine, it seemed to Cukor "that Judy's head snapped back like she'd been hit really hard. But since she didn't say anything, I let it pass. The next morning, the whole side of her face was bruised. But even though she had been hurt when Mason accidentally hit her too hard, she didn't tell anyone. That's being professional."

Cukor further exulted, "This was her first adult part, and it was very exciting to see her discover things in herself that she never knew she had. Once she had to scream; she had never screamed before, but when she finally summoned up the courage to let go, it was bloodcurdling." Judy's scream occurred when Esther furiously asks her goading accompanist to leave her alone following Maine's death. After Garland's first take, Cukor had her do another "for protection," in case something had been wrong with the film or camera. He then quietly expressed to her his awe at the power she had conveyed in both takes; with typical humor, she replied, "Oh, George, that's nothing. Come over to my house any afternoon. I do it every afternoon." Then she gave Cukor a look and added, "But I only do it *once* at home."

In a later reminiscence about Garland, the director noted, "Nobody ever says how intelligent she was, or how witty. Stories about her are frozen in a pattern, as if she had no life after 'Over the Rainbow.' She was the best raconteur, the funniest woman I've ever seen. The depth and perception she brought to *Star* were extraordinary. . . I marvel at her sensitivity." Mason agreed: "Judy was essentially a witty, lively, talented, funny, adorable woman. If the film went overbudget, only a very small fraction was due to her erratic timetable. She was by no means temperamental. [That's] usually a euphemism for selfish and bad-tempered. That sort can be a *real* time-waster. This was not Judy."

Luft, too, remembers Garland's pleasure at making *Star* and how "physically. . .very strong" she could be. "She had all this energy, and she'd work you hard enough so that *you* would drop. [Actress] Ina Claire came to the studio to watch Judy, and said, 'That girl should do one scene a day and then go home in an ambulance.' "

There were moments of friction, of course. Hugh Martin, hired as vocal arranger, stormed off the set after a row with Judy over her interpretation of *Star*'s most important song, "The Man That Got Away." There were delays as Garland, dissatisfied with some of her costumes, required additional designers. Many

BELOW: Rehearsal for "Lose That Long Face." BOTTOM: Rehearsal for the Academy Award sequence of the film.

ML-474 2/49

SHOOTING SCHEDULE

REVISED 6/25/54

Title "A STAR IS BORN" -Music Spot #6 No. 386 Director BARSTOW UNIT

Days Allotted 19 shooting, 7 Dress reh. & Rehearsal Asst. Dir. Graham

Start Shooting 6/30/54 Finish 7/29/54

DATES	SET, SCENE NOS., RESUME OF ACTION	PAGES	CAST AND WARDROBE CHANGE	LOCATION OF SET
Tue 6/29 (R1)	DRESS REHEARSAL & LIGHT SET: INT. STAGE & BACKSTAGE "Swanee" - Items 15, 3		Judy Garland 32 dancers 6 col. dancers 6 orchestra 6 children 2 stage grips	12-A
Wed 6/30 (1) Thur. 7/1 (2) Fri. 7/2 (3) Sat. 7/3 (4)	SHOOT INT. STAGE & BACKSTAGE "Swanee" - Items 15, 3		(as above)	12-A
Mon 7/5	HOLIDAY			
Tue 7/6 (5) Wed 7/7 (6)	SHOOT INT. STAGE & AUDIENCE (In front of tabs) "Born in a Trunk" - Items, 4,5		Judy Garland 18 orchestra Leader Bit Producer 4 Pages 67 audience	12-A
Thur 7/8 (R2) Fri 7/9 (R3)	REHEARSE BLACK BOTTOM # DRESS REHEARSAL & LIGHT SET: INT. STAGE & BACKSTAGE "Black Bottom" - Item 13		Judy Garland 15 girl dancers Stage Mgr. Female Star 2 Stagehands	12-A 12-A
Sat 7/10 (7) Mon 7/12 (8)	SHOOT INT. STAGE & BACKSTAGE "Black Bottom" - Item 13		(as above)	12-A
Tue 7/13 (R4)	REHEARSE ON STAGE & BACKSTAGE Items 8-9-10			12-A

TOP LEFT: Garland sings "Someone at Last." TOP CENTER: With Mason on the beach house set and TOP RIGHT: with Tommy Noonan during filming of the second version of "The Man That Got Away" sequence. ABOVE: First page of the Star *"Born in a Trunk" shooting schedule.*

scenes were retaken again and again at the request of the "perfectionists"—or Warner or Hart. Ronald Haver's comprehensive book *A Star Is Born: The Making of the 1954 Movie and Its 1983 Restoration* (New York: Alfred A. Knopf, 1988) provides a full account of the production, Judy's occasional absences from the lot, and all the rumors attendant to the film. The people he quotes, however, are unanimous in their memories of her hard work and how publicly apologetic she would be on those occasions when the pressure got to be too much and she would momentarily lash out at someone.

By February and March, the star had worn herself out and admitted to Luft she had increased her dosages of medication as production ground on. With his help, she quit her pills once again (in a painful, dangerous cold-turkey withdrawal) and returned to *Star* after two weeks for further retakes. The picture was planned as a three-hour road-show release with intermission, and there were additional delays when Transcona and Warner Bros. decided that none of the three Arlen/Gershwin songs written to conclude the first half of the film was usable. Luft turned to Roger Edens and his associate, Leonard Gershe, and they reworked an earlier Edens idea into a fifteen-minute medley of standards under the title "Born in a Trunk." Jack Warner loved it—despite the time it would add to the finished film—and agreed to the quarter-million-dollar cost of production. It took May, June, and July to plan, rehearse, design, costume, and prerecord and shoot the number. (Only Gershe received screen credit for "Born in a Trunk"; Edens's contract with MGM precluded any association with Warners.)

Principal photography ended around three o'clock in the morning on July 29 with an on-set party. Judy and Sid had more to celebrate than just the conclusion of *Star;* she was once again pregnant.

Warner rushed *Star* into two sneak previews in early August, but word got out when and where the film would be shown, and people lined up for tickets hours in advance. According to press reports, "the audience seemingly went crazy" when Judy's name first flashed on the screen, cheering in "the roar reserved for a champion." The excitement was compared to that at a Broadway opening, with cries of "Bravo" after musical numbers. When all 196 minutes of the rough cut were over, patrons called to a thrilled Garland, "Don't let 'em cut a minute of it. We could sit through four hours more!" Thousands waited in the street to laud her.

Sequences cut from Star*—either before or after the premiere.* CLOCKWISE FROM TOP RIGHT: *Garland with Jack Baker in "When My Sugar Walks Down the Street"; in "Lose That Long Face"; in "Here's What I'm Here For"; in the "Trinidad Cocoanut Oil Shampoo" commercial; and between her scenes as a carhop on location at Robert's Drive-In, Hollywood.*

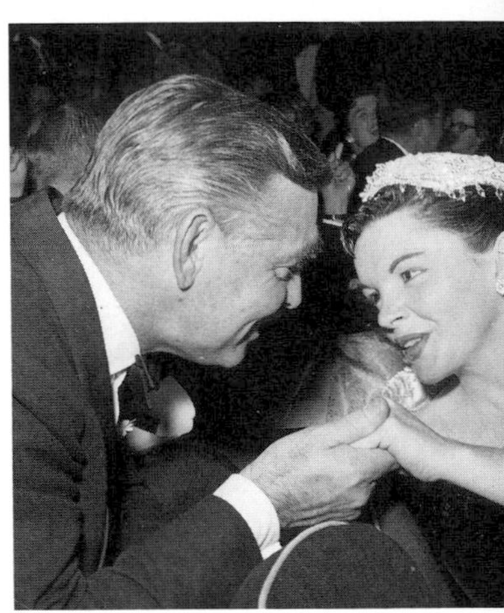

TOP LEFT: Singing "Swanee" during "Born in a Trunk." The Al Jolson standard quickly became one of Garland's concert triumphs. TOP RIGHT: With "dear Mr. Gable" at the Star *premiere. ABOVE: With Elizabeth Taylor and Michael Wilding at the post-performance Cocoanut Grove party. Although the studio system epitomized by* A Star is Born *was well on the wane by 1954—and despite the fact that Garland was slightly old for the part of Esther—the film remains for most critics her towering adult achievement.*

There were more exhibitor demands for *Star* than any previous Warner picture, and while Cukor attempted to polish the final cut, the studio began the largest ad campaign in its history. Publicity emphasized (in a positive manner) the "six-million-dollar" budget and ten-month shooting schedule; in truth, the actual cost of *Star* (before prints and advertising) came to $4.8 million. (Some $400,000 of that figure was incurred by the switch to CinemaScope; countless thousands more were spent in weeks of retakes and for overhead while the production shut down during selection of the first-act finale.)

Luft accurately points out, "*Star* took a long time to make because you have a long shooting schedule when your picture runs three hours. It was like making two movies." He admits too, that, in some ways, "we were so enthusiastic, we did too much of everything. Moss did a wonderful job, but he overwrote. [We] wrote too many songs. Too much movie, too much music. . . but it was a great too much."

Film tradesmen felt no apprehension. Warner received telegrams from exhibitors who previewed the picture, and every comment was rapturous: "[I] believe my experience in the business gives me the right to predict that *Star* will actually take in twenty-five million dollars and maybe more"; "The greatest hit in the entire history of Warner Bros."; "One of the greatest pictures of all time, if not *the* finest." One hundred theatre operators saw the film during an East Coast convention and notified Warner en masse, that "*Star* was the finest three hours and two minutes we have ever spent in a theatre." Press reaction was the same; much was made of the "unprecedented response" as newspeople applauded and wept.

Unfortunately, at the last minute, Warners decided not to road-show *A Star is Born* after all. Theatres were instructed to run the picture on a continuous basis in an effort to quickly recoup the film's expenses. It was the only area in which the studio refused to gamble, and it became the only aspect of *Star* to which many critics took exception: they felt the three-hour running time deserved at least an intermission if not special handling.

Nonetheless, the Pantages Theatre premiere on September 29, 1954, was lauded as the most elaborate in Hollywood history and a bigger night than the annual Academy Awards. The street-and-bleacher crowd was estimated at nearly thirty thousand and controlled by seventy policemen. A dozen radio programs broadcast from the lobby, and for the first time, a premiere was nationally televised in a live half-hour NBC production. Two hundred stars turned out, from Clark Gable to Joan Crawford, from Marlene Dietrich to James Dean. Warner hosted a Cocoanut Grove party after the premiere for eight hundred guests, and shared the head table with Garland, Luft, Sinatra, Bogart and Lauren Bacall.

In New York, *Star* was booked in two theatres in order to accommodate the expected crowds. The "dual premiere" at the Paramount and Victoria was telecast locally and broadcast on radio nationwide. Times Square was blocked off from Forty-third to Forty-sixth streets, and arriving first-nighters were showered with thousands of tiny stars. Fans broke police cordons when Garland arrived, and Barry Gray told his *Post* readers that, after the show, "Monday night crowds spilled over the gutters, and into Broadway. . . and rushed to Lindy's to spread the word. It was the biggest thing on film since D. W. Griffith's *Birth of a Nation.*"

Star grossed almost $700,000 at seventeen theatres in its first week of release—more than double its nearest competitor and, according to *Variety,* "a showing little short of phenomenal." Hundreds were turned away as it broke the first-day record for the Paramount (with or without a stage show). In San Francisco, the theatre scheduled seven showings on opening day, beginning at seven o'clock in the morning and ending at five o'clock the following morning.

Critical response to *Star* was all that Judy, Sid, or Warner Bros. could have wanted. Several reviewers cited *Gone With the Wind* as its only equal in ambitious effort and film entertainment. *Life* captured the spirit of dozens of major reviews: "The year's most worrisome movie has turned out to be one of its best . . . a brilliantly staged, scored, and photographed film, worth all the effort. Principal credit goes to imaginative, tireless, talented Judy [in] a film comeback almost without precedent." The London *Sunday Times:* "[Garland] displays an extraordinary maturing of her talents. Her singing has a new strength and edge. She shows a gift for parody which is brilliant. [Her] pathos has deepened, and her acting has a nervous tension which . . . held the house silent and tear-stained." Abel Green, editor in chief of *Variety* noted: "Boffola box office, period. It will not only mop up as a commercial entry [but] sets a number of artistic standards. Fort Knox, move over." *Saturday Review of Literature* added: "It is a bountiful, beautiful film [if] ultimately it becomes just too much for too little . . . [But] Miss Garland has the true star quality, that 'extra plus' which adds an indescribable poignancy and charm to everything she does. There is an ease and grace to her every movement, an originality and intensity in her gestures that go far beyond the merely skillful authority of the experienced actress. Her tremulous mouth, her voice always on the verge of tears, her large, brimming eyes can evoke any emotion at will. When she sings, it is with a felicity of phrasing, an inner awareness of both the rhythm and the meaning of her songs, that strikes straight to the heart of the listener." *Films in Review* decided that, "as film entertainment, it has everything. *Star* is an almost perfect example of what Hollywood can do when a big budget is *intelligently* spent on a script everyone believes in [and] also an almost perfect example of the kind of entertainment for which Hollywood is unrivalled anywhere in the world. Miss Garland sings, dances, mimes, and acts almost every kind of role. What picture will ever again give her such scope?" And *Time* beamed: "Everybody's little sister, it would seem, has grown out of her braids and into a tiara . . . She gives what is just about the greatest one-woman show in modern movie history."

BELOW: Garland took a full-page ad in the trades to express her gratitude to the Star *cast and crew and the media. The film opened across the country to over three times the average business. BOTTOM: At the Grove party: Judy, Sid, Jack Warner, Liberace, and Sophie Tucker.*

Chapter Six

Hang On to a Rainbow

The success of *Star* should have ensured Judy's future. Instead, her triumph was aborted within days of the premiere. A few exhibitors continued to resist the film's length and persuasively offered that a shorter version would mean an additional lucrative showing per day. In mid-October, Warner Bros.' president, Harry Warner, ordered *Star* arbitrarily cut by twenty-seven minutes. The excised footage was destroyed; even the *Star* negative was trimmed to conform to the new edit.

Few theatres ever played the complete film; only the short variant was made available. Business and positive word-of-mouth fell off. What had been produced, reviewed, and promoted as a unique moviegoing experience had been reduced to an imbalanced, even dissatisfying picture. Had *Star* been handled as originally realized—i.e., a road-show motion-picture event with intermission—the objections about its length could have been avoided. Instead, Warners fell subject to condemnation from the press, irate theatre managers, and filmgoers alike.

By year's end, *Star* was far from earning back its production cost. Future financial hopes rested on its Academy Award potential and critics' "best" selections for 1954. In the latter category, Warner Bros. received only new blasts. Notable was that from Bosley Crowther in the *New York Times:* "Every cut leaves a gaping, baffling hole. Not only the emotional pattern but the very sense of the thing is lost."

FACING PAGE: Publicity portrait, 1956. BELOW: Backstage at CBS after accepting the Look *award. The magazine's praise for Garland as Best Actress commended her "versatility and eloquence," noting her "place with the genuine artists who are wholly products of Hollywood training."*

Perhaps weary of the *Star* wars, Jack Warner mounted no Oscar campaign for the picture. Nonetheless, Garland was nominated as Best Actress (as were Dorothy Dandridge [*Carmen Jones*], Audrey Hepburn [*Sabrina*], Grace Kelly [*The Country Girl*], and Jane Wyman [*Magnificent Obsession*]). James Mason was nominated as Best Actor; *Star* was otherwise cited for art direction, costume design, scoring, and song ("The Man That Got Away"). The film and Cukor were passed by for Best Picture and Best Director nominations.

On March 8, 1955, *Look* magazine celebrated Judy as Best Actress in ceremonies during the CBS-TV Red Skelton program. In her advanced pregnancy, she was kept hidden behind a podium but offered, "It takes a lot of hard work on the part of a lot of people to make such a picture as *A Star is Born,* and I want to take this opportunity, if I may, to thank anyone who had anything to do with it—especially my old man, the producer." (Garland was also voted Best Actress in *Film Daily*'s poll and by *Box Office;* she won a Golden Globe from the Hollywood Foreign Press Association and topped the readers' poll of the prestigious British *Picturegoer* magazine.)

The Lufts planned to attend the Academy Awards ceremony on March 30, but five-pound eight-ounce Joseph Wiley Luft was born at 2:16 A.M. on the twenty-ninth, and Judy exclaimed, "I've got my Oscar already!" Doctors at first gave the child a fifty-fifty chance of survival; he almost unexpectedly rallied after thirty-six hours.

For months, Hollywood opinion had held that either Garland or Kelly would receive the Academy Award. As a result, NBC prepared to televise Judy's reaction should she win; she later relished the memory of their assault on Cedars of Lebanon. Her hospital room was suddenly invaded by technicians bearing television monitors. A three-story tower, holding camera, lights, and crew, was erected outside her window. Electric cable was strung "under my bottom, up my front, and down my nightie." Her nurse (who, as Garland remarked sardonically, "didn't know show *biz*") was taught to operate the venetian blind on cue. Even an NBC executive was "smashed down on the floor" so as to be out of camera range. When the big moment came, "I was leaning against the pillow, they opened the envelope and announced: 'Grace Kelly!' And I went, *'WHAAAAAAT?!'* But I didn't have time to be disappointed—I was so fascinated by the reactions of the crew: *'Kelly?! EHHH!'* They *tore* down the tower; they *ripped* out the wire; they took *away* the monitors. Nobody even said *'good night'*; they were so *mad* at me, because I didn't win! . . . But I was *nominated!*"

The loss of the Oscar brought the Lufts over a thousand telegrams and letters of condolence; Groucho Marx wired "This is the biggest robbery since Brink's." Bing Crosby, who'd joined Judy as a winner on the Skelton program, lost the Best Actor Oscar to Marlon Brando. His message to Garland read: "I don't know about you, but I'm renewing my subscription to *Look*."

Judy poses with cast members of her "Seven City Tour," July 1955. BELOW: Frank Fontaine later became an "overnight sensation" as a singer and comic on Jackie Gleason's 1960s television series. BOTTOM: The Wiere Brothers comedy trio join Judy in costume for the "Running Wild" first-act finale.

Judy publicly rose above her loss but felt deeply slighted by the dismissal of "her" film; its slow-to-recoup financial fate also meant the end of Luft's multi-picture deal with Warners. By June, with no money forthcoming from *Star*, Judy was back in rehearsal for a new stage show. Luft booked the three-hour revue into seven West Coast cities, and *Variety* termed Garland's opening performance in San Diego "dazzling. She has added a magnetic maturity to the old gamin quality." There was also appreciation for her "disarming frankness" in a casual query about her increased weight: "Do you think this kind of figure will *ever* come back?" The show played Long Beach four nights later; many of Garland's friends were literally bused in from Los Angeles by Frank Sinatra to cheer the show. At the finale, they joined her onstage, and Sinatra refused a request to sing: "I'm not going to follow this kind of an act."

Luft next planned to play the show cross-country, traveling by train and winding up on Broadway in late autumn. He was forced to cancel the entire project when some theatre managers—burned by lack of business done by other tours—refused to post the guarantee he required to make the trip viable. To break the contracts already in hand, he quickly sold Judy to CBS for a television show; each theatre agreement contained an "out" clause should Garland be offered a film or TV role. The network quickly slotted her as the premier performer on "Ford Star Jubilee," their first color "spectacular." The September 24 telecast was publicized as a ninety-minute version of Garland's Palace act; her fee was a record-breaking $100,000. There was much pressure on all concerned (and much preshow hoopla generated by both CBS and Ford), but the star felt the strain most of all. Concerned about her weight and the hazards of a live performance before millions of viewers, she had no desire to appear on television, despite the prestige of the showcase and Henry Ford's personal request that she inaugurate his series. Luft was aware of her terror and learned that, "when Judy was apprehensive about something, she was liable to get sick on you."

Garland gamely plunged into a month of preparation, but fighting laryngitis the day of the show, she walked through final rehearsals without singing a note. CBS production supervisor Harry S. Ackerman later said, "I just prayed to God

LEFT TO RIGHT: Judy sings the Palace medley, "Rock-a-Bye," and "Rainbow" on the "Ford Star Jubilee." Despite severe laryngitis, Garland was cheered by the press for her "personal triumph," "vibrant personality," and "customary verve and showmanship." "Rainbow" was called "a portrait come to life," and the New York World-Telegram *enthused, "There's never been anything like the one-woman show staged by Judy Garland."*

that she'd be able to appear." The corporate hierarchy was not aware that Judy, unable to sleep, had taken medication that morning in an effort to either rest or blot out her increasing fears. It took all day for her to work her way back from the effects; she told Luft she felt groggy and dizzy.

By airtime, adrenaline flowing, Garland was steady on her feet though her voice remained severely constricted. The tears that flowed during "Rainbow" were perhaps more real than ever before, augmented by her later-expressed feeling that "I've never known anything so terrifying. The voice went—everything went." The impact of her finale, however, was strong enough to be recalled almost twenty-five years later by a leading historian of popular culture and former professor of English at Boston University. Dr. Edward Wagenknecht wrote, "Garland's singing of 'Over the Rainbow' was perfect for *Oz* and for her as she was [in 1939]. But for subtlety and sophistication, it was far inferior to the way she sang it . . . on television. It seemed to me that, for a moment, the line between popular art and great art had been wiped out. This does not often happen with this type of entertainment."

The press for "Jubilee," while sympathetically acknowledging Garland's vocal problems, congratulated her. *Variety* was typical in its enthusiasm: "Nothing else mattered when she was on . . . that ol' black magic and magnetism came through in all its treasured nuances." Criticism was reserved for the overall production itself; the Chicago *American* referred to "Jubilee" as "a shoot-the-wad . . . imitation of [NBC] spectaculars. And Judy Garland was the wad CBS shot, without even granting her the consideration of a blindfold . . ." Their reviewer disliked the show's "sickly saccharine" nostalgia and Garland's "hideously deforming" Irene Sharaff costumes. Columnist Dorothy Kilgallen pleaded, "[Just] let her come out and lean against the curve of a piano, the way she's done at a hundred parties. That would [be] the true Judy—not a plump girl trying to look thin, not a young woman in old women's clothes, not a scared over-rehearsed actress. Judy Garland's a great talent. They shouldn't kick it around."

CBS, however, judged the show solely by public response and labeled Judy "the greatest personal triumph in [our] history. Our switchboards were still jammed twenty-four hours after the telecast. People from all over the country called *just*

TOP: Rehearsing at the Capitol Miss Show Business *sessions, August 1955. Judy recorded eleven songs and medleys for the album; one number—a new version of "On the Atchison, Topeka, and the Santa Fe"—was deleted due to time constraints. ABOVE: Between takes.*

to tell us how much they liked Judy. We've never had such an intimate personal reaction from viewers." Garland tallied a 34.8 rating (against 11.0 for the competition); forty million people had tuned in—the largest audience in history for a special. As a result, CBS signed Judy to an exclusive television contract.

Around the same time, Luft negotiated a deal for Judy with Capitol Records; it was the beginning of a ten-year association. Her first album, *Miss Show Business,* was conducted by Jack Cathcart and timed to coincide with "Jubilee." The sessions took place over four nights in August and September and provided a souvenir of Judy's stage and television acts. The finished product hit No. 5 on the charts, and Garland returned to the studio for three evenings in March 1956 for a follow-up. *Judy* utilized songs new to her repertoire, including those intended for her next CBS show; it also marked her first work with conductor/orchestrator Nelson Riddle. He remembered her as "*extremely* nice. I think she always wanted very much to leave a very pleasant image. . . always came prepared; she was never one to come to a session and learn the song [there]." With Roger Edens's vocal arrangement as a guideline, Riddle created Garland's classic "Come Rain or Come Shine," as well as a revered recording of "Last Night When We Were Young." He considered the latter a "tough" song and her rendition "a tour de force. I did [the song] with Frank Sinatra, which took thirty takes. I did it with Judy, which took less. [She had] great phrasing. . . in a totally true musical way, which is to read the lyric and find where you can breathe that will least interrupt the train of thought. She was a very canny, bright lady." *Judy* hit No. 17 on the charts, and critic Murray Schumach offered it as an "argument to show how artistic pop singers can be. It is quite possible that to evoke the pathos of her 'Any Place I Hang My Hat' requires as much artistry as, say, Kathleen Ferrier's in 'Das Lied von der Erde.' "

Judy's second TV appearance was scheduled as a half-hour concert, a special presentation of the "General Electric Theater" on April 8, 1956. The show, visually fashioned after a Richard Avedon photo session, was evidently planned with the "Jubilee" criticisms in mind. Garland lost weight, and James Galanos created a series of casual, almost rehearsal-style costumes for her, showing a maximum of leg. The songs (if in some cases standards) were those she had never before sung publicly. Her guests were dancer/choreographer Peter Gennaro and jazz pianist Joe Bushkin. (The Lufts had originally wanted Leonard Bernstein for the show, as he and Garland had teamed informally and successfully at parties, but CBS vetoed the choice.)

Whatever its innovative merits, the April show proved as ineffective as "Jubilee." The avant-garde production was curiously uneven and featured a star once more hampered by nerves and medication that impaired her singing. (Even the prerecordings used for several numbers were of lesser quality.) Judy later looked back on the program and humorously recalled, "One man kept worrying [during rehearsals] that we weren't going to hold the audience. 'They're gonna get beer,' he repeated constantly. After a few days of this, I was ready to *shoot* him." She had broken a bone in her foot a few weeks earlier and wore a cast until airtime. "I was supposed to dance in four-inch high heel shoes," she noted. "They took the cast off, I stepped into the shoes and went on live, hobbling. I looked like Nanette Fabray when she imitates a dancer in dire distress."

The ratings were again spectacular; it was the only special to place in the top fifteen programs for the week. But reviews made it apparent that Judy Garland

and television had yet to coalesce. "Not even sheer determination and hard work, of which she gave plenty, could bring this up to the standards of her full capability," opined *Variety.* A more trenchant writer described "a performer who only shows flashes of her one-time style," and asked that memories of her past work "be left undisturbed" by such programs.

Unfortunately, her two specials and the soon-to-multiply negative headlines about her private life served as a Judy Garland point of reference for millions of people in the late 1950s. In spite of her performance in *Star* and the success of her albums, the mass audience was exposed to Garland as a seemingly deteriorating TV singer or as the unstable, temperamental woman portrayed by the press—an old movie star who worked sporadically and seldom at her best. Ironically, she did some of her finest singing and most remarkable and ambitious work from 1955 to 1959. Normally terse critics were alternately inventive, wondering, or hyperactive in their attempts to describe her "incomparable" art or her effect on any crowd. She continued to command standing ovations and almost hysterical audience reactions—commonplace for pop and rock concerts in later decades but unheard of and unknown during this era. However, befitting the heritage of Baby Gumm, these hundreds of performances in the late 1950s were given onstage and not on television; the greater general public heard only about the Garland shows that were canceled or considered comebacks. In truth, Judy never stopped working in the late 1950s; along with Luft, Edens, Kay Thompson, Chuck Walters (or Robert Alton or Richard Barstow), she prepared and appeared in at least five different revue formats in five years, constantly varying her routines yet retaining many of the expected standards. (She later advised Tony Bennett to include at least three songs new to his repertoire whenever he planned a show; although Garland developed a reputation for seldom changing her own program, this was a rule to which she strictly adhered.)

After the April 1956 telecast, Luft arranged for Judy's Las Vegas debut at the New Frontier Hotel. She was guaranteed $55,000 a week, the largest salary ever paid a nightclub performer, and the new act included two elaborate production numbers with the Boy Friends: an almost balletic "Any Place I Hang My Hat" and a rowdy "Lucky Day" (in which Garland was picked up, tossed about, and carried off sideways for a finale). On opening night, July 16, the New Frontier scheduled one show instead of the customary two, and in an unprecedented move, every other major club in Las Vegas closed down so that Garland's fellow headliners could attend the premiere. *Daily Variety* offered, "[She]'s a singer's singer. Her style, her voice, and her delivery are the pride of her profession. There's no way to draw comparisons between [her] and any of her contemporaries, male or female." Weekly *Variety* testified: "Not only is she the tops in her field but likely champ entertainer as long and as often as she desires to play the bistro circuit."

The engagement was extended; Garland ultimately worked five weeks, some seventy performances, and broke all house receipt records. One night in August, the combination of hot, dry desert weather and cold, dry air-conditioning gave her "Las Vegas throat," a condition avoided by few who played the Strip. Luft pressed Jerry Lewis into service as a replacement, but Judy went on with him, playing silent partner to his ad-libbed comedy. As a finale, he sang her arrangement of "Rock-a-Bye" (with Judy whispering the lyric in his ear), and she did "Come Rain or Come Shine."

BELOW: Strutting to "I Will Come Back" on the 1956 special. BOTTOM: With Sid, Johnny Luft (left foreground), Lorna, and baby Joe, 1956.

TOP: With Jerry Lewis in Las Vegas; the comic had recently dissolved his professional partnership with Dean Martin, and his success as Garland's one-night replacement helped convince him he could establish a solo career. ABOVE: Judy arrives in New York for the second Palace engagement, September 17, 1956.

The Palace had been clamoring for Garland's return since 1952; during the Vegas stand, Luft arranged a four-week booking. Her schedule was set at Broadway's standard eight shows per week and, by opening night, September 26, much of the initial run was already sold out. (The day after the reviews appeared, tickets went on sale for an additional four weeks.) Judy's act was drawn largely from the Vegas show, but Edens prepared "Be a Clown" as the penultimate production number, putting her into circus garb for "Rainbow."

The premiere once again created a New Year's Eve atmosphere in Times Square, with thousands of fans behind police barriers and a celebrity-packed audience. The surprise of the first act was comic Alan King. He had nearly quit the show during rehearsals when the running order of supporting performers was shifted to highlight Nora Kovach and Istvan Rabovsky, a much-publicized dance team that had—as per their billing—"escaped to freedom through the Iron Curtain" and survived the sinking of the *Andrea Doria.* Though he relinquished the coveted next-to-closing slot, King was vindicated by making a big hit opening night. Still upset, however, he angrily strode past Garland, who had been watching the show from the wings. "I was in my dressing room for about five minutes—a knock on the door—it was Judy," King recalls. "She was wearing a terrycloth bathrobe that looked like it had been backstage for thirty years. I had not met her. She looked at me: 'You can close my show any time you like.' That's the first thing she ever said to me. And starting the next night, I closed the first half. We were together on and off for three years. It was the best time of my life."

Garland's entrance at the top of the second act was again designed to catch the audience off guard. The curtains parted to reveal a darkened stage. Suddenly, in the words of the *Hollywood Reporter,* "A spot picked her out of the pitch black background, and ten thousand volts of electricity shot through the audience." After a two-minute ovation, she launched into Edens's opening medley: "New York, New York," "Take Me Back to Manhattan," "Give My Regards to Broadway," and "The Sidewalks of New York."

By morning, the New York tabloids were front-paging Garland's return: "Judy Does It Again." The review headlines were equally declarative: "Judy Garland Now Owns Broadway," "Her Magic Nearly Lifts Palace Roof," or "All Broadway Bows to Judy." Walter Kerr exulted in the *Herald Tribune:* "It was perfect. [Her] barrel-house voice can bend the back walls into cyclotrons. The glorious steam-whistle that can shatter the chandeliers with a single, sustained note flung recklessly skyward is in great shape."

Garland became as hot a Broadway ticket as the current *My Fair Lady,* and Judy compared the performance to "a family party." That aspect was emphasized when weekend Palace audiences often saw the children onstage—Liza in a duet of "Swanee," Joe in Judy's arms for "Happiness Is a Thing Called Joe," and Lorna in appreciation of "Rock-a-Bye." ("Lorna," Mama explained, "likes the loud ones.")

October 16 brought a special highlight, five years to the day after Judy's original opening. During her final bows, she was joined onstage by RKO's Sol Schwartz, who told Garland and the audience, "We have had all the greats of show business appear here from Fanny Brice to the great Miss Barrymore. The biggest thrill of all is having Judy back again. For the first time in the history of the Palace Theatre, we are going to present someone with a gold key to the dressing room. A gold plaque with your name on it will be put on the door. From this night on, your dressing room will be called 'The Judy Garland Dressing Room.' We all hope you will consider this your home and, when you leave it and feel like coming home again, all you have to do is put the key in the door." He then asked her to reprise the Palace medley from 1951, "as I think that would tell the whole story of tonight."

Alan King's friendship with Garland deepened during the Palace engagement, and he retains special appreciation of her loyalty: "She had such respect for people with talent; she was very gracious, very kind." At one point, Luft and the Palace management decided the first act of the show was too long and planned to drop an act, the Spanish vaudevillian clowns Pompoff, Thedy, and Family. Knowing she would not have been consulted about the move, King casually mentioned it to Judy. "And she stormed out of the dressing room," he recalls, "screaming at the top of her lungs, 'Don't *nobody* get fired from my show, *nobody*. . .!' And Pompoff, Thedy and Family stayed."

King also cheered Judy when she wasn't feeling well or when her throat was bothering her. "I used to say to her—with honesty—'Judy, when you're bad, you're better than anybody else I ever saw.' [But] there were some nights when I didn't think she was going to get through. One [such] time, I sent Liza out. And the minute Judy saw her, *boy,* there was this *burst* of energy. They did a duet, and Judy then went on for another forty-five minutes." Despite such encouragement, however, there were occasions when Garland couldn't work. King later kidded her, "The reason you keep me with you is that nobody makes the speech—'Ladies and Gentlemen, Miss Garland will not appear tonight'—better than I." He also recalls that, in addition to vocal problems, Garland was frequently physically uncomfortable onstage in the late 1950s. Her weight had continued to increase, and this not only added to her fear of facing an audience but made movement an actual torment: "In order to make her thinner, which was impossible, they put her in dresses with steel stays—designed by the guy who did outfits for King Arthur's Round Table." Once cinched into such dresses, Garland would find even breathing painful. King remembers one particular evening when Garland was ill and unhappy, and "I was the only one she would let into her dressing room. She had laryngitis, and she was crying and whispered, 'Nobody believes that I can't talk. I can't go on.' Now, a lot of her laryngitis was very emotional—psychosomatic, I guess. So I said, 'Judy, you know the rumors about your drinking.' She didn't drink . . . she'd have a little white wine. But I said, 'Judy, everybody's going to say "Judy's drunk again." ' And she got very upset. I said, 'Let me bring you out. They're going to give the money back anyway. All you have to do is let them see that, obviously, you are not drunk. Don't even get dressed. Come out in this outfit.' She was wearing a pair of black silk Japanese pajamas, a little coat that covered up her weight. So we went out there. And they applauded, and I was holding her hand, and she was shaking. I made the announcement. Well, you know the audience: 'One, Judy! Just one!' And I was clowning around with her and ready to take her off. And she said, 'Very well, one.' And she started 'Rock-a-Bye.' She wouldn't let go of my hand, so finally, I just dropped [hers] and walked off. She stayed on for an hour and twenty minutes in those pajamas. Now she didn't really curse [in anger]. But when she got off, she screamed: 'I have never felt so comfortable onstage in my life!'" Unfortunately, Garland (or those around her) felt it important that she continue to wear ornate gowns for at least part of her act for the rest of the decade.

BELOW: Judy in the "Be a Clown" production number at the Palace, 1956. Variety's *editor-in-chief Abel Green labeled the star "the prime song belter of our times. . . . She makes a Brill Building lyric sound like a Shakespeare sonnet. She could sing Toots Shor's menu and have 'em hungry for more. She takes command of the rostrum as none does." BOTTOM: Onstage with Sol Schwartz on the fifth anniversary of her Palace debut, October 16, 1956.*

By December, the strain of giving eight all-out performances a week had become too much. Judy missed shows and even retired briefly to the hospital while the Palace closed for seven days. Her second engagement concluded after seventeen weeks on January 8, 1957, and the Lufts hosted an onstage farewell party for cast and staff.

Meanwhile, CBS announced Judy's next special for telecast in February or March, and sold the time slot to two sponsors. Their actions led to an historic court case and a series of ugly headlines that would further impair Judy's image. Although her contract called for network submission of a finished script, CBS offered instead a four-page outline, described as "a cross between her Palace and Las Vegas acts." When she rejected this both as a concept and for lack of a complete treatment, CBS was in a bind, and an anonymous network executive told New York *Herald Tribune* columnist Marie Torre, "[We're] ready to forget the whole thing." He referred to Judy's "highly developed inferiority complex" and commented that Garland "did not want to work . . . [possibly] because she thinks she's terribly fat."

Torre printed his comments and, six days later, CBS tore up Judy's contract, claiming she had not performed as requested. In March, Judy filed a $1,393,333 suit against the network, including as part of her case the "false and defamatory matter. . .CBS authorized" in the quotes provided to Torre. Litigation went on for three years; when the journalist refused to name the CBS executive who had been her news source, she was held in contempt and sentenced to federal jail for ten days. The United States Supreme Court declined to review her case, but the judge who questioned Torre sympathized with her, calling her the "Joan of Arc" of her profession. Such tribute, along with photographs of the writer leaving her two small children for jail, put Garland in the worst possible light. Little was made of Judy's expressed sympathy or Luft's point that "Miss Torre wouldn't be in jail if the CBS executive she is protecting had come forward in her behalf" (an idea with which Torre herself concurred).

In February and March, Judy returned to Capitol to record *Alone*. The album, completed in three sessions, featured the singer in a series of moody ballads and went to No. 17 on the charts. Its theme and Garland's work were lauded, although there was dissension over the Gordon Jenkins orchestrations. One writer

BELOW: Rehearsing Alone *with Gordon Jenkins. BOTTOM LEFT: Recording* Alone. *BOTTOM RIGHT: The Luft family Christmas card, circa 1956.*

LEFT: Singing "Lucky Day" with the Boy Friends during the 1957 U.S. tour. RIGHT: Backstage with Perle Mesta and Sid at the Washington, D.C., Capitol Theatre, moments before the September 16, 1957, opening of the Garland show. Famed hostess Mesta gave the post-performance party for Judy and two hundred guests.

thought the composer had "overwhelmed her fresh singing with vulgar arrangements. . . more concerned with creating unusual sound effects than with underlining the pathos [her] almost embarrassingly honest approach can evoke. Judy would have been better off alone."

In another new act, Garland reopened in Las Vegas on May 1 for three weeks at the Flamingo Hotel. One of her most requested songs at the Palace had been "The Man That Got Away"; here she added it to her permanent repertoire, initially in a song-and-dance treatment similar to that used earlier for "Any Place I Hang My Hat." Opening night brought a unique tribute. As Judy sang "Rainbow," the entire crowd rose and stood silently until the conclusion of the number. The *Hollywood Reporter* offered that "to explain [her] artistry is like trying to take into parts a globule of mercury."

Vegas was the beginning of a nine-week tour. Every critic trotted out the superlatives, although Garland was forced to pull out of a Dallas show one Saturday after four songs; her illness was later explained as a reaction to the death of choreographer Robert Alton four days earlier. (After the evening off, she "came roarin' back [the next day] in total command," according to the Dallas *Times Herald.*) When the Garland troupe opened the outdoor Los Angeles Greek Theatre on June 25, the *Mirror News* reported a capacity audience "mesmerized [by] her clear, full voice ringing on the soft summer evening air like a mockingbird serenading the moon." The *Hollywood Reporter* summarized, "The terrific hand she got [on her entrance] was nothing compared to the way she proceeded to put the crowd in the palm of it." One of Garland's most famous anecdotes grew out of the Greek engagement. "There are," she later explained, "an awful lot of insects involved, because the lights attract all kinds of bugs. One night, I got about one chorus into 'Over the Rainbow,' and a *moth* flew in my mouth. Now, in the middle of 'Get Happy,' you can go *'HCCHHHHYIIIICH!'*. . . but not during 'Over the Rainbow.' So I *parked* him in my cheek with my tongue—and he fluttered around for a chorus and a half. (I had a faster vibrato than ever that night. . .) When I finally finished the song and the lights went out, there was such a stomping and spitting. . . but I just had to let him stay once he was there!"

Judy made a much-anticipated return to England in October 1957, but, en route, was forced to play two stateside engagements in an effort to offset the prohibitively expensive seven weeks abroad (carrying conductor, dancers, et al.). The pre-London shows marked the onset of two years of increasing ill health and sometimes unsound behavior. The final performance in Washington, D.C., had

TOP: In the Dominion dressing room on opening night, October 16, 1957. ABOVE: With British pianist Winifred Atwell after the Dominion opening.

to be canceled when, confused and unaware from the combination of pills she had been taking, Judy quietly cut her wrists. (As on past similar occasions, she later had no knowledge of what she had done.) She opened on schedule in Philadelphia but, mid-engagement, twisted her ankle; she gave her next performance sitting down (the audience loved the informality of it all) but strained her voice, and the final shows were scratched. Such cancellations meant there were no profits to offset the expected London debt or even the money to transport Judy and company to England. Luft was bailed out by an unexpected insurance settlement on a racehorse and by a cash advance he received for committing Judy to a Brooklyn engagement the following March.

Judy reveled in her return to London and, on the first evening back, appeared at a rather formal press reception for some three hundred media representatives. The guests gave their names to a footman who made a bellowed pronouncement of their presence. Garland especially appreciated the moment that Gordon Jenkins, in London as her conductor, "found himself needing a men's room. He went up to the announcer—who was just *hooting* names through a megaphone—and asked quietly, 'Where is the men's room?' Well, the man didn't get the [first words] and just announced, 'MISTER MENSROOM!' And Gordon *ran* out of that building!"

Alan King had declined Sid's offer to join Judy's show in England, feeling "a British audience isn't going to understand a 'Catskill comic.' " But, as a favor to the Lufts (and as he was vacationing in Europe at the time), King agreed to do some advance work for them at the theatre. When he arrived, "there was an electric sign, several stories high: 'Judy Garland.' Underneath it, in seventy-five percent costar billing, was my name. It was the first time Judy had ever shared billing. She had tricked me. . . [and] I said I would open with her." As a result, King enjoyed "probably the greatest single success of my life."

Garland's show was booked into the refurbished, three-thousand-seat Dominion, and on opening day she told the *Daily Express,* "I have to be better than I've ever been tonight—it's a debt I owe. London gave me back my faith in myself." The ten Boy Friends once again introduced her; Edens's special routine for them listed "the famous falls of history" (Troy, Babylon, the Roman Empire, the Bastille) before musically mentioning ". . . *the memory we can't assuage: / She was taking her bow / When, like a clumsy cow, / She fell flat—on the Palladium stage*. . ." The chorus and curtains parted, and Judy was revealed ("taking no chances"), sitting flat on the floor and greeted by what one observer considered "a storm of applause unique in the theatre." Her act drew from the best of her earlier shows. Britain, which had never before seen a full, multi-costume and choreographed Garland production, was dazzled. At the finale, baskets and bouquets of flowers were presented to her onstage by Donna Reed, Petula Clark, and Vera Lynn.

Despite a few jabs at some of her gowns ("still the worst-dressed star") and the passing reference to her weight, reviewers termed her turn "devastating, [in a] brilliantly staged, irresistible production which leaves the audience screaming eagerly for more" *(Variety).* Maurice Kinn compared her effect to "a mass hypnosis [as] patients succumb to the administration of a crushing telepathy. No vocal performer in living memory had poured so much into a session." In the *News Chronicle,* Elizabeth Frank simply "wondered at the strange guises in which genius can appear to us."

Garland played four and a half weeks without missing a show despite severe vocal problems during the last two weeks. The sell-out crowds were virtually unanimous in their appreciation of her efforts, and Judy's humor invariably helped her over any rough spots ("I sound like Sophie Tucker's grandmother"). She was also bolstered by Jenkins's support and the estimation of her prowess that he published in *Melody Maker.* His article, headlined "A Miraculous Person," described her "tremendous musician[ship]; the whole band could tune up to her pitch . . . . [And] those electric crescendos are far beyond the scope of any mortal teacher; the talent of Judy Garland could never be learned. It must take a strange sort of person not to be moved by this great talent. I believe that people cry at Judy for the same reason that they do at sunsets, or symphonies, or cathedrals: when one is confronted with overwhelming greatness, it is impossible not to be touched."

One of King's favorite memories of "the Judy Garland days" rose from the star's continuing insomnia; she would often call him for company in the middle of the night. On one occasion during the Dominion run, they drove around London and ended up "on Curzon Street. . .where all the prostitutes used to go." Judy asked the driver to pull over and invited some of the girls for tea. "Five o'clock in the morning," relates King, "we walk into the Dorchester Hotel: Judy Garland and me and six hookers. We go up to the rooms, talked until seven o'clock. She wanted to know about them; she wasn't putting it down. It was amazing. When it was all over, I was dozing off. And she asked them, 'How much do you get for two hours' work?' And they told her. She gave me a little kick and said, 'Pay them.' And so I went to my pocket, and I gave ten pounds, and ten pounds, and ten pounds, and ten pounds. . . And then I went down to my room, alone."

Closing night saw a jubilant Judy perform the entire "Swells" routine twice after a call for an encore; two days later, she appeared in the Royal Variety Show, the 1950s equivalent of a Royal Command Performance. Introduced as "the first lady of American show business," she was recalled to the stage after her act and forced to apologize for not being able to give an extra song: "I'm told there isn't time, but it has been great fun—and a great honor." Count Basie and Mario Lanza were also on the bill, but the press proclaimed the event as "Judy Garland's Night." The Queen told her simply, "We missed you. Don't stay away so long next time."

BELOW: Rehearsing "Rock-a-Bye" at the Palladium for the Royal Variety Gala, November 18, 1957. BOTTOM LEFT: Receiving bouquets from Moira Lister, Petula Clark, Donna Reed, Alma Cogan, and Vera Lynn at the Dominion first night. BOTTOM RIGHT: With Queen Elizabeth II after the show; Mario Lanza is in the center background.

BELOW: Opening night at the Cocoanut Grove, July 23, 1958. Variety *observed, "There was no doubt. . . that the crowd was with her. It remained for Miss Garland to get ahead of the crowd and lead it, which she did; all the way. . . . She sang with open-throated power, the voice a pulsating emotional as well as musical instrument." BOTTOM: With Lana Turner after the first show.*

An exhausted Judy returned to the States, unhappily facing a season in Las Vegas. (Her engagement, opening December 26, covered the lucrative holidays, and the Flamingo refused to release her from the contract.) In addition to a new *My Fair Lady* medley, she worked in several numbers with dancer Bobby Van; *Variety* "found her in excellent voice and with a pleasing air of informality" at her premiere. Once past the opening, however, Judy encountered serious vocal trouble and canceled several shows. She returned New Year's Eve, but there was no entertaining some of the rowdy throng. She tried to reason with them, but several people threw paper hats over the footlights, inviting her to party; two women climbed onstage, began to dance, and had to be led off by the management. Increasingly distraught, Judy finally tried to shout down the crowd and was told to "shut up" by a ringsider: "Get outta here. You're too fat, and we don't wanna hear you anyway!" (Garland's later comment: "A thing like that makes it rather hard to go into 'You Made Me Love You' . . .") She left the stage and canceled the remainder of the engagement; the Flamingo unsuccessfully sued her for breach of contract, but the holiday fracas made headlines.

It was, in journalistic parlance, one of "Judy's recurrent bad times." Tired and upset with herself, her weight, and her health, she—in her own words—"just wanted to hide." There were new problems with alcohol and mounting problems with medication. Luft recalls she could charm many of those around her into procuring the prescription drugs she sought.

No small part of Judy's dissatisfaction stemmed from the ceaseless pressure to work and the constant financial crunch in which she seemed to find herself. Luft was committed to her well-being while simultaneously seeking a means to support their family and life-style; whether or not he regularly found such means, the Lufts continued to maintain a high-overhead existence. Judy's substance abuse caused family friction, as did Luft's sometimes heavy interest in horse racing. Garland filed for divorce in March 1958 (there had been a brief, earlier separation in 1956); then she and the children went off to Brooklyn for the previously arranged booking at the Town and Country. It was the first opening night she'd faced without Luft since 1951, and more difficulties developed.

There were the customary critical paeans on opening night ("Judy Garland made Brooklyn the capital of Show Business"), but she developed severe colitis and once again turned to a variety of medication. She began missing shows and, by the eleventh night, was fired by a weary club owner. Despite the dismissal, she went on that evening, sang two songs, and told the audience she'd been sacked. The microphone was abruptly turned off, and she left the stage. Subsequent rows between Garland, her agent, the club owner, and Luft (who had followed his family East) were intensified a few days later when New York State officials "escorted" Garland to court to answer a demand for back taxes. There were no funds to draw upon, and Judy was forced to turn over her jewelry and stage costumes in lieu of an assurance bond that she wouldn't leave town until the bill was paid. Luft eventually borrowed the required $9,000; by mid-April, the two had reconciled.

The media, surfeited with the Lufts' peccadillos, rushed into print with an extended analysis of Judy's woes. It was the direct (if simple) opinion of her former physician Francis Ballard that Judy required "a change of environment and associates. She's got to get out of show business, for a while at least. Fundamentally, she's strong: mentally, physically, and spiritually. If she had good, strong associates who had her well-being in mind, she could lead a normal, healthy life."

Whatever the public opinion of Judy's world, she had little recourse but to return to work. Ongoing financial demands included current and back taxes, old debts, the support of the children, and maintenance of the Luft home and necessary personal and professional staff. In May, she successfully played the outdoor Minnesota state centennial celebration, although some people in the audience suffered heatstroke in the mid-80° weather and had to be carried by stretcher from the stadium. (Garland was then accused of blasphemy by some locals, thanks to a casual between-songs comment, "My God, it's hot.") Back in Los Angeles, Capitol scheduled a new album of "happy songs" as a contrast to the preceding *Alone*. *Judy in Love* reunited her with Nelson Riddle; the eleven numbers were recorded over three nights in May and June.

Meanwhile, Luft booked her into the Los Angeles Cocoanut Grove. If successful, the show would do much to offset the months of unsavory personal and professional headlines. The American Guild of Variety Artists, however, stipulated that Judy do a one-woman show for fear supporting acts would again be thrown out of work should she fail to appear. As a result, Roger and Chuck helped assemble a one-act concert, including two new pieces of special material. The first, a wry, Garlandesque version of the "top forty" novelty "Purple People Eater," incorporated references to flying saucers, Sputniks, and such science-fiction films as *The Fly* and *I Was a Teenage Werewolf*. Even better was "When You're Smiling," in which Edens capitalized mid-song on Garland's recent crises: *"If your husband bluntly tells you you're too stout, / Don't you pout. / And for heaven's sake, retain a calm 'demeanah' / When a cop walks up and hands you a subpoena."* It made for the best kind of ingratiation; Garland used it as an opening song for several seasons.

The revitalized Judy opened at the Grove on July 23. She was heavier than ever before, but nothing seemed to matter in light of the "purest" act she'd ever offered: sixty minutes of song. The *Hollywood Reporter* asked, "What words fit Niagara and the Grand Canyon, tornadoes and volcanoes, sunsets and dawns, and Judy Garland at the top of her form? At the top of her gold-lined lungs, shoulders back, elbows out, fists clenched, [she] pelted our ears with the magic of that voice—an earthquake, a battering ram, a holocaust!" *Variety* offered a more technical appraisal: "On some notes, she opened at pianissimo and swelled to full fortissimo, a dramatic performance that few singers can match." The record-breaking business and reverberating raves were so strong that, on August 6, Capitol brought in a remote recording unit to capture the act in stereo. The strain of such steady vocalizing brought on laryngitis, however, and *Garland at the Grove* featured the singer in less than top form. (Capitol's liner notes falsely implied that the album had been made opening night.)

The media quickly labeled the Grove Judy's latest "comeback," and another resurgence evolved. Luft and Chicago impresario Henry Zelzer arranged to take Orchestra Hall for a week of similar Garland concerts in September, thus avoiding the expense of a full variety show and the hovering AGVA threat of two months earlier. The Nelson Riddle Orchestra and Alan King filled the entire first act, and King was overjoyed when asked to partner Judy for the "Swells" finale in act two. When it came time for rehearsal in Chicago, King remembers that "the only piano we could get was in the window of a Steinway piano store. They opened the store, and there we were, Judy and I, in the window, learning steps. Great

TOP: With Liza at the Grove opening night party, July 23, 1958. Judy had sung "Swanee" near the close of the show, then got her twelve-year-old daughter onstage for a duet reprise. When they finished, Judy wondered aloud, "What should I do next?"; Jerry Lewis carolled, "Why don't you sing 'Swanee,' lady?" ABOVE: Garland was greeted on her Chicago arrival by teenage fan Joan Finkler, September 1958.

BELOW: *At her Chicago press conference, September 1958.* BOTTOM: *With George Jessel at the Masquers Club salute; her plaque read, "To Judy Garland/Over the Rainbow/A Star Was Born." Jessel recounted his contribution to the Garland legend and added, "But she would be able to make you tingle when she sang, make you laugh and cry with her, if her name was Frances Gumm, Minnie Ha-Ha, or Algrena Handelpotz."*

fun." Garland opened to the biggest advance in the hall's history and played to 17,500 customers. Zelzer estimated that six thousand people had to be turned away, and the *Sun-Times* recorded "the kind of audience reaction usually reserved for the World Series. [The crowd] came running down the aisles to shake the hand of 'Miss Show Business.' " The act featured Judy's dry reminiscence of playing the Oriental Theatre "in 1872"; in another effective bit near the end of the show, she would ask someone in the front row for help in brushing the hobo blacking from her teeth. Edens's new finale arrangement of "Chicago" was replete with local references and proved to be the kind of showstopper that Judy could—and eventually did—sing everywhere.

Zelzer specialized in booking classical music artists, but he never forgot Garland's engagement ("my hottest ticket"). He put her picture on his office wall "between Toscanini and Schnabel. She's a real pro," he said, "and I'm proud to add her to the famous names." When local highbrow aficionados remonstrated with him, he retorted that Judy had done what classical music sometimes couldn't do—sell out Orchestra Hall at $7.50 a ticket.

Judy next took the new act to the Las Vegas Sands, where customarily blasé critic Ralph Pearl devoted a "creative writing" column to the show: "You sit there completely awed as your spine turns to jelly, and the roots of your thinning hair ache and stand straight up in the air. . . She stands up there, no bigger than a fair-sized jockey, [and] every other singer seems to fade into quiet but definite obscurity. She has no equal! Of that you can be assured!"

In an echo of the 1952 Friars' salute, the Hollywood Masquers Club celebrated Judy's new success at an October 24 dinner. George Jessel emceed and Sammy Davis, Jr., sang; but, with Edens at the piano, it was left to Judy to wrap up the evening. The *Hollywood Reporter* quietly compared her performance to "Margot Fonteyn dancing Giselle, [or] Laurette Taylor in *The Glass Menagerie.*" Judy repaid Davis's homage by joining him in a benefit for the San Bernardino Community Hospital on November 15. His introduction gave further indication of her reputation with her peers: "[She] holds a special place in the heart of everyone in show business. Not for any sentimental reasons, but purely and simply for what she is, what she gives, the tremendous talent that is hers. There will be other performers in the future, but none will ever equal her. She is one of a kind, there are no imitations, just one: Judy Garland, the greatest entertainer in the world."

From December through mid-January, Judy learned and recorded *The Letter,* a new musical score written by Gordon Jenkins. It was the composer's intention "to create a whole show written especially for records. . . [and] writing for a star of Judy's magnitude is just about the most exciting work anyone can have." Her songs traced a woman's memories of a Manhattan romance and were interspersed with narration by John Ireland as the lover who seeks a reconciliation with her by mail. Judy commented at the time, "I know that everyone involved in those long sessions feels that we were creating something very special." Garland especially enjoyed Jenkins's "The Fight," which included a kiss for the two protagonists. "We really kissed, you know—and I didn't mind at *all.* John's really quite good-looking. And Sid sat up in the technicians' booth and *glowered* at us!" Jenkins described her work as "beyond the capabilities of most singers," and Capitol packaged the album handsomely, even affixing to every jacket an envelope that included a transcript of Ireland's "letter." Reviewers, however, disliked Jenkins's

LEFT: With Gordon Jenkins and John Ireland at the Capitol sessions for The Letter, *January 1959. RIGHT: Garland and Alan King, "A Couple of Swells" at the Met, May 1959.*

"maudlin" storyline. One addressed Judy personally: "[This] might be all right for a lesser talent but, honey, not for you." Her voice, however, won unqualified praise.

Garland went on to her Miami cabaret debut at the Fontainebleau on February 17, and critics were astounded at the difference between the Judy they expected and the Judy they saw—a measure of the contrast between sensational headlines and sensational performance. Morris McLemore wrote in the *News*, "Frankly, I'm ignorant about the things Miss Garland is supposed to be guilty of. Mostly, it seems to me, she is guilty of packing in crowds of people to see and hear her despite the rather wide-spread belief that day-to-day living is too much for [her]." In the *Herald*, George Bourke labeled himself "a well-wishing doubtful Thomas at the start [and] a completely sold and devoted Boswell, eager to sing deserved praises, at the finish."

Luft meanwhile had signed Judy into New York's Metropolitan Opera House, another prestige booking and "the kind of show Judy believed she deserved." He arranged for Alan King and John W. Bubbles (the original Sportin' Life of *Porgy and Bess*) as her prime support, Jenkins as conductor, and "a company of one hundred"—singers, dancers, musicians—to assist. It was a vastly expensive production and the most ambitious revue Garland had attempted. But she voiced her joy at leaving "the night club racket: I hate doing two shows a night. It's wonderful and fun to work yourself up to a single performance, to give your all. But you can't generate that kind of excitement twice in the same evening—at least I can't."

There were, however, problems in the undertaking. In a later account of Judy's appearance, Rick Skye noted that no other popular singing entertainer had ever attempted a Met engagement. "Sir Harry Lauder performed for one evening in the 1920s, but he was primarily a comic and not under pressure to compete vocally in a musical temple like the Metropolitan. [Additionally] the staid Met Board of Directors had made it a practice to keep the house dark while the resident company was on tour, allowing only the occasional Bolshoi Ballet season or benefit performance." (Luft had gotten around the Board's stand by producing the New York engagement as a benefit for the Children's Asthma Research Institute at Denver.)

Judy at the Met, 1959: TOP: *"Swanee."* ABOVE: *"Born in a Trunk." The New York* Mirror *enthused, "The lyrical lady. . . glittered as she showered fans with vocal thrills. . . . When she gets into the singing groove, nobody—but nobody—can touch her."* Variety *commended her "vocal prowess, delivery, and projection, characteristic broken notes and all. . . amid cascades of handclapping fore, amidships, and aft."*

Edens and Leonard Gershe wrote a script that interlarded operatic jokes with the traditional Garland vaudeville: King entered with a brief parody of *Pagliacci,* and Bubbles soft-shoed to music from *Carmen.* When the chorus (in the guise of Met first-nighters) asked Garland to identify herself, the response came in the *La Bohème* melody for "Si, mi chiamano Mimi" ("I am called Mimi"): *"They call me Judy. . . but my children call me 'Mama.'"* King and Bubbles did some forty minutes of their comedy and dance specialties in the first act, but Edens had also provided Judy with an entire set of new solos: Cole Porter's "I Happen to Like New York," a remarkably rousing "Wonderful Guy," and a medley of "Almost Like Being in Love"/"This Can't Be Love." In a matching tuxedo, she joined Bubbles for "Me and My Shadow," following his choreography in pantomime. Their encore duet of "A Shine on Your Shoes"/"Shoe Shine Boy" involved much additional staging and—from underneath a partially raised curtain behind them—the legs of the chorus in accompaniment.

The second act was mostly Judy: "When You're Smiling," "The Man That Got Away," a medley from *The Letter,* and a virtually complete re-creation of "Born in a Trunk" (which encompassed multiple sets, a number of fast costume changes, and a full-stage reprise of "Swanee"). King came back for "A Couple of Swells," and Garland finished with the Olio, "Rainbow," and a five-song Jolson tribute.

Judy's "Opera House tour" broke in in Baltimore, and the local impresario called it "the best show we've ever had." Critics concurred but expressed surprise that Judy lipsynched to a prerecorded track for much of "Born in a Trunk." The approach had been adopted because of staging complexities, but after the notices, Richard Barstow restaged the medley with multiple microphones, and Judy thereafter sang the entire sequence live.

The show opened for seven nights at the Met on May 11, 1959; while enjoying the production, critics reserved their rhapsodies for Garland. The *Journal-American* declared, "Her full, thrilling, throbbing voice welled up in the vast cathedral of vocal culture, filling every bit of space above the orchestra, the boxes, and family circle. Not even Maria Callas ever got a better reception." In *The New Yorker,* Kenneth Tynan mused: "The engagement was limited; the pleasure it gave was not. When the voice pours out, as rich and pleading as ever, we know where, and how moved, we are—in the presence of a star, and embarrassed by tears."

Each evening after the show, fans filled the entire block around the stage door, offering a community sing of Garland songs. One night, climbing a "Swanee" crescendo, they slid in under pitch on the final high note. Sid Luft suddenly raised the dressing-room window above them and leaned out with a grin: "Judy says you're flat!" The crowd delighted in the criticism.

Box-office receipts for the Met topped $190,000 (per *Variety,* "One of the all-time one-week takes in any theatre"). The show moved on to the Chicago Civic Opera House, where critics—accustomed to the simplicity of Judy's 1958 concerts—were divided. "Miss Garland has been 'produced,' but no one needed it less," wrote Roger Dettmer. Richard Christiansen, however, found her "something for which theatres were built—a constant outpouring of the best a performer has to give that makes an audience roar with excitement and sheer joy."

Her ensuing stand in San Francisco was reviewed by the *Examiner* with the observation: "[Garland] had her audience in a state akin to the fever that hypoed the Oklahoma land rush. If they had taken out their uppers, removed their toupees, and tossed same over the footlights, it wouldn't have surprised me."

LEFT: Judy feeds baby Joe Luft while his sister Lorna perches on a makeup table, 1955. BELOW RIGHT: "A Couple of Swells" publicity portrait for Garland's TV debut, 1955. BELOW CENTER: David Stone Martin artwork used for Garland programs, posters, and ads in the late 1950s and early 1960s. BOTTOM LEFT: 1961 tour flyer for the "world's greatest entertainer."

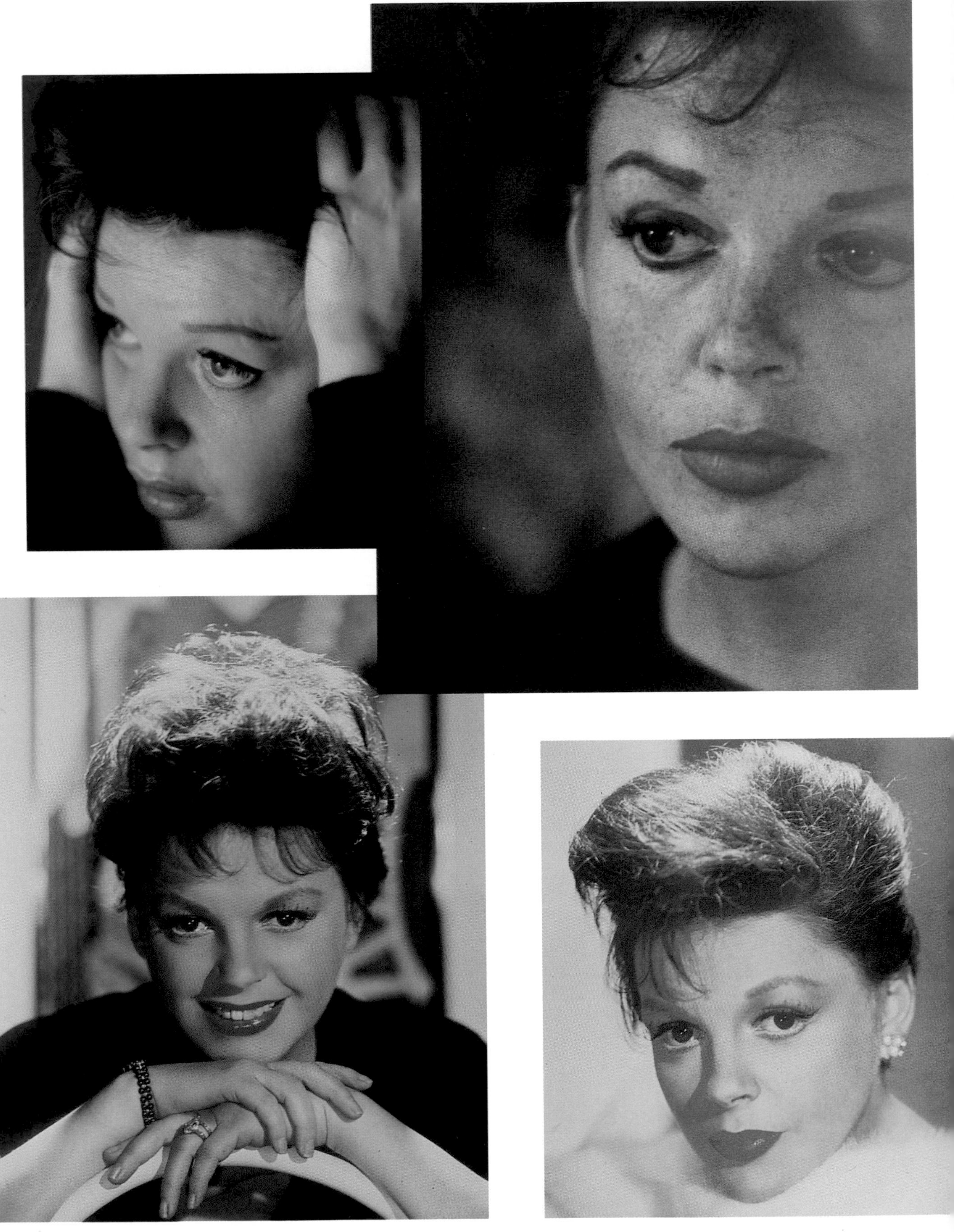

FACING PAGE: Publicity portraits, 1961–62.

Garland's second concert at Carnegie Hall, May 21, 1961. LEFT: Act one, BELOW RIGHT: act two, and BOTTOM RIGHT: final bows. BOTTOM LEFT: A jubilant Judy leaving the hall after her debut, April 23, 1961.

ABOVE: *Dean Martin, Judy, and Frank Sinatra at dress rehearsal for her TV special, January 1962.* *FAR LEFT:* *Ad art for the same show.* *LEFT:* *Publicity portrait, 1961.*

FACING PAGE: *Judy sings "When You're Smiling" in the opening segment of the program. Though telecast on CBS, the special was taped at NBC studios in Burbank, hence the camera insignia.*

DRINK
Coca-Cola
IN BOTTLES

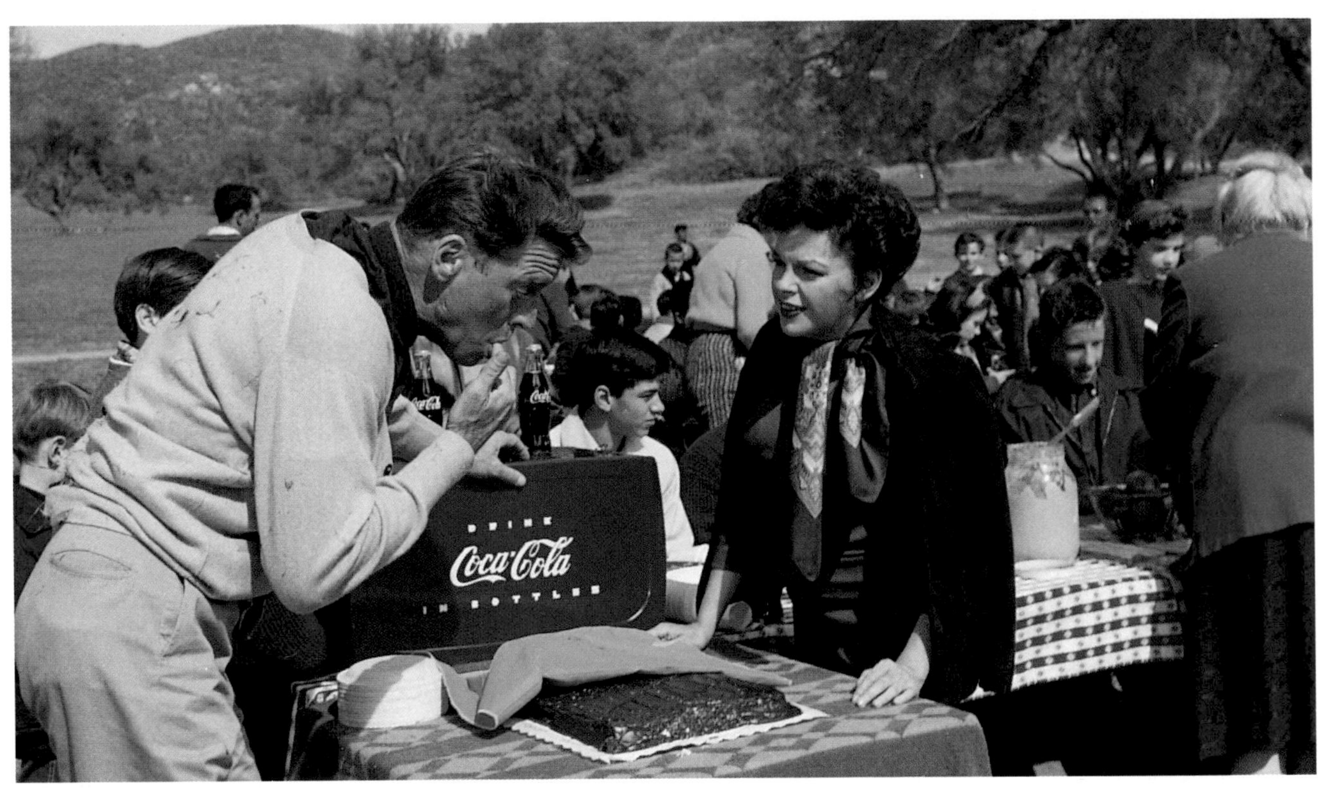

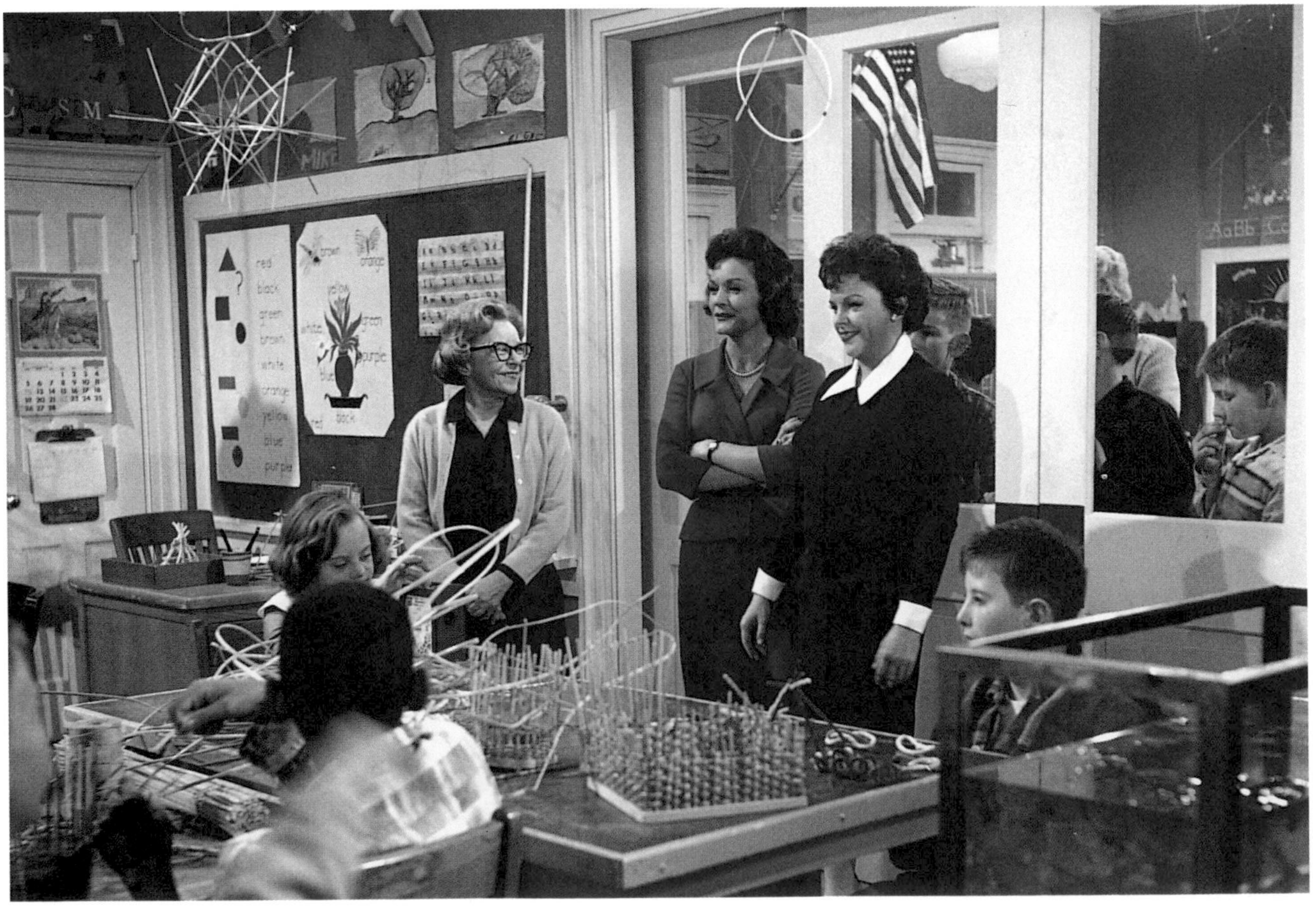
red
black
green
brown
white
orange
yellow
blue
purple

FACING PAGE, TOP: With Burt Lancaster and BOTTOM: with Gloria McGehee in A Child Is Waiting, *United Artists/1963.*

RIGHT: With Dirk Bogarde and BOTTOM LEFT: with Gregory Phillips and British schoolboys in makeup for "H.M.S. Pinafore" in I Could Go On Singing, *United Artists/1963. BELOW AND BOTTOM RIGHT: Singing "By Myself" in the same film.*

LEFT: "Jenny Bowman" arrives an hour late for her Palladium concert in I Could Go On Singing, *United Artists/1963. BELOW AND BOTTOM LEFT AND RIGHT: Onstage at the Palladium for the title-song sequence.*

That engagement also saw the debut of another appropriate Edens arrangement. Both he and Judy had been at MGM during the filming of *San Francisco* (1936), the melodrama in which Jeanette MacDonald heartened survivors of the 1906 earthquake with an impassioned hymn of hope. Edens rewrote and augmented MacDonald's title song for Judy, including a tongue-in-cheek verse that Garland performed with perfect irreverence: "*. . . I* never *will forget / how that* brave *Jeanette / just* stood *there—in the* ruins— */ and* sang. . . / [as a classical music trill:] A-a-a-a-and *sang: San Francisco, open your Golden Gate. . . !"* It became a permanent part of her repertoire.

The tour ended at the Los Angeles Shrine Auditorium, which, according to the *Times*, "echoed and trembled with applause, stomping and shouts. The best of the [Garland] acts are all here." Despite its popular and critical success, however, the show's costs and old debts once again eliminated any profit for the Lufts. What was more important was the growing problem of Judy's health. Throughout the tour, critics had, however gently, made reference to her "clearly desperate battle with the calories" and resemblance to a "seemingly terrified. . .oversized kewpie doll"; they found "her few, spare movements were automaton-like." Sonny Gallagher, a long-time admirer who knew Garland's work well, confirms each estimation: "For the most part, Judy just stood there and sang, raising one arm to accentuate song climaxes. [Her body] was unbelievably bloated, and the face appeared to be of plastic." Judy, of course, was more aware of all of this than anyone else. Dieting had become inexplicably ineffective, and performing took on new terrors when she sometimes felt so nauseous onstage she was afraid of becoming physically ill in front of the audience. Luft later commented, "Judy was so sick, and the show was so complicated and demanding of her, I don't know where the energy came from." King recalls, "Judy seemed to be in pain. She had such stage fright. . . You literally had to drag her out there."

By autumn 1959, Garland weighed more than 180 pounds, and her physical and emotional agonies were quite possibly heightened by whatever prescription medication she was taking to ease her fears. The increasingly alarmed Luft managed to get two doctors to the house, introducing them to Judy as business associates. After meeting her, they privately told him that Judy's weight was water retention and that she was dangerously ill.

Sid contrived to get her to a doctor whom she trusted in New York, and she entered Doctors Hospital on November 18. Tests revealed that her liver, affected by years of medication and alcohol, was inflamed and more than four times its normal size. She began emergency treatment for hepatitis, but her condition was increasingly critical. "I looked so big," Judy recalled, "you'd have thought I was going to have a million babies, and I was in such pain. My whole body was filled with poison." Several doctors felt sure the ailment would kill her; twenty quarts of fluid were slowly drained from her body.

After several weeks, Garland's chief specialist joined Luft at her bedside. The doctor felt she was beginning to rally, but gravely and regretfully told the thirty-seven-year-old woman, "For the rest of your life, all your physical activity must be curtailed. You are a *permanent* semi-invalid. It goes without saying that under *no* circumstances can you *ever* work again." Judy, who had listened quietly, attentively, fell back among her pillows. Then there was a weak but gleeful cry: "Whoopee!"

The Met Tour, 1959. BELOW: *Backstage in Chicago, dressed for her opening numbers.* BOTTOM: *Arriving in San Francisco. The San Francisco* Examiner *critic marveled, "The hold Miss Garland has on her audience is almost hypnotic and would put Mesmer to shame."*

Chapter Seven
World's Greatest Entertainer

FACING PAGE: *Onstage at the Sahara Hotel, Las Vegas, September–October 1962. Columnist Ralph Pearl reviewed Garland's appearances in the desert from 1956–67 and later called her "my absolute unequivocal choice as the greatest entertainer I ever saw. Talk about charisma, she invented the word. And it should have been retired from the English language as soon as she died."* BELOW: *Singing "It Never Was You" at the London Palladium, August 28, 1960. Dirk Bogarde had suggested the format of the show; in gratitude, she called him onstage while she performed "the song she knew I loved above all others."*

The doctor's dictum was not publicized, but it didn't matter. Given the preceding three years of negative headlines, Garland had already been written off. Popular and media opinion—comparatively in her corner after she left MGM in 1950—now held, in effect, that she had blown all her chances. (As Judy wryly put it, "I was someone who *had been* a movie star.") She finally left Doctors Hospital on January 5, 1960, but despite the uncertainty of her health and professional future, the subsequent months marked her most sound, relaxed, and secure adult interlude. Except for a small prescribed dosage of Ritalin, she was medication-free.

By April, she felt well enough to work on a limited basis, and although Luft vigorously pursued several business propositions of his own, there was—as ever—the pressing need for money. Judy's first job came when Columbia asked her to sing the André Previn/Dory Langdon "Far Away Part of Town" for the soundtrack of the musical film *Pepe.* (According to Langdon, studio executives felt Garland was too heavy to actually appear on screen.) In June, she spent three evenings recording a new Capitol album, *That's Entertainment,* later reviewed as "beautifully sung" by the *American Record Guide.* In July, flanked on the dais by John F. Kennedy and Adlai Stevenson, she appeared at a Democratic fund-raiser just prior to the 1960 national convention. Garland's refreshened voice and robust demeanor were such a hit that one columnist drily suggested she could win the vice presidential nomination.

Judy's newfound fitness was further demonstrated when she overcame a lifelong fear of flying and set off alone for a London and Rome vacation. A crowded press reception greeted her arrival in England, and the media came away with the impression that Garland "was the only calm person present." She told them, "I feel marvelous since I've gotten over my illness. I've had a chance to relax and take a good look at myself—I've lost a lot of my fears and anxieties."

In early August, she did four more nights of recording; the London sessions were devised to capture Garland's standards in stereo for the first time. At one point, she buoyantly encouraged her backup chorus of eight to "sing a little louder—you've got to sound like twenty-four people!" On "I Happen to Like New York," the chorus leader suggested he would have the group cut off their final note when Judy ended hers. She replied, "Oh, I don't stop. I hold it through to the end." The chorus collapsed in admiration. (Much of the material from the sessions was duplicated on a live recording made at Carnegie Hall the following April. As a result, most of the London tracks remained unreleased—except in limited 1970s issues—until 1991.)

Sid and the children eventually joined Judy in London, and they made plans to settle there permanently. Garland also decided she was ready to resume stage work, and close friend Dirk Bogarde suggested she return to the Palladium, encouraging her to appear without the supporting "Hungarians with dogs and ventriloquists: just you and a whopping big orchestra." Luft worried it might be too much; "I didn't want her to work, but she was in such good shape, it was kind

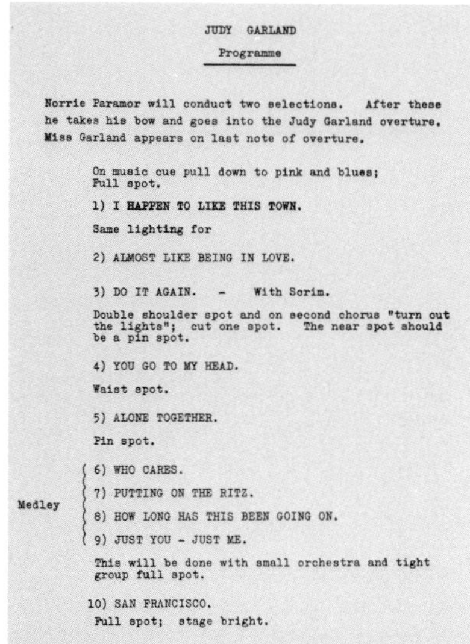

JUDY GARLAND

Programme

Norrie Paramor will conduct two selections. After these he takes his bow and goes into the Judy Garland overture. Miss Garland appears on last note of overture.

On music cue pull down to pink and blues;
Full spot.

1) I HAPPEN TO LIKE THIS TOWN.

Same lighting for

2) ALMOST LIKE BEING IN LOVE.

3) DO IT AGAIN. - With Scrim.

Double shoulder spot and on second chorus "turn out the lights"; cut one spot. The near spot should be a pin spot.

4) YOU GO TO MY HEAD.

Waist spot.

5) ALONE TOGETHER.

Pin spot.

Medley
6) WHO CARES.
7) PUTTING ON THE RITZ.
8) HOW LONG HAS THIS BEEN GOING ON.
9) JUST YOU - JUST ME.

This will be done with small orchestra and tight group full spot.

10) SAN FRANCISCO.

Full spot; stage bright.

11) YOU'LL NEVER WALK ALONE.

Blue lighting effect and a full spot.

12) THAT'S ENTERTAINMENT.

All lights up and full spot.

- Intermission -

13) WHEN YOU'RE SMILING.

Full spot.

14) I CAN'T GIVE YOU ANYTHING BUT LOVE.

Waist spot.

15) COME RAIN - COME SHINE.

Stage predominantly blue with a waist spot.

16) a) IT NEVER WAS YOU. b) ONE FOR MY BABY.
c) BOY NEXT DOOR. d) NEARER. e) IF LOVE WERE ALL.
f) A FOGGY DAY.

Only with piano. Scrim orchestra. Full pink spot.

17) ZING WENT THE STRINGS OF MY HEART.

Full spot; stage bright.

18) STORMY WEATHER.

Stage predominantly blue. Shoulder spot.

Medley
19) YOU MADE ME LOVE YOU.
Waist spot going into full spot on
20) FOR ME AND MY GAL.
staying in full spot for
21) TROLLEY SONG.

22) ROCK-A-BYE MY BABY.

Waist spot.
(In second chorus when Miss Garland raises her arm and sings "Oh, weep no more.." - full spot.)

- OFF -

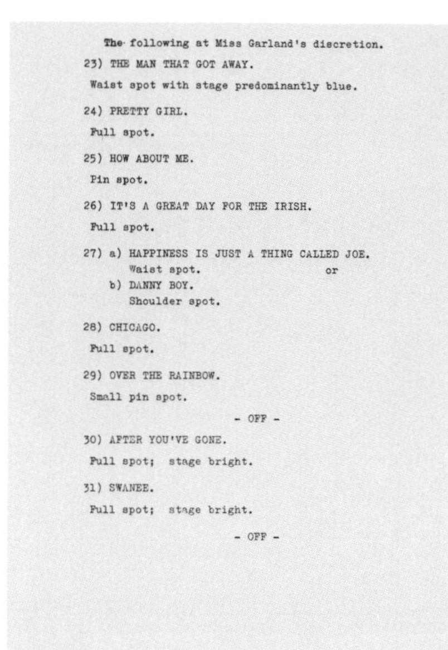

The following at Miss Garland's discretion.

23) THE MAN THAT GOT AWAY.

Waist spot with stage predominantly blue.

24) PRETTY GIRL.

Full spot.

25) HOW ABOUT ME.

Pin spot.

26) IT'S A GREAT DAY FOR THE IRISH.

Full spot.

27) a) HAPPINESS IS JUST A THING CALLED JOE.
Waist spot. or
b) DANNY BOY.
Shoulder spot.

28) CHICAGO.

Full spot.

29) OVER THE RAINBOW.

Small pin spot.

- OFF -

30) AFTER YOU'VE GONE.

Full spot; stage bright.

31) SWANEE.

Full spot; stage bright.

- OFF -

TOP, LEFT TO RIGHT: *Order sheet and lighting cues for Garland's first one-woman concerts, autumn 1960.* ABOVE: *In rehearsal in Paris, October 1960.*

of miraculous.'' He took the theatre for one night, and the date ''sold out in a day. It started another part of her career: instead of vaudeville or revue, it was now a concert.''

Backed by the orchestra of Norrie Paramor (who had conducted the Capitol recordings three weeks earlier), Judy gave her first one-woman show on Sunday, August 28: a two-hour-plus performance of some thirty songs. She planned the program herself for, as Luft points out, ''She had so much experience. She knew what an opening number was, and she knew what the second should be. She knew exactly what to do and where she was going—better than anybody.'' Dressed comfortably in a short black sheath and blue satin jacket, Garland offered a first act of twelve songs, highlighted midway by a jazzy, four-number jam session. (It was a self-admitted change-of-pace from her usual ''very sad, tragic songs—or *marches*.'') Just before intermission, she also sang a dramatic ''You'll Never Walk Alone'' in tribute to lyricist Oscar Hammerstein II, who had died five days earlier. For act two, she scampered out in sequinned top and black slacks and did another nineteen numbers, several with just the pianist in accompaniment.

The show marked a turning point for Garland. Her new physical strength and mental outlook produced onstage a woman somehow in greater command of her talent, humor, and personality—and unencumbered by dancers and production value. Though the ebullience, enthusiasm, and appeal of Baby Gumm and Dorothy Gale were never more apparent, they came with a self-awareness, maturity, and joy that gave a less sentimental, more authoritative adult aura to Judy's presentation. The Palladium audience was immediately aware of the difference, and their response indicated this as the show progressed; the London critics were overpowered. ''Incredible,'' wrote Jack Hutton, ''to see so many stars wallowing in unashamed admiration for another. Incredible to hear [her] magic set fire to the last chorus of some square old song and watch the audience burst at the seams and applaud bars before the end.'' The *Herald* recorded, ''Her reception shook stagehands hardened by years of hysterical audience reaction. The door keeper gasped, 'I haven't heard a reception like that since Nora Bayes was here in 1923.' ''

Judy repeated the show the following week in even more relaxed (and thus more hysteria-inducing) form; at the finish, the audience surged down the aisles to congratulate her over the footlights, much as they had at the Robin Hood Dell seventeen years earlier. Later, hundreds sang "For She's a Jolly Good Fellow" in the streets around the Palladium as her car drove off.

On the strength of such success, Luft arranged for Garland's Paris debut at the Palais de Chaillot in early October. He remembers having "to paper the house on opening night; the French couldn't make up their minds about Judy." But she came out to face a crowd of fans and Paris society with "Bon Jour, Paris" and, in the end, won eight curtain calls, an onstage embrace from Maurice Chevalier, and (per *Variety*) "one of the first standing ovations for a singing artist since the War. Her kind of gifts broke the lingo barrier with ease." Several papers ran their reviews on the front page—a unique acknowledgment of Garland's show as a major news story that would recur many times throughout the 1960s—and the Palais was mobbed for her second concert two nights later.

Luft booked Judy throughout the autumn, but her schedule was a light, easygoing one, and there were fewer than a dozen other appearances between early October and mid-December. On behalf of John Kennedy, she gave performances at United States military installations in Germany, urging enlisted men and women to cast absentee ballots for the Democratic presidential candidate. She also appeared at another Royal Variety Show at the Palladium and, after kicking off her high heels for "Swanee," made a memorable final bow in her stockinged feet to the Queen Mother. On December 10, Judy's "midnight matinee" in Amsterdam was broadcast live on Netherlands radio. When she ran out of orchestrations after twenty-eight songs, the crowd insisted she repeat "San Francisco" from the first half of the show. (Audience response during Garland's 1960–61 concerts frequently required such a reprise.) Dutch radio commentators stood in the wings and, between songs, described the onstage events to their listeners: "[She] gets more power as she goes further into her show. Everyone is walking to the stage to cheer and applaud, stamping on the floor. . . They can't get enough." By the finale, both stage and Garland were heaped with flowers.

LEFT: Advertising flyer for one of her "Koncerts for Kennedy." In addition to her standards, Judy offered the special material Kennedy campaign song, "High Hopes" by Sammy Cahn and Jimmy Van Heusen. RIGHT: At Wiesbaden.

KENNEDY
FOR PRESIDENT
RALLY
Wednesday October 26 2000 hours
KURHAUS WIESBADEN
HEAR
JUDY GARLAND
(in person)
SING YOUR FAVORITE SONGS
This gathering will be shown on Nation-wide T-V in the States!!
Here's your chance to let the folks back home see you!!
Fun for all!
EVERY BODY WELCOME
FREE ADMISSION

BELOW: Arriving in Amsterdam, December 9, 1960. BOTTOM: At the Golden Globe Awards with frequent professional aide Vern Alves and Polly Bergen (the latter was then married to Freddie Fields), March 16, 1961. Garland presented a special honor to Stanley Kramer, who noted, "It's not given to many people to receive an award from the world's greatest entertainer—Frances Gumm."

It was also in December that the resurgent Garland became a client of Freddie Fields Associates, a new artists' management company created by a former MCA agent. Occupied with business of his own, Luft was (at least initially) delighted to relinquish the job of handling Judy's career, and Fields immediately booked her for further European singing engagements. He also began negotiations for her appearance in the London production of *The Unsinkable Molly Brown.*

All his initial plans were canceled, however, when the momentum of Judy's foreign success brought her back to the United States on New Year's Eve, 1960. Stanley Kramer offered her "a brief, but highly dramatic" film role in the all-star *Judgment at Nuremberg,* and Fields quickly arranged for nineteen American concert dates to bookend the March 1961 shooting schedule. Garland's anticipated stage triumphs would not only help establish his office but enable her to chip away at some $300,000 worth of debts.

The second concert of the tour, at the Catskills' Concord Hotel on February 12, marked Judy's first association with Mort Lindsey—possibly her finest conductor and orchestrator. An old MCA client, Lindsey was summoned to rehearsals for the show by Fields's new partner, David Begelman, when the hotel's musical director was unable to handle Garland's difficult arrangements. Lindsey immediately evaluated the situation, brought in a new drummer, and was running down the charts when, as he affectionately remembers, Judy "came in in a fur coat; she looked like a little teddy bear." Although he had forsaken conducting chores to pursue music composition a year earlier, Lindsey was talked into doing the Concord show by Fields and Begelman. By the time Garland began the major portion of her tour two months later, he was installed as her permanent musical director and (eventually) orchestrator/arranger; together they went on to do well over one hundred live performances, two motion pictures, several recording sessions, and more than thirty hours of television. He recalls, "People would say Judy was difficult. I found her easier to work for than anybody. She appreciated what you did; she made your stuff come alive—even more than you'd hope. And she was just as kind as could be to my family and wife."

For many, Garland hit the apex of her adult career during the 1960–61 tour, especially given her recorded performance-for-posterity at Carnegie Hall on April 23. The show had been sold out since Fields announced it weeks earlier; a return date on May 21 was also sold out. Judy arrived at the theatre in a police-escorted limousine around 6 P.M. on the twenty-third, and she got her first look at the famous auditorium near the conclusion of Lindsey's six-hour orchestra rehearsal. "This is just beautiful," she marveled. "I've never seen anything like it." In hair curlers, slacks, and jacket, she sang "When You're Smiling" so that Capitol engineers could do a sound check; the label was recording the concert for a possible album. At one point during the brief rehearsal, Garland overheard a Capitol technician telling the brass section and drummer to "hold it down" so as not to come through too strong on the tapes. She quickly asserted, "Oh, no—this is my night. I want to hear the drums!" She later recalled, "The poor engineer went home with migraine!"

By eight o'clock, the streets around Seventh Avenue and Fifty-seventh Street were jammed. The crowd included virtually all of Broadway's top performers enjoying their Sunday night off; other stars had flown in from Los Angeles. The Carnegie doors were kept closed until the last possible moment, after which the audience filed in with an almost religious anticipation. By the time Lindsey raised his baton for the overture at 8:40 P.M., the atmosphere—as always at a Garland show—was palpably, tangibly electric.

Time later described the reaction to Judy's unannounced entrance: "She got, without opening her mouth, what it takes Renata Tebaldi two and a half hours of Puccini to achieve: a standing, screaming ovation that lasted almost five minutes." Garland could do little more than beam and bob her bows, finally approaching the microphone with a giggling "Oh, my. . . ," mock-clapping back at the crowd. The program and response were much the same as she had been giving and getting for the preceding eight months but here, before her peers and the New York press, she offered final, awesome proof of her new performance level. Roger Edens reflected, "I still don't believe anything like this could happen. She said, 'Let's do it,' as though she had never done it before." Kay Thompson felt that Judy had never "realized what she could do" until her 1961 appearances. And when the show-wise Carnegie audience became aware of her realization—and coupled that with their own vision of Garland the compleat artist and the seemingly healthy woman onstage—their reaction was best summarized by journalist James Goode: "Everyone had wanted her to be happy for so long that, when she was, it was more than they could stand."

Judy closed her first act with "San Francisco" and (as in the other concerts on the tour) exhaustedly made her way backstage for intermission. Her recuperative powers astounded those around her (she once quipped to Shana Alexander, "You know, I'm like Rocky Graziano"), and within twenty minutes, she was recoiffed and recostumed for the second act, bounding out onstage with "That's Entertainment." Two songs later, she won her second standing ovation for "Come Rain or Come Shine"; there was a third after "Rock-a-Bye." By then, hundreds of patrons were streaming down the aisles to the stage, and countless hands reached out to touch Judy as she swept along the footlights, taking her bows. Requests came from all over the house, and when she could be heard, Garland offered what became a legendary rejoinder: "I'll sing 'em all, and we'll stay all night." The roar in reply was shattering.

After "Rainbow," "Swanee," and a multitude of curtain calls, Judy left the stage, and the houselights were brought up. But the audience refused to retreat and called her back. Minutes later, she returned, admitting that she was nearly out of orchestrations: "We don't have much more." A voice from one of the boxes implored, "Just stand there." She wrapped up with "After You've Gone" and "Chicago," later confessing to Dirk Bogarde that she was, by that point, "dead beat. I couldn't get my breath. Then something fantastic happened. After the first verse [of 'Chicago'], when I sing 'And you will never guess *where*,' right there, in the silence, one voice from 'way out in the dark, called out *'Where?'*—right on beat—and saved me. I took it from him, and I *went!* I have tried to find out who he was to thank him . . . God sent that voice."

There were standing ovations after each encore; Rock Hudson lifted Liza, Lorna, and Joe onstage for a bow with their mother, and the concert finally ended at 11:20 P.M. More than a thousand people gathered at the stage door on Fifty-sixth Street; when Judy appeared in her dressing-room window to blow kisses, they shouted "Bravo!"

The Carnegie Hall concert became an immediate show-business legend. Those who participated in the event have, for more than thirty years, continued to wonder at the memory. Critic Rex Reed, then new to New York, flatly states, "I've never

TOP: Backstage in Buffalo, April 6, 1961. ABOVE: At the Carnegie Hall makeup mirror, May 21, 1961.

Judy at Carnegie Hall. LEFT: *During act one of the first concert, April 23, 1961.* RIGHT: *The second show, May 21. Judy later recalled that as she was standing in the wings before her debut, "I kept thinking of who was out front and kept telling myself, 'This ain't Dallas, kiddo! This is Carnegie Hall. . .and I ain't Heifetz or Rubinstein!' "*

seen an audience of more important, celebrated, influential, powerful, wealthy, jaded people in my life, grouped together in one setting, decimated to such a state of universal hysteria as I saw that night." Garland's publicist John Springer specifically remembers "Leonard Bernstein, the tears running down his face, screaming. . . [and] Hank Fonda, normally an impassive man, 'bravoing.' " Singer Anna Maria Alberghetti, soprano star of Broadway's *Carnival,* had been coerced into attending the concert; she always reserved Sundays to conserve her voice and strength for the eight performances of the week ahead. But, by Garland's third number, she recalls, she was "shouting and screaming along with everyone else, regardless of what I was doing to my voice." Mort Lindsey remembers, "This was her crowd—the first five or ten or fifteen rows were the cream of show business—and she sure delivered." Sid Luft had spent the twenty-four hours prior to the concert keeping Garland company, ensuring her peace of mind, seeing to it that she "got a lot of rest and wasn't disturbed by calls or anything." As a result, she "was in great, great spirits; the sound engineers said it was the most miraculous thing they'd ever heard at a recording session. With all her experience, she just gathered herself together and gave off all this unbelievable energy and timing; everything that was behind her in her life came bursting forth that night."

The reviews attempted to explain the quality of Judy's performance and the reaction it won: "The toughest town in the world broke down and cried Sunday night. It was a religious ceremony" (the New York *Post*). "I will probably be telling my children about it years from now. The condition in which Miss Garland left her audience is totally indescribable. She might have been a great faith healer endowed with magical powers, so urgent was their need to get close to her . . . There is no other woman in show business" (the Long Island *Daily Press*). "This is what singing popular songs was meant to be—not the masked, introspective interpretations singers these days affect" (the New York *Morning Telegraph*). "No other performer weaves that spell. Her fellow pros have no rivalry where

LEFT: Act two of Judy at Carnegie Hall. RIGHT: As the press put it: "Judy and Her Glad Hand," greeting fans across the footlights. Journalist Rowland Barber described "the spectacle that greeted her first entrance: three thousand people lifted simultaneously out of their seats as if by a massive, invisible magnet, and a deafening storm of applause." Garland decided "right away that they liked me and I loved them, and we had ourselves a ball."

she is concerned. All of them agree that *she is the greatest"* (the *Hollywood Reporter*).

Each of Judy's 1960–61 concerts garnered much the same audience response, and Garland was invariably in top (or near-top) form. Her approach throughout remained informal as she alternately sang at the microphone stand or strutted and danced across the stage. The songs were interspersed with perfectly volleyed replies to audience requests, or expertly told, self-deprecating stories about her comic misadventures with the British press, foreign musicians, hotel humidifiers, or the fancy hairdo she'd been given in Paris ("It went higher and higher and *higher,* and it had great *things* on my cheeks; spit curls, we used to call them in my day"). She could even joke about a bothersome zipper in her slacks: during one show, it refused to stay closed, "so I put in a great big *safety* pin—so that nothing too *gay* would happen! And the pin came undone as I sat down! I sang four numbers with the pin right. . ." , and she gestured to her posterior. "I've never sung so *high* in my life."

Fields and Begelman booked Judy for twenty-three further concerts in summer and autumn 1961, and she missed only two when downed by an ear infection and influenza. Her repertoire changed slightly; she added "Just in Time" to the show, replaced "You Go to My Head" with "Never Will I Marry," and put "Ooh, What a Little Moonlight Can Do" into the jazz medley in the first act. But audience reaction never dimmed; in many cities, even the orchestra rose to applaud at the end of the show, many of them having played parts of the performance with tears in their eyes. In addition to Lindsey, there were three traveling musicians on the tour, whom Mort would augment with twenty-five or more local instrumentalists in each city. After a concert, Judy often relaxed by playing poker with her resident trumpeter, pianist, and drummer.

By the time the tour ended in December, Garland had set box-office records that stood until the heyday of higher-priced rock concerts in the mid-1960s. She broke the attendance record at the Hollywood Bowl in September, when eighteen thousand people sat outdoors for over two hours in a steady drizzle and refused to leave after four encores. (She was once again forced to reprise "San Francisco" to cap the evening.) One hundred fifty thousand people saw her "live" during 1961; her worldwide fame was enhanced by millions more who heard her concert program on the *Judy at Carnegie Hall* recording. After editing more than a half hour of applause and Judy's anecdotes and interplay from the tapes, Capitol rushed the set into release in July. (Fields had to fight with them to include all twenty-eight songs on two discs rather than offering only highlights of the show on a single album.) By autumn, *Judy at Carnegie Hall* had topped every best-seller list; it remained No. 1 for thirteen weeks and stayed on the charts for ninety-four weeks altogether. At a list price of $11.98, it became the fastest-selling two-record set to date and, in 1962, won a Gold Record and an unprecedented five Grammy awards: Album of the Year, Best Female Vocal Performance, Best Engineering (Robert Arnold), Best Album Cover (Jim Silke), and a special artists and repertoire award for producer Andy Wiswell.

BELOW: With hairdresser Al Paul backstage at Carnegie Hall. BOTTOM: At Luchow's after the first Carnegie concert with, from left, Lauren Bacall, Hedda Hopper, and Adolph Green.

Garland's astounding comeback led to feature stories in *Life, Look, Show Business Illustrated, McCall's, Good Housekeeping, Redbook,* and *The Theater.* Such profiles were reverberations of the newspaper reviews she received in 1961, notices later described by author Rowland Barber as "a remarkable anthology of gee-whiz writing." A sampling of that critical consensus offers further proof that, from coast to coast, Garland not only topped herself but fulfilled her new poster billing as the "world's greatest entertainer." Dallas: "There haven't been many nights like it this first half of the century." Houston: "Unquestionably the greatest show ever given in Houston. Her magnetism is easily capable of lifting several tons of scrap iron." Buffalo: "The event was reckoned conservatively to be the outstanding demonstration of human enthusiasm since Lindbergh landed The Spirit of St. Louis on Le Bourget Field." Philadelphia: "[There were] cheers and bravos after every number. Callas and Tebaldi would be envious." Chicago: "Impresario Harry Zelzer had to go 'way back to the days of Caruso to [name] a comparable evening." Dallas/return engagement: "Now we know: Lightning can strike twice on the same stage. Her American theatre tour [has rivaled] just about any star tour of the century." Detroit: "Elvis Presley has had his moments, and Jascha Heifetz, but there never has been such a scene of thousands of people with tears in their eyes, on their feet, straining forward, begging to have the moment kept golden for them just a little time longer. She manages to turn ["Come Rain or Come Shine"] into something like out of *Aida* or possibly *Il Trovatore.*" Montreal: "What she does is always real singing, and often singing of a high calibre. Her musical timing was always as accurate as that of any member of the orchestra." And in Toronto, the critics outdid themselves: The *Globe and Mail* marveled, "[She] is the one star who never takes her ovations for granted or the affection which greets her. Her discovery of it is as spontaneous as her singing is. The house vibrated with the wonderment at [her] limitless power. . . [She] has one gift that came as a great surprise. She moves with grace and elegance. . . Any cool investigation of the Garland mystique goes by the board after you find that unexpected moisture in your eyes. All you wonder at is how, in that great, big, crowded, noisy house, Judy Garland can find you out and sing directly to you." The *Star* sent their sports writer, whose perspective was no less exultant: "They had a big hey-rube this summer about Roger Maris trying to hit sixty-one home runs so he would smash Babe Ruth's record. Judy Garland hit sixty-two home runs last night at O'Keefe Centre. And didn't swing anything heavier than a battered silk hat. As singers go, this doll starts where the rest stop." And the *Telegram* wonderingly, rhetorically asked: "How do you record that the massive pile of the Centre shook, that the air inside stirred and shuddered strangely, and that a host of citizens seemed supernaturally shocked with pleasure? How do you explain that it was due to the uncanny powers of one tiny woman singing songs? How do you measure miracles?"

Garland's status in 1961 was further enhanced by the December release of *Judgment at Nuremberg.* Producer/director Stanley Kramer had originally envisioned Julie Harris for the part but then realized that "Judy knew the suffering I want." She played a German woman called before the 1948 Nuremberg tribunal to testify against those who'd imprisoned her when she refused to lie about her relationship with an elderly Jew a decade earlier. Garland, though increasingly slimmer, was still near 150 pounds, which helped convey the required dissipation of a middle-aged hausfrau. Before flying to Los Angeles for eleven days of filming, she spent weeks perfecting an appropriate accent by studying with a Greenwich Village dialect coach recommended by Uta Hagen.

Sidney Skolsky visited the *Nuremberg* set and reported that her costars and even the film extras stayed to watch and applaud Garland's takes. Another journalist found her appearance "one of those rare moments on a big soundstage where everyone was caught up in the mood and emotion of the action." Spencer Tracy, playing the presiding judge at the trial, was uncharacteristically verbose: "Wasn't that a performance? I don't object to playing stooge to Judy; she's a great actress." Maximilian Schell, "alight with admiration," called Garland "fantastic; every dimension is there." (When he began praising her to her face, however, Garland jokingly rebutted, "Oh, horseshit, Max—just act the damn scene!")

Judy never stopped expressing the debt she felt to Kramer for entrusting her with the part. Most critics were astounded by her power; Bosley Crowther found her "amazingly real," and Arthur Schlesinger, Jr., writing in *Show,* praised Kramer for the "remarkable performances" of his actors: "Montgomery Clift, Garland, and Burt Lancaster far surpass anything I have ever seen them do before." Judy received an Academy Award nomination as Best Supporting Actress for *Judgment at Nuremberg,* but lost the Oscar to Rita Moreno of *West Side Story.* Once again, however, the Hollywood Foreign Press Association saluted her, this time with their annual Cecil B. De Mille Award for "outstanding contributions to the entertainment field throughout the world" in 1961.

Judy tallied another career first before the year was out. In November, she returned to Los Angeles for several weeks to record the singing and speaking voice of "Mewsette," a cartoon kitten in the animated feature *Gay Purr-ee.* The assignment included five songs written especially for her by Arlen and Harburg. Upon hearing Garland's renditions, Arlen wrote, "Judy is a treasure; she does a superb job, and one's musical creation could not be in better hands." (When *Purr-ee* opened in November 1962, it was frequently double-billed with an inferior picture, and business was only fair. But reviewers, while bemoaning its slight script and lack of humor, praised the film's innovative artwork, score, and Garland's "patented verve, oomph, and feeling." The cartoon has since become a children's television and video favorite.)

Judy capped off 1961 by flying to Berlin for the December 15 world premiere of *Judgment at Nuremberg* and then spent the holidays with Sid and the chil-

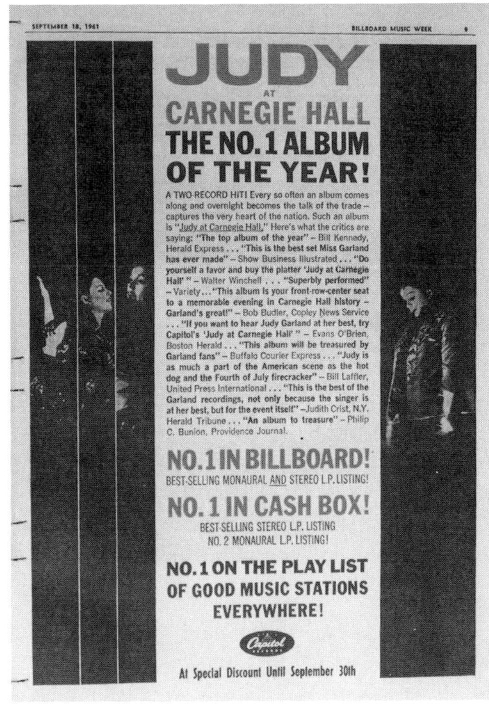

SEPTEMBER 18, 1961 BILLBOARD MUSIC WEEK

JUDY
AT
CARNEGIE HALL
THE NO. 1 ALBUM OF THE YEAR!

A TWO-RECORD HIT! Every so often an album comes along and overnight becomes the talk of the trade—captures the very heart of the nation. Such an album is "Judy at Carnegie Hall." Here's what the critics are saying: "The top album of the year" – Bill Kennedy, Herald Express . . . "This is the best set Miss Garland has ever made" – Show Business Illustrated . . . "Do yourself a favor and buy the platter 'Judy at Carnegie Hall' " – Walter Winchell . . . "Superbly performed" – Variety . . . "This album is your front-row-center seat to a memorable evening in Carnegie Hall history – Garland's great!" – Bob Budler, Copley News Service . . . "If you want to hear Judy Garland at her best, try Capitol's 'Judy at Carnegie Hall' " – Evans O'Brien, Boston Herald . . . "This album will be treasured by Garland fans" – Buffalo Courier Express . . . "Judy is as much a part of the American scene as the hot dog and the Fourth of July firecracker" – Bill Laffler, United Press International . . . "This is the best of the Garland recordings, not only because the singer is at her best, but for the event itself" – Judith Crist, N.Y. Herald Tribune . . . "An album to treasure" – Philip C. Bunion, Providence Journal.

NO. 1 IN BILLBOARD!
BEST-SELLING MONAURAL AND STEREO L.P. LISTING!

NO. 1 IN CASH BOX!
BEST-SELLING STEREO L.P. LISTING
NO. 2 MONAURAL L.P. LISTING!

NO. 1 ON THE PLAY LIST OF GOOD MUSIC STATIONS EVERYWHERE!

Capitol

At Special Discount Until September 30th

Trade paper ad for the "Album of the Year." "It's the first of my records that I've really enjoyed listening to," Judy said at the time. "I get a big kick out of it. The excitement of the night comes through. . . . And I forgot all about the recording when I went on—luckily—or I'd have been self-conscious. . . and concentrating on my 'pear-shaped tones'! There are a couple of things I would have done over, but with the spontaneity of the evening, you wouldn't pay any attention to them. [The 1961 tour has] been terribly exciting all over, but Carnegie Hall was a special night. . . one of those perfect nights."

Judgment at Nuremberg. CLOCKWISE FROM TOP LEFT: *Between takes with Spencer Tracy; on the set with an unidentified technician; as Irene Hoffman on the witness stand; at the Berlin premiere, December 1961; after the premiere with (from left) Montgomery Clift, Stanley Kramer, West Berlin Mayor Willy Brandt, Richard Widmark, and Maximilian Schell. The latter played the defense attorney in the film; before their scenes, Garland told him, "Hit me hard, Max, so I can get my tears."*

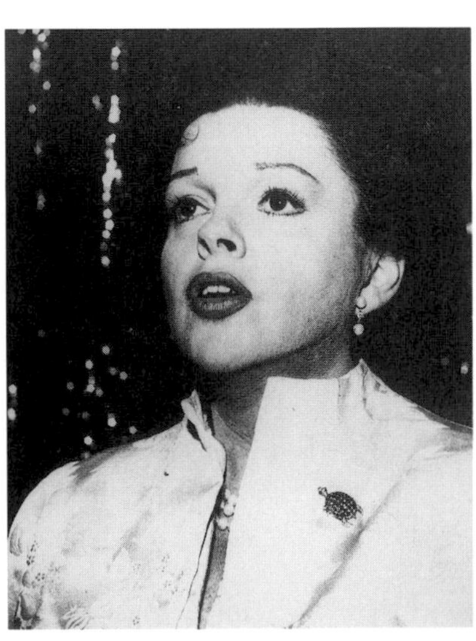

dren at a rented home in Scarsdale, New York. It was a reunion for Garland and Luft; they had separated on and off during the year, and he was increasingly wary of the expanding control Fields and Begelman seemed to exert over her life.

Looking back on 1961, however, Judy commented, "Every once in a while you seem to earn a year where everything goes right." It was outwardly true, of course, but the work and renewed physical and emotional demands also took their toll. The "permanent semi-invalid," so healthy and fit the year before, was devitalized by the end of 1961. Personal ambition may well have played a part in her herculean effort, but it is more probable that she agreed to such concentrated labor in an effort to become solvent and provide for her children. She (perhaps foolishly) agreed to every job possibility and kept a pace equal to—if not surpassing that—of any earlier period. As a result, her debts were supposedly paid off, and she had never been a greater star, more in demand, or more highly respected. But if Fields and Begelman were responsible for paving the road back, the increasingly taxing series of challenges they arranged seemed to come without the necessary understanding that such demands would seriously impair Judy's long-term health and stability. A nonstop work schedule was always detrimental to Garland's well-being, and there had already been a few instances on tour when the stressed-out Judy behaved temperamentally or irrationally (whether as a reaction to the pressurized schedule or as a result of brief overmedication). Her success, however, had quickly established her new managers and their agency. On the basis of Garland's return, Freddie Fields Associates evolved into the prestigious Creative Management Associates; CMA would later become International Creative Management, a major show-business force. (With tongue-somewhat-in-cheek, Judy later gibed, "I can remember when CMA was an answering service—at my apartment!")

The same back-to-back schedule was already established for Garland deep into 1962. Fields had settled the cross-courts legal battle between Garland and CBS; in January 1962, Judy, Frank Sinatra, and Dean Martin joined forces for her comeback TV special. Taped over three nights, the program provided Garland with a nationwide capper to eighteen months of work, re-creating highlights from her concerts on a lighted runway or in front of a blazing backdrop of lights that

The 1962 CBS-TV special. BELOW: Rehearsing with Frank Sinatra. BOTTOM LEFT: Between takes. BOTTOM RIGHT: Rehearsing for the finale.

TOP: Rehearsal for the 1962 special. ABOVE: Singing the opening numbers. One—her version of "Just in Time"—was the result of an eight-hour session the preceding summer in which Garland, Kay Thompson, and Mort Lindsey created an intricate arrangement that soared through two choruses and four musical keys.

spelled JUDY. Norman Jewison artfully produced and directed the show, which he later termed "the most exciting television I ever did." His reaction to Garland was similarly declarative: "I simply couldn't believe that an artist could stir so many people with the sound of her voice. You literally felt the waves and radiations of emotional response." When "The Judy Garland Show" was telecast on February 25, 1962, it pulled virtually unanimous raves from critics and the highest rating of any entertainment program in CBS history. *Show* felt that even Sinatra "suffered by comparison" to Garland; other critics found both guest stars "pleasantly unnecessary," and the *New York Times* decided they were "around just to give Miss Garland time to change clothes." The *Los Angeles Times* called it "a beautiful hour [with] moments. . . as memorable as any that television has ever given us." *Life* predicted "[Judy's] 'Man That Got Away' will unloose a nationwide flood of tears which would make Noah start packing," and *TV Guide* flatly stated, "Nobody can match her." Judy herself was "terribly proud" of the show—"and I usually don't like my own work." The program was repeated by popular demand and amassed four Emmy nominations, including Program of the Year. It later won the international television award at the Montreux Festival.

From the taping of the special, Garland segued immediately into a costarring role with Burt Lancaster in *A Child Is Waiting.* The thoughtful film about a school for mentally retarded children was produced by Stanley Kramer and directed by John Cassavetes; Judy played a misfit music teacher whose sympathetic emotional attachment to one of her pupils is deemed detrimental to the self-sufficiency such children must be taught. Given a 1949 encounter with similar youngsters while at Peter Bent Brigham Hospital, Garland felt it was "wonderful to bring [such] a story intelligently to the screen."

Child was filmed between late January and mid-April, and Cassavetes was forced to shoot around Garland on a number of occasions when the exhausted actress feared facing the cameras. Her work was nonetheless pleasantly low-key, and the London *Times* found her "quiet performance all the more effective for the fact that her well-known, well-loved mannerisms are kept in check. She has seldom been better." Overall, the film won mixed response and minimal box-office returns when released in early 1963; some critics were limited in their understanding of the problems facing both the children and the schools that sought to help them. Others were compassionate in their comprehension of Kramer's intent; *Daily Variety* found *Child* "poignant, provocative, revealing. . . a distinguished attraction." Although the central role of Garland's pupil was expertly played by actor Bruce Ritchey, most of the other youngsters were actual students from Pacific State Hospital, which gave a joyful poignancy to the school scenes. Their participation provided *Child* with its major effectiveness, and *Saturday Review* praised, "Wonderful, too, is the way [Garland and Lancaster] work with the children; [they] radiate a warmth so genuine that one is certain that the children are responding directly to them and not to some vaguely comprehended script." On her first day of work with the students, Garland had to smile through tears when the children clamored for autographs from "Dorothy."

With no break, Judy flew to New York in mid-April and entered the hospital for a rest. By April 23, she was out and, three nights later, attempted a live recording session before one thousand invited guests at Manhattan Center. "Judy Takes Broadway" was conceived as a thirteen-song concert of new material, and Mort Lindsey "worked three months on it. I flew out to the coast; we discussed all

A Child Is Waiting. TOP LEFT: *With Burt Lancaster and John Cassavetes.* FAR LEFT CENTER: *With an unidentified technician.* CENTER: *Meeting her "students" during filming of the opening sequences.* BOTTOM LEFT: *Scene with Gloria McGehee deleted from the release print.* BELOW: *Wardrobe test for her role as Jean Hansen.*

the arrangements. Then I went back to New York and wrote on my own; the charts were going to be kind of a surprise for her." Garland energetically and good-naturedly made her way through the ninety-minute session, but an obvious case of laryngitis marred each take. She got through nine of the songs, kidding with the crowd about her voice ("I sound like a great whiskey tenor") and reprimanding herself for her stops and starts over the new tunes ("Oh, I'll never stop singing so long again and do these terrible *dramatic* pictures!"). Finally, she offered heartfelt thanks to the crowd for its patience: "I'll get there someway, if you'll stay with me. And you usually have—that's what's kept me alive." The audience was thoroughly captured by her all-stops-out performance, but the album was scrapped. (Material recorded that night was not released—except on pirated issues—until 1989.) In its place, Capitol hastily assembled *The Garland Touch,* bringing together two singles Judy and Lindsey had recorded the preceding October, two tracks from *Judy in Love,* and six selections from her unreleased London sessions of 1960. Compilation though it was, the album spent fourteen weeks on the charts and was rated by *High Fidelity* as "a superlative disc. . .one of [her] finest."

There was little time for regret over the aborted album. After a much-headlined altercation with Luft (wherein he branded Garland an unfit mother, and she had him restrained at the Hotel Stanhope while she rushed Lorna, Joe, and Liza to the airport), Garland arrived in England in late April to begin another film. *The Lonely Stage* was based on a 1958 CBS teleplay starring Mary Astor; producers Stuart Millar and Lawrence Turman noted they had "wanted to adapt the vehicle for Judy since its original telecast. We always had our own faith in her talent and our own hunch she'd come back." Garland's role in the script was reworked from that of a dramatic actress to a popular concert singer, visiting London to appear at the Palladium and meet again the British surgeon with whom she'd had an illegitimate son thirteen years before. Dirk Bogarde played (as Judy put it) "the man that got away," and Jack Klugman re-created his TV role as the star's manager. Just prior to release, the film was retitled *I Could Go on Singing,* as United Artists wanted to exploit the picture as one in which Garland sang.

LEFT: At the Judy Takes Broadway *recording session, New York, April 26, 1962. The proposed album was to include songs from* Sail Away, West Side Story, Bells Are Ringing, Greenwillow, My Fair Lady, Wildcat, The Most Happy Fella, Gypsy, The Music Man, Show Girl, *and* Spring Is Here. *RIGHT: On the set of* I Could Go On Singing.

It's Judy!
lighting up the lonely stage
STUART MILLAR and LAWRENCE TURMAN
JUDY GARLAND DIRK BOGARDE
"I COULD GO ON SINGING"
JACK KLUGMAN
MAYO SIMON ROBERT DOZIER
HAROLD ARLEN and E. Y. HARBURG RONALD NEAME
STUART MILLAR and LAWRENCE TURMAN
SAUL CHAPLIN MORT LINDSEY EASTMANCOLOR PANAVISION

PRECEDING PAGE: *Performing the title song for* I Could Go On Singing, *United Artists/1963; inset shows the film poster.*

THIS PAGE AND FACING PAGE: *Judy at the Sahara, Las Vegas, September/October 1962. A columnist mused, "Any theatregoers who pass her up hate themselves. If you were around and hadn't seen Babe Ruth or Ted Williams, you weren't a baseball bug. If you missed Man O' War, you're not a racing nut. Forget fighting if you could've but never saw Dempsey. Same with Judy. . . . While the jam-packed audience yelled requests, a shrill voice screamed, 'What's the difference, sing anything.' That sums it up."*

Two publicity portraits for "Judy and Her Guests," Garland's 1963 CBS-TV special.

FACING PAGE: Judy reminisces about MGM with guest Mickey Rooney during dress rehearsal for the first episode taped for her 1963–64 CBS-TV series, "The Judy Garland Show," June 1963.

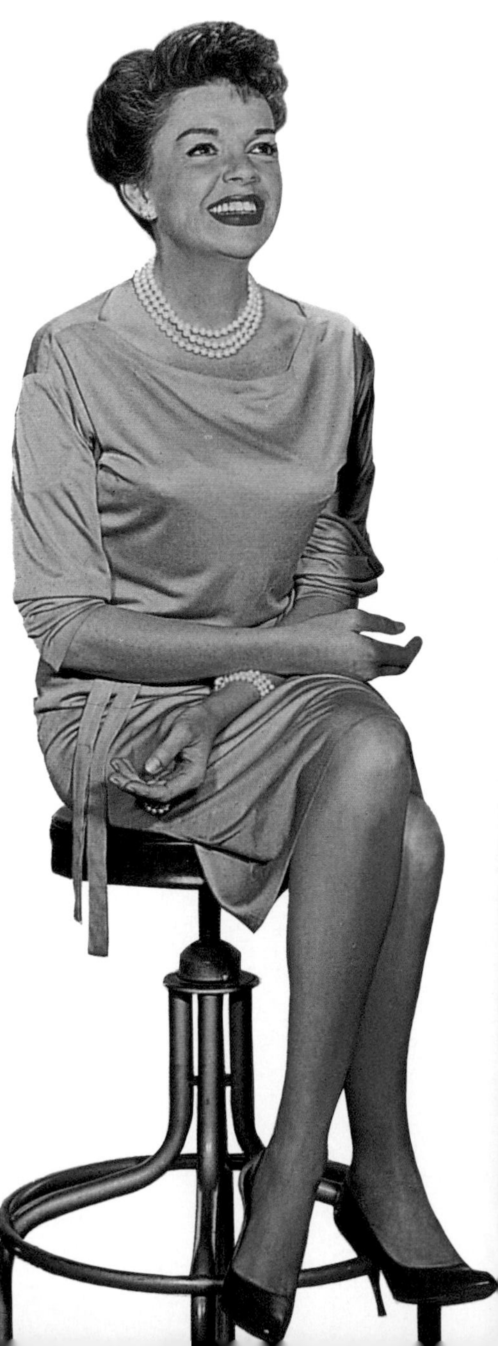

LOT

"The Judy Garland Show" CBS-TV series. FACING PAGE: *Judy chats with Lena Horne, July 1963.*

TOP, ABOVE LEFT, AND FAR RIGHT: *Judy in performance (and between takes) of "Seventy-Six Trombones," January 1964.* RIGHT: *Singing "Paris Is a Lonely Town," January 1964.*

FOLLOWING PAGE: *Seventeen-year-old Liza Minnelli joins her mother for "I Will Come Back," July 1963.*

Singing took eleven weeks to complete, and the shooting schedule was interrupted many times. Garland was often depleted, unable to get to the set. There was a brief hospitalization after a fall in her home, another after a minor overdose of medication. She was engaged in preliminary child-custody battles with Luft. She felt overbooked by CMA and overlooked by the busy Begelman (with whom she had supposedly fallen in love). She disliked the film script, and it wasn't until Bogarde began rewriting it (with her help) that she regained enthusiasm for the property. Similarly, Mort Lindsey recalls, "She really wasn't feeling well, and we didn't know what to do." Begelman had Lindsey lay down orchestral tracks for several of her numbers, took the tape to her, and Garland—thrilled by Mort's work—was again spurred on to perform. But she was alternately convivial or hostile with both Bogarde and director Ronald Neame, terrified of being unable to produce what was required. Added to this was the self-imposed necessity of dieting for the camera and her fear of increasing dependence on pills.

Klugman remembers the insecure Judy clutching his arm as they watched the rushes of the film—he laudatory, reassuring, and unbelieving that she was unable to see the extraordinary quality of her work, despite the soap-opera plot and off-camera tensions. Bogarde recalls her sometimes illogical behavior and the manner in which she totally alienated a film crew that had been initially in her thrall. However, after completing her final shot, Garland looked at the assembled staff and, as if acknowledging both the situation and her capabilities, said with laser directness, "You'll miss me when I'm gone." Neame and Bogarde both agreed. The actor admits, "A few weeks later, another actress came over. . .and the unit said, 'If only we had Judy back!' Because the other was worse—and they knew the value of Judy. When she delivered, there was absolutely *nothing* like it."

Garland's work in the film was laced with such delivery. For all its script and visual imperfections (the latter primarily in Judy's occasionally unsuitable wardrobe and hairstyles), *Singing* captured some of the essence of her concert work, particularly in an almost documentary retelling of her opening-night en-

I Could Go On Singing *captured something of Garland's concert persona.* TOP LEFT: *With Al Paul and Jack Klugman as she prepares to face a Palladium audience.* TOP RIGHT: *The standing ovation at her entrance, with Mort Lindsey as her beaming conductor.* ABOVE: *Singing "Hello, Bluebird."*

trance at the Palladium. With Lindsey on-screen conducting her overture, Garland's character waits in the wings, clapping and growing to the music, finally propelling herself onstage, eyes and smile sparkling; the energized audience can do nothing but rise to her. Garland sang four numbers in the film, and she called Lindsey's orchestration of "By Myself" her "favorite of all time." The number itself was shot one night after Garland had stayed all day in her trailer, refusing to work. When told that the day crew was about to give way to a night crew, she ordered supper for everyone, came out to join them for the meal, and—finally feeling well enough to perform—completed the entire, difficult routine in a matter of minutes.

There were pivotal dramatic scenes as well: Garland offered a poignant telephone monologue, surrendering her son to his father, and then demonstrated her personal charm when, an hour late for a concert, she wins back a waiting crowd. She and Bogarde spent three days writing and revising their final moments of on-screen confrontation, rehearsed the dialogue for a full day, and then shot it once. An awed member of the crew termed the segment and the work that went into it "a miracle"; Garland's character, propped up in a hospital emergency room, moved from drunken, owlish humor to defiance to a tearful breakdown and recovery—all in one six-minute take.

Singing enjoyed an extraordinary London premiere in March 1963; crowds stretched for blocks on either side of the Plaza Cinema, rocking Garland's car in joyful hysteria when she arrived. Though dismissing the mawkish plot, the critics' estimation of Judy was unparalleled. She jestingly suggested that they were awash in "spastic Garland mania," but the general consensus was that expressed by *Time:* "Her acting may be the best of her career." The London *Telegraph* pronounced, "She is the very best there is," and Penelope Gilliatt wrote, "She is a harrowingly good actress. [The hospital scene] should be in every drama-school library; [it's] a thrilling piece of technique." *The Listener* found Garland "incandescent—an enchantress," and Penelope Houston stated bluntly, "There is no counterfeiting this sort of talent." One of the few professional dissenters

I Could Go On Singing, *1962.* LEFT: *A technician stands by during Garland's bravura scene with Dirk Bogarde. Note the quilt used to smother any camera sound and the key light aimed directly at Garland's eyes.* RIGHT: *A drained Garland between rehearsals.* FACING PAGE, TOP: *Rather than lipsync to a prerecording, Judy sang "It Never Was You" live in one take for this sequence on a studio mock-up of the Palladium stage. Her accompanist was David Lee, pianist for portions of her 1960 tour.* FACING PAGE, CENTER LEFT: *With Ronald Neame and Gregory Phillips as her son on location at Stoke Poges.* FACING PAGE, CENTER RIGHT: *Garland's fortieth birthday was celebrated on the set.*

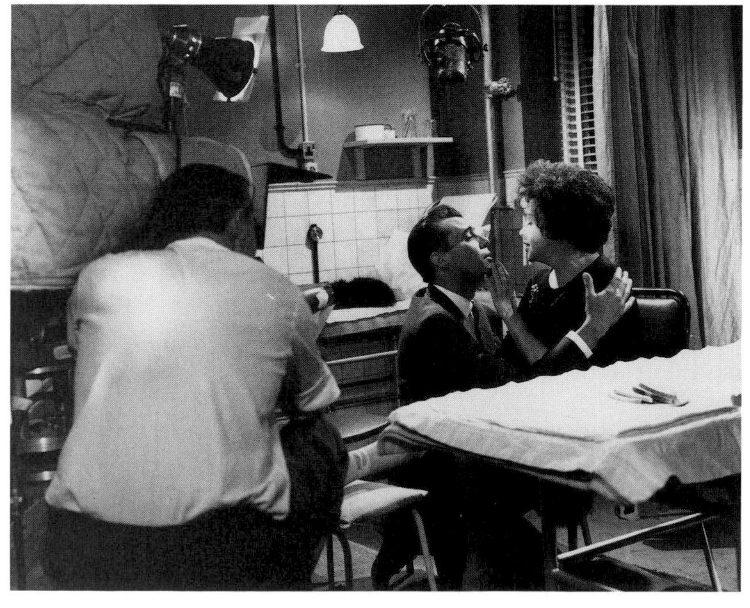

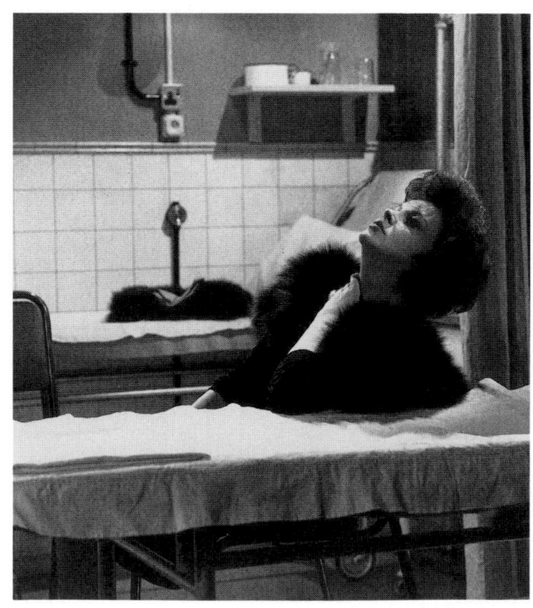

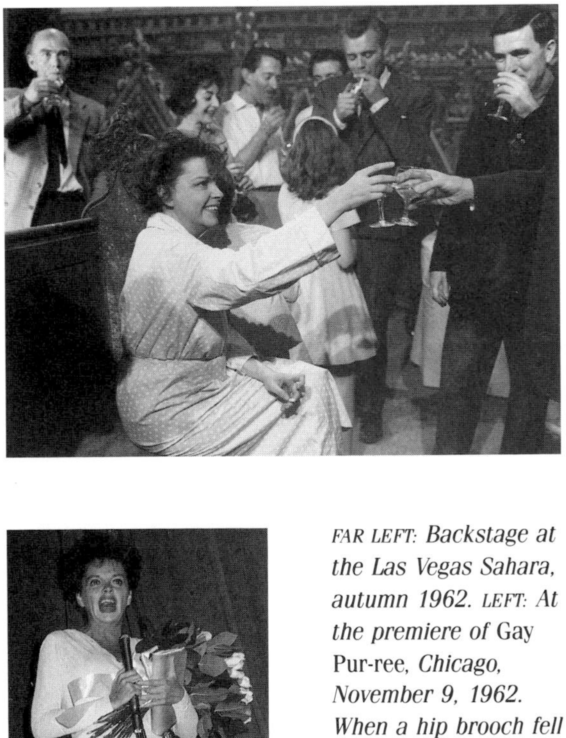

FAR LEFT: Backstage at the Las Vegas Sahara, autumn 1962. LEFT: At the premiere of Gay Pur-ree, *Chicago, November 9, 1962. When a hip brooch fell from Garland's dress, the film's producer picked it up and tried to hand it back to her. Deadpan, she responded, "Isn't that yours?"*

was Bosley Crowther, who seemed to be expecting a musical comedy; yet his reaction was the popular one, for *I Could Go on Singing* did little business despite the praise for Garland.

Judy returned to the States in August 1962 and recklessly embarked on a thirty-day fast to lose the last of her overweight. As a result, she was hospitalized for a kidney attack but came out—at a trim one hundred pounds—to open a scheduled three-week engagement at the Las Vegas Sahara on September 18. She did one show per night at eight o'clock; management extended the booking for another week and then—for the first time in Vegas history—invited her to stay two weeks more for a regular 2:30 A.M. concert. "It's New Year's every night!" was Judy's comment. "I'm always awake [then] anyway, and you've never seen such crowds!" The act, in Hedda Hopper's words, consisted of "just Judy, the band, and the customers fighting to get in." *Variety* found Garland "more dramatically electric than ever, giving her stylized tones a virtual tour de force as she sobs, shouts, caresses her songs." A columnist mused, "Judy splits every note, like they did with the atom. Then she dissects each split, and every segment becomes a trilogy. Kind of resented the deafening applause. Should have been a hush like for Lincoln at Gettysburg." Garland garnered a quarter million dollars for the gig and, on closing night, joked, "In case you hear a loud noise during the show, it's the sound of people fainting—the same people who said I wouldn't last one week!"

In November, she flew to Chicago for the premiere of *Gay Purr-ee* and gave what became a legendary show at the Arie Crown Theatre. Battling severe laryngitis, she went on to face five thousand people and, given her nonstop clowning and determined animation, voice mattered least. The *Chicago American* ser-

Jack Paar introduced her simply, ". . . She's pure magic. So—abracadabra: Judy Garland." BELOW: *Robert Goulet sings "Mewsette" with a jubilant partner.* BOTTOM LEFT AND RIGHT: *Paar and guest. He finally told her, "I don't even belong in the same building with you."*

monized, "People choked the aisles screaming 'More!' And Judy, who already had sung to them for more than two hours with her bad throat and her great voice, sang more. We wondered how Judy Garland, a human, can exist. It's almost unfair to heap one living person with such love because we think it is impossible for any person to live up to it. But thank God for someone like Judy Garland, who makes us feel like standing up and smiling at life and believing there is something special waiting over the rainbow—for all of us."

In early December, Garland enjoyed one of her finest hours as special guest on "The Jack Paar Program." Greeted by a standing ovation from the studio audience, she provided "a picture of mental and physical health. . .a highly rewarding and gratifying display" (*Variety*). It was the first time the mass public had seen the newly slender Judy, as well as its first exposure to her famed humor. She was, as Paar trumpeted, "one of the great talkers in show business," and whether accurate or embellished for effect, her anecdotes were uproarious and impeccably delivered. The host called it simply "the most enjoyable night I've ever had." Judy and costar Robert Goulet then spent three nights on a whirlwind bus tour of New York theatres playing *Gay Purr-ee*. On December 6, she sang for President Kennedy after the premiere of *A Child Is Waiting*, a Washington, D.C., benefit for the Joseph P. Kennedy Foundation.

Garland's landmark achievements had continued to flourish in 1962. She was delighted and gratified but drained. By the end of the year, she dreamed only of a three-month vacation (in the unexpressed hope it would restore her health). But the signal successes of the 1962 TV special and Paar appearance provided final impetus for Fields and Begelman's master plan: a weekly Garland TV series beginning in the 1963–64 season. After negotiations with all three networks, they cut an agreement with CBS, and on December 28, Judy signed what was termed "the biggest talent deal in TV history." If all contract options were exercised, Garland's production company would be paid $24 million for four seasons of variety programs. In further concessions, CBS agreed that Judy would retain all rights to the shows; they also gave her the freedom to bow out of the program after the first thirteen episodes if she so desired. (The network, however, could not cancel the show at that time.) Despite the anticipated work load, Garland was sold on the idea as a means of gaining ultimate financial security and the chance to establish a permanent job and home with her children. For CMA, "The Judy Garland Show" meant maximum financial compensation as well. They would collect a packaging fee, plus agency percentages of the salaries for Garland as well as any of their other talent booked on the show as guests or staff.

The series was scheduled to begin production in June 1963. Meanwhile, Judy spent five nights in January taping another CBS special for telecast March 19. The program emphasized new songs and new aspects of the Garland talent, pairing her with Phil Silvers and Robert Goulet. "It was time," felt producer Burt Shevelove, "to break away from nostalgia, from the long parade of classics identified with Judy." Taping ran into the early hours of the morning, and the weary Garland caught rest whenever she could. Mort Lindsey, aware of her fatigue, sympathetically remembers that "the orchestra stayed on the stand six hours while she took a nap." As a result of her exhaustion, Judy sang somewhat huskily, but the program showcased her slim figure and versatility. Her duets with Goulet were musically memorable (if, in the quip of critic Don Freeman, "almost friendly enough to be released as an Italian movie"), and for the first time since the

TOP: During a 1962 visit to the Oval Office, Garland casts a radiant glance at her friend, President John F. Kennedy. She would occasionally call him for professional advice; he would reciprocate with a request for a telephone rendition of "Over the Rainbow." ABOVE: In New York, Judy poses with CBS-TV vice-president Hubbell Robinson after signing a contract for her own series.

The 1963 CBS-TV special. LEFT: *"Almost Like Being in Love"/"This Can't Be Love."* RIGHT: *A love song medley with Robert Goulet.* BELOW: *"Hello, Bluebird," with Phil Silvers and Goulet.*

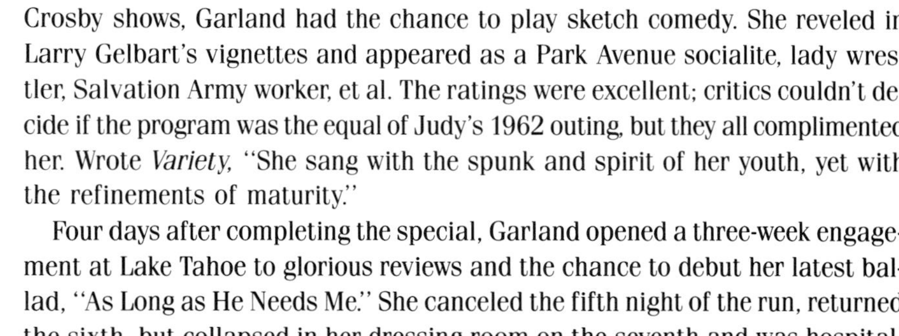

Crosby shows, Garland had the chance to play sketch comedy. She reveled in Larry Gelbart's vignettes and appeared as a Park Avenue socialite, lady wrestler, Salvation Army worker, et al. The ratings were excellent; critics couldn't decide if the program was the equal of Judy's 1962 outing, but they all complimented her. Wrote *Variety,* "She sang with the spunk and spirit of her youth, yet with the refinements of maturity."

Four days after completing the special, Garland opened a three-week engagement at Lake Tahoe to glorious reviews and the chance to debut her latest ballad, "As Long as He Needs Me." She canceled the fifth night of the run, returned the sixth, but collapsed in her dressing room on the seventh and was hospitalized with slight paralysis. (Leighton Noble, orchestra leader at Harrah's, remembers that Judy's problems stemmed from exhaustion and overmedication.) The hospital, besieged with phone calls from the media and fans, was forced to bring in extra switchboard help. Although she made a quick recovery, Garland yielded the rest of her engagement to Mickey Rooney and then began another attempt at reconciliation with Luft. There had been months of headlines about their divorce and custody cases; the reunion lasted until July, when they separated for good.

In March, Judy flew to London for the *I Could Go on Singing* premiere and appeared live on television in "Sunday Night at the Palladium." Her salary was the largest ever paid on the variety hour, and she donated it to the Thalidomide Fund (which provided artificial limbs for children born with birth defects). Garland won enraptured laughter from the theatre audience when she blithely admitted missing a song cue and asked Lindsey to begin again: "We can even stop on television—I can make just as many mistakes!" The program also marked the debut of his orchestration of "Smile"; Judy's rendition was later excerpted from the Palladium tape and telecast on "The Ed Sullivan Show." It became a Garland classic, and Sullivan reran the number several times in the 1960s and 1970s.

In May, work began in earnest on the TV series; CBS scheduled the Garland show for Sunday nights at nine o'clock—an enormously prestigious but inherently dangerous time slot. The top-rated "Bonanza" was Judy's NBC competition, and although her 1962 special had won double the Western's audience, many network and business insiders felt that such a masochistic maneuver signified what little hope CBS had for the Garland program. She was, however, the most legendary name in entertainment in spring 1963, and the staff chosen to work on the show was determined to ensure her success.

The inspirational and devastating story of Garland's TV series has been told in *Rainbow's End* by Coyne Steven Sanders (New York: William Morrow and Company, Inc., 1990). Brilliantly researched, the book details the corporate intrigue to which Garland fell victim. Although Judy's health, medication, and occasional alcohol problems were detrimental to the show's potential, Sanders points out that almost everyone connected with the program recalls her resolute and sometimes superhuman efforts to make it succeed. They lay primary responsibility for the show's demise at the feet of network president James Aubrey, vice president Hunt Stromberg, Jr., and Fields and Begelman. Indeed, Sanders's methodical investigation brings new perspective to the difficulties that beset Garland's program, providing a much different view than that previously accepted as fact. (Historical opinion of the series was shaped for years by *The Other Side of the Rainbow,* Mel Tormé's account of his work as composer of the show's special material. Largely self-serving, his book nonetheless won critical praise and acceptance in 1970 from those unfamiliar with the program's chronology or quality. The memories of those who spoke to Sanders handily dispel many of Tormé's assertions.)

During its twenty-six episodes, "The Judy Garland Show" went through two directors, a passel of writers, and three executive producers. The first of these, George Schlatter, completed five programs, each of which showcased Garland as the larger-than-life "world's greatest entertainer." CBS, however, wanted Garland's image recast as a palatable-to-the-hinterlands Dinah Shore girl-next-door; the network was infuriated by Schlatter's attempt to make each program a special event. They dismissed him and his writers and (remembering the successful 1962 special) hired Norman Jewison for the next eight programs. Jewison also disagreed with the CBS concept but, in a conscientious effort to make Garland a hit, endeavored to supply familiar TV guests and folksy features.

BELOW: Rehearsing "Smile" in London. BELOW CENTER: Ticket to the first "Garland Show" dress rehearsal. BOTTOM RIGHT: With initial guest, Mickey Rooney. BOTTOM LEFT: Rehearsing a solo for the first "Garland Show."

CBS TELEVISION NETWORK
TELEVISION CITY
7800 BEVERLY BLVD., HOLLYWOOD, CALIF.
Entrance: 1 Block South of Beverly on Fairfax
STUDIO 43
SUNDAY JUNE 23 1963
7:30-9:00 p.m.
Doors Close 7:10 p.m.
FREE PARKING
THE JUDY GARLAND SHOW
DRESS REHEARSAL
Children Under Twelve Will Not Be Admitted
№ 229

BELOW: *Between takes of a holiday medley, November 1963.* BOTTOM LEFT: *Rehearsing "As Long As He Needs Me" and* BOTTOM RIGHT: *dueting "The Best Is Yet to Come" with Liza Minnelli, July 1963.* FACING PAGE: *Music for a classic duet and scenes from the show guesting Barbra Streisand and the Smothers Brothers, October 1963.*

Meanwhile, with eight episodes of varying format already taped, "The Judy Garland Show" premiered on September 29, 1963, trouncing "Bonanza" in the ratings and winning occasionally qualified but generally laudatory reviews—especially for Garland herself: "She has always had talent, looks, poise, grace, intensity, a warm and witty comic sense, good legs and endearing face—a rare performing flair—and last night, she used them all. Her show was beautifully produced," wrote Jack O'Brian in the New York *Journal-American.* But that Jewison episode was actually only fair television and, if fulfilling the CBS vision of the series, presented a star far removed from the charged and unforgettable Garland of the preceding three years. Her airtime seemed less than that of guest Donald O'Connor, her voice was momentarily under strain, and her exhilarated stage gestures unnerved some viewers.

The next telecast found Garland in top form, meeting head-on the challenge of her personally chosen guest, a fledgling Barbra Streisand (plus an unbilled walk-on by Ethel Merman). *Show* lamented the premiere ("[Judy] got lost in a tangle of guests and devices") but cheered the second show and pinpointed the reason for its supremacy: "All that was really needed was more Judy." The viewing public had returned to "Bonanza," however, and the Garland series foundered. Its composition enigmatically changed on the air each week as the network alternated telecasts of the "superstar" Schlatter episodes with the less reverent Jewison programs.

After thirteen programs had been taped, the show took a hiatus, and a new executive producer, director, choreographer, and writers were signed. Some viewers and columnists had continued to berate the program, taking exception to the fact that Garland was no longer the vocal equal of her Carnegie Hall—or *Wizard of Oz*—days. Investigative reporters for national magazines haunted the set, delighting in news that Garland skipped workdays and seeking proof that she drank. After her three years at the top, there seemed to be an understanding

JUDY–BARBRA
THE JUDY GARLAND SHOW #9
GET HAPPY / HAPPY DAYS
Slow – Smooth
JUDY
BARBRA
Ab Bbm7 Cm7 Bbm7
FOR-
SING HAL-LE-
Bbm7 Cm7
Bbm7
ON GET HAP- PY
THE LORD IS

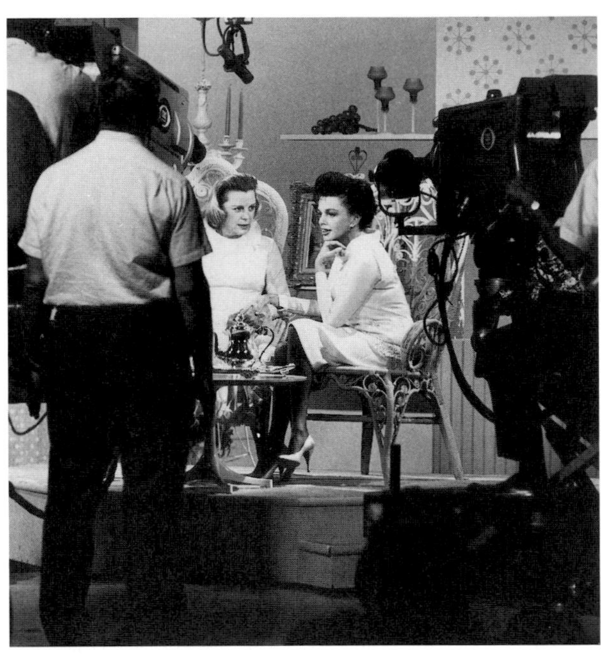

LEFT: Judy and June Allyson, September 1963. They irreverently reminisced about MGM and their twenty years of friendship in a hilarious (if Liebfraumilch-laced) conversation. (Two years later Judy quipped, "June got kinda drunk, but I didn't know it—I got kinda drunk myself!") RIGHT: Ethel Merman and Shelley Berman join Judy for "Everybody's Doing It," December 1963. Merman had made an October "surprise" appearance on the show, leading Garland and Streisand in a trio of "There's No Business Like Show Business." (The series provided Judy the opportunity to work with such stars as Count Basie, Donald O'Connor, Peggy Lee, Jack Jones, Bobby Darin, Bob Newhart, Steve Allen, Ray Bolger, Jane Powell, and Martha Raye. But, as Mel Tormé later said, "One of our top problems [was] who could we get to equal Garland? [CBS] would only have been satisfied if Kennedy had done a soft shoe with her, after which we would have cut to Winston Churchill painting her picture.")

somewhere that it was time to tear her down. But even a dirt-grubbing *Newsweek* stringer had to report that Judy was "a pro in giving an interview—charming, gay, ebullient." Garland herself echoed the comments of the majority of her staff (both then and since) by asserting, "I've worked hard on this show to make it a hit," and she was candid and self-aware enough to admit, "Sometimes rehearsals are missed, but I've been around long enough so I can pick things up quickly."

The majority of the public, the media, and the Garland Show's staff had no trouble in determining the real reasons for the sorry ratings—seemingly with more sense than the network ever exhibited. There was continuing protest over her time slot; not only was she opposite "Bonanza" but back-to-back with another hour of variety ("The Ed Sullivan Show") as her CBS lead-in. (The following season, both Sullivan and Danny Kaye—the latter a mild CBS hit with his own show in 1963—refused to "inherit" Garland's "suicide slot.") There was additional widespread furor over the CBS-inflicted phony formats, the jokey debasing of Garland's reputation, and the inappropriate guest stars and scripting—along with wonderment and praise that the show had developed into a product of frequent and genuine quality after a few volatile weeks. Journalist Lloyd Shearer pointed out that the show was merely a "statistical failure. . . incorrectly targeted by network masterminds." But Aubrey, Stromberg, and their associates refused to move the show to another night and, in effect, wrote off "The Judy Garland Show" early in its existence.

The strain on Garland can be imagined. According to those around her, Fields and Begelman had to some extent defected—whether in weariness over her demands for reassurance or in abandonment of a sinking show. But Judy continued to persevere—even amidst the backstage turmoil, network interference, lack of cooperation, and a work load that would have been difficult had she been medication-free. If not possessed of the robust voice and impeccable control of two years earlier, the paper-thin Garland was far from past her prime and (eventually) made each format work in her own way. There were scores of unforgettable Garland solos during the twenty-six episodes, many new to her repertoire. The series also gave her the opportunity to work with other exemplary talents, and she invariably topped any competition.

Bill Colleran was the fortuitous choice for final executive producer of the show. He and Garland "hit it off at once. But I got real nervous with what [CBS] was doing with her—too many little bitsy pieces that were not Judy. I had to do my first shows with the guests that were already signed; then I paid off some of the rest of them and said, 'That's it; what this girl does better than anyone in the world, anywhere in history, is sing.' There's nobody that could even touch her. So I gave her a mike, added ten men to the orchestra, and let her sing for an hour. CBS was furious! [But] the show was wonderful from then on."

The concert programs were the last seven of the series, and by the time they were taped, CBS had already canceled the show. A grass-roots Save "The Judy Garland Show" Campaign had sprung up in New York, too late to make a difference but capable of tallying ten thousand letters and cards, over two hundred telegrams, and numerous petitions (each signed by hundreds of people), all within days of its formation. When she heard about the plan, Garland gleefully exhorted, "Get as many as you can; I'm all for it!" But the network encouraged Judy instead to save face and announce she was quitting "to give my children the time and attention that they need."

The press and public were not fooled; indeed, they were irate. Even before the all-music format was implemented, Garland and Colleran had produced additional worthy episodes, especially an elegantly casual Christmas show with Liza, Lorna, and Joe. Another highlight came in Judy's rendition of "The Battle Hymn of the Republic," taped in unspoken tribute to John Kennedy three weeks after the presidential assassination. Mort Lindsey recalls, "CBS didn't want her to do it; they felt it was too heavy or political. But that was one [arrangement] she devised from top to bottom; she knew exactly where she wanted to go." Colleran calls it "one of her greatest performances of all time; if you didn't cry, you were dead."

He also labels Judy's concert-show series appearances as "the most personal she ever gave. Her heart was right out there on the line, every single time. And

BELOW: Memories from George Jessel, September 1963. BOTTOM LEFT: Judy, Tony Bennett, and Dick Shawn provide a buoyant finish to "Yes, Indeed," July 1963. BOTTOM RIGHT: Vic Damone makes his third series appearance, here in a Kismet *medley with his hostess, February 1964. In earlier shows, the stars sang excerpts from* Porgy and Bess *and* West Side Story.

CLOCKWISE FROM TOP RIGHT: *Singing "The Battle Hymn of the Republic," December 1963, three weeks to the day after the assassination of John F. Kennedy. The studio audience rose and cheered Garland's rendition; beaming her thanks after a taping, July 1963; in an unaired opening number, "If Love Were All," July 1963; with Mort Lindsey as he conducts "Make Someone Happy," January 1964.*

when she looked at you with those incredible eyes, and she said what she said, you believed everything. She had an incredible ability to tell you exactly what she meant and felt so deeply—and make you feel it." Echoing the majority of Garland's associates throughout her lifetime, he remembers "how dear she was, how bright, and how funny—a very fine, wonderful human being in every way, with a great deal to give that she gave continuously."

If James Aubrey was delighted to be rid of her, Garland and the series nonetheless won four Emmy nominations, and most critics were again quick to place the blame for the cancellation squarely on network interference and disinterest. Terry Turner summarized the overall situation in the Chicago *Sun-Times:* "They hired Judy because she was a star, and then they wouldn't let her be one." The show's overall superiority was also recognized in the San Francisco *Chronicle,* where a clear-eyed Terrence O'Flaherty enumerated Garland's troubles but called her show "the most crisp and stylish musical series of the season. In fact, I cannot recall any in television's history where the production was so polished or where the star burned with any brighter intensity." Perhaps the most succinct and prophetic comment came from a columnist whose postmortem concluded, "The tapes of these twenty-six TV shows, with close-ups and medium shots of Judy singing songs identified with her and standards, are priceless [and] destined to become a golden section of the Judy Garland story." Even one of Garland's sponsors made public pronouncement about the program; in a singular and unprecedented tribute, Menley and James decided to forgo a final advertisement on the last telecast and devoted their concluding moments of commercial time to a special voice-over announcement: "The first half of 'The Judy Garland Show' has been brought to you by Menley and James Laboratories, who wish Judy continued success and happiness. We have enjoyed bringing you 'The Judy Garland Show.' "

Garland was proud of much of her series work and agreed with the critics' condemnation of CBS: "The time slot was impossible," she told *TV Guide,* and added (with network-mocking candor), "They wanted me to be the girl-next-door. But they couldn't find the right house or the right door." The demise of the program was personally devastating, however; with it went her hopes of a permanent home and steady income. (Her later plan to syndicate the shows collapsed in a morass of lawsuits.)

The final show included five song clips taken from an earlier episode; despite two sessions, a distraught Judy had been unable to tape a complete hour. Although never telecast, her finale for the series was the Cy Coleman/Carolyn Leigh "Here's to Us," from Broadway's *Little Me.* It was a personal favorite, and for her rendition, Garland inserted an original lyric—just seventeen words—prior to Leigh's concluding phrase. It was a potent reminder of her lifetime of entertainment and genuine gratitude for her audience support:

And here's to you
For letting me do
What I'll do to the end of my days. . .
Here's to us — forever and always.

TAPE #26 "THE JUDY GARLAND SHOW"

1.	OVERTURE (Long)	(1)
2.	"AFTER YOU'VE GONE" Judy	(2)
5.	"THE NEARNESS OF YOU" Judy	(6)
6.	"LOVE WALKED IN" Judy	(7)
7.	"TIME AFTER TIME" Judy	(8)
8.	"THAT OLD FEELING" Judy	(9)
9.	"CAROLINA IN THE MORNING" Judy	(10)
11.	Travel & Opening Talk Judy	(13)
12.	OPENERS	
	a. PARIS: "BON JOUR PARIS" Judy	(14)
	b. LONDON: ""BACK IN LONDON" Judy	(16)
	c. LOEWS STATE: "BACK TO MANHATTAN" Judy & Male Chorus (o.c.)	(18)
	d. PALACE: "PALACE OPENING" Judy	(24)
	e. PALLADIUM: "I FINALLY GOT HERE" Judy	(29)
13.	Talk About Closing Judy	(31)
14.	"THE LAST DANCE" Judy	(32)
16.	"BORN IN A TRUNK" MEDLEY Judy & Girl Chorus (o.c.)	(35)
17.	a. ½ Hour Closing Billboard	(45)
	b. Station Break	(45)
	c. ½ Hour Opening Billboard	(45)
18.	FOURTH COMMERCIAL	(46)
19.	"SUPPERTIME" Judy	(47)
20.	"ALMOST LIKE" & "CAN'T BE LOVE" Judy	(49)
22.	Billy Barnes Talk Judy	(52)
23.	"HAVE I STAYED TOO LONG" Judy	(53)
24.	"SOMETHING COOL" Judy	(55)
25.	SIXTH COMMERCIAL	(57)
26.	"WHERE IS THE CLOWN" Judy Pantomime, Male Chorus (o.c.)	(58)
27.	"HERE'S TO US" Judy	(62)

TOP: The first draft rundown—sans commercials and station breaks—of the last show. The exhausted, disheartened Garland was only able to complete eleven of the scheduled nineteen routines. ABOVE: Judy in "Where Is the Clown," which was deleted from the air tape.

CHAPTER EIGHT

HERE'S TO US

Despite the demise of the series, Garland's professional standing remained essentially intact in spring 1964. CMA booked her in Australia, after which she hoped to star in London and on Broadway in a new comedy, *The Owl and the Pussycat.* Her escort on the tour and proposed costar for the play was actor Mark Herron, whom she'd been dating since their introduction on New Year's Eve.

Judy's arrival in Sydney was greeted by a press turnout larger than that accorded Queen Elizabeth a year earlier, and she was publicized as the highest-paid entertainer ever to appear in Australia. Though physically frail (her weight well below one hundred pounds), she "won the greatest audience ovation in the history of Aussie show biz" at her opening on May 13. Critics acclaimed her performance "bouncing, bubbling. . . gay and witty and charming" as she offered more than twenty songs from the Carnegie album and TV series material. Working center ring in a sold-out, ten-thousand-seat site usually reserved for sporting matches, Garland impetuously adapted the verse of "When You're Smiling" to fit the venue: *"And for heaven's sake, retain a calm 'demeanah,' / When you're stuck up here in this old wrestling arena."* Even a passing reference to *The Pirate* brought applause, and Judy quipped, "You're the only ones who saw it. . ."

The critics found her second concert on Saturday, May 16, an even bigger triumph: "Some of the songs could not be heard above the tumultuous roar of the crowd." Her voice was reviewed as "the glorious Garland article of old with a mature huskiness added," and backstage at the conclusion of the show, the exhausted Judy was rabidly complimented by producer Henry Miller. But—whether in flustered excitement over the audience reaction or indelicately demeaning in his phrasing—he continued, "Only a jerk singer like you could get a response like that." A stunned Garland slapped him and walked away. He tried to save matters by taking a heart-shaped ad in the press to declare his appreciation, but everything seemed to deteriorate after that. By the time she arrived in Melbourne for her final show, the overwrought Judy had not slept for several days. (She had been forced to adjust to unfamiliar medication in Australia when all she had brought with her from the States was confiscated in Customs on her arrival.) When she finally managed to get some rest the day of the concert, she woke with no voice—the result of the dry heating system in her hotel or its effect combined with that of the foreign medication. She made lengthy attempts to use a vaporizer to clear her throat, and the management at Festival Hall was called and asked to explain and apologize for her delay. Garland was further detained by press and fans outside the hotel and theatre, and she arrived an hour late for the sold-out show. As if to reassure the crowd of seven thousand that she was indeed ready to perform, she took stage immediately, clowning with Mort Lindsey and the orchestra mid-overture. But no explanation or announcement had been made to the throng, and a small proportion was in no mood to welcome her. As she prepared to begin her first number, voices called out "You're late," and one man shouted, "Have another brandy." Supportive factions in the

FACING PAGE: *Closing night of "At Home at the Palace," August 26, 1967.*
BELOW: *Fresh from a Hawaii vacation, the tanned and freckled Judy meets the press in Sydney, May 1964.*

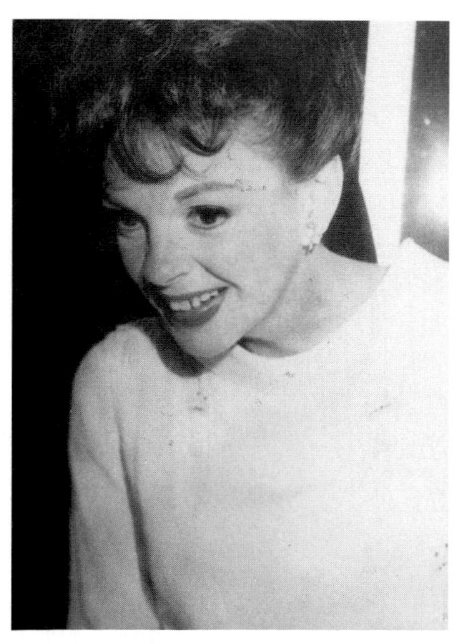

BELOW: Walking the aisle of Sydney Stadium to center ring for her first concert, May 13, 1964. BOTTOM: Arriving at the Palladium for "Night of 100 Stars," July 23, 1964. She is escorted in both instances by Mark Herron.

hall began to holler as well, but Judy, highly vulnerable and unsure in such a situation, was ill-prepared to cope with even the encouragement. She quickly won over the house with her initial songs, but when she began to joke between numbers, the restive comments began again. After a long intermission and some heated exchanges, Garland wept through "By Myself" and fled the stage.

The furor over the concert created international headlines, and there were front-page, rancorous accusations in the Australian press that Judy had been drunk or drugged. Hostile dialogue flew between the reporters and Garland, her entourage, and supporters, although more intelligent and sympathetic analysis of Judy's problems surfaced as well. Much was made of the local rivalry and "extreme jealousy" between Sydney and Melbourne. One writer pointedly offered, "Most Australian premieres take place in Melbourne because theatrical managers. . . know that [if] Sydney [is] given preference, Melbourne just doesn't want [the show]. The promoters should have presented Judy in Melbourne first. It would have been a different story if they had." Another, who attended all three Australian concerts, found the behavior of the Melbourne audience "thoroughly rude, disgusting and embarrassing. If [they] had been a little more civilized, they would have seen the Garland that Sydney saw." One reporter felt Garland was ill and asked why she had been allowed to perform: "Calling off the show would have saved a lot of sadness. . . and anger."

Although similar situations could and have happened to other performers, the worldwide press leapt upon it as an indication that Garland was washed up. She and Herron fled to Hong Kong where, terrified during the onslaught of a typhoon, she took an overdose of sleeping pills and was rushed to the hospital in critical condition. At one point, she was given up for dead but rallied yet again; an attempt to pump her stomach damaged her throat, however, and she was told not to sing for a year. The recent years of overwork, underweight, malnutrition, and increasing fragility took an additional, irrevocable toll as well. For the rest of her life, Judy would be forced to fight for her health; medication would often affect her voice and her emotional and mental behavior much more than before.

Upon her release from the hospital, Garland announced that she and Herron had married. Given the tumult created by the news—plus the fact that she had not yet divorced Luft—she recanted a few days later and said they were engaged; she credited Mark with saving her life in Hong Kong. The couple moved to London, where Garland was hospitalized with cuts on her wrists and arm. Within hours, however, she left a nursing home to appear at the annual "Night of 100 Stars" benefit at the Palladium. According to critic John London, "She received a fantastic reception. I doubt whether there has ever been anything to equal such a spontaneous outburst of affection." Scheduled merely to take a bow, Judy received a standing, screaming ovation at her entrance. When the cheers subsided and the show was about to continue, the audience suddenly, impulsively, and en masse began to chant, "We want Judy." She had to take a second bow before the next act could go on, and when he later tried to conclude the evening, compère Richard Attenborough was drowned out by shouts of "Judy!" "Sing, Judy, sing," and "We love you." She came forward, expressed her thanks ("It's nice to be home again") and offered impromptu renditions of "Rainbow" and "Swanee." The worldwide press headlined her "comeback"; much was made of the fact that Garland's appearance overshadowed every other star performer on the bill (including the Beatles in the first flush of their historic popularity).

PRECEDING PAGE: *Each episode of the CBS-TV "Judy Garland Show" closed with a "Born in a Trunk" segment.*

TOP: *Judy sings "Something's Coming" and* *ABOVE LEFT:* *"Tonight" with Vic Damone, December 1963.* *LEFT:* *Newspaper art for the series.* *RIGHT:* *Garland during production of the fourteenth episode, December 1963.*

FACING PAGE, TOP LEFT: *Judy offers "San Francisco" and* *CENTER LEFT:* *"I'm Old-Fashioned," January 1964.* *TOP RIGHT:* *Between takes.* *BOTTOM:* *With Diahann Carroll in a Harold Arlen/Richard Rodgers medley, January 1964.*

FACING PAGE, TOP: Judy with Jane Fonda, Roddy McDowall, and Henry Fonda at the Cocoanut Grove, 1963. BOTTOM LEFT: With Mark Herron at the Academy Awards, April 5, 1965. BOTTOM RIGHT: Backstage with two young fans, Randie and Shawn Williams, at the Circle Star Theatre, San Carlos, California, August 31, 1965.

LEFT AND CENTER LEFT: Garland and Sammy Davis, Jr., during two episodes of his TV series, February and March 1966. BOTTOM LEFT: Judy in concert at the Diplomat Hotel, Hollywood, Florida, February 1966. BELOW RIGHT: Singing "What the World Needs Now" as hostess of "The Hollywood Palace," April 1966.

"Judy Garland: At Home at the Palace." RIGHT AND BOTTOM RIGHT: *Singing solo and* BELOW LEFT: *with fourteen-year-old daughter, Lorna, during the record-breaking third engagement, July/August 1967.*

FACING PAGE, TOP LEFT AND RIGHT: *Judy at the Palace.* BOTTOM LEFT: *Judy at the Felt Forum, Madison Square Garden, Christmas 1967.* BOTTOM RIGHT: *Poster art for 1968 Lincoln Center concert.*

JUDY GARLAND
LINCOLN CENTER PHILHARMONIC HALL
SUNDAY FEB. 25, 8:30 PM ONE PERFORMANCE ONLY

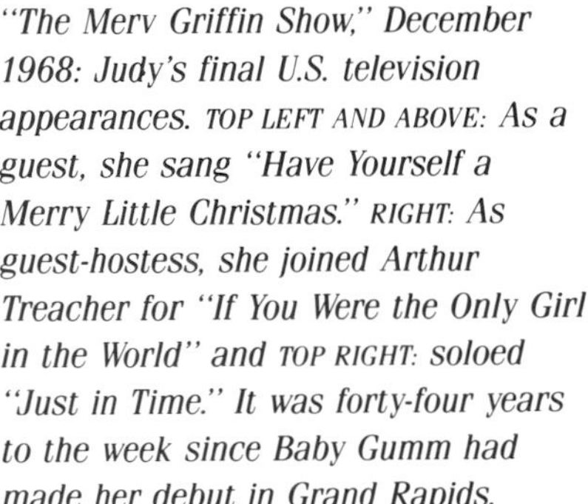

"The Merv Griffin Show," December 1968: Judy's final U.S. television appearances. TOP LEFT AND ABOVE: *As a guest, she sang "Have Yourself a Merry Little Christmas."* RIGHT: *As guest-hostess, she joined Arthur Treacher for "If You Were the Only Girl in the World" and* TOP RIGHT: *soloed "Just in Time." It was forty-four years to the week since Baby Gumm had made her debut in Grand Rapids.*

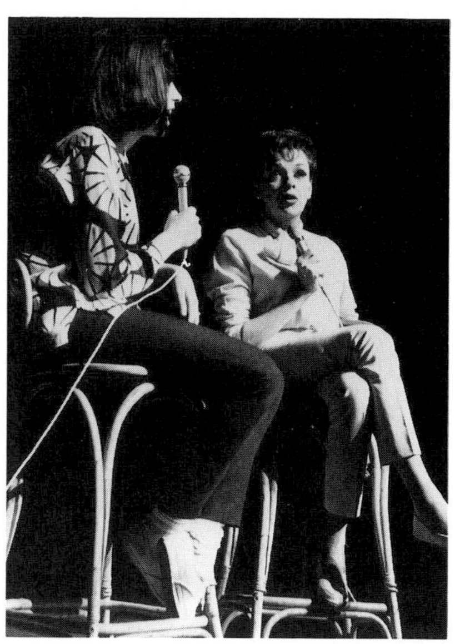

Rehearsals for Judy and Liza at the Palladium, November 8, 1964. Garland's solos included "Once in a Lifetime," "Maggie May," "As Long As He Needs Me," "Just in Time," "It's Yourself," "Smile," "Never Will I Marry," "What Now, My Love?" "The Music That Makes Me Dance," "Joey, Joey, Joey," "Make Someone Happy," "The Man That Got Away," "Rock-a-Bye," "San Francisco," and "Rainbow."

Attenborough recalled, "The magical thing was that every single artist on that stage wanted the limelight on one person only—Judy. They were as excited, if not more excited, than the audience." And Judy herself said the experience "left me so terribly grateful. These people were taking the trouble to show me that, to them, all the things that have happened in the past, all the things that have been said about me, didn't matter. They wanted me to know that they really cared."

In October, delighted by Liza's increasing success in theatre and on records, Judy invited her daughter to join her for a Palladium concert on November 8. Although initially reticent, Liza capitulated when Judy announced the show to the press. The theatre sold out before the performance could be advertised, and an additional appearance was added to accommodate ticket requests. Capitol arranged to record the first night for an album; the independent ITV network signed to videotape the November 15 "midnight matinee" for a television special.

Mother and daughter chose their own solos for the two-hour show and selected their duets together. After several days of rehearsal (including a five-hour orchestra call on the afternoon of the eighth), the pair offered a fifty-song program. Judy's fourteen numbers included much new material, including the showstopping premiere of "What Now, My Love?" Liza's nine solos were climaxed by a five-minute salute to her mother, parodying eight numbers and concluding with "My Mammy" *("I'd trade a million votes / For one of those notes. . .").* They dueted on more than twenty other songs, including the two medleys Garland had done with Streisand on the TV series.

The fans were enraptured from the beginning of the overture, although as the *New York Times* noted, "the audience was there to be captured. Miss Minnelli held her own with [them]. . . but it was Miss Garland who turned cheers into ovations." The *Daily Mail* commended Liza for her "scatty, off-beat interpretations of most of her songs," and concluded, "To talk about Judy Garland rationally is about as difficult as describing magic. Apart from still being the greatest of them all, through every routine it was apparent that she is also an accomplished actress. And if, to the very critical, the voice is no longer always what

TOP LEFT: In rehearsal. TOP CENTER: Backstage prior to the second show. TOP RIGHT: Mother and daughter duets included some of their songs from the series, "Hello, Dolly," "The Whole World in His Hands," "When the Saints Go Marching In"/"Brotherhood of Man," "Chicago," "Don't Rain on My Parade," and "Swanee." ABOVE: In her dressing room after the second concert, November 16, 1964.

it used to be, she still has that elusive 'star quality' which makes her the most-loved performer in the world today." (After the arduous rehearsal, Judy's voice was indeed somewhat frayed; Capitol's two-record set of excerpts from the concert offered proof of that fact, although the album rose to No. 19 during its months on the charts.)

The second concert was even more ecstatically received: the *Daily Sketch* reviewer could "actually feel the electricity crackling through the galvanized ranks of paying customers. This is not so much an entertainment as an experience." When Garland's voice again became worn by the end of the show, she asked the audience to sing "Rainbow" for her. They complied instantly for what *Variety* termed "the most moving moment in a heady mixture of slickness and emotion." Unfortunately, the ITV telecast five weeks later consisted of only 50 minutes of the 130-minute concert. The poorly edited excerpts omitted most of the performance highlights and included instead the entire twenty-minute finale when Garland was vocally at her weakest.

An odd legend has sprung up around the Judy/Liza concerts—in part because of the record and TV show and in part because of Liza's innocent remembrances of her mother's astonishment at the power, pizazz, and professionalism her daughter had acquired. "She was proud," Liza recalls, "but there must have been that threat at the same time. It was like competition, but with enormous love [and] a sense from both of us of 'I'm dealing with a power out here.' " With great humor, Liza sums up the situation by noting the difference in her costar before and after Liza's first set of songs: "My mother walked off the stage. *Judy Garland* walked back on!" Over the years, much fabrication has grown out of the misinterpretation of such comments. One biographer claimed that Minnelli, "shrieking hostility, deliberately provoked [and] challenged her mother"; Garland, in retaliation, supposedly "pushed Liza off-stage" in anger at the end of the show. No one who attended either concert, however, witnessed or reported anything but affection and enthusiasm between the two, onstage and off. Both reporters and audience members remember Garland encouraging all her own backstage visitors to "go and see" and praise Liza after the show.

Financial demands, work permits, and legal difficulties meant Garland had to return to the States in December. Prior to leaving London, she taped an interview with Jack Paar for telecast on his NBC program, and he has since affectionately written that she was "high on everything [that] night: from 'uppers' to a little white wine and perhaps Vicks VapoRub. It turned out to be a marvelous show." What played extremely well in the studio, however, translated poorly on the home screen. Garland was in poor voice and, though extraordinarily funny in her anecdotes, seemed somewhat hazy and wan. Coupled with all the negative personal and professional headlines of the preceding year, her appearance on the Paar show virtually obliterated much of the general public goodwill gained since the Carnegie Hall era.

CMA, however, began booking concerts for 1965, and Judy had already selected her own opening act. While in Hong Kong, she'd heard the Allen Brothers, a singing/dancing duo of unrelated Australian performers, Peter Allen and Chris Bell. She imported them to London to work in cabaret under her aegis and quickly earmarked Allen as a potential suitor for Liza. (Their engagement was announced in November 1964, a month after they met.) In early February, Garland agreed to appear on the CBS-TV talent-scout program "On Broadway Tonight" to introduce the Allen Brothers to America. Producer Irving Mansfield later confirmed he'd received twenty-seven thousand requests for the eleven hundred seats in the studio. The live audience—seemingly comprised of fans delighted to have Judy back home again and determined to offset any fear she might have about her reception—rose to greet her and applauded the beginnings, middles, and endings of her solos. The program won surprisingly good reviews, the notices referring to Garland "in top form" and to her segment as "magic time." In truth, her performance was improved over that on the Paar show, but she had lost much of the television ease she'd learned during the run of her series, and her voice seemed vibrato-heavy and tight.

BELOW: Singing "Never Will I Marry" on "The Jack Paar Program" from London, November 1964. BOTTOM: Singing "Almost Like Being in Love" during "On Broadway Tonight," February 1965.

That vocal condition developed into a severe head cold by the time she opened at Toronto's O'Keefe Centre several days later. She drew good houses and responsive audiences from the outset but garnered critical notices: "Judy's Voice Is Gone But They Still Love Her." Laryngitis forced her to cancel two midweek shows; her return was positively reviewed ("Judy Works Old Magic. . ."), and she finished the week in fine fashion. The Toronto engagement, however, saw the onset of a fifteen-month period of heavy professional obligation, sometimes uneven work, and occasionally mixed reviews—seeming evidence of the toll taken by her Hong Kong illness.

There was first a highly successful ten-day return to the Miami Beach Fontainebleau Hotel in March ("Garland Belts 'Em Out in Best Form"). Then, back in Los Angeles, Judy went into rehearsals for the April 5 Academy Awards presentation. Unfortunately, the medley she sang that night was hardly the vehicle with which to impress her largest television audience in three years. For the first time, Roger Edens let her down; his vocal arrangement of a dozen Cole Porter songs was plodding, unimaginative, and unwieldy—and Johnny Green's orchestration was its match. Garland was well rehearsed, in reasonably good voice, and, despite the expected nerves, worked hard at presenting a happy, controlled image. But the general effect was much depleted by the material, though several critics were

TOP: *The Cole Porter medley, April 1965. Conductor John Green later asked, "Could there be a better actress than Judy? She was a real honest-to-God musical-theatre performer. Sang like an angel. A great showman. Hell of a dancer and a heartrending actress."* ABOVE: *Judy with broken arm at the Greek Theatre, September 1965.*

FACING PAGE BOTTOM, LEFT TO RIGHT: *On Gypsy Rose Lee's talk show, August 1965; singing "Once in a Lifetime" on "The Hollywood Palace," October 1965; a rundown of that show, presented to those in the studio.*

appreciative and accurately noted that she "received an ovation fit for Mrs. Norman Maine."

Vocal difficulties developed during spring concerts in Charlotte and Chicago. In Cincinnati, Judy developed a high fever and rash prior to the show but insisted on going on. She completed the first half in rare vocal form but, by intermission, "was shaking like a leaf" when helped from the stage by her manager. After an hour's intermission, she returned with a doctor and apologized for canceling the rest of the appearance. Most of the audience of five thousand left quietly, but a few dozen troublemakers assaulted the Garland dressing room.

The illness in Cincinnati (and a May divorce from Sid Luft) again gave Garland the impetus to rid herself of her dependency on medication. In June, she checked into the UCLA Medical Center and successfully quit the pills she had been taking. Then she was forced to leave the hospital to fulfill a prearranged Las Vegas booking. She had an almost immediate allergic reaction to another prescribed medication just prior to leaving Los Angeles, followed by convulsions at the Vegas Thunderbird Hotel on the afternoon of the opening. Unbelievably—typically—she did the show on schedule. The *Sun* headlined: "First Nighters Go Wild Over Judy; Wins Standing Cheers," and declared, "[She] is the most exciting performer in the entire history of show business." *Variety* summarized, "In the distinctive tones hoped for, she socked across [her opening number]. It was as if she had hit a home run with the bases loaded." Garland's two-week engagement played to capacity, outdrawing every other hotel on the Strip.

She followed Vegas with a triumphant show at New York's Forest Hills Stadium in July. Despite heavy rain during the day and several light showers during the performance, Judy drew more than ten thousand to the outdoor venue. "Trim, confident, and buoyant," praised *Variety,* "she could have gotten away with 'The Internationale' sung in Russian." In good, if not great voice in the clammy night mist, Garland "generated a record ovation" at the stadium. For nearly thirty minutes after her twenty-song, ninety-minute concert, thousands of fans remained in the stands to chant "We want Judy!" until she returned for a bow.

August brought a week's engagement outside San Francisco at the Circle Star Theatre, and her first appearance in-the-round gave Judy much nervous vocal difficulty on opening night. This was passed off by some critics and duly noted by others ("Miss Garland trembled on the brink of utter disaster all evening. . . . Sometimes her struggle through the songs seemed almost unbearable"). By the second night, she was in excellent voice "and sang the roof off" the theatre. Lorna and Joe joined her onstage at several performances; the girl singing and the boy playing drums. There was a sterling September return to the Greek Theatre ("This was Judy back home looking and sounding better than in her 1957 appearance" wrote the *Hollywood Reporter*), but she fell and broke her arm after the opening. She went on the next night, assisted by Mickey Rooney, Martha Raye, and Johnny Mathis, but trouble with her cast and severe pain forced cancellation of the remaining four shows.

There were contrasting television appearances early that fall as well. On a September "Andy Williams Show" (taped in July), Garland was vocally slow to warm up in their duets and prerecorded for a comparatively ineffectual, pseudo rock 'n' roll solo of "Get Happy." Though she provided some good comedy both in line readings and during a pantomime makeup sketch with Williams, her limited vocal range only added to public speculation about her diminishing talent. Surprisingly, she then turned up in October on a live "Ed Sullivan Show" and, in *Variety* parlance, "sang in the old wham style if with less voice." It was the closest Garland had come in eighteen months to her earlier TV series presence and timing. Two weeks later, she taped an even more successful appearance as guest hostess of the "Hollywood Palace," singing effectively and introducing the guest acts with humor and reasonable élan. But such vintage arrangements as her 1951 Palace medley were by this time a key or two out of her comfortable range; it remains a mystery as to why, in this instance and many others in succeeding years, the orchestrations weren't transposed slightly to accommodate her.

On November 14, Judy married Mark Herron during a quick trip to Las Vegas. Her opening at the Sahara two weeks later brought out all the superlatives. If television viewers had recently seen a Garland who vacillated in vocal quality, live audiences were witness to what *Sun* columnist Paul Price surmised "may well have been the most fabulous night in show business. . . and I've never been much of a fan." In the same paper, Ralph Pearl reported, "Hubby Mark Herron sat at ringside, watching a Judy he'd probably never heard in such great voice or seen in better spirits." Garland was by this time healthily chubby once again, quite possibly because she had worked hard at resisting overmedication. As a result, her voice was full and rich. A subsequent one-night stand—as the first solo performer to work in concert at the enormous Houston Astrodome—was also a vocal triumph. The public came out in even larger crowds than they had for her 1961 Houston shows, despite well-founded misgivings about the suitability of the Dome's sound system for a musical show (and the incongruous booking of The Supremes as Garland's opening act).

There was a happy return to Florida in February, playing the Diplomat Hotel, and even the sole critic who thought Garland below par on opening night returned later and found her singing "flawless, incredible." Another concurred: "The night I saw her, there was never such singing since the world began. What would this century be without Judy Garland singing?" Judy displayed some of her regained vocal power during solo moments on the February Perry Como "Kraft Music Hall"

Singing "A Wonderful Day Like Today" on "The Andy Williams Show," July 1965.

HOLLYWOOD
PALACE
PRESENTATION ON ABC-TV
SATURDAY, NOVEMBER 13, 1965

PROGRAM

NOTE: The position which an act is allotted on the program does not in the least reflect upon its merit. When a bill is made up almost exclusively of headliners — a frequent occurrence at the Hollywood Palace — every number is worthy of the "star spot" on ordinary vaudeville bills. It is only fair to the artist, therefore, to judge his work solely upon its merits.

OUR HOSTESS JUDY GARLAND Her Majesty Of Music Visits The Palace

LYONS FAMILY LIFTS WITH FATHER

GENIAL GENIE OF GAGS GENE BAYLOS

Glamorous CHITA RIVERA DANCING BEAUTY FROM BROADWAY

Italy's THREE BRAGAZZI MEDITERRANEAN MUSICAL MADNESS

JUDY SINGS "A COUPLE OF SWELLS"
THE QUEEN OF SONG PLAYS A QUEEN OF THE ROAD

VIC DAMONE DOING WHAT COMES VOCALLY

"WEST SIDE STORY" WITH A HAPPY BLENDING JUDY & VIC

SCHREIBER & BURNS A CAR-FULL OF FUN

"JUDY AT THE PALACE!"
A NIGHT TO REMEMBER

Mitchell Ayres and the Hollywood Palace Orchestra

A ZODIAC PRODUCTION
Executive Producer - NICK VANOFF
Producer - WILLIAM O. HARBACH

BELOW: An ad for Judy at the Astrodome, 1965. BOTTOM: Onstage that night. (Despite the billing, Judy was not filling in for Diana Ross. The Supremes were Garland's warm-up act; they had not yet expanded their name to highlight Ross.)

TV show; she sang "What Now, My Love?" and, according to a Seattle critic, "sounded like she was ready to lead the second charge of the Light Brigade." A week later, laryngitis affected her taping of a "Sammy Davis, Jr. Show." Nonetheless, she won ovations from the studio audience, and dressed in tramp costumes, she and Davis performed a superbly arranged medley of her film hits. On camera, he asked her to return for his next show. Her vocal trouble was even worse by that point, although she and Davis again effectively clowned through a minstrel medley. In April, Judy taped another "Hollywood Palace" but with less happy results than before. On camera, she was good-humored (if slightly slurred in delivery); her voice varied from fair to harsh. But, in a rage, she tore up the star dressing room after the show, and when word got around about her behavior, it effectively blacklisted her from future prime-time television work.

There were reasons if not excuses for her actions. The marriage to Herron was already foundering; by May, they had separated, as the actor had been warned that he would be responsible for half of Judy's tax debt for the year if they stayed married longer than six months. Garland was unable to handle the burden of the separation, the responsibilities of home and children, and especially her increasing financial problems. Her recent record royalties and television and concert salaries had been attached for tax debts, and she was threatened with repossession of her home. Understandably, she had difficulty in comprehending the fact that, after fifteen months of work at top salary, she had gone further into arrears with each job she took.

Her public reputation in 1966 was also at a new low, suffering by comparison to the glories of the earlier part of the decade. The public was near saturation level in their ability to assimilate the up-and-down aspects of her life, and there was very little explanation offered for the extremes. To the press, a successful appearance was always a comeback; a personal disaster, illness, hospitalization, or canceled performance was decried (according to one omniscient journalist) "as if it were a breach of faith" by Dorothy Gale. During Judy's lifetime, there was no public understanding of the effects of prescription medication—nor were there Betty Ford Clinics or public praise and canonization for those who admitted and sought help for substance abuse. There was also no awareness of the managerial reasons for Garland's tangled financial status. The public only read about or witnessed the excesses of Judy's behavior, and they were soon overwhelmed with such reportage and conduct—no matter how she tried to rise above the situations or how she labored.

Given her tax problems, Judy simply refused to work through much of the remainder of 1966. There was a single further booking: a two-week Mexico City nightclub engagement in August that promised cash payment and began in hysterical triumph. The scheduled thirty-minute premiere lasted ninety minutes, and the press was jubilant. "Glorious, extraordinary, electrifying, and magnetic" wrote the critic in *Exito* before invoking such names as Josephine Baker, Maurice Chevalier, Marian Anderson, Lawrence Tibbett, and Jascha Heifetz to conclude, "I have never before experienced the strange emotion of seeing the little giant, Judy." But the altitude of Mexico City and Garland's medication combined to give her laryngitis; she struggled through the second night but, unable to talk, was forced to bow out after that.

She planned another attempt at autobiography, this time assisted by her new escort, publicist Tom Green. (An earlier effort, with Fred Finklehoffe in 1960,

had never been completed.) Judy spent the Christmas holidays with Green's family in Massachusetts. Meanwhile, Sid Luft had once again reentered the picture in an effort to help straighten out her financial affairs. In October 1966, she joined him in a multimillion-dollar suit against CMA, Fields, and Begelman, charging that they "deliberately and systematically misused their position of trust so as to cheat, embezzle, extort, defraud, and withhold" monies from her.

In February 1967, 20th Century-Fox offered Garland a supporting role in the film adaptation of Jacqueline Susann's novel *Valley of the Dolls.* A runaway bestseller, the roman a clef included among its protagonists a character much inspired by Garland's personal and professional history. In a couple of sections of the book, Susann merely rewrote contemporary fan-magazine articles on Garland as she created a drug-addicted entertainer named Neely O'Hara. Garland accepted the film role (as an Ethel Merman prototype) purely for the money. When she finally read the script prior to her first day of filming, she realized the picture would be far from a cinematic masterpiece. Her sudden unwillingness to participate was also influenced by medication, and after several days of refusing to leave her dressing room when required on the set, Garland was fired by Fox. (The subsequent headlines implied that she had lost another major opportunity.) She quickly traveled to New York to appear on an NBC-TV Jack Paar special, but gaunt, blurry, and in unbecoming hairstyle and makeup, she provided medicated (if funny) commentary. Coming on the heels of the *Valley* dismissal, the performance was another public disaster.

Luft next managed to secure her three one-week concert bookings on the summer-stock circuit. She opened at Long Island's Westbury Music Fair in June 1967 to fine reviews and an almost messianic audience response; she was described by *Variety* as "the object of veneration of a kind that will probably not be seen again for a long time." Vocally, it was an increasingly difficult time for Garland. Though there were nights when she was in comparatively fine voice, her primary medication continued to be Ritalin, and the excessive doses she would sometimes take dried out her vocal chords. Singing apart, however, she was very much the consummate professional during her 1967 tour. As one critic later noted, "She seemed to be saying if she only sang half as well as before, then she would

TOP, LEFT TO RIGHT: "Meet me in Mi—ami, Sammy," sang Garland to her host on the Davis show, February 1966; after a duet of "Mr. and Mrs. Clown" with Van Johnson on "The Hollywood Palace," April 1966; closing the same program with "By Myself." ABOVE: At home in Brentwood, 1965.

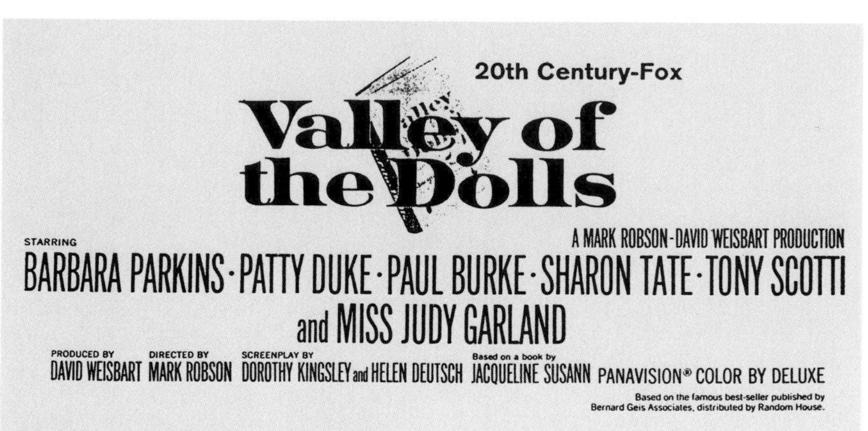

TOP LEFT: Trade paper ad for Valley of the Dolls *before Garland left the cast, April 1967. (Judy had scanned a packed press conference assembled to hear about her job in March and gibed, "Usually when there's this big a crowd, it's because I've been fired.") TOP RIGHT: With Lorna and Joe in publicity for the Palace show, July 1967. ABOVE: Backstage at the Palace.*

perform twice as well." Her vibrancy, happy attitude, and fully charged personality induced tears and chills for thousands who flocked to see her despite the *Dolls* and Paar debacles. More than ever before, her audiences also included hundreds of children and teenagers, weaned on annual teleshowings of *The Wizard of Oz,* the programming of her other MGM films by local stations, and the TV series and guest appearances.

In July, Sid was able to book Judy into the Palace for the third time. She was exultant though faced with some harrowing facts. The theatre was only available for four weeks, so there was no hope of an extended run. The show would open July 31, the peak of midsummer heat and the worst time of the year for New York theatre. She would once again face the severest critics in the country. And, as two shows a day were by now difficult for her, Luft booked seven evening shows a week, which meant that she would have to perform twenty-seven consecutive nights.

Miraculously, Judy again pulled it off. Thrilled to return to "her" theatre—the act was billed as "Judy Garland at Home at the Palace"—she provided a full seventy-five- or eighty-minute show each evening. Her "surprise" entrance for the engagement brought Garland in from the lobby of the theatre and down the center aisle of the Palace amidst a crowd invariably on its feet in acclamation. She sang a mélange of past and present hits, adding new material in "How Insensitive," Cole Porter's "I Loved Him," and duets with Lorna on "Bob White" and "Jamboree Jones." Lorna also offered a solo medley of "Singin' in the Rain" and "Happy Days Are Here Again," Joe played drums, and both daughter and son joined Mama for "Together." The show was staged by Richard Barstow, and he brought John Bubbles (again part of the first-act bill) into Judy's act to reprise "Me and My Shadow" from the 1959 Opera House tour. The routine was expanded to introduce Lorna and Joe as well.

Once again, Times Square was a cordoned-off mob scene for the opening. Critical estimation of Judy's reappearance was almost unanimously laudatory, despite occasional minor reservations about her voice and the rabid behavior of the audience. Every review responded in force to Garland's personality, the planned or candid humor, the joy and ebullience she inspired. In the *Post,* Jerry Tallmer referred to himself as "an aging critic, shuddering happily with tears coursing down his cheeks as talent and the times are once again, beyond belief, reborn. Judy for the thousand and first time has come all the way back." Lee

Silver in the *Daily News* found that the "one thing that came through, despite the audience's roar of cultish adulation, is that she is as great a performer as they think she is. Time, instead of taking its toll, has given an even greater authority to her stage presence and a more dramatic quality to her vocal control." The public responded as well, breaking the Palace box-office record for vaudeville and bringing the four-week gross to over $300,000. Theatre management even opened up the second balcony to accommodate the crowds.

The press interviewed, profiled, and celebrated Garland once again, and Luft negotiated a new recording contract for her with ABC-Paramount. *At Home at the Palace/Opening Night* included live excerpts from the act and spent several weeks on the charts, although only side one was taken from the July 31 performance; side two was drawn from an appearance later in the first week.

As the run progressed, an animated Judy made every night celebrity night and informally brought to the stage such associates as Duke Ellington, Joel Grey, Barbara Harris, Joan Crawford, and Beatrice Lillie. Liza returned from appearances abroad for the last two evenings of the show and joined Judy to chat and (on closing night) to duet "Chicago" and sing "Cabaret" (to which Judy danced). Minnelli had just done a charity benefit in Monaco, although Princess Grace had been in Hollywood at the time. "Maybe," quipped Judy, "she went back to get her Oscar regilded." At the end of the final performance, after singing "Auld Lang Syne" and watching the final curtain fall, most of the audience remained to chant "We want Judy." When she reappeared for a final bow, she said simply, "Never forget that I want *you*, too."

From the Palace, Luft booked Judy on a ten-city, sixteen-show tour, which saw her range in vocal quality but never performance power. (On evenings when Garland had rested, eaten, and/or been able to limit her intake of Ritalin, her singing was invariably refreshened.) Midwestern critics were harsher in their ap-

Closing night at the Palace. LEFT: *"Me and My Shadow" and* RIGHT: *with Liza. Garland's partner John Bubbles had earlier sighed to a reporter, "Ain't Judy something else? She's the only one I know of in all my travels who can fill the spots of all the other acts missing on the bill." Just back from a tour, Liza was brought up onstage by a doting mother and impishly asked, "How was* Australia? *You know I want to hear about* that!"

praisals of Judy's voice, but almost uniformly in awe of her impact on audiences and communicative ability and humor. Highlights of the tour included her spontaneous offstage visits to military hospitals in Boston, Chicago, and Bethesda, where she performed impromptu concerts and went from ward to ward to chat with, kiss, and bolster hundreds of servicemen wounded in Vietnam. A free-to-the-public open-air concert on Boston Common on August 31 drew Garland's largest live audience, a crowd estimated at 108,000 people. They began arriving thirteen hours before showtime (waiting through two torrential downpours), sang "Hello, Judy" to her as she danced between numbers, and thundered approval when Mayor John Collins presented her with an engraved Paul Revere bowl.

It was during this era (especially in East Coast cities) that some percentage of the Garland audience seemed to want to put itself into her act, occasionally demonstrating to excess. The tumult came from all ages and types, and Garland was grateful (if wary) and usually adept at handling it. But the overall behavior of some of the more hysteric and unrestrained cultists astounded the rest of the audience. The situation was inflamed by a *Time* report on Judy's Palace return. While almost grudgingly commending her, the reviewer snidely slid into amateur analysis over the "disproportionate part of her nightly claque [that] seems to be homosexual." Garland took offense at the tone of the piece, telling later audiences and interviewers, "For years—since I was a *fetus*—I've been misquoted and rather brutally treated by the press! But I'll be damned if I like to have my audiences mistreated." It was a difficult stance for her to take, as the tenor of the times was far from a liberated one. She had, in fact, already summed up her public attitude about her gay following when a San Francisco columnist had pointedly, negatively tried to make an issue of it in 1965. Garland gently, almost chidingly replied, "I sing to *people*."

Judy next returned to Vegas for a Caesars Palace engagement and, five nights after the November 30 opening, missed her first performance since the tour began in June. As she was preparing to go to the stage, she heard a television news broadcast about the death of Bert Lahr, and the inconsolable Garland collapsed. Palace management was indignant, but she worked again the next evening and, just before her "Rainbow" finale, said, "This I am singing to my dear Cowardly Lion. God bless him."

After six months of steady work, Garland had neither the strength nor the

BELOW LEFT, CENTER, RIGHT, AND FACING PAGE, TOP: Judy Garland—"At Home at the Palace." The elaborate sequinned pants suit had been designed for Valley of the Dolls, *but when a baiting first-nighter bellowed, "Where'd you get that outfit?" the cagey Garland blithely riposted, "I made it myself."*

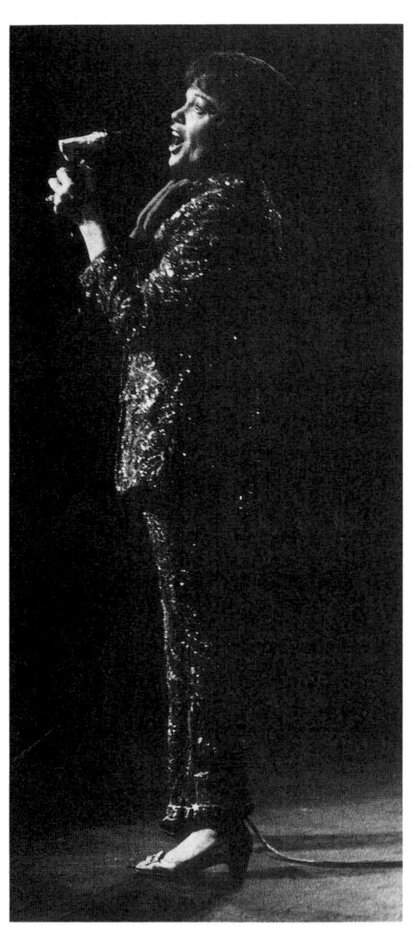

inclination to fulfill Luft's final booking of the year, a Christmas stand at the Madison Square Garden Felt Forum. Nevertheless, she rehearsed a new show (including numbers with Lorna, Joe, and a children's chorus) and played the first four nights; plagued by an obvious cold, she still managed to evidence more voice than on many earlier occasions during 1967. By midweek, however, she entered the hospital with bronchitis, and the final three performances were canceled. The media, in turn, accused her of "losing her professional sense of obligation to the audience."

Despite the press's attitude, Judy had tallied seventy-nine concerts in seven months, but after the arduous ordeal of touring (and the burden and fear of facing thousands of people on many occasions without much voice), there was again nothing to show for her efforts. The "Group V" corporation Luft had formed to afford her financial protection was impotent against the IRS; they had taken most of her income as well as proceeds from the sale of her Los Angeles home. In early 1968, Garland was locked out of a New York townhouse when she could not pay the rent; the same thing happened in May at the St. Moritz Hotel, and her possessions were impounded.

She did only two formal concerts in early 1968, the first a grievous one-night stand in Baltimore. Whether overly medicated or (as she attempted to explain to the audience) suffering from food poisoning, Judy was unable to sing. She fought her way through a performance, encouraged by fans who had run to the apron stage; the majority of the audience was saddened and quietly horrified that she had been allowed to go on. A week later, she gave a satisfactory show at Lincoln Center in New York, but the vigor and goodwill of the preceding year had been dissipated by debts, medication, ill health, and her disillusionment with Group V. Judy's attempt to be the first Broadway replacement in *Mame* had also come to naught. Although songwriter Jerry Herman and several of the producers dreamed of seeing her in the vehicle, Garland was not well enough to sustain eight strenuous performances a week.

Other nadirs were hit that spring. Tom Green had been Judy's on-and-off-again fiancé for nearly a year when she had him jailed in April for stealing two of her rings; he had actually pawned them at Garland's request so as to pay one of her hospital bills. (Green later estimated that he spent $50,000 providing for Judy from 1966–68.) Another disaster occurred in Boston. Booked for two May concerts, Garland first visited Chelsea Naval Hospital and, at her premiere the next night, offered a nonstop two-hour show with force and strength (if little voice). The second night, with patients as special guests, an obdurate Garland refused to appear. Over the phone, Lorna tried to cajole her mother into performing, citing the wounded veterans: "Mama, they've wheeled them all in here." Judy replied, "Well, if they can wheel 'em in, they can wheel 'em out."

A five-night June engagement at the newly opened Garden State Arts Center in New Jersey proved another fiasco. On her opening and fourth nights, Garland gave vital, admirable performances. The second and third nights, she was ill and unable to sing on key. During her third song on closing night, she fell asleep and had to be helped from the stage and hospitalized. Once more, Garland sought treatment at Peter Bent Brigham Hospital in Boston, and spent several weeks in their withdrawal program. As a result, her appearance at Philadelphia's outdoor J.F.K. Stadium on July 20 was one of her finer efforts of the era. Refreshed and in good form after the hospitalization, she zipped from one song to the next,

ABOVE: Greeting fans on the Boston Common. Garland's banter with anonymous voices in the crowd provided highlights in her concerts. In 1968, one man impulsively called out, "Marry me!" Without missing a beat, the star echoed, "Marry you? *With* my *record?"*

TOP LEFT: At a Cleveland press conference, September 1967. TOP RIGHT: With Bernard Johnson and his family in New York, December 1968. The designer created Judy's outfit for her hostess stint on "The Merv Griffin Show." ABOVE: Garland cajoled entertainer Danny LaRue into a quick guest spot on opening night at London's Talk of the Town, December 1968.

happy and in full control of her program and raving audience. An ensuing appearance on the syndicated Mike Douglas TV show gave evidence of an again-revitalized voice, although she did not look her best.

There was little additional work for the rest of the year. When CMA approached her with a check they held for accumulated royalties, she agreed to drop her portion of the suit against them in order to receive the funds. She took an apartment by herself in Boston; Lorna and Joe went to live with Sid in Los Angeles, and Liza was increasingly busy with her own career and marriage to Peter Allen.

In autumn, Judy briefly returned to New York as one of the first women invited to appear in the Blackglama mink-coat ad campaign, "What Becomes a Legend Most?" In October, she was also introduced to pianist/songwriter Johnny Meyer, who got her work singing in a small club for $100 a night and arranged for her successful November appearance at a Lincoln Center ASCAP salute to Harold Arlen. In December, Meyer booked Garland on several New York TV talk shows and for an engagement at London's Talk of the Town nightclub. Her appearances with Dick Cavett, Johnny Carson, and Merv Griffin were boisterously received by studio audiences, and the increasingly fragile Judy ranged from poor to good voice as she introduced four of Meyer's songs.

Their brief relationship was over before she left for England, however; just prior to her departure, she announced her engagement to discothèque manager Mickey Deans, whom she had first met in 1967. Deans accompanied her to London, and they were greeted by a writ attempting to prevent Garland's cabaret appearance. Earlier in 1968, Luft had assigned her Group V employment contract to two businessmen to acquire a loan. When Sid and his partner were unable to repay the money, Judy's services became the province of the businessmen. But after she claimed to have no knowledge of the assignment, the British judge threw the case out of court, and Judy enjoyed a successful if somewhat under-rehearsed opening at the Talk of the Town on December 30. Every star in London was present to cheer her on, and the reviews were predominantly panegyric. *The Stage* decided, "There are very few artists who create an emotionalism—almost amounting to hysteria—minutes before they actually set foot onstage. Of these, probably the greatest is Judy. [Even before she made her entrance] the atmosphere was so electric that one felt as if it would be possible to shovel it into boxes and sell it to less fortunate places of entertainment." Sheridan Morley found her "one of those rare singers who seem to call for dramatic rather than musical criticism. For a definition of theatrical magic, one need look no further." The *Financial Times* labeled her "the Maria Callas of popular music. Her voice still holds its tremendous charge of suppressed excitement."

Judy got through the first three weeks of the engagement victoriously, though finding the smoke-laden atmosphere of the club extremely hard on her voice. Lorna Smith, serving as her backstage adjunct, attempted to smooth the way for Garland each night, although from the moment she first saw Judy, it was apparent that Garland's health had become a serious problem. Smith regarded it as a miracle that the entertainer was able to go on each evening, "drawing herself together to become as much of 'Judy Garland' as her worn-out constitution would allow."

As a favor to the producers of the "Sunday Night at the Palladium" TV show, Garland agreed to fill in for an indisposed Lena Horne on January 19. But it was her own one night off from the Talk of the Town and a challenge beyond her. She insisted that her overture be played, which put a three-minute orchestral medley into the middle of a fast-paced variety show with no explanation; many viewers assumed something had gone wrong. When Judy appeared and stumbled over the words to her first song, the impression was compounded. Although she was in relatively good form, it was Britain's first mass exposure to the kind of TV work that many in the States had seen over the preceding four years. As a result, there was much conjecture in the press about Judy's condition.

At the Talk of the Town, however, the only continuing problem concerned Judy's consistent late appearances. According to Smith, Garland was actually unaware that she was arriving past her scheduled show time. (The club had agreed she could make up at her hotel and then go directly onstage from her car.) Her health was so bad one evening that she was told by her doctor to cancel the performance. A replacement was found but Garland insisted on singing as well and, though late, took the stage to elated applause. Two nights later, however—and aware that she was an hour late—she was forced onstage when feeling terribly ill. As in Melbourne, she thought the situation had been explained to the audience and that she had apologized in advance for the delay. When she arrived at the club and went out singing, several ringside customers berated her; others called out, "Give the girl a chance." But the rude faction continued to razz Garland, throwing bread sticks and crumpled cigarette packets at the platform. According to witnesses, they were more motivated by alcohol and rowdiness than by any real rancor toward the star. One man stood up and took the microphone from her as she neared the edge of the stage. Judy, failing in any attempt to placate the handful of ruffians, finally walked off as one of them shattered a glass across the dance floor. Backstage, Garland was distraught and then horrified when told her apology had not been made before she went on. Her doctor ordered her to bed, and the club management (already under fire because of the lateness of the show on other evenings) announced that Judy would not return until declared medically fit.

Garland took Friday and Saturday off, but returned to cheers on Monday and played out her final week while jesting, "What's the matter? Can't a legend have the flu?" Despite everything, her engagement broke all records at the Talk of

Judy at the Talk of the Town. Journalist Clive Hirschhorn raved about her "splendid performance [as] a capacity audience kept yelling for more. [And] who can blame them? When she is on form, there is no star in the world today more exciting to watch or more thrilling to listen to."

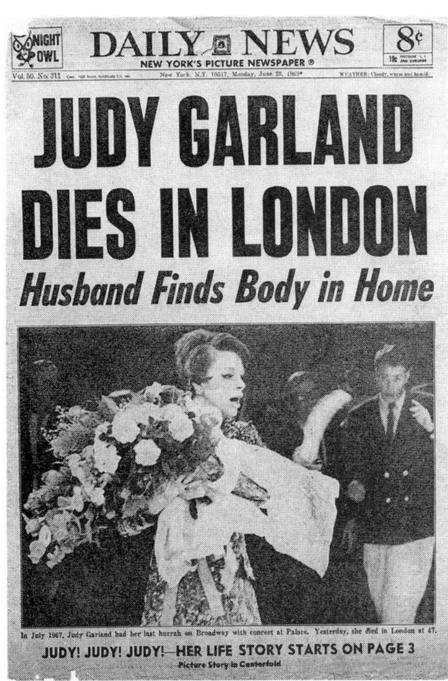

NIGHT OWL

DAILY NEWS

8¢

NEW YORK'S PICTURE NEWSPAPER ®

Vol. 50. No. 311 New York, N.Y. 10017, Monday, June 23, 1969

JUDY GARLAND DIES IN LONDON

Husband Finds Body in Home

In July 1967, Judy Garland had her last hurrah on Broadway with concert at Palace. Yesterday, she died in London at 47.

JUDY! JUDY! JUDY!—HER LIFE STORY STARTS ON PAGE 3

Picture Story in Centerfold

TOP: A month prior to her death, Judy and Mickey Deans were photographed as they briefly left their new home in London for a business trip to New York. ABOVE: Newspapers around the world featured similar front page headlines on Monday, June 23, 1969.

the Town and received more press coverage than that of any other performer in the club's history.

Judy married Deans in London on March 15, shortly before embarking on a four-city tour with singer Johnny Ray as her opening act. They debuted in Stockholm, where Garland got a ten-minute standing ovation at the conclusion of the show, but their second appearance (in Gothenburg) was canceled when she took too many sleeping pills in an effort to rest, and the promoter was afraid she wouldn't wake in time. The two final shows—in Malmö and Copenhagen—were successfully completed, although Judy was ever more frail and ill, her voice strong but tired. At the supper club where she performed in Malmö, she was pelted with flowers by the crowd; the Copenhagen concert won similar response. Despite fears over her health by those around her, film footage taken onstage and backstage shows her happy and very much the hard-working veteran—having her hair done, applying her makeup, kidding with photographers. It provides at least one alternative view to the many legends that circulate about her terror before a performance and the implication that everything had to be done for her.

Illness forced Judy to cancel a Paris concert in early May, but later in the month, she and Deans made a brief business trip to New York. He planned to license her name for a chain of movie theatres, thus providing some steady income without the pressures of performing, but the deal fell through, and they returned to England. Lorna Smith visited Judy on June 16 and, dismayed by her weakened condition, hoped to establish a group of friends who would see that she was eating, had company, and was being looked after.

Mid-morning on Sunday, June 22, however, Deans found Judy in the bathroom of their tiny mews cottage in Cadogan Lane, her head cradled in her arms. She had taken her customary Seconal sleeping pills the night before, awakened in the night to take more, and in her weakened condition, had been unable to survive the dosage.

Her death, the subsequent autopsy and inquest, her wake, and interment once more made international headlines, and Judy Garland topped radio and television newscasts for the next six days. The overriding tenor of the reports concentrated on the tragedy of her life. Her extraordinary body of work was frequently lost in the (sometimes inaccurate) litany of addictions, hospitalizations, domestic problems, cancellations, firings, and implications of a (finally realized) suicide attempt. Adding to the drama, a British doctor who had briefly treated Garland in 1964 stated that she had cirrhosis and was living on borrowed time.

Much of the media and public were thus surprised by the findings announced at the Garland inquest on June 25. Pathologist Dr. Derek Pocock offered a lengthy, formal statement in anticipation of any questions, first noting, "There is no question of alcoholism. No effects of alcoholism could be found on her body: no cirrhosis of the liver, no effects of chronic alcoholism." He continued: "The question of self-poisoning with sedatives is not a matter of clear-cut finding. It is not a black and white affair, and there are a great many grades between purely accidental overdoses and the ones taken by a person who is habituated or perhaps gets a little incautious. [But] there is absolutely no evidence from the findings of the doctors and the evidence generally to suggest that this was a deliberate action on the part of Miss Garland. She had taken more barbiturates than she could tolerate. This is quite clearly an accidental circumstance to a person who was accustomed to taking barbiturates over a very long time."

Garland's body was flown home to New York, and the media turned its attention to the twenty-two thousand mourners who waited up to four hours to pay their respects at Frank E. Campbell's Funeral Chapel. Eighty-first Street between Madison and Fifth avenues had to be closed to traffic, and Deans eventually requested that the parlor remain open all night to accommodate the men, women, children, and teenagers who paid tribute during the seventeen-hour wake. Hundreds of floral arrangements arrived from stars and fans, including a huge spray from MGM and another from the Palace.

On Friday afternoon, June 27, James Mason gave the eulogy at a private service; a heartbroken Mickey Rooney left even before it began. The co-workers and friends in attendance included Kay Thompson, Freddie Bartholomew, Alan King, Ray Bolger, Lauren Bacall, Harold Arlen, Johnny Mercer, Betty Comden and Adolph Green, Patricia Kennedy Lawford, and Mayor John V. Lindsay. The assemblage sang "The Battle Hymn of the Republic," and Liza's conductor played "Here's to Us."

Judy's family received thousands of condolence messages, but perhaps the most warming memorials came in the reactions of two anonymous children. After the service, Garland's casket was taken to Ferncliff Cemetery in Hartsdale, New York, and hundreds of local residents lined the driveway as the limousine passed. One solemn little boy in shorts said to a supervising policeman, "I don't think I'm dressed respectful enough." The patrolman lifted up the boy so that he could better see what was happening and told him, "Respect is from the heart, son." A nine-year-old girl cut out her favorite poem, mounted it on a piece of cardboard, and offered it as her gratitude. It concluded:

To one. . . who shares my joys.
Who cheers when sad.
The greatest friend I ever had.

Judy Garland's final performance had been given three months earlier. The March 25 concert at Copenhagen's Falkoner Centret marked her first appearance in Denmark, although critics there had for years heard the negative professional and personal rumors surrounding her name. But despite her advance reputation—and despite the fact that Judy was far from well—the reviews of that show give final testimony to the communicative ability, the natural talent, and the genius that Baby Gumm retained to the end of her life. The critics offered: "We found her last evening to be an enchanting entertainer, an exquisite artist in her field" and noted that "her distinctive personality was intact, her mode of delivery strong and glowing, her personal charm indisputable. People streamed down the side aisles to applaud as near to the star as possible." One summarized, "The air was thick with rumors that the star was no longer a star, that she had not only lost her voice, but that she could no longer even get through her program. Suddenly she stood on the enormous stage and disproved all the rumors in the world. Her voice [was] under control and bright with infectious vitality—it struck sparks. After a large number of curtain calls, she finally gave in to the deepest wish of the audience. She sat down on the stage floor and began to sing 'Over the Rainbow.' It was as though she sang it for the first time, with fervent innocence and sweetness. Tears came to one's eyes. All the spectators arose and cheered Judy Garland. She had a great triumph."

Garland remained a major news feature for a full week. After her wake, Variety *rather pointedly noted that the quoted comments of "waiting mourners. . . all seemed intelligent, touching, and sincere. They were there because they had to be; she was like a member of the family. She was someone not pitied, but loved."*

DAILY NEWS 8¢
NEW YORK'S PICTURE NEWSPAPER

JUDY'S PEOPLE DIDN'T FORGET

FINAL
DAILY NEWS 8¢
NEW YORK'S PICTURE NEWSPAPER

AN ALL-NIGHT VIGIL FOR JUDY

NIGHT OWL
DAILY NEWS 8¢
NEW YORK'S PICTURE NEWSPAPER

JUDY WAS STAR IN FINAL ROLE

Hundreds Linger After Funeral

CHAPTER NINE

THROUGH THE YEARS

By June 1969, Judy Garland's professional and personal travails had in many ways overwhelmed the general public. Seeing only the final rocky television appearances and reading the sensational headlines, few were aware of the financial burden or frailty and illness behind Judy's behavior; little sympathy could be summoned for her situation. It would take years for the saturation to ease and for the extraordinary quality of Garland's body of work to rise slowly through the sorrowful legend.

Still, when she died, there was some immediate recognition. Judy Garland passed away before the era in which stars of her caliber were given commemorative (if hastily assembled) late-night television tributes following network newscasts. But in the days and weeks after her death, countless learned and not-so-learned analyses of Judy's life and times were published or broadcast; the personal eulogies were almost invariably more accurate and generous than the initial wire-service news reports. ("Strangely enough, the fact that she was a very good, very talented performer has not been mentioned much in the general rush to the wailing wall" was the comment of Richard Christiansen in the Chicago *Daily News.*) Among the outpourings were scores of newspaper editorials, often in small-town journals, where one would—perhaps unfairly—expect appreciation for Garland's talent to take a distant second place to disapproval of her problems. Despite the fact that her professional image was at its lowest ebb, much of the commentary indicated that her passing was a personal loss to many, many people.

The Lock Haven (Pennsylvania) *Express* spoke of the "incandescent memory" she would leave behind; the New Britain (Connecticut) *Herald* called her "an entertainer without peer." The Birmingham (Alabama) *News* quoted the memories of a veteran Broadway stage manager who attended Garland's Palace debut in 1951 but "really couldn't see her" because of the tears in his eyes. The editorial concluded, "The rest of us loved Judy, sang with her, stood with her, wished her all the best and, even now, some of us are having trouble seeing." Among other observations were those of the Morristown (New Jersey) *Daily Record:* "We will remember her for the days when no one was capable of sharing the spotlight with her"; the Cincinnati *Post and Times-Star:* "[She] dedicated her life to entertaining people. And in that she succeeded as few others have"; and the Boston *Record American:* "[She was] an artist with a voice like all the trumpets of Joshua." In *Life,* Budd Schulberg classified her as "a little Mozart of song and dance," and the Cleveland *Plain Dealer* stated simply, "She had few peers and no superiors in the art of rekindling emotional embers. . . Seldom has one succeeded in bringing so much happiness to others. [She was] one of the rarest of rare talents." In North Vernon (Indiana), the *Plain Dealer* summarized, "Her whole life was in response to a powerful voice that told her, 'Sing it beautiful and thrill and entertain millions. Lift them for the moments of the song from their little selves. Paint vocally in a bewitching way the stuff their dreams are made of. And in the process. . . break your own heart into a million never-to-be-put-together pieces.' "

FACING PAGE: A 1961 portrait reflecting the theme of Judy's favorite song, "(I'll come to you, smiling) Through the Years" by Vincent Youmans and Edward Heyman. BELOW: The acknowledgment card sent by Liza Minnelli to those who offered condolences to Garland's children in June 1969.

The family of
Judy Garland
gratefully acknowledges
your kind expression of sympathy

Chicago Tribune

JUDY GARLAND DIES AT 47

Munitions Car Blast Kills 11

Twisters Kill 6, Injure 35 in Midwest

JUDY MOURNED

Singer Dies Suddenly in London

PREVIEW

Los Angeles Times

LATE SPORTS

RACE RESULTS

JUDY GARLAND DIES

Singer, 47, Found in London Home

Natural Cause Blamed by Scotland Yard

In addition to similar headlines, press notice of Garland's passing also included personal tributes. A New Zealand fan took a full paper page to quote Noel Coward's lines from "If Love Were All," ascribing to Judy a legendary "talent to amuse." In a trade paper, Tom Green paid similar homage, excerpting "Rainbow," and in Variety, *Richard Barstow simply reprinted Ira Gershwin's "Man That Got Away" phrase, "The stars have lost their glitter."*

Vincent Canby provided a compassionate *New York Times* assessment of Garland's private difficulties with the trenchant observation that "Judy lived [her life] and died still worrying about money, and Jacqueline Susann wrote it, as if it were a comic strip, and made a million dollars." Wayne Warga of the *Los Angeles Times* decided that "the word to remember is legend: bigger than life, twice as talented, and much more vulnerable. She wasn't indestructible after all. Those were real tears in her voice. Yet I can somehow hear her say, if she could comment on her own death, 'Do you suppose they'll close Bloomingdale's for the day? Or maybe Schraffts?' "

Judy was also immediately revered in myriad letters to the editor. "An Ex-Marine Who Remembers" in Louisville wrote of his memories of Garland the performer before concluding, "But above all I remember the Judy who had the time to call a worried mother two thousand miles away and let her know her son was okay, wounded but okay." A Las Vegas reader took exception to media carping about Garland's unreliability by pointing out that "Albert Einstein . . . had the habit of keeping people waiting and sometimes not showing up at all. But once in his office or workroom, he [too] 'did his thing' rather proficiently." A theatregoer bluntly stated that Judy's "legend as the Greatest Star erred only on the side of conservatism"; another self-chastisingly wrote: "You know that you were one of those who asked her for everything she had, and watched her give it, then asked for more, and watched in incredulity as she gave that, too."

There were enormous changes in popular entertainment throughout the 1960s. But despite the onslaught of percussive music and realistic film, the next decade brought increasing exposure and appreciation of Judy Garland's talent. In 1970, *Cue* saluted "the finest performers and works" of its thirty-five years of publishing and selected Judy as its choice for outstanding female singer: "Adulation and notoriety aside, [she was] a superb artist whose voice will outlive the triumphs and the tragedies." *The Wizard of Oz* was by then a film legend, enjoying in 1970 its twelfth highly rated and (virtually) annual national telecast. The picture would continue to serve as an extraordinary introduction to Garland for each succeeding generation. In its first teleshowing after her death, *Oz* was hosted by Gregory Peck, who offered that "Judy left behind a legacy of performances perhaps unequaled by any star of our time." The continuing magic of the Garland/*Oz* combination was further accented when, in May 1970, MGM auctioned off hundreds of its vintage costume and prop pieces. A pair of Judy's ruby slippers commanded a price equaled only by that of a full-size showboat—$15,000.

The first of many commemorative tributes took place in June 1970, when the London-based Judy Garland Club arranged a memorial service at St. Marylebone Parish Church. The Mass was conducted by the Reverend Peter Delaney a year to the day after he officiated at Garland's New York funeral. More than two hundred people gathered, in Delaney's words, "to give thanks for the life of Judy Garland . . . whose greatest quality was the quality of being human." The reverend, a decade-old friend of Judy's, described her as a "person of the most tremendous humility, a person with an immense capacity to love and an immense need to be loved . . . a person of joy." Reflecting on the preceding June, he remembered "the most touching event of those tense days." As he led Garland's rose-covered coffin into the street from the Manhattan chapel, "the thousands who lined the [route] suddenly dropped their voices into silence. And as I looked at the faces peering from windows and lamp-posts, I realized that these were people who had lost a friend." He concluded, "Hers was a life and talent shared by millions—and that life and that talent continue in the people throughout the world who *will* not, and *cannot*, forget Judy Garland."

Three weeks later, on July 20, the British club dedicated a plaque to Garland, mounted on the wall of the Queen's Staircase, which leads to the Royal Box at the London Palladium. It was an unprecedented tribute; the theatre had never before accepted such a permanent honor for any performer. The plaque, inscribed "in loving memory of the incomparable Judy Garland," was unveiled by Sir Richard Attenborough as he recalled her electrifying 1951 and 1964 Palladium benefit appearances. In reviewing Judy's career, Attenborough testified that she "changed the manner of our profession for all time—she brought something that no one has ever equaled."

Garland received another singular tribute in February 1973 when the National Association of Recording Merchandisers made her the posthumous recipient of their Presidential Award for "outstanding creative achievement." Normally considered the least sentimental representatives of the recording industry, the NARM convention delegates roared their approval at the surprise presentation. The dedication read, "In loving memory of the great lady of music whose magnificence as an artist dominated the entertainment world for four decades. As long as music is heard in our land, she will never be forgotten."

Judy's movies, first shown on television in the 1950s and 1960s, continued to be revived, with increasing admiration for the inherent style of some of the Freed Unit musicals. (The originally praised virtuosity of such films was taken for granted in the 1950s, regarded as somewhat quaint in the 1960s, and finally respected as a unique achievement in popular entertainment by the 1970s.) Full-scale retrospectives of the Garland canon were mounted at the British Film Institute/National Film Theater in 1971, at New York's Eighth Street Playhouse in 1979, at the New York Regency in 1987, and at the Los Angeles County Museum of Art in 1986. In its article about the 1979 festival, the New York *Daily News* summarized Judy's impact: "She dazzled us all—on the screen, on recordings, on the stage, singing, dancing, or just talking. . . There was only one, [and] she added new dimensions to the word entertainment."

By that point, the MGM movie-musical magic specifically purveyed between 1929 and 1958 had already been celebrated in the 1974 release *That's Entertainment!*. Executive producer Jack Haley, Jr., assembled a two-hour-plus compendium of excerpted song and dance highlights that won rapturous reviews, broke box-office records, and introduced Garland to thousands of new fans. She was the only star afforded two segments in the picture. Mickey Rooney narrated the scenes chosen from their films, and Liza Minnelli later appeared to introduce other highlights—from "La Cucaracha" (1935) through "Get Happy" (1950). The triumph of *That's Entertainment!* was particularly that of Judy, Fred Astaire, and Gene Kelly. The *Washington Post* found that their passages "put this compilation on the level of genius." Garland's "Rainbow" and "You Made Me Love You" were described as "emotionally stirring and liberating routines. . . Not one of them depends on 'production values.' " *New York* magazine added, "[She] was special because Hollywood for once recognized her unique abilities and used them properly. She is the central star of [the film] simply because she contributed the most to MGM's musical personality." A sequel, *That's Entertainment,*

BELOW: In the wings at the Palladium with Al Paul and Jack Klugman between takes of I Could Go On Singing, *1962. BOTTOM: "I'm Dorothy Gale—from Kansas," 1939.*

TOP AND ABOVE: *Mid- and late-1930s publicity photos taken to promote MGM's featured player.*

Part 2, was released in 1976, and Gene Siskel enthused, "A few performances speak for themselves. And the person whose performances speak best is Judy."

In November 1982, the Academy of Motion Picture Arts and Sciences celebrated Garland in an evening of film clips and reminiscences. The *Los Angeles Times* observed that she was "still making history": her tribute was "sold out two weeks in advance, a record for a public event" in the eleven-hundred-seat AMPAS theatre. The *Times* reporter (to her surprise) discovered that Garland's professionalism seldom allowed any offstage problems to intrude on her finished work: "Hardly ever did we see the agony. . .the bolts and jolts, the temper tantrums, the unpredictable Garland. Throughout a career spanning four decades, she was always the hugely talented Garland, the hypnotic Garland who sang, danced, and acted with seemingly effortless charm."

The Academy benefited from the Garland talent to a much greater extent in 1983 when, on their behalf, Hollywood historian Ron Haver produced a "restored" version of *A Star is Born.* Despite Harry Warner's 1954 command to destroy the excised footage, Haver believed that the material had to be somewhere in the Warner Bros. holdings. After an arduous, months-long search, he managed to reassemble most of the original three-hour soundtrack, the footage for three lost musical numbers, and portions of dialogue scenes. (Where he could find no film, Haver used stills over the soundtrack for transition.) His *Star* debuted on July 7 at New York's Radio City Music Hall to a capacity crowd that had paid up to $150 a ticket. Producer Luft, costar Mason, Liza Minnelli, and Lorna Luft were among those introduced. Academy president Fay Kanin gave special recognition to George Cukor, who had died six months earlier—the night before he was scheduled to view the first samples of Haver's work. Kanin also exulted at the audience's seeming interest in the Academy's film preservation program: *Star* was the proclaimed beginning of a ten-year endeavor to seek out, reclaim, restore, and protect vintage or missing motion pictures. But the crowd was there for, and the night belonged to, Judy. Rex Reed wrote, "Who else could draw six thousand people to a one-night showing of a movie made twenty-nine years ago? You could hear the cheering all the way to Fifth Avenue."

Her performance, the reestablished *Star,* and the electricity generated by the Music Hall audience ultimately won worldwide wonder and press. Roger Ebert called the evening "a revelation" and the film "a landmark of Hollywood melodrama." *The Village Voice* marveled at "the sociocinematic event of a lifetime," noting that "if Aeschylus or Shakespeare lived in the twentieth century, one of them would certainly have written *Star.* It's *the* tragedy of the modern era." Subsequent benefit showings for the Academy in five other cities won equal box-office response—so much so that Warner Bros. (somewhat haphazardly) threw the picture into general release that autumn. Where local theatre managers promoted the film's appearance, *Star* did excellent business, and the restored print also became a sensational success on the international film-festival circuit for the remainder of the year. In 1984, it was released with great success on the home video market.

Critical estimation of the reemerging picture was frequently laced with awe. Gene Siskel raved, "Count me among the many who consider this to be the best musical drama ever made. If you have ever questioned Garland's appeal, see *Star.* She is an extraordinary talent in a modest, almost everyday package. . . *Star* is refreshingly adult. If you have despaired of ever seeing a mature film about people again, take heart." The critic for the Seattle *Post-Intelligencer* had "seen [the film] on television and never much liked it. But on the big CinemaScope screen and in its full length, I found this legendary movie so extraordinarily beautiful, so emotionally powerful, so perfect in almost every department, that it literally took my breath away." (The reissue also produced an ideal, witty summation of the 1954 *Star* edit when the Baltimore *Sun* marveled, "It's difficult to imagine a publishing house lopping thirty pages out of an already-released best-seller to make it 'a faster read,' but that's essentially what Warner Bros. did.")

Garland's memory was initially somewhat less well served by television documentaries. A profusion of well-chosen film clips provided saving grace for both the BBC "Omnibus/Impressions of Garland" (1972) and Barry Norman's "Hollywood Greats" (1978), but the shows were seemingly fashioned to explain the difficulty and implied waste of Judy Garland rather than acknowledge her ability. Norman's profile was particularly geared to such an approach; "Where," asked one critic, "was the star who brightened all our lives?" Slightly more successful was a seventeen-minute "60 Minutes" profile in 1975. Avowed but clear-eyed admirer Mike Wallace hosted the CBS piece and conducted the interviews, including conversations with Liza, Lorna, and Joe. The *Christian Science Monitor* noted, "What comes through triumphantly. . . is the legacy of love and affection [Judy] left behind with her three children. One has only to listen to their words, watch the glow in their eyes when they talk about 'Mama,' to sense the true depth of the complex relationship Judy has with her family as well as with the world." The Garland segment turned out to be a favorite of the show's staff and was repeated the following season.

Throughout the 1970s and 1980s, her television work was invariably regarded as a highlight of any historical examination of the medium. This newfound respect perfectly exemplified the increasing appreciation for Judy Garland—oftentimes, the performances involved had been ignored or dismissed by the original reviewers. Such retrospectives also revealed that Garland at her best had no rivals. In November 1986, NBC offered an hour-long, prime-time special, "Jack

BELOW: Between takes of the abandoned "Paging Mr. Greenback" in Presenting Lily Mars, *1942. BOTTOM LEFT: A poignant pose on the Shepperton mock-up of the Palladium stage, taken the day Garland filmed "It Never Was You" for* I Could Go On Singing, *1962. BOTTOM RIGHT: January 1963 publicity portrait.*

Paar Comes Home." There were brief clips of the host's encounters with brothers John and Robert Kennedy, Oscar Levant, Richard Nixon, Richard Burton, Bill Cosby, the Beatles, and Billy Graham. But the show built to two complete segments—twenty minutes in all—devoted to Paar's 1962 interview with Garland. He later referred to the special as "the best of everything I ever did" and to Judy as "one of the world's greatest entertainers."

Rights to Garland's own TV series and 1962/63 specials were tied up for years in litigation. Random syndicated showings garnered excellent response beginning in 1974. When Sid Luft finally won control of the material five years later, he began a gradual release of several programs and compilations to cable and home video. From 1990–92, the Disney Channel offered six such shows, led by the 1963 Christmas episode of the TV series. Among many laudatory notices, *Newsday* praised, "Belying the 'tormented soul' legend, Garland shines as the warm and enthusiastic mother her children always recall so fondly. The show appropriately closes with 'Over the Rainbow,' sung to the younger kids as a loving lullaby. Perhaps the most telling legacy of this hour is that afterward, you'll want Judy to tuck you in too."

The most successful and popular Garland television retrospective to date came in 1985, when PBS devoted a "Great Performances" program to "Judy Garland: The Concert Years." The ninety-minute show concentrated solely on the entertainer and her work during the post-MGM era, drawing specific praise for a format that allowed Judy to sing sixteen complete songs and portions of sixteen others. Produced by Joan Kramer and David Heeley and hosted by Lorna Luft, the show won universal acclaim for Garland, several international television awards and an Emmy nomination, and brought in hundreds of thousands of pledge dollars for public television. (In its initial New York telecast, "The Concert Years" outrated all the local independent TV fare and surpassed even the heralded finale of "The Jewel in the Crown" as a fund-raiser.) The Newark *Star-Ledger* described the show as "just about the best thing we have ever seen dealing with Judy. . . a brilliant reminder that she was the absolute best in her class." The *Boston Globe* called the program "a towering posthumous triumph," and the *New York Times* noted its "uncommon abundance of thrilling moments. Time has hardly dimmed the emotional impact of a Garland performance." A lengthy feature in the New Orleans *Times-Picayune* headlined, "What becomes a legend most? 'The Concert Years,' " and found the show "a love letter. . . [which] displays Garland at something approaching her peak. She looks great here: mostly slim and as lovely as she'd ever be, with those enormous orphan eyes, Peter Pan hairdo, and glittering Ray Aghayan costumes. Among the interview quotes, Tony Bennett calls Garland 'the greatest singer of the century.' That takes in a lot of territory, and even hard-core fans might stop short of such a declaration. But when the musical sequences begin, Bennett's hyperbole seems justified."

Unfortunately (if understandably), most of the dozen or more books published about Garland since 1970 have sidestepped accurate or complete assessments of her work to concentrate on personal drama. There have been exceptions, of course—notably the volumes on the creation of *Oz, Star,* and the TV series *(Rainbow's End);* the Thomas J. Watson & Bill Chapman *Judy: Portrait of an American Legend;* and Christopher Finch's *Rainbow.* The latter is especially intelligent in its delineation of Judy's vaudeville and MGM days. But most of the biographical recountings to date have added to the frequently inaccurate life-legend, taking

Judy and her associates. BELOW: *Van Johnson helps adjust Garland's skirt on the set of* For Me and My Gal, *1942. (She is costumed for the ultimately replaced finale routine.)* BOTTOM: *Between takes of* Presenting Lily Mars, *Judy goes into a dramatic dance with Gene Kelly, in costume and on the set for his* DuBarry Was a Lady, *1942.*

as fact both Garland's embellished or unhappy quotes, or the occasionally self-serving memories of those who surrounded her. (Several key players in the complicated scenario have also refused comment on their Garland association.) As a result, the balanced, full story of her turbulent times has yet to be completely told.

Similar problems have beset the proposed film and stage projects based on Judy's life. Many have been planned, most abandoned, and those that reached production were invariably criticized for concentrating on offstage trauma and missing what made Judy Garland important in the first place. The most publicized of the suggested film biographies was rumored as a 1970s Vincente Minnelli picture which would star daughter Liza. (Both vehemently denied that they would consider such a project.) Authors ranging from Mario Puzo *(The Godfather)* to Leonard Gershe ("Born in a Trunk") have been announced as possible scenarists for other Garland films, but only one such project has actually been produced to date. In 1978, NBC offered a two-hour television movie based on a portion of Finch's *Rainbow.* The show detailed Garland's life from 1932–39 and was alternately described as "tedious and lusterless" (by the *Chicago Tribune*) and as "a sadly moving drama with a first-rate cast" (by United Press International). Piper Laurie and Don Murray played Ethel and Frank Gumm; Martin Balsam, Rue McClanahan, and Michael Parks appeared as Louis B. Mayer, Ida Koverman, and Roger Edens. The film was directed with care and insight by Jackie Cooper, and young Judy was played by Broadway's original Annie, fifteen-year-old Andrea McArdle. But the assignment was beyond McArdle at that point: Cooper remembers her as "cold and unresponsive," lacking in respect, and at odds with her mother. Her reviews were mixed ("She acts like a zombie drugged on Sominex" was one estimation), and Judith Crist echoed a general response: "The 'remake' of lives of stars who still exist on film is a pointless exercise."

Onstage, a number of presentations built around Judy Garland have been realized. Some offered new characters based on her legend: Neil Simon's *The Gingerbread Lady* (later revised and filmed as *Only When I Laugh*) won a 1971 Tony Award for Maureen Stapleton in the story of an alcoholic entertainer and her teenage daughter. The next year, Johnny Meyer's *When Do the Words Come True?* played the Bucks County Playhouse and starred Gloria De Haven as "Janet Hartman," a pill-addicted chanteuse with tax problems. Other vehicles have ranged from one-woman or full-cast theatre pieces to simple nightclub shows and showcase/backers' auditions. There have been productions titled *Rainbow* in New York, *There's No Place Like Home* and *Born in a Trunk* in Chicago, *Beyond Rainbows* in Rochester and Buffalo, *One More Song* in Atlanta and Millburn, New Jersey, *Judy* in Toronto and Philadelphia, and *From Gumm to Garland* in Seattle. The most extravagant of the attempted stage retellings was *Judy,* a 1986 London amalgam of ballads and traumatic events from Garland's life. *Variety* found it "a sick-for-kicks act which only diminishes a sublime artist whose great performances are all that history needs." Nonetheless, Lesley Mackie won the coveted Olivier Award for her virtuoso performance in the title role, and the show continues to be revised and performed in such diverse locales as Japan and Denmark.

Probably the two most successful and warming tributes came at extreme ends of the nightclub spectrum. A lavish stage review, *Hallelujah, Hollywood!,* ran for several years in the 1970s at the MGM Grand Hotel in Las Vegas, and Garland songs or film clips were utilized in the "Dear Mr. Gable," *Meet Me in St. Louis,*

TOP: With Crosby, Dinah Shore, and Sinatra at a radio rehearsal. Bing later called Judy "a great dramatic actress [and] a tremendously gifted comedienne, one of the most amusing women I ever knew. I had some wonderful times with Judy. . . a joyous, talented, dear girl." Sinatra has said, "Judy will have a mystic survival. The rest of us will be forgotten—never Judy." In the mid-1940s, he tried to fathom the personal cost of performing the way she did: "Every time she sings," he explained, "she dies a little." ABOVE: Garland and Astaire during Easter Parade, *1948.*

Garland and her associates. TOP, LEFT TO RIGHT: *With Laurence Olivier on the set of* Pride and Prejudice, *1940; with Shirley Temple at a party at the home of Robert Stack, 1940; on the set of* Ziegfeld Girl *with Lana Turner and Jimmy Stewart, 1941.* ABOVE: *With John Garfield, 1944.*

and *The Pirate* segments. A grand Ziegfeldian finale built to an even more evocative recognition. After their bows, the scores of onstage performers quietly doffed hats or extended hands to salute a spotlit, empty entrance at the top of a grand staircase and then stood in silence as Garland's "Over the Rainbow" was played.

A smaller-scale but more specific homage came in *Julie, Julie, Julie,* a 1986 New York cabaret act featuring Julie Sheppard as Garland and Ricky Ritzel as a Manhattan pianist. The seventy-five-minute presentation placed Judy in the fictitious setting of a New York bistro in April 1961, where she is spontaneously coaxed to sing; fifteen numbers were interspersed with typical Garland banter between singer and accompanist. Staged and directed by Bruce Warren, the show was commended by *Variety* for its "laudable attention to detail" and the expert performances of Sheppard and Ritzel. Most of Garland's signature tunes were purposely avoided and, at its best, the production provided a reminiscent glimpse of a funny, buoyant entertainer at a healthy juncture in her life and career. Such ebullience was enough to turn the anticipated four-week booking into a seven-month engagement.

Sheppard was one of countless female and male performers who built routines or entire acts around their impersonations of or takeoffs on Garland. Even while Judy was alive, such stars as Kaye Ballard, Carol Channing, Sheila MacRae, Allen Sherman, and Lucille Ball offered comic Garland vignettes onstage or television. The most successful of the "illusionists" has been Jim Bailey, whose award-winning turn plays everywhere from Carnegie Hall to the Palladium. (Garland saw Bailey's work in the late 1960s—prior to his national fame—and went backstage to tell him, "I had no idea I was so *pretty*!") In 1972, Bailey's Judy was joined onstage in Las Vegas by Liza Minnelli for a one-time-only re-creation of the original mother/daughter act. They won accolades from a surprised audience and critics; Liza described Bailey as "a great talent with a gift from the angels." (One less-than-enchanted journalist later commented, "I can think of one angel who must be spinning. . .")

Not surprisingly, the procession of Garland re-creations makes many audiences long for the real thing. As a result, most of Judy's commercial recordings have been repeatedly repackaged and recirculated on tape and disc, with the legitimate Decca, MGM, and Capitol issues augmented by a seemingly ceaseless supply of bootleg material. The latter includes Garland's TV soundtracks and alternate takes, radio performances, rehearsals, movie cuts, and concert performances ranging from the Palace closing night in 1952 to her final American concert in 1968.

The most successful Garland recording remains that of the Carnegie Hall appearance. The album's twenty-fifth anniversary in 1986 brought several hours of radio tributes in major cities. In New York, WNEW's Jim Lowe reminisced about the "privilege" of attending the show and devoted his April 23 program to concert excerpts. Midway, the host took an on-air call from lyricist Sammy Cahn, who spoke of Judy's "impeccable taste in music." Ironically, during the finale of Lowe's show, he received and broadcast the news that Harold Arlen had died that afternoon.

In late 1986, Capitol decided to issue *Judy at Carnegie Hall* as a compact disc but deleted four tracks from the recording in order to squeeze the release onto one CD. The label was immediately swamped with critical and public complaint; one irate writer compared Capitol's action to "printing the Constitution of the United States with several paragraphs missing and then saying, 'This is history. Sort of.' " In response to the continuing cry, the company redid the issue on two CDs three years later, augmenting all of the originally released songs with portions of Garland's anecdotes, song introductions, audience interplay, and additional applause.

Capitol has continued to release its Garland albums on compact disc, including, wherever possible, additional or deleted material from Judy's original sessions. In November 1991, the company produced a three-disc compilation, *Judy Garland/The One & Only,* and *USA Today* stated flatly, "These are some of the classiest pre-rock pop recordings ever made. The fascinating thing is how elegant, restrained, and precise Garland seems compared with singers who have taken her emotive style several steps further. . . Unlike them, Garland stops short of dismantling a song for the sake of visceral excitement. Even her most seemingly spontaneous moments are conveyed with great eloquence and precision."

Similarly, a boxed set of three videotapes—*Meet Me in St. Louis/The Harvey Girls/Easter Parade*—appeared for Christmas 1991 from MGM/UA Home Video, Inc. The Garland package was one of ten in a promotion saluting great film stars. It outsold all the others, including those featuring Elvis Presley, Clint Eastwood, Bette Davis, and Humphrey Bogart. By spring 1992, *Pigskin Parade* was the only one of Judy's thirty-two feature films not available for home video. Many of her MGM titles had at that point been on the market for over a decade, in some cases remastered and reissued with selected shorts, deleted numbers, or promotional trailers.

The Wizard of Oz remains Garland's most successful video. By 1988, it had sold nearly two million units worldwide; the next year, a special package produced to celebrate the film's fiftieth anniversary sold three million additional units. This was especially astounding in that *Oz* has also endured as an annual television event. An unprecedented two showings in 1991 gave the film a total of thirty-four network airings by 1992, and its estimated worldwide audience has long since passed the one-billion mark. The picture has become a cornerstone of American popular culture, heralded as the film seen by more people than any other. This was officially acknowledged in 1989 when the United States government selected *Oz* as one of four 1939 films to be honored with a first-class postage stamp; the selected image showed Judy Garland as Dorothy. Later that year, the film was one of twenty-five designated as a "national treasure" under the National Film Preservation Act of 1988.

The *Oz* fiftieth anniversary was celebrated in massive merchandising; the film,

BELOW: In New York with First Lady Eleanor Roosevelt at a Greek Resistance Benefit, February 1941. BOTTOM: With Mickey Rooney between takes of Babes on Broadway, *1941; the picture epitomizes the observation made about Garland by Mrs. Ira Gershwin: "Wherever she went, there was laughter." Today Rooney says of Judy, "She was the best in the world. No one has ever given so much of herself for her profession to everybody in the world."*

BELOW: Judy and Marilyn Monroe, spring 1962. Monroe often played Garland's recording of "Who Cares" to bolster her own self-confidence; Judy had also served as an informal vocal coach for her during production of Some Like It Hot. *BOTTOM: "Together (Wherever We Go)"—anthem of mother and daughter on "The Judy Garland Show," July 1963. "When you'd sit and talk with her," says Liza, "you really felt that nobody else existed. That nobody was funnier; that nobody was wiser; that nobody could ever love you more; and that you never could ever love anybody more. They're the dearest memories I have."*

Oz books, and Garland have long been recognized as among the most desirable Americana collectibles. This was underscored when, in 1988, Christie's East in New York auctioned two more pairs of Judy's ruby slippers. The final sale price for each pair was $165,000, the highest amount paid up to that time for any item of movie memorabilia.

Annual *Oz* festivals sprung up in several small towns in the United States during the 1970s, as did a Judy Garland Festival in Grand Rapids, Minnesota. Local artist Jackie Dingmann began to campaign for recognition of the town's most celebrated daughter in 1975. In 1989, the Judy Garland Festival was a nine-day, internationally publicized event, drawing more than twenty thousand visitors to musical events, film showings, and a parade. The Grand Rapids Historical Society has since founded the Judy Garland Historical Center, purchasing the home in which the Gumm family lived during Judy's four years in town. A Garland museum now occupies the third floor of the old Central School building as well. Unfortunately, the Grand Rapids events have had to contend with as much controversy as success; some factions among the eight thousand locals remain strongly opposed to celebrating someone whose personal life-style they find distasteful. The debate has been picked up by the national media, thus doing Garland's reputation as much harm as good. Differing viewpoints from around the country have been reported at length by the Grand Rapids *Herald-Review;* finally, in October 1991, the paper printed a letter from a Garland fan in Houston that simply and accurately pointed out that, in Grand Rapids, "neither side, for or against . . . cares in the least about Judy Garland. Interest centers completely on the idea of capitalizing on [her] memory."

Since her death, Garland's history has inspired additional controversy, most notably in the brief intrafamily friction caused by a 1978 sale of her personal effects and professional memorabilia. Even then, however, the Los Angeles event drew a crowd possessing "an emotional involvement you don't see at auctions," according to one promoter. The *New York Times* noted the absence of the "hard-edged, greedy" patrons who'd attended an earlier Joan Crawford sale. The Garland event, if somewhat melancholy, managed to maintain overtones of yet another (albeit low-key) tribute.

A happier, unique homage came in the 1975 christening of the Judy Garland Rose, cultivated in Britain and named for her by R. Harkness & Company at the request of the Judy Garland Club. The flower went on to international European honors and, when finally imported in 1991, sold out across the United States. In 1992, the Pennsylvania-based Judy Garland Memorial Club and the City of New York Parks and Recreation Department joined forces to create a Judy Garland Rose Garden of nearly two hundred bushes. Commemorated by a large bronze plaque ("In celebration of Judy Garland, 1922–1969"), the garden overlooks Manhattan and the Statue of Liberty from the entrance of the Brooklyn Heights Promenade Park.

Garland's seventieth birthday anniversary was also observed by the New York Public Library for the Performing Arts with "Judy Garland: A Celebration." The ten-week retrospective exhibition in the Amsterdam Gallery featured two dozen of Judy's film, stage, and television costumes; posters, scripts, programs, photographs, and other career memorabilia.

In the last two decades—whether fairly or not—the work and impact of many top box-office stars of the past have been forgotten or dismissed. But the 1969 editorials and commentary about Judy Garland were just the beginning of a growing series of tributes to her achievement and musical influence. Shortly after Judy died, veteran Hollywood journalist and scenarist Adela Rogers St. Johns called her "our one great genius"; St. Johns then eulogized Garland at length in the 1974 book, *Some Are Born Great,* a paean to "gallant. . .women of irrepressible spirit who accomplished nothing less than miracles." *Life* must have concurred with St. Johns's estimation; a "special report" issue of the magazine two years later saluted Garland as one of 136 "Remarkable American Women, 1776–1976." There was similar praise in 1987 when *People*'s special issue, "One Hundred Years of Hollywood," rated Judy one of film history's "twenty-five most intriguing stars. . . [the] endearing, magically gifted Girl with the Golden Throat." John Fisher's 1976 *Call Them Irreplaceable* saluted twelve matchless entertainers: Jolson, Crosby, Coward, Astaire, Dietrich, Kaye, Durante, Chevalier, Sinatra, Hope, and Benny. In such company, the chapter on Garland begins with utmost simplicity: "She may well have been the greatest star." Ethan Mordden offered much the same judgment in *Movie Star,* his 1983 book on screen actresses: "Garland, of them all, is most genuinely legendary, like her or not. It's no great deal in film to leave a name behind one, but to remain a working *experience* after death is true stardom." In 1990, he expanded on his thoughts for a lengthy monograph on Judy for *The New Yorker:* "To watch Jolson or [John] Barrymore today is to enter a museum," he offers. "Garland is ageless. . . [and] comparable to no one, not only the first of her kind but the last." Finally, journalist Gerald Clarke (at work on a Garland biography in 1991) wrote about the Grand Rapids conflict for *Fame* and stated, "It can be argued that Garland was the greatest American entertainer of this century—or, most probably, any century."

Judy's costars and co-workers have been equally laudatory. Most of them directly state or imply that their experience with Garland stands as the highlight of a career, in spite of any other celebrated associates and no matter at which point in her own chronology Judy was encountered. Prior to his death in 1973, Arthur Freed mused, "You just couldn't mistake that talent; there was so much of it. She interpreted a song better than anyone in the business. When she was on, there wasn't anything she couldn't do—[because] this girl was real."

In 1991, Barbra Streisand remembered her duets with Garland on the TV series as "sheer bliss," and defined Judy as "miraculous. . . soulful. . .divine." Gordon Jenkins told a television interviewer in the early 1970s that he "wouldn't trade two of *any* [other performer] for one Judy Garland." Mort Lindsey has written, "I have served as musical director for many stars. It is not belittling or demeaning to any of them to state that Judy Garland was head and shoulders above them all." When someone once deprecatingly told Tony Bennett that Garland's success had been due to the vociferous acclaim of a claque, Bennett agreed by riposting, "Yes—the whole world was her claque." He has since specifically called Judy's rendition of "Last Night When We Were Young" "the finest record I've ever heard," and offered the general estimation, "If you want to learn how to sing, you have to sing like Judy Garland. That's the proper way to sing American popular music."

During his interview for "The Concert Years," Alan King was asked to rank Garland in the show-business pantheon, and he defined her as "the best live vaudeville stage performer I have ever seen." He acknowledged that some industry veterans "always say: 'Jolson—the greatest.' " But King concluded, "I saw

TOP: On her Christmas TV series show with Lorna and Joe, 1963. With simplicity and tenderness, Joe says today, "I loved her very much"; Lorna quietly, proudly feels that "My mother was the most important figure in American music history." ABOVE: Backstage at the Americana Hotel after sharing a benefit bill with (among others) Alan King, May 15, 1966. He offers now, "She had such great soul. There was no other artist like her. . . there'll never be another one like her."

LEFT, CENTER, RIGHT, AND FACING PAGE: Judy at the Las Vegas Sahara, September–October 1962. Several years and scores of concerts later—and after a particularly powerful number one evening—she joshed, "They call me a belter*. . . and I don't know* why!*" When the audience's laughter abated, she mischievously trailed off, ". . . Because I stopped making* belts *a long time ago."*

Jolson . . . he would have *opened* for Judy Garland." Rex Reed told the show's producers, "Maybe once every century a performer comes along who is able to communicate through voice so much emotion that it connects directly with the heart of the person who's absorbing that talent. There's been no one who could do that before [Judy Garland]; there's been no one who could do that, to that extent, since. You can listen to [others] sing the purest, most beautiful notes in the world, and you feel nothing, because there's nothing going on there. And the proof that [Garland] will live forever is the fact that I get letters today from kids who say, 'We've just heard our first Judy Garland record. Do you think you could talk her into singing "New York, New York"?' They don't even know she's dead. All they know is that they've heard this woman's voice, [and] they're so moved by it, they want her to sing the songs that they think are right for her. People are going to discover her again and again until the end of time."

Reed's appraisal has been borne out by the enthusiasm for Garland from contemporary rock and pop performers. Cyndi Lauper, Boy George, Michael Jackson, Bette Midler, Barry Manilow, Peter Allen, and Melissa Manchester are only some among those who cite Garland as an influence on their musical lives. Lauper refers to her as possessing one of "the voices that have soothed me from when I was a child." Manchester laughingly claims that, as a teenager, she so often played the *Judy at Carnegie Hall* album that "you could see *through* it." She more seriously and simply adds, "Judy will be given a tremendous place in the annals of musical history because she did all of the creators great service by being around."

The career and achievement of Judy Garland have been a singularly enduring, continually affecting part of American life in the twentieth century. When the American prisoners of war came home from Vietnam in the 1970s, Harry Reasoner did a television special in which he enumerated things that had changed in their absence. One of these, the newscaster noted, was that they returned to a world in which there was no longer a Judy Garland. Reasoner, of course, was literally correct. But whether discussing the 1970s or the 1990s, it remains virtually impossible to find anyone over the age of two who doesn't know Dorothy Gale of Kansas—or who, in well-educated, succeeding years, doesn't come to know the "real" Dorothy Gale. It's the same word carefully chosen by Arthur Freed; Frances (Baby) Gumm made forever "real" countless emotions, songs, experiences, and characters: the Esthers Smith and Blodgett, Lily Mars, Betsy Booth, Jenny Bowman—and the (by actual definition) incomparable Judy Garland.

It's probably true that the turmoil and trouble of her life can never be completely divorced from her prodigious artistic abilities and qualities. But knowledge of her difficulties has nothing to do with thrilled appreciation for her talent, her intelligence, her humor, her compassion, her warmth, and her joy. As the years go by and Garland's gift becomes ever more irreplaceable and important, it's possible that those difficulties are best categorized and viewed as a leavening, unavoidable part of the package of genius.

The Broadway musical *Follies* opened in 1971. Its soon-to-be-legendary merits were extolled in the *New York Times* by critic Martin Gottfried, who concluded, "I am convinced that *Follies* is monumental theatre. Not because I say so, but because it is there for anyone to see." His last phrase can easily be taken out of context for anyone who might require an explanation for Judy's billing and reputation as the world's greatest entertainer.

But an even simpler rationale is also possible. The revered National Film Theater in London made a similar, quiet claim about Garland in 1971, calling her "the greatest star in the history of popular entertainment." The remark, they later noted, "did not go unchallenged." Then they added a gentle dismissal of any further dissent: "But once, not so long ago, people disputed that the world was round."

In 1968 an interviewer asked Judy Garland what she would like people to think about her. Her reply was soft but direct: "I would like them to know that I have been in love with them all my life, and I've tried to please. I hope I did."

Bibliography

Judy Garland's career spanned five decades; as a result, she figures prominently in the history of twentieth-century entertainment and popular culture. This bibliography highlights books that were helpful in weaving the textual story of her work and notes in passing many of the other volumes about her. There is also a list of some in which she—briefly or at length—plays a prominent part. (The feelings expressed about certain titles are strictly personal opinion; different readers may well have different reactions.)

The best Garland books:

Finch, Christopher. *Rainbow.* New York: Grosset & Dunlap, 1975. Probably the definitive Garland biography to date. Although Finch rushes through the last fifteen years of her life, his insight and work on the Baby Gumm and MGM eras is resourceful and excellent.

Fordin, Hugh. *The World of Entertainment.* Garden City, New York: Doubleday and Company, Inc., 1975. The occasional factual flub scarcely impairs this richly detailed history of MGM's "Freed Unit."

Haver, Ronald. *A Star Is Born.* New York: Alfred A. Knopf, 1988. Although occasionally lacking in perspective, Haver provides an excellent day-by-day examination of how Garland's film classic was assembled, dismantled, and restored.

Sanders, Coyne Steven. *Rainbow's End.* New York: William Morrow and Company, Inc., 1990. A brilliantly detailed and researched account of the 1963–64 CBS-TV series, "The Judy Garland Show."

Watson, Thomas J., and Bill Chapman. *Judy: Portrait of an American Legend.* New York: McGraw-Hill Book Company, 1986. A concise, lightweight but accurate outline of Garland's professional life, illustrated with glowing photographs.

Also:

Dahl, David, and Barry Kehoe. *Young Judy.* New York: Mason/Charter, 1975. A detailed, evocative (if not completely accurate) account of Gumm family life through Frank's death less than two months after Baby signed her MGM contract.

DiOrio, Al, Jr. *Little Girl Lost.* New Rochelle, New York: Arlington House, 1973. A fan's fervid biography, with excellent photographs and some then-groundbreaking appendices.

Frank, Gerold. *Judy.* New York: Harper & Row, 1975. A highly detailed account of Garland's life and times, done with usually helpful, sometimes hindering, cooperation from her family. Lacks the distance from participants that gives Finch's *Rainbow* its sheen.

Fricke, John, Jay Scarfone, and William Stillman. *The Wizard of Oz: The Official 50th Anniversary Pictorial History.* New York: Warner Books, 1989. The saga of *Oz,* told in accurate, chronological detail and over five hundred illustrations.

Harmetz, Aljean. *The Making of The Wizard of Oz.* New York: Alfred A. Knopf, 1977. Subsequent research has disproven chunks of Harmetz's journalism, but her book is valuable for its interviews with veterans of the studio system.

Meyer, John. *Heartbreaker.* Garden City, New York: Doubleday & Company, 1983. A one-sided account of life with the Legend for two months late in 1968. For those who care, it provides a look at Garland's latter-day humor and survival instincts.

Minnelli, Vincente, with Hector Arce. *I Remember It Well.* Garden City, New York: Doubleday & Company, Inc., 1974. The film director relates some telling anecdotes about his professional and personal relationships with Garland.

Morella, Joe, and Edward L. Epstein. *Judy: The Films and Career of Judy Garland.* New York: The Citadel Press, 1969. A scrapbook survey of Garland's career, concentrating on her films.

Smith, Lorna. *Judy With Love.* London: Robert Hale & Company, 1975. Notable for its superlative accounts of Garland at work, both from the audience's perspective and behind the scenes.

Tormé, Mel. *The Other Side of the Rainbow: With Judy Garland on the Dawn Patrol.* New York: William Morrow and Company, 1970. Worthwhile solely for its accounts of Garland interacting with her fellow professionals on the TV series.

Simply for the record:

Barson, Michael S. *Judy/Liza, The Myth and the Madness.* Cresskill, New York: Sharon Publications, Inc., 1985. Makes Spada and Parish (see below) seem like Bernstein and Woodward.

Coleman, Emily R. *The Complete Judy Garland.* New York: Harper & Row, 1990. An excellent and worthwhile premise gone seriously awry. The listings and analysis of Garland's work are so often incomplete and larded with error or misinformation that the final product is rendered fairly useless.

Deans, Mickey, and Ann Pinchot. *Weep No More, My Lady.* New York: Hawthorn Books, Inc., 1972. Garland's last husband describes her life before and after their marriage.

Edwards, Anne. *Judy Garland.* New York: Simon and Schuster, 1975. Edwards presents her point of view replete with astoundingly faulty research and lack of general Garland knowledge; the book only comes to life in a retelling of Judy's sad final six months.

Juneau, James. *Judy Garland.* New York: Pyramid Publications, 1975. A brief career retelling.

McClelland, Doug. *Down the Yellow Brick Road.* New York: Pyramid Press, 1976. *Oz* stills accompany secondary source information in telling the story of the film.

Melton, David. *Judy: A Remembrance.* Hollywood: Stanyan Books, 1972. Drawings and poetic tribute.

Parish, James Robert, with Jack Ano. *Liza.* London: W. H. Allen, 1975. On par with Spada.

Petrucelli, Alan W. *Liza! Liza!* New York: Karz-Cohl Publishing, Inc., 1983. Schizophrenic biography.

Spada, James. *Judy and Liza.* Garden City, New York: A Dolphin Book/Doubleday & Company, Inc., 1983. Mostly a trash rehash of the legends behind mother and daughter.

Steiger, Brad. *Judy Garland.* New York: Ace Books, 1969. A quickie paperback, rushed out after Garland's death.

Books that include material about Judy Garland and/or were of much-appreciated help in providing details for this volume:

Allyson, June, with Frances Spatz Leighton. *June Allyson.* New York: G. P. Putnam's Sons, 1982.

Astor, Mary. *A Life on Film.* New York: Delacorte Press, 1967.

Bogarde, Dirk. *Snakes & Ladders.* New York: Holt, Rinehart and Winston, 1979.

Cooper, Jackie, with Dick Kleiner. *Please Don't Shoot My Dog.* New York: William Morrow and Company, 1981.

Fisher, John. *Call Them Irreplaceable.* New York: Stein and Day, 1974. Celebrating a dozen legendary popular entertainers.

Geist, Kenneth L. *Pictures Will Talk.* New York: Charles Scribner's Sons, 1978.

Hemming, Roy. *The Melody Lingers On: The Great Songwriters and Their Movie Musicals.* New York: Newmarket Press, 1986.

Hepburn, Katharine. *Me.* New York: Alfred A. Knopf, 1991.

Higham, Charles. *Celebrity Circus.* New York: Delacorte Press, 1979.

Higham, Charles. *Warner Brothers.* New York: Charles Scribner's Sons, 1975.

Hirschhorn, Clive. *Gene Kelly.* Chicago: Henry Regnery Company, 1974.

Hopper, Hedda. *The Whole Truth and Nothing But.* Garden City, New York: Doubleday & Company, Inc., 1963.

Hotchner, A. E. *Doris Day: Her Own Story.* New York: William Morrow and Company, Inc., 1975.

Jablonski, Edward. *Happy with the Blues.* Garden City, New York: Doubleday and Company, Inc., 1961. A discerning biography of Harold Arlen, the composer of Garland's *Oz, A Star is Born,* and *Gay Purr-ee.*

Kobal, John. *Gotta Sing, Gotta Dance.* London, Spring Books, 1983. A history of film musicals.

Leigh, Janet. *There Really Was a Hollywood.* Garden City, New York: Doubleday & Company, Inc., 1984.

McClintick, David. *Indecent Exposure.* New York: William Morrow and Company, Inc., 1982. David Begelman stars in a 1970s "Hollywoodgate" scandal, and his check-cashing "aberrations" are traced back to the era in which he was managing Garland.

Mordden, Ethan. *Movie Star: A Look at the Women Who Made Hollywood.* New York: St. Martin's Press, 1983.

Morley, Sheridan. *James Mason.* New York: Harper & Row, 1989.

Murphy, George, with Victor Lasky. *Say. . . Didn't You Used to Be George Murphy?* New York: Bartholomew House, Ltd., 1970.

Otash, Fred. *Investigation Hollywood!* Chicago: Henry Regnery Company, 1976. A private eye's view of the 1958 battle between Judy and Sid Luft.

Paar, Jack. *P. S. Jack Paar.* Garden City, New York: Doubleday & Company, Inc., 1983.

Pasternak, Joe. *Easy the Hard Way.* London: W. H. Allen, 1956.

Pearl, Ralph. *Las Vegas Is My Beat.* New Jersey: Lyle Stuart, Inc., 1973.

Pleasants, Henry. *The Great American Popular Singers.* New York: Simon and Schuster, 1974.

Rooney, Mickey. *Life Is Too Short.* New York: Villard Books, 1991.

Rose, Helen. *Just Make Them Beautiful.* Santa Monica, Calif.: Dennis-Landman, 1976.

Shipman, David. *The Great Movie Stars: The Golden Years.* New York: Crown Publishers, Inc., 1978.

St. Johns, Adela Rogers. *Some Are Born Great.* Garden City, New York: Doubleday & Company, Inc., 1974.

Steen, Mike. *Hollywood Speaks.* New York: G. P. Putnam's Sons, 1974.

Tucker, Sophie. *Some of These Days.* Garden City, New York: Doubleday, Doran and Company, Inc., 1945.

Whiting, Margaret, with Will Holt. *It Might As Well Be Spring.* New York: William Morrow and Company, Inc., 1987.

Wilk, Max. *They're Playing Our Song.* New York: Zoetrope, 1986. Interviews with and profiles of American popular songwriters.

ACKNOWLEDGMENTS

My thanks go first to the Turner Entertainment Company: to Roger Mayer, who once again said "Yes"; Carole Orgel Postal, who stood beaming encouragement; Diana Brown, who epitomizes professionalism and goodwill; and to Joe Swaney, Dick May, Scott Perry, Beverly Laufer, Irma Kraus, Kim Velinsky, Leroy James, Rob Johnson, Ron Lane, Dennis Millay, Sara Powers, Camille Jeffery, Maureen Reay, Bernice Gettler, and (especially) Cathy Manolis.

This book was born at the Academy of Motion Picture Arts and Sciences during a February 1990 research trip, and I'm indebted to Robert Cushman and all the staff who made a score of visits both comfortable and memorable. I'm equally indebted to Ned Comstock and Leith Adams at the University of Southern California Cinema-Television Library and Archives of Performing Arts, and to Joan Pierce and Judith Singer at (respectively) United Artists and Warner Bros.

George Feltenstein at MGM/UA Home Video, Inc., has been boundlessly enthusiastic; his expertise and friendship are invaluable. At Capitol Records, I thank Wayne C. Watkins, Sujata Murthy, and Brad Benedict for sharing their talents—and Bud O'Shea and Jane Arm for introducing us.

In 1984–85, I had the chance to work with Joan Kramer and David Heeley on "Judy Garland: The Concert Years." I thank them for the opportunity to learn, to help—and their faith ever since.

I reiterate my gratitude to those who entrusted their one-of-a-kind artwork to me, especially Donald F. Smith, Mrs. Wallace Worsley, Allen Lawson, Gary Bell, Tom Boghossian, Max Preeo, Pam Wulk, Marvin Paige, James Auer, Paul Chopak, Dale Namio, Kim Lundgreen, Christian Matzanke, and Les Perkins. Woolsey Ackerman worked tirelessly both through his offices at Turner and in his capacity as an unofficial collaborator. I am deeply grateful to both Fred McFadden and Bill Chapman for our association and for trusting me to try to do right by both Garland and their collections.

Many "Judy friends" contributed to this project—some in art, some by writing about her in the Garland magazines, some in thirty years of sharing our mutual regard: Max Preeo, Dana Correll Dial, Jim Spearo, Sonny Gallagher, Lorna Smith, Charlotte Stevenson, Gwen Potter, John Gordon, Ken Sephton, Peter Gannaway, Sue LeBeau Perry, John Walther, Sherry Kamps Biggart, Neva Foley, Randy Henderson, Dee Goldstein, Roslyn Portnoy, Pat McMath, Barbara Reeve, Nancy Barr Brandon, Jenny Wheeler, the late Beth Kanzer, Anne Suter, Richard Leslie, Robert Rosterman, Tommy Cooper, Don Koll, Jerry Waters, Ron O'Brien, Margaret Augustine, and especially Betty Welch, who extends herself again and again in fellowship. I'm also grateful to Sean Kelley, Scott Fisher, Joe Fonseca, Scott Schechter, Elaine Willingham, Sidney Myer, John Meyer, Linda Kellogg, Kim and Rudy Rudolph, Bill Reid, Dave Kenney, Jan Kiley, David Krauss, Mitchell Kessler, Alan Herskowitz, Stephen Sisters, David Goldstein, John Lecher, Harry Forbes, Tom Garofolo, Steve Young, Vickie Jennings, Tom Jones, Gina Valentine, Dan and Pat Thome, Judy Thompson, Joe Tyler, David Shipman, Felix Brenn, Tom Lynch, Barry Monush, Stephen Lynch, Tom Watson, Richard Brock, Brian Stamp, Richard Skipper, Danny Sherman, Christopher Rogers, Victor Mangum, Anthony Morelli, Taylor Maddux, Ethan Mordden, Barry Leighton, Sue Balfe, Doug Lembke, Tony Landini, Roberta and Hank Bauman, Doug Becker, Michael Benson (coproducer of the New York Public Library's 1992 exhibition "Judy Garland: A Celebration")— and Fern Formica, Margaret Pellegrini, Meinhardt and Marie Raabe, and Jerry and Elizabeth Maren.

My appreciation for support and incomparable bolstering to: Boots and Fran Pedersen, Bronson Pinchot, Donald Stannard, Mrs. Ethel Fricke, Dennis Cleveland, Patty Tobias, Judy Tucker, Rainie Cole, Jon McNeal, Ned Price, Sue Procko, Kris Larson, Bob Cancellare, Paul Lim, Jerry Herman, Peter Vogt, Jack Haley, Jr., Michael Patrick Hearn, Eddie Gualtieri, Tom Gualtieri, Barbara, Bob, Autumn, Ashley, and Andrew Evans, John Green, Gerald Clarke, Chuck and Sheila Goldsmith, Bill Van Camp, Kristen Weigle, Richard Mikell, Steve Cox, Mike Emyrs, Colonel James and Dorothy Tuttle Nitch, Bill and Dorothy Raye Parker, Dorothy Scott, Marguerite "M&M" Novak, Jean Nelson, Michael Feinstein, Andy McGibbon, Skip Carozza, Barry Alden Clark, Kevin Cassidy, Dorothy Collins, Tim Brown, Matthew Berg, John Burke, Judy Bieber, Dave and Jo Bostedt, Fred Barton, Charles Busch, Eric Myers, Scott Britton, Dr. Dan Brook, Tom Babbitt, Eileen, Brian, and Andrew Muller, the late William J. Schuessler, Michael Gessel, Steven Dale, Tommy Femia, Will and "Baby" Friedwald, Tom Kidd, Marc Lewis, Robin Olderman, Richard Hayes, John Van Camp, Chris Sterling, Philip Gamble, Bob Sixsmith, David Rambo, Ted Heyck, David Morgenstern, Nick Riviezzo, Barbara Koelle, Jim Jensen, Dick Jordan, Billy Barnes, Craig Jacobs, Tammy Jones, Doug Marconnet, Stuart Bloom, Finn Antonia Handel, Scott McKee, Jane Albright, Tod Machin, Leslie Smith, Barbara Stratyner, Rob Marx, Don Vlack, Herb Scher, Eric Stephen Jacobs, Wendy Roth, Jim Randazzo, Paul Kelly, Fred Meyer, Fred Martin, Rob Roy MacVeigh, Mark Porter, Jody Thomas, Karl Taylor, John Patrick Schutz, Joshua Smith, Andy Stowinski, Steve Quandt, Andy Potts, David Youse, John Wuchte, Larry Cox, Paul Massirio, Craig Dawson and the faction at Sam's, Lynne, Dan, Alison, and Colin Smith, Marguerite Heiden, and Helen Fisher. Special thanks to Father Raymond Wood, Pastor E. W. and Juanita Neuenschwander, and the Reverend Dale D. Hansen.

For professional assistance in preparing the book, I thank Matt Sartwell, Michael Schau, and Dan Gutman. For past assistance, I thank Jim Frost, Ann Milburn, Ellen Herrick, and Karen McDermott for continuing inspiration.

My gratitude goes also to friends in New York who provided computer advice: Richard L. Wall, Michael Rose, Michael Williamson, John Lytton, and Patrick McCarty. I thank Douglas Welty, Jim Winston, and Erick Neher for their hours of company, compassion, help, humor, and editorial presence. A special citation goes to six other friends, heaven-sent with much love and laughter: Ann Dorszynski Caird, Shelley Pedersen, Russell Adams, Dave Peters, the late Mike Fastert, and (especially) Dave Rebella.

There are others who read the manuscript as it materialized and furnished analysis (coupled with encouragement). Frank DeGregorie not only took and provided some of the 1967 Palace photographs herein, but participated in the life of this book whenever possible. Brent Phillips was the ideal presence, sharing an unparalleled zeal, intelligence, and anticipation. Rick Skye has been "my buddy" for more than a dozen years; his friendship and generosity throughout have been overwhelming. There are none better than these gentlemen.

The late John Graham knew more about Judy than anyone, and his research made possible the revisionistic accounts of Baby Gumm's debut (largely drawn from interviews with Jimmie Gumm Thompson), Clark Gable's birthday song, and much hitherto unpublished material. John was a challenging friend for fifteen years; his knowledge and insights are missed.

Throughout much of this work, Steve Sanders has been three thousand miles away, yet he remained omnipresent with his concern and by hovering (in the best sense of the word). There's no way to thank him for the tangible work he did to help—or the intangibles that, in some ways, provided even more.

For many years of extended kindness, I thank Lorna Luft, Jake Hooker, Joseph Luft, and Sid Luft, who so painstakingly preserves so much of Judy's work.

I'm grateful to many people at Henry Holt for their perseverance and contribution: Bruno Quinson, John Macrae, John Jusino, Barbara Miller, Verna Shamblee, Amy Robbins, and Lottchen Shivers.

Sylvain Michaelis and Irene Carpelis bore up remarkably well under the onslaught of material for use in their design of this book. I thank them for their understanding and skills—along with those of Marianne Palladino, Rachel Geswaldo, Jonette Jakobson, and especially Joe Bartos, whose steady talent literally put it all together and helped to realize the book you now hold.

This project would have foundered many times had it not been for the personal and professional expertise, aid, and intervention of Mitchell Rose. As an agent, he never failed to provide support, guidance, intelligence, and common sense. As a friend, he never failed to provide encouragement, compassion, and humor. His quiet ability to help one realize any amount of potential is priceless; his is the credit for seeing *Judy* through (with gratitude as well to his compatriots, Carol Fitzgerald and Justin Evans).

To conclude, I thank family:

. . .Walter and Dorothy Fricke, who after my initial Ozzy exposure in 1956 saw nothing strange in having a five-year-old enraptured by a singer of their generation—and found less strange in waking me up anytime there was a Garland movie on the late show. I was always unfailingly encouraged, tempered, and championed; I could not be more aware of my fortune in having them.

. . . My brother Mike and sister-in-law Linda, who share their own family so willingly: Erin, now eight and fresh from a sojourn as Dorothy in a school play; and Noel, now two, who fell in love with her *Wizard of Oz* videotape at precisely the right inspirational moment to kick me into the final stretch.

. . . And especially to Patty, my on-the-spot New York sister, who riffled through all the pages, exulting and challenging and reacting and supporting and, always, understanding. She was best of all—and, best of all, always present at moments I needed to share.

There are two last expressions of debt. The first goes to Judy Garland herself. When she died in June 1969, I had been a fan for nearly thirteen years. A letter expressing my contemporary emotions turned up in December 1969 in a memorial journal compiled by Lorna Smith, Judy's great good support in England. I'd never remember now what I wrote then had Lorna not excerpted it. But with much gladness I expressed my gratitude that I had been "chosen" to be a Judy Garland fan. Years later, my appreciation has only soared—along with my admiration and a still-growing gratitude. Her art continues to enrich my life.

And, finally, to my friend. Christopher O'Brien was largely responsible for getting me through the *Oz* book in 1988 and 1989. Together we celebrated the offer for this one when it came through in September 1990; I told him that night that *Judy* would be "his." Five days after the book contracts were signed in January 1991, he died. The finished product has become ever more his—largely because his was the belief that made anything possible. Not surprisingly, "anything" took much longer than anticipated in this case; working for the first time in eight years without a combination conscience and cheerleader was daunting at best—and impossible the rest of the time. But now the book is here—as he unfailingly was and has been. It's meant for everyone who loves Judy. . . and with thanks and love for Judy Garland herself. But most of all, with joy and heart, it's for Christopher.

PHOTO CREDITS

Much of the art in this book comes from its working association with the Turner Entertainment Company or from the author's collection. But a large group of other collector/archivists also share credit for the unique pictures herein. The professional care and expertise—and the personal cooperation and enthusiasm—of these people has been of substantial aid. Some of their contributions are listed below, but whether acknowledged in detail or (per their requests) thanked more succinctly, all have provided otherwise unobtainable material. Paramount among these friends are Fred McFadden and Steve Sanders, whose files and excitement for the project provided dozens of historically notable illustrations. Others who gave of their own research include: Paul Chopak, Al DiOrio, Scott Fisher, John-Michael Flate, Sonny Gallagher, Susan Glattstein, Randy Henderson, Kim Lundgreen, Christian Matzanke, Gary Moon, Dale Namio, Les Perkins, Donald F. Smith, and Eric Tasker. Wayne Martin, "Judy's Number One Fan," originally amassed and protected much extraordinary art. Finally, in years of love for Judy Garland, John Graham, Jim Squires, and Richard Connolly made major contributions to the investigation, study, and safety of materials that otherwise would have been lost. Before their premature deaths and over years of friendship, these men were exceptionally kind about providing access to remarkable photographs.

It is with sincerest gratitude that additional acknowledgment is here offered for the following illustrations: Max O. Preeo: pages 9, 192 (left), 227 (bottom), 228 (top), 231 (top center). The Enstrom Studios of Bovey, Minnesota: pages 10, 12, 14 (left). Dona Massin: page 18 (right). (Dona not only participated in the Kusell revue but went on to assist choreographer Bobby Connolly on *The Wizard of Oz* and to appear in the film as personal attendant to the Cowardly Lion in the Wash & Brush-Up Co. sequence.) Pam Wulk: pages 16 (left), 29 (bottom right), 45 (left column), 47 (bottom left), 66 (bottom left), 103 (bottom right), 161 (left and right), 206 (bottom left), 232 (top right), 236 (top left). Woolsey Ackerman: pages 29 (top right), 55 (top right), 61 (top left), 108–109 (various). Gary Bell: pages 34 (right), 37, 83 (right). The Rick Skye Collection: pages 34 (left center), 35, 36 (bottom left and right), 39 (bottom right), 40, 58 (bottom left), 61 (bottom), 82 (various), 83 (top left), 84 (left), 86 (top), 87, 88 (top), 105 (left), 108–109 (various), 112 (top left), 134, 135 (top left, bottom right), 137 (center), 139 (left), 140 (top), 144 (bottom), 193 (inset), 222 (top and bottom right), 223 (top left). [The last three photographs were taken by Fred Orlansky.] Brent Phillips: pages 36 (top), 58 (top), 61 (top right), 106 (top right), 108–109 (various), 229 (bottom left). Mrs. Wallace Worsley: pages 46 and 47 (bottom right). Allen Lawson: pages 47 (top left and right) and 140 (bottom). The Michael Benson Collection: pages 58 (bottom right), 62, 63, 64, 81, 82 (various), 105 (top and bottom right), 108–109 (various), 172 (left center and bottom). Tom Boghossian: pages 60, 84 (right), 108–109 (various). Marvin Paige, Motion Picture and Television Research Service Archive: pages 85 and 108 (top left corner). Bob Willoughby/Sygma: pages 129, 130, 131 (bottom right), 132 (top and bottom), 133, 136. Stephen Cox: pages 138 (top) and 158 (bottom). Capitol Records: rear dust jacket and pages 156, 160 (left top and bottom), 167 (left), 170 (top right), 184 (top right), 185 (left and right), 187, 194 (top left; right top and bottom), 199 (top; center bottom), 218 (center; bottom right), 219 (top left; bottom), 240. Gary Smith: page 172 (top). Douglas Kirkland/Sygma: page 173. James Auer: pages 175 (left center and bottom, bottom right), 176 (bottom left), 193 (right), 196 (left and right). The John F. Kennedy Library: page 205 (top). Frank DeGregorie: pages 214, 233 (left and right), 234 (center and right), 235 (top). Nancy Barr Brandon: page 221 (left column: top, center, and bottom). Gerald Waters: pages 222 (left) and 223 (top right). Albert Fisher/Fisher Production Group: page 224. Newspaper clippings on pages 11 and 13: copyright ©1924 by the Grand Rapids *Herald-Review*. Reprinted by permission. Newspapers on pages 238 (bottom) and 239: copyright ©1969 New York *Daily News*. Reprinted by permission. Chicago *Tribune*: page 242 (top), copyright ©1969 Chicago *Tribune*. Reprinted by permission. San Gabriel Valley *Daily Tribune*: page 242 (center), copyright ©1969 The San Gabriel Valley *Daily Tribune*. Reprinted by permission. Los Angeles *Times*: page 242 (bottom), copyright ©1969 Los Angeles *Times*. Reprinted by permission.

The following photographs are reproduced through the courtesy of the Academy of Motion Picture Arts and Sciences/Margaret Herrick Library: from the Metro-Goldwyn-Mayer Collection: pages 25, 26 (right), 28 (bottom), 31 (top left), 41 (bottom), 42 (center), 43 (center), 44 (right), 45 (center), 48 (top and bottom left; bottom right), 49 (left), 51, 52, 56 (top left), 70 (top), 71 (bottom left), 74 (top), 77 (right center), 89, 90 (center right), 94 (top left), 95 (top center, bottom right), 113 (top right), 122 (bottom), 244 (top), 249 (top); from the John Truwe Collection: pages 56 (bottom left), 68 (top left), 70 (bottom), 71 (top left), 80 (left top and bottom), 92 (right), 98 (bottom left), 99 (bottom right), 101 (bottom), 113 (bottom right), 115 (top left), 120 (top); from the George Cukor Collection: pages 146 (bottom right), 147 (bottom), 148 (top center), 149 (bottom left); from the General Collection: page 127 (center). "Academy Award®" (or "Oscar®") is the registered trademark and service mark of the Academy of Motion Picture Arts and Sciences.

Illustrations on the following pages are reprinted courtesy of the University of Southern California Cinema-Television Library and Archives of Performing Arts: from the Arthur Freed Collection: pages 80 (bottom right), 90 (top right; top and bottom left), 117 (bottom left); from the Charles Walters Collection: pages 102 (bottom right), 104 (bottom right), 113 (top left), 120.

A final heartfelt gratitude goes to Bill Chapman. He has shown warm, selfless kindness in offering access to his remarkable collection, and has provided the illustrations on pages 5, 7, 28 (top), 29 (bottom left), 32 (bottom), 33, 34 (top and bottom left), 39 (top left), 66 (top left and right), 68 (bottom left), 69 (top left), 71 (top right), 72 (top left), 75 (left center and bottom), 79 (right), 92 (left), 98 (top left), 100 (bottom), 102 (top left), 104 (top and bottom left), 106 (bottom left), 112 (bottom left and center right), 114 (bottom right), 116 (top right), 118 (top), 122 (top), 131 (top left), 135 (right top), 149 (right center), 150 (top right), 151 (bottom), 159 (bottom), 164 (top and bottom), 169 (top left), 170 (bottom right), 175 (top right), 176 (top left and right; bottom right), 178, 186 (top), 194 (bottom left), 203 (bottom left), 207 (top and center right), 208 (bottom left), 220 (bottom left), 243 (bottom), 244 (bottom), 245 (top), 246 (top and bottom), 247 (top), 249 (bottom), 250 (bottom), 252 (top, left to right), 253.

MGM publicity pictures and stills, production photos, and original ad art from the following films appear through the courtesy of the Turner Entertainment Company: *Andy Hardy Meets Debutante* ©1940 Loew's Incorporated. Renewed ©1967 Metro-Goldwyn-Mayer, Inc. All rights reserved. *Babes in Arms* ©1939 Loew's Incorporated. Renewed ©1966 Metro-Goldwyn-Mayer, Inc. All rights reserved. *Babes on Broadway* ©1941 Loew's Incorporated. Renewed ©1968 Metro-Goldwyn-Mayer, Inc. All rights reserved. *Broadway Melody of 1938* ©1937 Metro-Goldwyn-Mayer Corporation. Renewed ©1964 Metro-Goldwyn-Mayer, Inc. All rights reserved. *The Clock* ©1945 Loew's Incorporated. Renewed ©1972 Metro-Goldwyn-Mayer, Inc. All rights reserved. *Easter Parade* ©1948 Loew's Incorporated. Renewed ©1975 Metro-Goldwyn-Mayer, Inc. All rights reserved. *Every Sunday* ©1936 Metro-Goldwyn-Mayer Corporation. Renewed ©1963 Metro-Goldwyn-Mayer, Inc. All rights reserved. *Everybody Sing* ©1938 Loew's Incorporated. Renewed ©1965 Metro-Goldwyn-Mayer, Inc. All rights reserved. *For Me and My Gal* ©1942 Loew's Incorporated. Renewed ©1969 Metro-Goldwyn-Mayer, Inc. All rights reserved. *Girl Crazy* ©1943 Loew's Incorporated. Renewed ©1970 Metro-Goldwyn-Mayer, Inc. All rights reserved. *The Harvey Girls* ©1945 Loew's Incorporated. Renewed ©1973 Metro-Goldwyn-Mayer, Inc. All rights reserved. *In the Good Old Summertime* ©1949 Loew's Incorporated. Renewed ©1976 Metro-Goldwyn-Mayer, Inc. All rights reserved. *Life Begins for Andy Hardy* ©1941 Loew's Incorporated. Renewed ©1968 Metro-Goldwyn-Mayer, Inc. All rights reserved. *Listen, Darling* ©1938 Loew's Incorporated. Renewed ©1965 Metro-Goldwyn-Mayer, Inc. All rights reserved. *Little Nellie Kelly* ©1940 Loew's Incorporated. Renewed ©1967 Metro-Goldwyn-Mayer, Inc. All rights reserved. *Love Finds Andy Hardy* ©1938 Loew's Incorporated. Renewed ©1965 Metro-Goldwyn-Mayer, Inc. All rights reserved. *Meet Me in St. Louis* ©1944 Loew's Incorporated. Renewed ©1971 Metro-Goldwyn-Mayer, Inc. All rights reserved. *The Pirate* ©1948 Loew's Incorporated. Renewed ©1975 Metro-Goldwyn-Mayer, Inc. All rights reserved. *Presenting Lily Mars* ©1943 Loew's Incorporated. Renewed ©1970 Metro-Goldwyn-Mayer, Inc. All rights reserved. *Strike Up the Band* ©1940 Loew's Incorporated. Renewed ©1967 Metro-Goldwyn-Mayer, Inc. All rights reserved. *Summer Stock* ©1950 Loew's Incorporated. Renewed ©1977 Metro-Goldwyn-Mayer, Inc. All rights reserved. *Thoroughbreds Don't Cry* ©1937 Metro-Goldwyn-Mayer Corporation. Renewed ©1964 Metro-Goldwyn-Mayer, Inc. All rights reserved. *Thousands Cheer* ©1943 Loew's Incorporated. Renewed ©1970 Metro-Goldwyn-Mayer, Inc. All rights reserved. *Till the Clouds Roll By* ©1946 Loew's Incorporated. *The Wizard of Oz* ©1939 Loew's Incorporated. Renewed ©1966 Metro-Goldwyn-Mayer, Inc. All rights reserved. *Words and Music* ©1948 Loew's Incorporated. Renewed ©1975 Metro-Goldwyn-Mayer, Inc. All rights reserved. *Ziegfeld Follies* ©1946 Loew's Incorporated. Renewed ©1973 Metro-Goldwyn-Mayer, Inc. All rights reserved. *Ziegfeld Girl* ©1941 Loew's Incorporated. Renewed ©1968 Metro-Goldwyn-Mayer, Inc. All rights reserved. Additional illustrations are reproduced by permission of the Turner Entertainment Company on pages 23 (bottom), 77 (top left), 118 (bottom), 119 (top).

Stills from *Pigskin Parade* ©1936 Twentieth Century–Fox Film Corporation. All rights reserved. Stills and production photographs from *A Star is Born* ©1954 Warner Bros. All rights reserved. Stills and production photographs from *Judgment at Nuremberg* ©1961 RoxLom Films, Inc. All rights reserved. Stills and production photographs from *A Child Is Waiting* ©1962 Larcas Productions, Inc. All rights reserved. Stills and production photos from *I Could Go On Singing* ©1963 Millar-Turman Productions, Inc. All rights reserved. Special thanks to Erin Scully and The Robert F. Kennedy Memorial Foundation for permission to quote from material written for Judy Garland by Roger Edens.

The majority of the special interior photography for the book (posters, lobby cards, rotogravure pages, trade ads, and magazine covers) was done with elan, patience, and buoyant grace by Michael Chan in New York. Similar work was handled in expert fashion in Los Angeles by Producers Photographic Laboratory, Inc., and in Milwaukee by Black and White Labs.

Photograph of Christopher O'Brien by Nick Granito.